SEMANTICS

SEMANTICS

ANATOL RAPOPORT
University of Toronto

with the collaboration of Leo Hamalian,
The City College of the City University
of New York

 Thomas Y. Crowell Company
New York   Established 1834

Library of Congress Cataloging in Publication Data

Rapoport, Anatol, 1911–
 Invitation to semantics.

 Includes bibliographical references.
  1. Semantics. 2. Languages—Philosophy.
I. Title.
P325.R3   412   73-8620
ISBN 0-690-00285-8

Manufactured in the United States of America

1 2 3 4 5 6 7 8 9 10

To Gwen

preface

Language can be examined from two points of view: as an object of interest in its own right and in relation to other things. The study of language in its own right is the concern of linguists. They describe the structures of languages, how they are related and how they differ, and they trace the evolution of languages. To the linguist, a language is what an organism is to an anatomist or a physiologist—primarily a system to be understood in terms of its own internal logic, how it is put together and how it works. By comparison, the language philosopher inquires into the relation of language to other aspects of human existence. From his point of view, language is a component of human behavior, a product and possibly a determining factor of human psychology, of social organization, and of history.

This book attempts to connect the two approaches to the study of language. Semantics is the junction. It is the branch of language study that deals with *meaning*, hence, in a way, the focus around which language science develops.

If, for the purpose of definition, the area of semantics must be circumscribed, one could say that semantics is concerned with a fluctuating relationship: that is, the one between words and what they stand for. Indeed, this was the sense in which "semantics" was understood when M. J. A. Bréal introduced the term in 1897.* This definition may serve the purpose of the linguist. For the language philosopher, however, meaning is more than a relation between words and their

---

* His *Semantics, Studies in the Science of Meaning* was first translated into English in 1900. (*Essai de semantique, science de significations*, P. Hachette, 1897.)

referents. Studying language as a human activity, the language philosopher relates meaning to the entire range of human experience. This broader view of meaning—the role of language in human affairs—has become increasingly a central concern also of psychologists, sociologists, anthropologists, and political scientists; that is, those who study man, his psyche, and his works.

If the social scientist views language as essentially an instrument of communication, the philosopher of natural science (also a product of human activity) sees it as an instrument of cognition. We obtain knowledge about the world around us by *telling ourselves* what we have observed and what we have deduced from our observations. Therefore, how language conveys meaning deeply interests not only the social or behavioral scientist but also the philosopher of natural science.

Concern with the various aspects of meaning has considerably broadened the scope of semantics. This broadened scope will be reflected in this book. On the one hand, we shall assume the linguist's point of view in examining the structural underpinnings of meaning, how meaning emerges from the way in which the so-called units of language are combined. On the other hand, we shall assume the language philosopher's point of view in examining also the cognitive and behavioral aspects of meaning, the role of language as the unique characteristic of the species Man. Semantics thus becomes a tool for understanding ourselves and for understanding the process of understanding.

In the United States, the student of the so-called "communication arts" (composition, rhetoric, literature, speech, general semantics, etc.) is at times exposed to this latter point of view to the neglect of more technical matters that do not measure up to the "human interest" expectations of student. The quality of instruction in this area varies. It becomes questionable when obfuscated by insufficient penetration. Specifically, discussion (better said, mere mention) of the importance of certain esoteric scientific and mathematical theories without provision for sufficient background often serves to confuse rather than to enlighten the student.

In my opinion, there is no doubt that the theories of language philosophy raise fundamental cognitive issues in modern science. However, the task of explaining, say, non-Euclidean geometry or the theory of relativity to a reader without an adequate background is not a simple one. I have found it necessary to devote Part III of this book to such matters, and in so doing may have taxed the patience of the reader. Indeed, it may be difficult for the reader to see why a discussion of formal logic, mathematics, or mathematical physics should be included at all in a book on semantics. I flatter myself in the expectation that a reader ready to expend some intellectual effort (for which, I maintain, no specialized knowledge is necessary) will find such effort rewarding. In understanding the language of science, he grasps how one very important function of language (the cognitive) is *supposed* to work. Part III, therefore, is to be viewed as the background for the ideas expressed in the other three parts. Why it is placed where it is will be made clear in Part I.

Parts I, II, and IV treat matters discussed in linguistics, the psychology of language, and language philosophy, including general semantics.

I am deeply indebted to four ladies, who, by providing "feedback," helped me keep the "general intelligent reader" in mind. They are my wife, to whom this book is gratefully dedicated; my assistant, Claire Adler, who, as on several former occasions, has given invaluable editorial help; Doris J. Humphrey, a teacher of English; and Dorothy Williams Malan, who typed and retyped the manuscript in its several phases. Needless to say, any errors or inadequacies of exposition are to be debited entirely to me.

ANATOL RAPOPORT

contents

/I
MAN
AND
HIS
LANGUAGE

1/the symbol user

Throughout the ages philosophers have grappled with the problem of defining man. To what purpose? Ordinarily we go about defining something in order to distinguish it from something else. Clearly, philosophers, searching for the definition of man, could not have such a purpose in mind because there is no problem of distinguishing a human being from something else. Any three-year-old can do it instantly without benefit of a definition. Why, then, do philosophers persist in these herculean efforts to answer the question "What is man?"

I think the most likely reason is that philosophers have been traditionally preoccupied with discovering the "essences" of things. Philosophy is the oldest systematized search for general knowledge, and knowledge begins with bringing some sort of order into our observations. Our observations tell us that the world is extremely diverse, but also that there seems to be some unity in diversity. Everything is different from everything else, but some things are more different than others. Consequently some things belong together, and the world can be divided into *classes* of things. Things in the same class have some characteristics in common. The search for an "essence" is the search for *the most important characteristic* that the things of a class have in common.

Many philosophers believed that the discovery of these "essences" imparted wisdom. This conviction persists to our own day. People still pose philosophical questions like "What is the essence of freedom?" or of "love" or of "treason" or of "education." Note what is assumed by such questions. It is assumed that there *exists* something in the world, not necessarily a class of things but perhaps a class of conditions, that constitutes "freedom" or "education" or "blasphemy" or "genius"; further, that these conditions or properties distinguish freedom from license, education from training, genius from talent, blasphemy from heresy, and so on; finally, that by discovering the most essential of these conditions or properties we gain insight into the "essence" of "freedom" or "sanity" or "progress" or "loyalty" or whatever—and thereby become wiser.

Whether inquiries of this sort are indeed paths to wisdom is a question interesting in its own right, and we shall examine it in Chapter 19. First, let us see what it means to pursue this sort of inquiry with respect to man.

An inquiry into the essence of man differs in two important respects from similar inquiries into the essence of "patriotism," "prejudice," and considerations of that sort. First, man exists in nature regardless of what we know or think we know about him. The same cannot be said about "alienation" or "justice" or "tyranny." These are states of mind at least as much as combinations of objectively demonstrable conditions. Second, all concepts mentioned are *derivatives* of man's existence. Therefore, if inquiries into essences are worthwhile, an inquiry into the nature of man is certainly a fundamental one. Reliable knowledge on this subject is more likely to shed light on the concepts *produced* by man—if only because man antedates all of the concepts he has produced to describe the human condition. Let us therefore examine definitions of man that have been proposed.

Twenty-three centuries ago, Aristotle set forth a formula for making definitions. Select, he wrote, some characteristic of the thing defined that will place it in a class; then point out further characteristics that will distinguish it from other members of the same class. Following this formula, some one—whether seriously or not—proposed to define man as a "featherless biped." A salient characteristic of man is that he walks on two legs. This makes him a biped, a member of a class of living beings. But birds are also bipeds. So the definition has to distinguish men from birds. Man differs from birds in that he has no feathers: hence "featherless biped."

It does not take long to see the inadequacy of this definition. Leaving aside many dinosaurs that used to walk on two legs, as well as kangaroos—all featherless bipeds which may have been unknown to Aristotle—the definition fails to distinguish a man from a plucked chicken. Clearly neither the number of legs nor the absence of feathers captures the essence of man.

There has been no lack of definitions in which the so-called mental or spiritual qualities of man are brought out. Man has been called a rational animal, a being with a soul, a being intermediate between angels and beasts, and so on. All of these definitions suffer from the same defect. They define something familiar and recognizable, namely man, in terms of something far less familiar or far less recognizable, like "angels" or "rationality" or "soul." Actually a definition should do the reverse; it should explain the unfamiliar in terms of the familiar. If there exists some hitherto undiscovered characteristic of man that is his "essence," his most important distinguishing feature, then, if this characteristic is to be made known, it must be derived from already known properties of man. To define man in terms of "soul" or "rationality" is to do little more than attach labels to the presumed distinguishing feature, which is what we are looking for in the first place.

There remain two definitions of man that avoid this error of putting labels on unknown or vaguely conceived characteristics. One of the definitions defines man as a *tool maker*. Tool making is a clearly recognizable activity. Moreover, while tool *using* is not a uniquely human activity, tool *making* is. Although monkeys have been observed to use coconuts as missiles and, occasionally, sticks as tools, no animal besides man has ever been observed to *fashion* a tool for future specific use. So the definition does single out a uniquely human characteristic. But it misses the *social* aspect of human existence. It evokes an image of an ancient lone inventor who stumbled on the idea of an axe with a handle or a bow and arrows. Of one thing, we may be sure: our ancestors were social animals long before they became men. Inventions came about in the course of social interactions.

However, the social way of life is certainly not uniquely human. All mammals live in family units at least some of the time, and many animals far removed from mammals phylogenetically live in communities. Certain of these communities are so close-knit that some biologists view them as organisms of a higher order in which the individuals are analogous to cells of a biological organism. For example, worker bees are sexless. They "work" (forage for food and build honeycombs) but they do not reproduce, whereas the drones and queens reproduce but do not work. Among ants, differentiation goes even further: some individuals take on the function of defense with appropriate modification of anatomy, the so-called "soldier ants." In short, complex social life is not a uniquely human invention.

A definition of man that combines the social aspect of man's existence with a possibly unique characteristic is "Man is a talking animal." Talking is certainly a social act. Man talks because and only because he lives with others of his own kind. Whether talking is uniquely human and whether it is an essential characteristic depends on how we define language. All social animals communicate with each other by means of signals of some kind. Some signals are odors, such as those that emanate from one individual to inform another that a potential mate is in the vicinity. Some are visual as gestures or postures. Some are tactual. And some are aural, like the cries of mammals and the songs of birds. There is evidence that some sounds uttered by animals are differentiated and produce differential effects, such as mating calls and warning cries. Therefore, without further qualifications of what we mean by "talking," the definition of man as a "talking animal" may not be adequate in capturing the uniqueness of man.

If, however, we modify the definition to say "Man is an animal with a symbolic language," we may have a definition that serves this purpose. It turns out that man is indeed the only animal that uses a symbolic language as a means of communicating with others of his kind and, what is most important, with himself. Moreover, many thinkers have come to believe (and I agree) that the use of symbolic language is not only unique but also an essential aspect of being human; that more can be learned about the nature of man by studying symbolic language and its role in human existence than from any other characteristic of man. Understanding how symbolic language works (and often fails) as a means of communication provides a key to many questions summarized in a single one: "Why do we behave like human beings?" or, for that matter, "Why don't we behave like human beings?" Let us, then, see what is meant by "symbolic language." We shall begin by defining a symbol.

I shall call a symbol something that satisfies three conditions. First, to be a symbol, something has to be recognized as a unit. Second, it must stand for something else. Third, what it stands for cannot be inferred from the symbol itself; it is a matter of established habit or social agreement or convention.

This definition can be elucidated by examining some things that are symbols and some that are not. Take a dark cloud. It often portends rain. It can therefore be said to be a *sign* of rain. It is also recognizable as a unit (since it is named). But a dark cloud is not a symbol for rain because its connection with rain is a relation given in nature, not established by social convention. On the other hand, a picture of a cloud with slanting lines below it on a weather chart is a *symbol* of rain, being a *conventional* way of depicting rain. If a picture of a knife and fork is meant to depict simply a knife and a fork, it is not a symbol because what is depicted is clear from the picture itself. But on European highways, a picture of a crossed knife and fork stands for a restaurant. The connection is established by convention. Here we have a symbol. Similarly, a bed is a symbol for a hotel, a monkey wrench for a garage, a red cross for a first-aid station, and so on. A pair of sticks at right angles to each other is only a pair of sticks, but in certain contexts a pair of sticks stands for Christian faith. This is a symbol. We recognize a blindfolded woman holding aloft a set of scales as a symbol of justice, a rooster as a symbol of France, two snakes entwined on a staff as a symbol of medicine. None of these meanings can be inferred from the pictures themselves. They are meanings by agreement only.

The letter M is recognizable as a unit. It stands for the sound "m." The connection between the shape of the letter and the sound is only a matter of convention. There is nothing inherent in either the shape or the sound that connects them with each other. Therefore the letter M and, of course, all of the remaining letters of the alphabet are symbols.

We recognize words as units. A word stands for something other than its sound or its appearance in print. Moreover, the connection between a word and what it stands for is purely a matter of social agreement among people who speak the same language. Those who speak another language will not generally be able to guess what a particular word stands for. Therefore, words are symbols.

Now we are ready to define symbolic language, that which we said makes man what he is. A symbolic language is a system of communication in which each message (or act of communication) is a combination, usually a sequence, of symbols.

If we examine the systems of communication used by animals other than man, we see at once that they are not symbolic languages. A cricket issues sounds that are signals to other crickets. But these

sounds are not "symbols" because their "meaning" is inherent in themselves, not established by convention. Communication among animals
may be quite elaborate. The so-called dance language of the bees
conveys information from "scouts" to others, not only about the
presence of food in the vicinity, but also about the direction and the
approximate distance of the source. But, again, what a communicating
bee does and how what she does affects her sisters are entirely determined by the way the bee's nervous system is constructed. The signal
cannot be pried loose, so to speak, from the situation that initiates it;
nor can the response to the signal be anything but what it is. Neither
the way of transmitting the signal nor the response to it is learned by
the bees.[1] They are "built-in." Using computer jargon, we would say
today that the bee is *programmed* once and for all to go through
certain gestures after feeding abroad or to respond to these gestures
by flying to the indicated spot to gather the food.

Some animals, to be sure, especially those that live with man, can be
taught the "meaning" of some words, in the sense that they acquire
habits of reacting to the sounds of the words in specified ways. Mr.
Smith can teach his dog to bark when he says "thief"; so, in a way, the
word has acquired "meaning" for the dog. Mr. Smith has a friend,
Mr. Jones, and, if Mr. Smith's dog is exceptionally intelligent, Mr.
Smith can get him to run to Mr. Jones every time he says "Jones." So
the word "Jones" has also acquired a "meaning" for the dog different
from that of "thief." So far so good. However, it is quite impossible
for the dog to combine the two meanings. No matter how many times
Mr. Smith repeats "Jones—thief" to the dog, the dog will not get the
idea that "Jones is a thief" and will not bark at Jones the next time
Jones comes around.

The example illustrates the distinction between signals and symbols.
For the dog, the word "thief" becomes a signal to bark, and the word
"Jones" a signal to run to Jones when Jones is present. Signals cannot
be combined and recombined to become signals for something else.
Symbols *can* be combined and recombined to acquire new meanings.
Words, for example, can be combined and recombined to form sen-
tences, and sentences acquire meanings that are more than just the
meanings of the individual words that compose them. It is the acquisi-

1. Recent experiments suggest that some learning may be involved in the bee's acquisition of her "language." Nevertheless, *what* the bee learns is predetermined by her
genetic makeup, not by the "speech community" in which she happens to grow up.
as is the case with human beings. This is the fundamental distinction between human
and nonhuman languages.

tion of new meanings through combinations that makes the range of ideas communicated by symbolic language practically limitless. A typical human language has fewer than 100 distinct sounds. But combinations of these sounds make thousands of words, and combinations of words make a practically limitless number of sentences. It is almost certain that you have never previously read the sentence I have just written. But you nevertheless understand it because you are able to gather its meaning from the meanings of the words in it and, above all, from the way the words are put together.

There is no question, then, but that symbolic language, unlike signal languages that many animals possess, is a uniquely human characteristic. Do we have reason to believe that it is an *essential* human characteristic?

Survival for any form of life depends upon adaptation to its environment. In nonhuman species, adaptations are traced almost entirely through modifications in anatomy and physiology. A beast of prey has teeth and claws appropriate to its predatory life; the grass eaters can live on grass because they can digest cellulose, which does not yield to the digestive processes of the meat eaters. Fish are streamlined; birds have very light bones and very strong forelimb muscles, and so can fly. Man can do a little of what most animals do, but nothing very well. He can run, but not as fast as a deer or a cheetah; he can climb, but not as surely as a monkey or a squirrel; he can swim, but not as well as a seal. He eats meat, but his teeth are not as well adapted to meat eating as a tiger's. His claws are practically worthless for the purposes for which claws are used. His skin is almost bare. Naked and without fire, he could survive only in the tropics. As a child, man is helpless for a longer period than the young of any other animal species.

Even more striking is the paucity of man's instinctual adaptation to one particular way of life. The bird's command of the art of nest building is built-in. Birds kept in isolation from birth have been observed to build nests of the same materials, of the same design, and on the same engineering principles as all others of their species. They don't have to take courses in nest building. Instructions in how to build a nest are inscribed on the chromosomes of the fertilized eggs of the particular species. By comparison, practically everything man does he has to be taught how to do.

It would seem, then, that among all creatures man is the most underendowed by nature. However, symbolic language enables man to do something no other animal can do, namely to transmit experience across generations. Many animals with sufficiently developed nervous systems are able to accumulate experience so that older animals become more proficient in their life activities. Possibly young lions have to learn to approach their prey upwind. So there is an accumulation of personal experience in the life of some animals. However, there is no *generational* accumulation of experience. Each generation must learn the same things over and over again. Not so with man. Each human generation can absorb comparatively quickly the accumulated experiences of the preceding generations and go on from there. Symbolic language makes this possible by allowing man to communicate not only about here and now but also about what has already happened, about what is going to happen, about what may happen, and about what might have happened.

A cricket's song says only one thing: "I am here now." A dog or a bird may warn others of danger provided the danger is of the moment. A cat can make her mistress understand that she wants to go out, but only at the door. No cricket can say "I can't tonight; meet me tomorrow night." No cat can say "Leave the door open as you go out; I may want to go out later." We can say such things because symbolic language allows us to combine and recombine symbols so as to impart *emergent* meanings to the combinations. In this way symbolic language frees the act of communication from a particular relevant situation. Symbolic communication *evokes* situations in the minds of the communicants, and there is practically no limitation on the range of situations that can be so evoked. Knowledge imparted by evoking images, independent of a particular situation, makes possible the accumulation of experience by successive generations. This accumulated experience and its products, artifacts, customs, techniques, beliefs, laws, and institutions is called culture. Man is the only animal that produces culture and is, in turn, shaped, at least psychically, by his culture.

So now we seem to have found what we are looking for—a definition of man that brings out his unique and most essential characteristic —the use of symbols. Man is a symbol-using animal, or, if you will, a culture-producing animal, which is saying the same thing because culture is preserved and transmitted by symbols. Also, cultural change is passed along from one generation to another by symbols, whether we view such change as instigated by changes in man's material environment or by changes in his attitudes, beliefs, and outlooks.

Symbols, then, play the part of a new "hereditary substance," as it were.[2] Like the biological hereditary substance, symbols are carriers of both constancy and change in the condition of human existence, but they are independent of either the constancy or changes in man's biological make-up. This "new dimension of evolution" can be seen most clearly in the evolution of language itself. Languages evolve just as biological species do. In fact, the taxonomy of languages (their classification into families, groups, etc.) parallels the classification of living organisms into phyla, classes, genera. The taxonomy of languages is based on the same principles as those of living organisms, namely on the closeness of kinship, which, in turn, depends on descent from common ancestors. Yet the evolution of languages in no way depends on changes in man's biological make-up. It has *its own* mechanisms of both conservation and change. The same is true of culture in general. Man can be credited, therefore, with introducing a new principle into evolution: the symbol user as a creature that evolves without waiting for his genetic complex to change.

What, if anything, follows from this definition of man? Philosophers sought "essences" because they thought that knowledge of "essence" was a means of understanding the true nature of things. With regard to man, understanding his nature has often been identified with the knowledge of what is *proper* for man. In this way, the problem of defining man was linked to moral as well as to natural philosophy.

Alfred Korzybski (1879–1950), for example, was quite explicit on this point. Korzybski distinguished plants, animals other than man, and man by their principal survival mechanisms. He called plants "energy binders" for their ability to capture solar energy and to harness it for their survival needs. He called animals "space binders" for their ability to move around in space and so actively seek survival-enhancing locations, as in searching for food and for mates and in escaping from enemies. Man is a "time binder." His time binding is the ability to utilize the time dimension (generational accumulation of experience— language) as a survival mechanism. The identification of language as a survival mechanism indicates also a basis for "language hygiene"—the

2. Information that determines how an organism will develop is coded on minute particles called *genes*. In reproduction, genes are transmitted from parents to offspring. Thus we can imagine that the genes constitute in their totality the hereditary substance, or germ plasm, of a species that has a continual existence across generations and manifests itself in a succession of *somata* (bodies). The mystically inclined may take this to be a realization of the doctrine of the transmigration of souls.

proper use of language. We shall have considerably more to say about this conclusion in Chapters 19 and 21.

Definitions of man that place him at the summit of an evolutionary process are essentially optimistic definitions. They are based on the assumptions that there is a creative perfection-seeking process in nature; that man himself is a product of that process and, through introducing a new dimension into evolution, has himself become a carrier of "progress."

There have, however, been other conceptions of man. In one myth, man is said to have been created in God's image, that is, essentially perfect (or innocent), and is then to have "fallen." Plato (427–347 B.C.) pictured a Golden Age, in a distant past, from which mankind *regressed*. Plato's political tract, *The Republic*, is essentially a description of a society made perfect by guarding *against* change. In this view, change is regarded as essentially degenerative, not as progressive. The basis of ethics, hence what is proper for man, appears in this outlook to be a matter of preventing change. There is no room in this ethics for growth, development, or "progress."

The concept of progress as a prime mover of change is comparatively a recent one. It came to the forefront following the Industrial Revolution in Europe when a rapidly expanding technology came to be recognized as a source of riches by the greedy and as a means of improving human life by the idealistic.

With the publication of Darwin's *The Origin of Species* (1859), the idea of progressive change acquired a profound philosophical interpretation. In the light of evolutionary theory, man no longer appeared as a creature who was once perfect because he was created in God's image and who had "fallen," but, on the contrary, he came to be thought of as a product of a "biological progress." By analogy, cultural change was now seen not as a regression from idyllic "good old days" but as a creative process driven by man's own aspirations, striving toward perfection. Cultural anthropologists of the late nineteenth century wrote about "stages" of cultural development. They pictured human society evolving from the stage of savagery to that of "barbarism," itself a transitional stage passing into "civilization." [3]

The idea of progressive biological and cultural evolution tended to alleviate the shock of realizing that man was not as important in the scheme of things as religious beliefs had made him out to be.

3. Cf. Lewis H. Morgan, *Ancient Society* (Chicago: Charles H. Kerr and Company, 1910).

In the myths that man had invented to explain the world, the earth was, as a rule, tacitly or explicitly assumed to be the center of the universe and man the crown of creation. As the horizon of knowledge widened, the earth was recognized for what it was—an insignificant lump of matter in a vast, indifferent universe; and man himself was revealed as a descendant of creatures not essentially different from other beasts. Yet the conviction that man is something special persists even in the outlooks based on those discoveries. This "special" feature of man is sometimes identified with man's *awareness* of what is happening, his capacity for inquiry, especially his quest for self-knowledge. Believers in progressive evolution see the emergence of this faculty as a continuation of a creative process that led to the emergence of living organisms from inert matter, to the emergence of *purposeful* activity in living organisms with nervous systems, to the emergence of consciousness and, finally, of curiosity (exploration of experiences) in higher animals. In man this new drive was turned inward and was transformed into a capacity to ask questions about himself.

This positive view of evolution is eloquently expressed by Julian Huxley[4] and taken as a basis for a universal ethics. Good is that which is in harmony with the direction of evolution from inert matter to life to purposeful activity to curiosity to an appetite for understanding and, finally, for self-knowledge.

At the time Julian Huxley wrote, total self-destruction of mankind was still not thinkable. Now it is. If such an act of self-destruction does occur, what could an "outside observer" conclude about the particular branch of the evolutionary tree that terminated in man, the erstwhile "crown of creation"? Assuming that this "outside observer" witnessed the entire history of life on this planet up to the extinction of man, he might describe what happened as follows.

"Man was just another form of life that was viable for a while but finally became unviable. This had happened many times before. The dinosaurs were once lords of creation. For 180 million years they were admirably adapted to their environment, and their massive bulk and armor made them invulnerable to enemies. But the environment eventually changed. The climate became colder and drier. Being cold-blooded, the giant reptiles lacked a temperature-regulating mechanism

4. Sir Julian Sorell Huxley, *The Uniqueness of Man* (London: Chatto & Windus, 1941); *Evolution: A Modern Synthesis* (London: George Allen & Unwin, 1942); *Essays of a Humanist* (New York: Harper (reprint), 1964).

to cope with the changing climate. Another life form, the mammals, appeared. They were much smaller than the terrible lizards and no match for them in open combat. But mammals had built-in thermostats and could cope with the new climatic conditions. And they had a different way of reproducing. Instead of laying fertilized eggs, the females carried the young inside them and cared for them when they were born. In this way a greater proportion of the young survived to reproduce in turn. The mammals also probably preyed on the unprotected eggs and on the newly hatched young of the reptiles. The mammals forged ahead of the erstwhile, dominant reptiles in the struggle for existence. The reptiles were reduced to relative insignificance.

"Still later, man appeared among the mammals. He developed an altogether different survival mechanism—symbolic language. This mechanism enabled man to accumulate knowledge across generations and, on the basis of this knowledge and the changed world outlook resulting from it, to create complex forms of social organization. Man survived not by adapting himself to his environment but by changing the environment to suit his own needs. Accumulated knowledge enabled him to harness the forces of nature and placed immense power in his hands. Thereby the attention of men was turned toward accumulating and increasing their own power. But the complex forms of social organization designed by men never encompassed the whole of humanity. Instead, rival centers of power called 'nations' or 'alliances' appeared. From time to time, some of these attempted to destroy others, seeking thereby to increase their power or to prevent others from doing the same. Thus man became the *war-waging animal*.

"The outbursts of organized mutual destruction increased in intensity. The harnessing of the forces of nature was turned more and more toward improving methods of destroying men and the products of their labors. In wreaking this destruction on others of their own species, men believed that they were thereby protecting themselves. These beliefs were rooted in the symbolic descriptions of relations among men, in the definitions of friends and enemies, of loyalty and duty, of good and evil. In the course of development of destructive technology, devices finally appeared which, in addition to destroying men and their artifacts on an unprecedented scale, made the planet uninhabitable for human beings. And so the species *Homo sapiens* became extinct.

"The history of man, then, was not unlike the history of other species that became extinct when the environment changed, except for one thing: the change in environment that led to man's extinction was man's own doing. Many other species perished with man, but many that were immune to the changes of environment produced by man survived, among them the cockroaches, which were immune to large doses of radiation. The cockroaches had been around for about 40 million years, perhaps a thousand times longer than *Homo sapiens* and forty times longer than genus *Homo*. Evolution will go on without man. Evidently man was not on the main trunk of the evolutionary tree. He was on one of the branches that had to terminate in extinction: an unsuccessful experiment. In inventing symbolic language, man put his bet on the wrong survival mechanism."

Such might be the comments of an "impartial outside observer" on the rise and fall of man. We, however, are not impartial. Moreover, we are not yet extinct. Being human, we cannot easily rid ourselves of the idea that we are somehow "special." And if we ask ourselves why we believe this, a possibly defensible answer is that we are special because we are the only beings that can ask the question "Why are we special?" Let us, therefore, not prejudge the issue of whether man's "reason," derived from man's unique survival mechanism, symbolic language, is a blessing or a curse. Let us try to get a better understanding of how it can be both.

The potential of symbolic language to evoke mental images of situations not immediately experienced nor ever experienced has three important consequences.

First, as has been said, it makes possible the transmission of experience by means of language alone, thereby vastly increasing the amount of knowledge that can be stored in the collective memory of a culture. With the invention of writing, the storage of knowledge becomes independent of even the collective memory. Libraries can now serve as extracorporeal memory banks of vast capacity.

Second, symbolic language enables us to imagine the possible, and so to anticipate future events. It enables us to compare what is with what might be. It gives us the capacity to hope and also, be it noted, to fear. A message can transport us to ecstasy or plunge us into despair without in the least changing the physical situation in which we find ourselves. Joy derived from sensual experience and misery imposed by physical pain are comparatively infrequent occurrences in our lives.

Most of our joys and sorrows come from remembrance of the past and anticipation of the future. It has been said that motivation to act comes from some imbalance in the state of an organism. In non-humans, this imbalance is primarily physiological: hunger, thirst, pain, sexual tension, and so on. Human beings, however, can be in a state of imbalance even if all the physiological variables are in equilibrium precisely because human beings "take stock" not only of the actual state of affairs but also of anticipated or potential states of affairs. Man has fewer occasions to be content, hence inactive, than any other animal.

Third, symbolic language enables us both to transmit and to believe *false* or "not true" messages. A being not charitably disposed to the human race might well call man the "lying animal." And indeed man alone among animals can lie, wittingly or unwittingly, to others and to himself. Symbolic language being a freewheeling language, "emancipated," as it were, from the situations to which it refers, makes falsehood possible. By falsehood, I mean here not only deliberate deceit but, more generally, any serious discrepancy between the images that are evoked by what we say, hear, read, and write, and actual states of affairs.

From what has been said, one might infer that symbolic language, like all human inventions, is a mixed blessing. On the one hand, it has made possible a tremendous accumulation of experience, and through it an extracorporeal arsenal of tools (technology) which has enabled man to mold his physical environment to his needs instead of molding his own body and psyche to the physical environment. There is little doubt that this reversal of the adaptation process is responsible for man's survival so far. On the other hand, it is symbolic language that generates the tremendous excess baggage of false knowledge cluttering up our existence: obsolete myths and superstitions, unfounded hatreds and fears. It is symbolic language that makes possible the manipulation of the many by the few. It is the power of the word that has vested in a few individuals the power of life and death over the entire population of the globe.

This is literally true. For it is only necessary for one man in Washington or in Moscow to speak a few words over a telephone to trigger a chain of events that will turn the world into a radioactive inferno. For, if certain words are pronounced by the president of the United States, they will serve as signals to people who stand ready to react to them by pronouncing certain words in turn. These words, which are physically only little puffs of air, will, in turn, stimulate some hundreds of people to perform specific acts and to send specific messages. These messages will, in their turn, stimulate some thousands of people to perform certain other acts. To someone unaware of what is happening, none of these acts will appear particularly sinister or violent: young ladies operating switchboards and typewriters, people getting into cars or trucks, gates opening and shutting, pieces of equipment being moved, and, finally, people throwing switches or pushing levers. All of these acts in their proper sequence *have already been prepared.* Only a signal is required to set them in motion. And if they are set in motion, they will add up to an orgy of death and destruction. The killing will not be done solely by human beings. It would probably not be possible to induce so much murder if it had to be done by human beings. There are not enough people capable of killing to kill every one.

There are comparatively few people who can strangle or stab a child. Hardly anyone could press a child's arm to white-hot metal while the child screams and struggles to tear himself away. But "normal" young men drop napalm bombs on villages, and napalm was invented not only to burn human flesh but also to resist all attempts of the human to get the burning stuff off his body. Chemists keep working to "improve" napalm; that means, to make it even more difficult to save one's self once one has been splattered with it.

The reason "normal" human beings are able to do such things to others is that a screen of symbolic language is interposed between what people believe themselves to be doing and the results of their actions. The chemist is not torturing a child; he is "working on a scientific problem." The flyer who drops napalm bombs is not injuring or killing anybody; he is "fighting in defense of freedom" or simply "doing his job." Technology and symbolic language separate killers and torturers from their victims and so make possible the organization and execution of murder, mayhem, and destruction on a limitless scale.

And so, the total murder of the human race now is not only possible but has actually been prepared for and organized, awaiting only a signal to be carried out. This possibility was created by applied science and by the complex forms of human organization that we call civilization, both products of symbolic language.

It has become possible to kill in a matter of hours hundreds of millions of people only because each of the participants in this prospective mass murder, prepared in advance, has, by virtue of being human, learned to internalize *verbal definitions* of situations. If at any time while he is carrying out his assigned activity he were asked why he is doing what he is, he could reply, "It is my job to do so-and-so when commanded by legitimate authority." Ordinarily his assessment of the situation would go no further. But even if we could pursue further analysis of each participant's actions, the analysis would not get very far. It would quickly come up against the impenetrable wall of verbally induced and verbally defined compulsions and beliefs. "Is the authority legitimate?" we might ask. Of course it is, might be the answer. The order was given by my superior. But his legitimacy, we might say, depends on the legitimacy of the organization that defines the chain of authority. "Is the organization legitimate?" Of course it is. The armed forces were established by government directives. "Is the government legitimate?" Of course it is. Here, if our respondent is an American and imbued with the philosophy of American constitutional law, he might go on to point out that the legitimacy of government derives from the sovereignty of the people, that the sovereignty of the people is the essence of democracy, and that democracy is the essence of liberty. This "reasoning" would not be possible if it were not guided by images evoked by symbols, that is, by verbally defined situations.

If man destroys himself, then symbolic language will have contributed to his undoing as much as it served to enhance his survival. For it is primarily through symbolic language that man perceives reality, and if his perceptions drive him to destruction, then clearly the perceptions are distorted. Our language acts like a screen between us and reality. For the most part, we see only what is on the screen, not what is behind it. The screen filters and distorts what comes to us. Images often appear on it that are no more than shadows of other images, not projections of underlying reality. That is to say, verbal descriptions of reality acquire a life of their own and proliferate as fantasies and myths. The history of human folly is largely a history of man's preoccupations with images that he himself has created by virtue of the limitless capacity of symbolic language to generate "meanings" unrelated to anything real.

In Jonathan Swift's savage satire on the human race, *Gulliver's Travels,* there is an account of how two warring factions developed in the empire of Lilliput over the proper way to break eggs eaten in the shell. One party maintained that the smaller end should be broken; the other favored the larger end. The emperor declared for the small-end party and issued an edict commanding all his subjects to break their eggs at the small end. The Big-endians would have none of this and rebelled. Pacification was accomplished at the cost of 11,000 Lilliputian lives. The story has a familiar ring, of course, except that many more than 11,000 human beings have perished for saying the wrong words or performing the wrong symbolic acts, whether in prayer or in politics. The Nazis alone massacred several million men, women, and children because a certain label deprived them of the right to live. The shameful race relations that have besmirched United States history were rooted not in differences of skin color but in the label that was attached to people of a certain ancestry.

It appears, then, that the essential characteristic of man, that is, his possession of and dependence on a symbolic language, underlies both his success and his failure as a social animal. The fanciful definition of man as a being between the angels and the beasts, if taken figuratively, may have something to recommend it, provided we are willing, in fairness to the beasts, to extend the range of human depravity considerably beyond the capabilities of beasts. At the upper reaches, imagination, compassion, a sense of the future, an appreciation of beauty—all these semidivine aspects of the human psyche, derived from symbolic representations of experience, give us a sense of pride in being human. Human reason, having blossomed into science, emancipated man from drudgery and so made possible cultivation of the spiritual faculties that endow human existence with meaning. At the same time, hatred, ethnocentrism, superstition, fears unrelated to demonstrable threats, and the attending destructive urges are likewise rooted in symbolic experience. Our enemies are those who have been *defined* as our enemies, not those who have actually done us any harm. We fear what we have been taught to fear by use of language alone, not by actual experience. Man's cruelty to man based on labels that men attach to each other exceeds anything observed in the so-called world reddened by tooth and claw. As Mephistopheles says of man in Goethe's *Faust*:

Life somewhat better might content him,
But for the gleam of heavenly light which Thou has lent him:
He calls it Reason—thence his power's increased,
To be far beastlier than any beast.[5]

Whom will subsequent history vindicate—the nineteenth-century prophets of progress, or the misanthropes like Jonathan Swift and Goethe's Mephistopheles? If we ask the question seriously, we ought to examine the peculiar feature of the human species called "reason" more closely. How can we do this? Would it help us to examine man's "organ of thought"—the brain? Let us see.

When we want to understand how something works, we usually examine its structure. For example, in order to understand how a piano or a flashlight or an automobile works, we look to see how it is put together. But discovering merely the structure often is not sufficient. For instance, in the case of the piano, we must not only see how the parts fit together but must also understand the principle of the lever, how depressing a key sends the hammer flying upward to hit the string. We must also understand the connection between the length or the tension of the string and the pitch of the tone it produces. All these connections can be easily demonstrated. In the case of a flashlight, the situation is more complicated. We must understand how the chemical reaction in the battery generates an electric current and how the current heats the thin filament in the bulb to incandescence. The theory of these processes is more involved than the mechanics of levers and the physics of sound. The automobile is a much more complex system than either a piano or a flashlight and, accordingly, more must be learned to understand how the automobile works.

Pianos, flashlights, and automobiles are all accessible to our understanding because it was we (human beings) who put them together in the first place. It is a different matter with the brain. The structure of the brain has been studied by neuroanatomists in great detail and has been minutely described. Quite a bit is known also about what happens when the constituent units of the brain, the neurons (brain cells), are functioning. Essentially a brain cell acts by producing an

5. Johann Wolfgang von Goethe, *Faust*, trans. Bayard Taylor (New York: Modern Library, 1912), p. 10.

electrical discharge and, under certain conditions, the resulting electrical and chemical changes in the vicinity of the discharging cells activate other cells or, on the contrary, prevent their activation. The work of the brain is essentially the production of patterns of activation among the brain cells.

It is known that the activation of certain brain cells results in the transmission of impulses along nerve fibers and that these can cause muscles to contract. It is also known that stimuli acting on our sense receptors (organs of sight, hearing, etc.) start nerve impulses that travel toward the brain. The courses of the impulses traveling in both directions have been charted. Certain areas of the brain have been discovered to be associated with specific sensory and motor functions. Experiments on animals have revealed the role of certain brain areas in comparatively simple mental processes such as memory retention, perception of shapes and patterns, and so on. However, the gap between this sort of knowledge and knowledge of just how the brain functions as an "organ of thought" (which we are convinced it is) is still immense. No one has yet established a connection between events in a brain and the simplest voluntary actions requiring genuine thought, for example, reading a sentence or adding two plus two. We have no knowledge that would enable us to distinguish between the brain of an Albert Einstein and an Al Capone, between the brain of an Adolph Hitler and a Mahatma Gandhi, between the brain of a paranoid schizophrenic and a clinically normal person.

It seems, therefore, that the study of the actual (material, physical) "organ of thought" is not likely for quite some time to provide us with hints as to how human reason works, particularly how human thought differs from that of other animals with brains, or what it is that has made us so unique in the world of living beings.

The same difficulty arises in trying to understand "how a piano works." Assuming that we have understood all the mechanical details, how the depressing of the key propels the hammer, how the impact of the hammer initiates the vibration of the string, and even how the resulting vibrations of the air are perceived as a tone, we still have not answered the question "What is music?" This question may be of no interest to the piano maker or the physicist, but it may have been the question that instigated our investigation of "how the piano works" in the same way the question "What is man?" may have instigated an investigation of "how the brain works." Both investigations led to a gap, still unbridged, between understanding of how an event happens and understanding its "meaning."

The fact that the gap has not been bridged does not mean that it cannot be bridged. Perhaps someday the entire sequence of events, from the depressing of the piano keys in certain combinations and sequences to the vibrations of strings to the perceptions of tones to the emergence of "musical meaning" to our emotional reactions to it, can be fully described. If, however, we are interested in the last links of that chain and if the gap still exists, then we must begin our investigations somewhere on the side of the gap where our interest lies. The question is, where?

So it is with the study of man. Granted that man is what he is because he has a very special brain, an examination of the brain will not, at this stage of our knowledge, carry us across the gap from physiology to psychology, let alone to sociology, anthropology, economics, politics, ethics, and aesthetics, all of which examine matters pertinent to the question "What is man?" We must begin on the "psychological" side of the gap.

A study of language seems to be a good place to begin. Language is directly involved in all of man's specifically human activities. At the same time, we can study language in sufficient detail to gain some knowledge of "how it works," that is, how it generates and transforms ideas and, through these, directs human behavior.

Although a language is not a material thing like a brain, it nevertheless has a distinct structure. A language can be "dissected" as a brain can and its constituent parts seen in their relation to each other. Understanding the structure of a language helps us understand how it "works"; that is, how it functions in communication among human beings. Moreover, the relationship between the structure of language and that of human thought is much more apparent than the connection between the structure of a brain and that of thought. By examining their verbal outputs, we *can* distinguish an Erasmus from a Savonarola, a Hindu from a Jew, a Communist from a Republican. Verbal output, not only of a person but of a whole people, is often the most important key to their mental and emotional make-up. Conceivably the total verbal output of the human race may one day provide us with insight into our nature and our fate.

To say that "a man is what he eats" is rarely enlightening except possibly as a hint to understanding the chemistry of the human body, which is not radically different from the chemistry of many other animals. To say "Man is what he utters" comes much closer to revealing the truth about our essential nature. In order to get at that truth, we must be able to interpret human utterances. But how can we? The utterances are language and language is the only tool we have for making interpretations. Can we understand language if we must use language as an instrument of analysis? Are we caught in a vicious cycle? We are and we are not. Language has many levels, and to a certain extent we can use the higher levels to understand what is going on at the lower ones. Whether in attempting to understand ourselves we can ever escape from language altogether is a question I am not competent to answer; nor is it relevant to the purpose of this book. A great deal can be learned about language while using language as a tool of analysis, and we shall so proceed.

APPLICATIONS

I. The following are some other definitions of man (cf. p. 4) culled from a variety of sources:

a) Man is an animal that can talk about talking.
b) Man is an animal aware of his own existence.
c) Man is an animal that knows it will die.
d) Man is the only animal without instincts.
e) Man is a biped born without fur or feathers.
f) Man is a naked ape.
g) "Man is the only animal that cooks its food." *Claude Lévi-Strauss*
h) "Man is the only total omnivore on earth: he will, or has, or can, eat virtually anything" *Dr. William Watson*
i) "How like a god!" *William Shakespeare*
j) "How like a dog!" *Ivan Pavlov*
k) "Man is a rope, fastened between animal and Superman—a rope over an abyss." *Friedrich Nietzsche*

l) Assume that you are visiting Mars for a weekend in the year 2046 and that your Martian hosts (who speak English) have asked you, "What is man?" Using any one (or a combination of several) of the above definitions as a point of departure, respond to this question in about 1,000 words.

2) Assume that you are a Martian visiting the planet Earth for the first time. After a stay of one month, you are writing a letter to your family on Mars, explaining and/or describing what a man is.

3) Behind each of the definitions listed above lies a submerged philosophical position. Develop the implications of one position and its antithesis in a dialogue between two speakers. Plato's *Republic* will serve as a model. For further information, see one or more of the following titles: Desmond Morris, *The Naked Ape*; Friedrich Nietzsche, *Thus Spoke Zarathustra*; Claude Lévi-Strauss, *The Raw and the Cooked*; William Watson, *Man the Omnivore*; B. F. Skinner, *Beyond Freedom and Dignity*; Ernst Cassirer, *An Essay on Man*; Feodor Dostoyevsky, *Notes from Underground*; Alexis Carrel, *Man the Unknown*.

II. B. F. Skinner, the behaviorist, has said, "We have not yet seen what man can make of man," and Jean Paul Sartre has asserted, "Man invents himself every moment." It would seem as though both the behaviorist and the existentialist believe that "Man"—or "human nature"—is an abstraction that has meaning only *after* we have observed human behavior or existence, not before, as many thinkers of the past maintained. Often people buttress an argument by saying, "As we all know, it is only human nature to blah-blah-blah-blah."

1) Do you believe there is such a universal as "human nature"?

2) Read Chapter 7 on "denotation" and "connotation." Can you support your arguments by reference to "denotative" meanings? If you cannot, does this mean that your arguments are invalid? For additional suggestions, read B. F. Skinner, *Verbal Behavior*; Jean Paul Sartre, *Existentialism as a Humanism*; and Alexis Carrel, *Man the Unknown*.

III. "Man is indeed the only animal that uses a symbolic language as a means of communicating with others of his kind and, what is most important, with himself." (page 6) Do you think the author can "prove" this assertion? Using what evidence? Is there evidence to the contrary? Consider the following pieces of "evidence" to the contrary:

1) St. Francis allegedly communicated with the birds in their language. Birds may have a symbolic language that we humans do not understand.

2) Marine biologists report that dolphins appear to communicate with one another by a series of clicks, beeps, and grunts emitted from an orifice in the head. There is a record of whale sounds that suggests a system of communication between these sea mammals.

3) Dogs dream (as any pet owner can testify). Since the language of

dreams is symbolic (Freud), it would seem to follow that dogs must possess some rudimentary form of symbolic language.

4) Some scientists think that intelligent animals can learn to perform menial tasks in the service of their human masters. That would suggest at least a *potential* for understanding symbolic language.

Before you commence arguing, examine the "evidence" carefully and, if you have the time, consult Susanne Langer, *Philosophy in a New Key*; Robert Yerkes, *Chimpanzees: A Laboratory Colony*; and John Lilly, *Man and Dolphin*.

IV. Related to symbolism (page 6) is a rhetorical device called *synecdoche* in which a part of a thing is used to represent the whole. When successful, it presents an idea through a concrete image that enables us to see the subject. For insance, "He commands three hundred tanks" is a synecdoche for "He commands an armored division." In the following instances, *A* is a synecdoche and *B* is a literal statement. Circle your choice of alternatives in each of the following pairs and answer the question: "I prefer (*A*, *B*) because it is (clearer, more vivid, less ambiguous, less pretentious, etc.).

1) A. One hundred and twenty mailed horses were ready to ride.
   B. A company of cavalry was ready to ride.
2) A. Cannon to the left of them, cannon to the right of them.
   B. Artillery to the left of them, cannon to the right of them.
3) A. He had ten thousand rifles trained on Vicksburg.
   B. He had ten thousand infantrymen surrounding Vicksburg.
4) A. There are six sails in the harbor.
   B. There are six sailboats in the harbor.
5) A. Fifty thousand pairs of eyes followed the ball.
   B. Fifty thousand spectators watched the ball.

V. In a recent book by Alvin Toffler called *Future Shock*, it is argued that too much change in our environment or our lives causes derangement of the physiological and psychological processes. The total self-destruction of mankind may come about according to Toffler, not from the lack of change, but from overchange. Too much stimulation of the human organism or of human society creates the condition of "shock." Does this position differ from the position taken in this chapter?

VI. "By falsehood, I mean here not only deliberate deceit but, more generally, any serious discrepancy between the images that are evoked by what we say, hear, read, and write, and actual states of affairs." (page 16) Are there degrees of "lying"? In *Cat on a Hot Tin Roof*, Tennessee Williams has a tirade against "mendacity"—by which he means about the same thing as the definition you just read. But in *The Art of Lying*, Oscar Wilde asserts that all fantasy (that is, literature) is a form of lying, and that Americans tend to be uncreative and unimaginative because they chose for their national hero a man who reputedly could not tell a lie. D. H. Lawrence, in "The Spirit of Place" says: "An artist is usually a damned liar." Discuss the following questions:

1) Plato would have denied the poet access to the ideal Republic precisely because he told persuasive lies. Is literature indeed a form of "lying"? If so, does this mean that literature is either useless or dangerous?
2) People used to speak about "white" lies and "black" lies (the color symbolism here is worth the semanticist's attention). Do you, in fact, tell lies yourself during the course of a normal day? Can a lie be necessary or constructive? Count the number of lies ("white," of course) you tell during any given day.
3) What do you think D. H. Lawrence means when he says in the same essay, "And out of a pattern of lies art weaves the truth"? Read his *Studies in Classic American Literature* in which he penetrates behind the "lies" of American literature to the "impeccable truth."
4) Read "The Benefits of Poor Communication" by Charlotte Kursh in *Intellectual Digest* of December 1971. Do you agree with the point of view expressed in this article?

VII. There is yet another reason (in addition to the screen of symbolic language) why the chemist can develop napalm and the flyer can drop it: physical distance creates psychic distance. People who live in Los Angeles have noted this about themselves. What contributions has technology made toward *reducing* distances between people and between people and events? It has been said that in the future television will make impossible another war like the one in Vietnam. Do you agree with this statement? In other words, can technology be used to counteract the influence of symbolic language?

VIII. One of the definitions of sanity used to be the ability to tell the real from the unreal. In the past, verbal descriptions of reality acquired a life of their own and proliferated as fantasies and myths (the Western outlaw, the innocent Sleeping Beauty). What do you think will happen to the definition of reality when an economy (such as the American), in search of a new purpose, seriously begins to enter into the *production of experiences* for their own sake, experiences that blur the distinction between the vicarious and the nonvicarious, the simulated and the real? Some sociologists predict that ours will become the first culture in history to employ technology to manufacture that most transient, yet lasting, of products— the human experience. Of course, this manufactured experience will be adorned with symbolic significance that may no longer surround our manufactured products, especially as they become more perishable. That is, you may have an "experience" of Africa without ever leaving Los Angeles, of the eighteenth century at Disneyland, of "love" and "affection" at the nearby massage parlor.

1) Can you think of any "packaged experiences" that simulate reality? Have you experienced them? Do they seem to weaken your sense of reality?
2) Is Bob Dylan a "real" rebel or is he a "manufactured" one for the sake of record sales? Is it disturbing to you that he has repudiated the "message" of his songs that appeared to influence large numbers of young people in the late sixties? That is, that he described and created a reality for them which he later confessed no longer existed—and perhaps never did?

IX. One of the classical debates in the field of neurology is whether the "mind" can be conceived of apart from the "brain." Sir Charles Sherrington, a Nobel Prize winner in medicine, maintained that the mind was distinct from the brain. Ivan Pavlov, the Russian behaviorist, scoffed at the distinction as a "capitalist fable" (this was during Pavlov's last days under the Soviet government).

1) Do a brief research paper on the "Sherrington-Pavlov Controversy." Begin with the *Dictionary of National Biography*. Express your own position at the end of the paper and the reason for taking that position.
2) Pavlov's remarks about the Sherrington view suggest a political overtone to the controversy. Is Pavlov guilty of what the semanticist regards as "name-calling," or is there something more to his accusation? For further information, read Grey Walter, *The Living Brain*.
3) Is there a difference between "imagination" and "reason"? What is it?
4) Would it be accurate to say that the scientist employs "reason" and the artist uses "imagination"? Cite examples to support your point.

X. The great French chef Brillat-Savarin once remarked, "Tell me what you eat and I will tell you what you are." Assuming that he meant something by this observation, what do you think he meant? Some zoologists now consider this statement can be extended into studies that will reveal what man has been, how he evolved, and where he is going (that is, eating is an index of one's psychological state; mothers express oral sadism by forcing children to eat foods they hate; "leftover" scavenging impulses energize self-service in stores where products lie about in profusion; man "hunts" in supermarkets, eats in cavelike restaurants, etc.). Can you add other instances of the "eating game"?

XI. The fundamental question of this book is raised at the end of the chapter and deserves to be repeated here: "Can we understand language if we must use language as an instrument of analysis?" After you have finished reading this text, you may have an answer to this question. Do you have one now? It would be useful to jot down your response now and then to reexamine the question when you have completed the book.

2/linguistic innocence and linguistic awareness

We know next to nothing about how a child acquires the ability to speak and understand his native language. Explanations of this amazing feat amount to little more than putting word labels on what occurs. Some say the child learns "by imitation." So does a parrot, when he is "learning to talk." But we cannot converse with a parrot, whereas we can with a three-year-old child. Clearly, then, there is a difference between what each of the two has learned. But what is this difference?

Even if we assume that both the child and the bird learn "by imitation," is the ability to imitate innate or is it also learned? We know that the child can imitate before he learns to speak. We clap our hands, and the baby does the same. Somehow the baby already "knows" that his hands are "the same things" as our hands. How does he know this? It can't be only because he sees that his hands look like our hands. If it is, then how can we explain that a baby will touch his ear or his nose, which he does not see, when we touch ours? Can a baby do this only if he has had access to a mirror? In India a superstition forbids showing a mirror to a child before a certain age, and some people have no mirrors at all. Hence the appeal to mirrors will not do as an explanation of how a young child recognizes the correspondence between his (unseen) body parts and those of others. So the very process of imitation remains a mystery.

Another explanation of how a child learns language is "by association." The child supposedly learns to "associate" words with what they stand for. To be sure, the child's first words are names of objects (including persons). Yet very soon the child learns to use words that have no relation to objects, words like "if," "or," "the." Evidently much, much more than the use of correct word labels for objects is involved in learning a language.

Somehow the ability to use language is acquired in the first few years of life. Moreover it is acquired without any awareness of "linguistic principles" such as grammar or semantics. The very young child does not know what "meaning" means. Ask him "What is a telephone?" and most likely he will think the question silly. "A telephone is a telephone" is a young child's common reply. What does he mean—that everything is identical to itself? Or does he mean that a "telephone" is a telephone, thinking of the *word* "telephone" first, then the object, telephone? If he thinks that the question is silly (which we may infer from his giggles), does he think it is absurd to ask a question to which the only answer is a tautology? Or does he think it absurd that an adult does not know what a telephone is?

Most likely, for a very young child, the question "What is the meaning of a word?" does not yet make sense. Words are either familiar or unfamiliar. Unfamiliar words are ignored until they become familiar. They become familiar by being linked to things or events that accompany their use. For the young child, then, a word *is* the thing or event to which it is linked. Meaning is an identity, not a relation. Therefore, when we ask a child "What is a telephone?" he does not understand the question as a request to connect the *word* telephone with the appropriate object. If he did, he would point to a telephone and say *"This* is a telephone." Instead, the child thinks of the *object* telephone (with which he has identified the word), and for him the question becomes "What is (the object) telephone?" The only answer to this question is that the object telephone is itself. And since there cannot possibly be any other thing that the telephone can be, the question seems "funny."

The Swiss psychologist Jean Piaget has made extensive studies of juvenile semantics. Some of his experiments are startlingly revealing. For example, Piaget would ask a young boy (who had one brother) "Have you a brother?" The answer would usually be "Yes." Then he would ask "Has your brother a brother?" Boys below a certain age frequently answer "No." It is reasonable to conclude that the little boy thinks of "brother" not as a *relation* between him and his sibling but as the *identity* of his sibling. It does not yet occur to him that he himself is his brother's brother.[1]

In another experiment, Piaget would ask, "Suppose everyone called the sun 'moon' and the moon 'sun.' Would that be all right?" Up to a certain age, the child's answer is usually "No." To the question "Why not?" the answer would be something of this sort: "Because the sun is in the daytime and the moon is at night." Or "Because the sun is brighter than the moon." Or "Because the sun is not the moon and the moon is not the sun." All these answers point to an inability to dissociate an object from its name.[2]

The idea that things have "real" names, and that reality is ignored if they are called by other names, is remarkably persistent. A joke attributed to Abraham Lincoln goes like this: "If you called a dog's tail a leg, how many legs would a dog have?" If the answer is "Five," the rejoinder is "Wrong. A dog has four legs no matter what you call his tail." But is this so? How many fingers does a man have? If you count thumbs as fingers, ten; if not, eight. Russians use the same word for finger, thumb, and toe. Are Russians justified in saying that a man has twenty fingers? If so, then why not say that a dog has five legs if the same word ("leg") is used for all five extremities?

In one of Plato's dialogues, a character named Hermogenes argues that the names of things are not arbitrary, that things have "true" names. "I should explain to you, Socrates, that our friend Cratylus has been arguing about names; he says that they are natural and not conventional; not a portion of the human voice which men agree to use; but that there is a truth or correctness in them, which is the same for Hellenes as barbarians." [3] We also read in Genesis (2:19): "And whatever Adam named every living thing, that was the name thereof." The idea seems to be that Adam *guessed* the "true" names of animals.

Identifying words with objects generates a belief in word magic. The belief is rooted in early experiences. Saying "Mama" often makes Mama materialize. Wishes can at times be gratified by pronouncing words. The practice of pronouncing words in the hope that the words

1. Jean Piaget, *Judgment and Reasoning in the Child* (New York: Harcourt, Brace and Company, 1928), pp. 75 ff., 104 ff.
2. Jean Piaget, *The Child's Conception of the World* (Totowa, N.J.: Littlefield, Adams & Company, paperback, 1967), pp. 81–83.
3. Plato, *Cratylus*, in Roger Brown, *Words and Things* (Glencoe, Ill.: The Free Press, 1958).

uttered will make things appear or happen is deeply incorporated in all human beings. Men everywhere use incantations, blessings, curses, and prayers.

Verbal taboos have a similar origin. Certain beings, real or imagined, are objects of awe or fear, and their names are avoided in speech. The assumption is that pronouncing a name makes contact with what is named. Contact with exalted or terrible beings is best avoided. In the Hebrew Old Testament, the name of the deity is Yahweh. In reading the Old Testament aloud, however, pious Jews must pronounce the word Adonai. Both Yahweh and Adonai refer to the same being, but Yahweh is his "real" name and therefore taboo.

Taboos sometimes extend to names of animals as well. The Russian linguist A. A. Reformatsky notes the variety of euphemisms for "bear" among Russian commercial hunters. Actually even the common word *miedvied* is an old euphemism; its literal meaning is "honey eater." Eventually secondary euphemisms developed: *khoziain* (landlord or boss), *lomaka* (he who breaks things, like bones maybe), *mokhnach* (the shaggy one), *liesnik* (the forest dweller), or simply *on* (he).[4]

These circumlocutions seem to be remnants of ancient reluctance to pronounce names of dreaded beings for fear of making them appear. They are a vestige of word magic. We still say "speak of the devil" when someone about whom we were talking makes an appearance.

In many preliterate cultures, the "real" names of persons are never used in addressing them or in referring to them. Some other names are used instead. Sometimes the "real" name of a person remains a secret. The underlying belief is that knowledge of the "real" name confers power over the thing or being named. Recall the story of Rumpelstiltskin, where the wizard's power over the queen was broken when she found out his name.[5] According to a Jewish superstition, changing

---

4. A. A. Reformatsky, *Vvedenie v Yazykoznanie*. [Introduction to linguistics] (Moscow: State Scientific-Pedagogical Publishing House, 1955), p. 70.

5. Another example is T. S. Eliot's engaging verse:
   When you notice a cat in profound meditation,
       The reason, I tell you, is always the same:
   His mind is engaged in a rapt contemplation
       Of the thought, of the thought, of the thought of his name:
           His ineffable effable
           Effanineffable
   Deep and inscrutible singular Name.
T. S. Eliot. "The Naming of Cats," in *The Complete Poems and Plays, 1909–1950* (New York: Harcourt, Brace and Company, 1952), p. 149.

the name of a sick person may save his life by confusing the Angel of Death.

Closely related to the notion that things have "real" names is the conviction of primitive people, first coming in contact with foreigners, that the strangers cannot talk. The Slavic word for Germans is *niemtsy*, which means "mutes." The word Slav probably derives from *slovo*, which means "word" in most Slavic languages.[6] Even when extended contact with foreign-speaking people finally drives home the idea that different people use different words to denote the same things, the notion often persists that one's own names are the "correct" ones. Jim argues Huckleberry Finn into a corner when he challenges Huck to explain to him why a Frenchman "doesn't talk like a man."

Eventually people resign themselves to the fact that foreigners do speak differently. They also perceive that one can communicate with strangers if one learns their language. The primitive idea about learning a foreign language is that the main problem is to learn "their" names for things.

Lemuel Gulliver, in his travels to exotic lands, quickly learns the language of the Lilliputians, of the Brobdingnagians, of the Laputians, and even of horses. In Part III of his *Travels*, Gulliver describes his method of acquiring a foreign language. He points to things and has his native teacher say their names. These he writes down in his notebook (using the English alphabet). The implication is that, having mastered a sufficient number of words, Gulliver is able to converse in the newly learned language.

A character in a Russian novel uses the same method to learn several languages at once. He is an enthusiastic young Red Army man who believes that the world proletarian revolution is imminent and that when it occurs the Russian workers will be teaching their class allies in Germany, France, and England how to liquidate the bourgeoisie. To prepare himself for this task, he is collecting English, French, and German words which he writes down in parallel columns with their Russian equivalents. He makes some surprising discoveries: for example, that the English word "revolution" has apparently been borrowed from Russian (the Russian word is *revolutsia*). He even entertains a psycholinguistic theory to explain the difference in the pronunciation: because of their dislike for revolution, the English capitalists have introduced a hissing "sh" sound into it.

6. Another possibility is that "slav" is related to *slava* (fame or glory).

In the sixteenth century, a Spanish bishop undertook to decipher what he thought was Mayan writing (apparently a sample of pictographs). Pointing to the sample, he asked a captive Indian "¿Qué es A?" (Which is A?). The captive, probably realizing that failure to reply might result in unpleasant consequences, pointed to something in the sample. "Muy bien," said the bishop; "¿Qué es B?" Proceeding in this way, the bishop completed his linguistic research.[7]

Frederick the Great (1712–86) is said to have performed an "experiment" to determine the "original" language spoken by man. He ordered several newborn babies to be completely isolated, except for feeding by silent attendants, in the expectation that when they started to speak, they would speak the "original" language. Some scholars said it would be Greek; others thought it would be Hebrew.

In short, linguistic innocence is rooted in ignorance of the arbitrary and accidental way in which any linguistic community, including our own, has come to project experiences onto symbols and to organize symbols into a language. For several centuries, Latin and Greek grammars were taught in European schools, not only because it was considered necessary for educated people to acquaint themselves with the writings of the Greeks and Romans, but also because these grammars were thought to be models of clear thinking. The vulgate grammars—English, German, and so on—were thought to be variants (often corrupted ones) of the supposedly perfectly "logical" classical grammars. Even today the names of grammatical categories (cases, tenses, etc.) in German, Danish, and other Continental languages are designated by their original Latin names.

In the 1911 edition of *Encyclopaedia Britannica*, one reads the following in the article on philology:

> To [the Indo-European family of languages] belongs incontestably the first place, and for many reasons: the historical position of the peoples speaking its dialects, who have now been the leaders in the world's history; an abundance and variety and merit of its literatures, ancient and modern, which, especially the modern, are wholly unapproached by those of any other division of mankind; the period covered by its records; and, most of all, the great variety and richness of its development.

7. At any rate, this is the method attributed to Bishop Diego de Landa (?–1579) by his severe critic, Dr. Phillip J. J. Valentini, a nineteenth-century scholar of the Mayan language. Cf. Cyrus Thomas, *A Study of the Manuscript Troano* (Washington, D.C.: Government Printing Office 1882), p. xxv. Incidentally, after "deciphering" Mayan script, the pious bishop ordered all the manuscripts burned, having decided that Mayan learning was the work of the devil.

In contrast, the "monosyllabic" languages of Southeast Asia, to which Chinese belongs, are described as "destitute of formal structure."

It seems to the speakers of English that Chinese is "ungrammatical."

The *Britannica* article reflects two sources of bias in assigning "degrees of importance" to the various language groups. One is the old ethnocentric and racial bias that has until quite recently characterized comparative studies undertaken by Europeans in whatever field. The other is the bias imposed on early linguistics by its origins. The field from which linguistics sprang was called *philology*. Early philologists were students of literature. Knowledge of literature, especially classical literature, was then a principal motivation for studying languages. In other words, interest in a language was stimulated by its *literary* product rather than for its own sake. For this reason a language or a group of languages was assigned a degree of importance in accordance with how its literature was valued.

The situation changed toward the end of the last century when linguistics emerged as a subfield of anthropology—the study of man. Anthropologists became interested in the rich diversity of life-styles of various human groups. They could not avoid being impressed with the diversity of languages. Interest was awakened in "exotic languages" of out-of-the-way tribes. What was striking about these languages was their often exquisite complexity and intricacy. The notion of "primitive" tongues was quickly dissipated. Different as the various languages were, there seemed to be no simple criteria by which they could be ranked in order of "complexity," "sophistication," or whatever dimension.

With that realization came new methods of study. The student's own language no longer served as a framework in which the language studied had to be fitted. The structure of the language studied had to be inferred from usage in *that* language, somewhat in the way the child internalizes the structure of his own language through *usage*, not through comparison with some model language. Yet the anthropologist studying an exotic language could not, even if it were possible, simply relive the experiences of the child learning to speak. For the anthropologist had also to *describe* the language he was to learn, something a child cannot do.

Let us see how one would proceed to study a language "firsthand," as it were, instead of through the prism of one's own tongue. An ideal way of doing this would be to put oneself in a position where only

the strange language was at one's disposal for communication purposes. After the language was mastered in this way, the anthropologist
could describe it by generalizing his experiences with it. The approach
would naturally be extremely time-consuming; so a compromise is
made. The investigator uses a native speaker as an informant. He is
careful, however, to avoid the Spanish bishop's crude error of assuming that the strange language is a "literal" (that is, letter by letter)
translation of his own. The first things an attentive student of language discovers is that the sounds in another language are different
from those of his own. There may be more or fewer of them, and,
what is most important, differentiations may be made in the strange
language that are not made in his own and, conversely, differentiations
in his own language may not be made in the other.

Once, when I tried to learn Bengali, I was baffled by the distinction
made by the Bengalese between two kinds of "t." To me they sounded
exactly alike. Only when my "informant" explained to me that one
"t" is produced by touching the roof of the mouth with the tongue
while the other is made by touching the teeth, and only when I myself produced the two "t's" did I begin to hear the difference.

In the same way, grammatical distinctions in one language are difficult for a speaker of another language in which they are not made.
We have four ways of expressing past action: *I was going, I went, I
have gone, I had gone*. To us these distinctions are meaningful because
each form brings out a different "view" of the past action. In some
languages these distinctions are not made (and perhaps others are
made instead). It takes considerable effort to reorganize one's perceptions to learn these distinctions. Only when one has *internalized* the
distinctions made in a language does one acquire "fluency" in it. One
has then learned to "think" in that language, that is, to see the world
through *its* prism.

Phonemic and grammatical analysis brings out a cardinal principle
that one must adopt in any serious approach to the study of language.
One does not learn to pronounce the words of another language by
simply putting together the sounds of one's own tongue in another
way. Nor is it possible to translate from one language to another by
simply translating words. Each language represents a different way of
organizing the muscular movements that produce the basic sounds of
the language, a different way of organizing the sounds into meaningful units, and, what is most important, a different way of organizing

meaningful units into larger ones. Different languages may have widely different grammars, and it may not be possible simply to translate one grammar into another because different grammars represent different *methods of organization.* To grasp the structure of a language far removed from our own, we must often get rid not only of our habits in making sounds (usually difficult enough) but also of preconceived ideas about what is meaningful and what is not, what is to be distinguished and what is not.

A concrete illustration was given by Dorothy Lee, who studied Wintu, an American Indian language.[8] Many American Indian languages are characterized by a strong tendency to combine elements into more or less inseparable units. In English, too, we make such combinations by means of prefixes and suffixes. These parts of words cannot stand by themselves. Thus "un" and "ness" cannot be used as independent words, but they are nevertheless meaningful units. "Un" means "not," as in "unworthy" or "unbending"; "ness" means "something that has the property of," as in "happiness" or "laziness." On the other hand, our sentences are composed of words which can stand by themselves. In many American Indian languages, "one-word sentences" may predominate; that is, sentences in which the words are so tightly stuck together (like our prefixes and suffixes) that they cannot be pulled apart to stand by themselves. Wintu is one such language.

Here are some "one-word sentences" in Wintu together with their approximate meanings.

puqeda	I just pushed a peg into the ground.
olpuqal	He is sitting on one haunch.
poqorahara	Birds are hopping along.
olpoqoyahe	There are mushrooms growing.
tunpoqoypoqaya	You walked short-skirted, stiff-legged ahead of me.

Note that every one of these expressions has a common stem, namely "poq" (or "puq"). In much the same way the English words *propose, depose,* and *expose* (and some others) have a single stem, "pose." After some reflection, we may guess the meaning of that stem and thereby the common "kernel of meaning" in the three words. "Pose" has something to do with "position" or with "putting." Thus,

8. Dorothy D. Lee, "Linguistic Reflections of Wintu Thought," *International Journal of American Linguistics* 10 (1944): 101-7.

to *pro*pose means "to put something *forward*"; to *de*pose a dictator means "to bring him *down* from his high position"; to *ex*pose a plot means "to bring it *out* in the open," and so forth.

Now let us see whether we can guess the meaning of "poq," the common stem in the Wintu one-word sentences cited above. I submit it is not easy.

Actually "poq" refers to a mushroom shape. Pushing a peg into the ground evokes a mental picture of a hand (like the cap of a mushroom) over a peg (the stem). Mushrooms are mushroom-shaped. Admittedly the resemblance to mushrooms of hopping birds and of a man sitting on one haunch is far-fetched, but it is there to some extent in the general appearance of something thick being supported by something thin. As for the short-skirted, stiff-legged lady, a schematic picture of her lower half reveals the resemblance quite clearly (Figure 1).

Figure 1

Possibly the sentence "There has been an atomic explosion" could be expressed in Wintu by a word with "poq" in it. Bizarre? Hardly, when we reflect that we too have adopted the phrase "mushroom cloud" to refer to an atomic explosion.

In English we also have "shape words" that refer to many otherwise unrelated things, events, or situations. We eat with a "fork." The farmer tosses hay with a "pitch fork." The piano tuner and the a cappella choir conductor use a "tuning fork." We speak of "forked" lightning and of a "fork" in the road. To a chess player, a "fork" is a position where a knight or a pawn threatens two pieces at once. All of these situations have only one thing in common: a configuration that reminds one of a stem with branches.

Linguistic awareness involves a realization that historical accident, related probably to what at some time has been of importance in their experience, determines how and what people will abstract from their experiences and how they will express in their language what they have abstracted. One way of abstracting is no more "natural" than another. Only familiarity with our own abstractions and unfamiliarity with the abstractions made in other language communities make other languages seem bizarre while we are still linguistically naïve. Thus the designation of some languages as "primitive" by the early philologists was simply a manifestation of linguistic innocence.

Similar considerations apply to theories of grammar. We learn in school that a noun is a name of a person, place, or thing, and that verbs denote actions. But what we take to be a "thing" or an "action" is determined by our "grammar" more than by any inherent property of what is named. Are we prepared to defend the notion that "blasphemy" is the name of a person, place, or thing? Is lightning a thing? Or does the fact that these words are nouns lead us to extend the definition of noun to "acts" (like blasphemy) or "short-lived events" (like lightning). Again, in the sentence "In Spain it rains mainly on the plains," "rains" is a verb. In the sentence "The rains in Spain stay mainly on the plains," "rains" is a noun. The difference is only grammatical. The two sentences say practically the same thing. The one kind of "rains" is no more an action or a thing than the other. Only the grammatical form of the first sentence makes it appear that in the one case something ("it"?) is doing something, while in the other, something "stays" somewhere.

For this reason, modern grammarians (who have acquired linguistic awareness) have dispensed with the *semantic* definitions of grammatical categories (that is, definitions related to the meanings that grammatical categories are supposed to express). Instead they have confined themselves largely to *structural* definitions. In English a noun is something that can be preceded by an article or can take a plural or something like that. A verb is something that can vary with tense or can end with an "s" in the third person or something like that. In English, incidentally, words that look exactly the same in their uninflected forms can as a rule be either nouns or verbs. Consider the following: block, rule, pipe, paper, brief, stick, paste, kill, house, stem, lift, cry, swell, board, table, chair, book, fire, feed, cripple.

Many words can be both adjectives and nouns: brief, black, iron, good, evil, criminal.

One can go on indefinitely. However, in some languages more highly inflected than English (for example, Russian), this is not the case. The complete word usually consists of a stem (which often cannot stand alone) and a suffix, which by its form reveals the grammatical category to which the word belongs. On the contrary, in other languages less inflected than English (Chinese, for example), there

are no structural distinctions according to which words can be classified as "verbs" or as "nouns." And so the modern grammarian aban-
dons these categories in describing the grammars of these languages.
He does not try to fit all grammar into a familiar model.

In later chapters, we shall be concerned with another kind of linguistic innocence, namely that of philosophers who tacitly assume that
whatever has been given a name exists and that one of the main tasks
of philosophy is to inquire into the nature of what has been named.

The simple-mindedness of this philosophy is reflected in the failure
to distinguish between different senses of the word "exist." Few will
deny that the moon "exists." But whether we are willing to admit that
virtue "exists" depends on how we choose to understand existence. If
we do admit that "virtue" exists, we should at least recognize that its
mode of existence is not the same as the moon's. In particular, while
it seems reasonable to wonder about the "real" nature of the moon
regardless of what people think it is (for example, whether it is alive
or not, whether it shines by its own or by reflected light), one is on
shaky ground if one wonders what virtue "really is" regardless of
what anyone thinks it is. One can defend such questions, of course,
but only if one makes some far from self-evident assumptions—for
instance, that virtue is something that can exist apart from virtuous
human beings or possibly as something that existed even before there
were any human beings.

One naturally wonders how philosophers came to ask questions
such as "What is virtue?" and others of this sort mentioned on page 3.
It is not unlikely that they found themselves facing such questions as
a consequence of a conceptual jump from a familiar word to an imagined thing for which the word is supposed to stand. The conceptual
jump, in turn, is propelled by a tacit conviction that whatever is
named must have an existence (or else it would not be named). This
way of thinking (like any other) is contagious, and the contagion is
carried by language. One philosopher writes a learned dissertation on
the nature of virtue; another will eventually be compelled to reply. A
controversy ensues, a contest in which men try to demonstrate—to
each other, to themselves, and to whoever is reading or listening—their
reasoning power, their erudition, or their perspicacity. Under these
circumstances, it becomes difficult to challenge the meaningfulness of
the central question (for example, What is virtue?). For to challenge
the meaningfulness of a question that philosophers take seriously is to

challenge the philosophers' self-image as men engaged in important pursuits. Few men can squarely face such a challenge.

The obverse of assuming that whatever has been named "exists" is to deny the existence of anything that cannot be directly made apparent to the senses. Such denial also reflects a simple-minded notion about the meaning of "existence." In this view, if something does not "exist" in the way the moon or snow or traffic lights exist, it doesn't exist at all. To discourse on the nature of such chimeras is to talk "non-sense." In later chapters we shall also examine this attitude more closely.

Actually, the fact that virtue or despotism or the capitalist system depends for its "existence" on ideas and notions generated by men does not deprive these words of *all* meaning. Nor does it mean that they exist only "in the minds of men." There may very well be demonstrable situations or conditions to which words like "virtue," "despotism," or "the capitalist system" can be applied more or less consistently. The degree of consistency in the use of such "abstract" words is a very important question indeed and is related to the degree of "meaningfulness" we can ascribe to these words. However, to declare abstractions meaningless simply because it is hard to pin down what they are abstractions of is to evade a difficult problem, not to solve it. If abstractions were meaningless, then we could talk sense only about "things."

In Swift's *Gulliver's Travels* the fixation on the "concrete" meanings of words is satirized by driving it to its absurd conclusion. Some philosophers in the mythical land of Lagado decided that, since words are only names of things, language could be dispensed with altogether. Eliminating language, they argued, would prolong human life by saving wear and tear on the lungs. Philosophers intent on putting this theory into practice walked about the city with sacks on their backs containing all the possible things about which they would have occasion to talk. On meeting, they would put down their sacks and pull out things which they showed to each other in silent conversation.

. . . which hath only this inconvenience attending it [Swift comments] that if a man's business be very great and of various kinds, he must be obliged, in proportion, to carry a great bundle of things upon his back, unless he can afford one or two strong servants to attend him.[9]

9. Jonathan Swift, *Gulliver's Travels* (New York: Harcourt, Brace and Company, 1920), p. 190.

In summary, linguistic innocence stems from the failure to appreciate the complex relations between words and what words stand for. Children and so-called primitives often implicitly identify words with their referents. The identification leads to a tacit assumption that everything has a "right" name and even that a name can often be substituted for its referent as in word magic (practiced both by children and by primitives). Singling out a particular language (one's own) as "natural" reflects the persistence of the "right name" delusion, even after the speech of strangers has been given the status of "another language" rather than gibberish. Even then, the notion persists that, although other people call the same things by different names, one's own grammar is more "logical" than other grammars or that the sounds of one's own language are more melodious or more expressive than those of others.

On the philosophical level, linguistic innocence is reflected in ascribing existence to everything for which one's language community has a name. A reaction against this notion is the denial of existence to "abstractions." Linguistic awareness comes with the recognition that our language plays an important part in organizing our thinking; that the way the thinking of a language community is organized depends on many factors, some probably related to demonstrable historical experiences of the community, some without discernible origins. Once we appreciate the diverse ways in which thinking can be organized, we recognize the possibility of a wider disparity between the "logical structure" of a language and the structure of "reality" that the language is supposed to depict. For, if different languages reflect different perceptions of reality, none of the perceptions may be a dependable "map" of reality. And since we think of the world around us (and within us) in terms of language, we may be seriously deceived if we are not aware of the distortions that language puts into our perceptions. For this reason, language awareness is a necessary step on the road to self-knowledge as well as to knowledge of the real world (see Part III).

APPLICATIONS

I. Cite some instances that exemplify in one way or another "the primitive identification of words and objects" and discuss whether or not they seem to generate a belief in "word magic." After you have collected a few examples of this sort, you should be able to recognize similar practices in the language of your friends and colleagues and perhaps in your own thought as well. In analyzing these passages, try to identify the unspoken assumption behind each one.

The following is an example:

"Come to where the flavor is. Marlboro Country." (Cigarette advertisement) SAMPLE ANALYSIS. The cigarette is called Marlboro (the word). There is apparently a place in the West known as Marlboro (object) where all harassed Americans yearn to be, on horseback and free as the wind. Since we cannot actually go to Marlboro, if we smoke a Marlboro, by some kind of magic we will be transported to that place through our experience with the cigarette.

II. Hucksters, scholars, civil servants, and technicians have always had their own jargon, but the current American linguistic practice of never calling a thing by its most familiar name is so pervasive that we have euphemisms for every man and every occasion. *Newsweek* provides this example:

She and her husband—a successful *mortical surgeon*—live in a *planned community*. Their place is not just a furnished apartment: it's a *garden apartment* containing *oversized rooms* furnished with *quality appointments* and done in *decorator colors*. They prefer to drive a *preowned car*. Like most *young moderns*, she suffers mildly from *hair fatigue*, *problem skin*, and *overacidity*, but she has licked her *figure problem* and is again down to *graduation-day size*. Someday, of course, she and her husband will become *senior citizens* and retire to a *leisure village*. "I'm no *overachiever*," she likes to say. "All I want from life is to become a happy, *fully realized person*."

In the same mood, *The Statesman* of January 11, 1957, invited its readers to invent six pretentious names for jobs demanding little or no skill or to mask six unpleasant things with names which conceal their unpleasantries. Here are some of the entries:

racing tipster:	equine velocity estimation specialist
snow shoveler:	seasonal clearance officer
night watchman:	noctician
baby-sitter:	infant security deputy
window cleaner:	fenestral obscurity remover
streetwalker:	gainfully itinerant amorist (female)
park custodian	peripatetic discarding wrapping/newspaper impaler

Guess what the following refer to: a) crowd engineer, b) carboniferous fuel operator, c) retail trades distributive official, d) custodial engineer, e) vertical transportation equipment superintendent.

There are even euphemisms for euphemisms. As the pleasant way of saying things becomes more and more familiar, new euphemisms have to be invented. The term "stroke" was once a euphemism for apoplexy; now strokes are being called "cerebrovascular accidents." The word "finalize" supplanted the simple word "end" a few years ago. Now space technicians have found a new euphemism: "definitize." Ron Zeigler, President Nixon's press relations man, called an inaccurate statement of the president's "non-operative." Read the front page of any newspaper if you wish to find a few of your own. What are some that you know?

III. The concept of the "shape word" may give us a clue about the process by which the poet invents metaphors. For instance, in *King Lear* Shakespeare calls man "a poor forked creature" (a configuration that reminds one of a stem with branches). The metaphor is particularly appropriate to the lightning-struck heath with its naked trees and withered foliage. A modern novelist writes about a female character: "She had legs like Italy."

1) Look through *A Concordance to Shakespeare* for fifteen minutes and see whether you can find any leads to "shape words" in his work. Compile a list of them. Do they have anything in common?
2) Many seventeenth-century poets, and Dylan Thomas among the moderns, wrote "shaped poetry"—a cross, a tree, wings, a diamond are some of the shapes into which the words are formed. Read five or six of these poems. Do you see any point in the shape?
3) Examine Emmett Williams's *Anthology of Concrete Poetry*. Do the poem shapes have meaning? What meanings?

IV. A system of *structural* definitions of grammatical categories would be very helpful to those people learning English as a second language. Until one knows a language, *semantic* definitions are largely meaningless.

1) Starting with the suggestions in the text, work out a system of structural definitions that encourages better identification of grammatical categories.

a) *noun*: something that can be preceded by an article
b) *verb*:something that can vary with tense (*ed* or change of vowel or auxiliary *is, are, has, have been* preceding)
c) *pronoun*:
d) *adjective*:
e) *adverb*:
f) *article*:

It may be convenient to work with the conventional categories above, but you are free to create your own (for instance, you might prefer "modifier" to "adverb" and "adjective").

2) Now, if you know a language other than English, try these structural categories with its grammar. What modifications do you have to make, if any?

V. A key word in an important philosophy developed since World War II is "existence." As intended by existentialist thinkers, the meaning of the word is more abstract than it is in this chapter, and certainly cannot be made directly apparent to the senses. The existentialist also attaches a special meaning to a word used in Chapter 1, "essence." These two common words form the basis for the French school of existentialism: "Existence precedes essence." The existentialist believes that man's freedom was limited by the assumption that essence precedes existence.

For further information, read Jean Paul Sartre's *What Is Existentialism?* (also known as *Existentialism as a Humanism*); Maurice Merleau-Ponty's *Sense and Non-Sense*, especially the chapter called "The Battle over Existentialism"; William Barrett's *Irrational Man*; or Jean Wahl's *Existentialism*.

1) Are these men "discoursing over chimeras"?

2) By now, the word "existentialist" is in common usage. What do *you* mean by the word? If you don't use it yourself, what do you perceive it to mean as used by others? Is there a "territory" for this "map"?

3/levels of language analysis

It was said (cf. p. 20) that to understand how something works, we must first understand how it is put together (its structure) and, in addition, some principles that account for a chain of events (causal connections). So, to understand how a bicycle works, we must know how its parts fit together and, in addition, some principles of mechanics, say, those of the lever, the gear assembly, and the way a rolling wheel is kept from toppling over by minute adjustments of its direction of motion.

Language has to be approached in the same way, the difference being that the structure of a typical language is vastly more complex than that of a bicycle; moreover, to decide whether or not a language is "working properly" is far more difficult than deciding in the case of a bicycle. The "function" of a bicycle is to enable a person, while using his own muscular power, to move at speeds up to about five times his walking speed. We can say that the bicycle is working properly if it can perform this function. It is easy enough to *say* what the function of language is: to communicate our thoughts and to express our feelings to others. But it is far from easy to decide whether or not language is performing these functions properly because we cannot directly compare our thoughts with those of others. Nor can we always be sure that our internal communication (thinking in terms of words) will not drive us to a false conclusion or into a blind alley.

The *structure* of language, on the other hand, can be described in great detail. For this reason the branches of language analysis that deal primarily with structure have been developed further than those that deal with the function of language as an instrument of communication.

We shall have to deal with both the structural and the functional aspects of language. Because the development of language science has been uneven (with further advancement on the structural side), the level of our discussion will necessarily shift. At times we shall be talking about things that are easily demonstrable but seem to have little bearing on the principal theme of this book (the role of language in human existence). At other times we shall be touching on matters of deep concern to us as human beings, but our discussion will be on the level of speculation or conjecture.

The same would be true if we approached our subject by examining the *act* of communication rather than its vehicle (language). The act of communication, like language, can be studied on different levels.

At one level there is the *signal*, an event initiated at one place (for the purpose of communicating something) and reproduced at another. Communication takes place when the party receiving a signal is able to infer *what signal was sent* (or, in a special case, *whether* a signal was sent). For instance, the military operations of the American Revolution (so the story goes) were initiated by a signal sent from the Old North Church in Boston to Paul Revere on the other side of the Charles River. By prearrangement, it was understood that a *single* light in the church tower would convey the information that the British were marching by land; *two* lights, that they were advancing by sea. The communication problem here was simply to ensure that the two signals were *distinguishable*. It would have been unfortunate for the American revolutionists if the two lanterns had been so close together that their light blended into a single light.

The communication problem in telegraphy is larger but of the same sort in principle. Letters of the English alphabet are coded upon sequences of short and long electrical impulses (the Morse code). These are transmitted over a wire, and the original message is reproduced (decoded) at the receiving end. Neither the telegraph operator nor the communication engineer is concerned with the *content* of the message or its meaning. All they are concerned with is the arrangement for transmitting impulses in such a way that the events at the destination enable the recipient to infer what sequence of impulses has been sent. The *meaning* of the impulses does not enter into this picture.

The situation in telephony, radio broadcasting, and television is even more complex but again the same in principle. The main problem is to reproduce faithfully at the receiving end events initiated at the transmitting end; that is, to achieve fidelity. What is said, the quality of the message or entertainment, and so forth, do not concern the technicians. On *this* level, communication science is a branch of engineering. It deals with the physics of signal transmission—for instance, with the propagation of electromagnetic waves and with acoustics. It deals with disturbances that distort signals—such as static and other forms of "noise." It poses the problem of utilizing efficiently the capacity of a given channel (the medium through which signals are sent), that is, of maximizing the amount of "information" that can be transmitted accurately in a given time. The word "information" is used here in its strict technical sense: it has to do only with the number of distinguishable signals sent, not with the meaning of the signals. As an example, the message sent to Paul Revere carried one "bit" of information, namely only that bit which enabled Revere to resolve the uncertainty as to which of two equally probable signals ("one if by land, two if by sea") was sent. How the information was interpreted and used would have been of no concern to the "engineer" charged with arranging that (very simple) communication system.

Of course, the goal of communication involves much more than the mere transmission of signals. We think further of communication as the transmission of impressions, ideas, even feelings, from "mind to mind." This is another level of communication, considerably higher than that of the engineer, but in a way not too different from the problem of the communication engineer. To describe it, one must go further back to the origin of the signals with which the communication engineer is concerned.

The act of communication originates in someone's mind as an idea to be communicated. From what we know (or conjecture), the presence of ideas or of any mental processes (in short, of consciousness) in a mind is associated with certain patterns of activity in a brain. If the idea is to be communicated, these patterns must stimulate certain nerve impulses. The impulses travel along nerve fibers to the appropriate muscles, say, those that activate the tongue, the lips, the vocal cords (organs of speech). Patterned movements of these organs form sound waves. These travel through the air from the mouth of the speaker and impinge on the eardrum of the hearer. The resulting patterned vibrations of the eardrum stimulate corresponding patterns of nerve impulses traveling toward appropriate centers in the hearer's brain. The activity of these centers (we assume) generates ideas. Thus the broader communication situation presents the same problems as the narrower one with which the communication engineer is concerned: the problem of accurate (or adequate) reproduction at the receiving end of events initiated at the sending end. The entire chain of events is the following:

Ideas—activity in a brain—nerve impulses—patterned movements of speech organs—sound waves—patterned vibrations of an eardrum—nerve impulses—activity in a brain—ideas.

The total act of communication is successful if the last link of the chain (the ideas generated in the hearer) is somehow in proper correspondence with the initial link (the ideas originating in the brain of the speaker). The communication engineer has singled out only the middle links in that chain, especially in those cases when the sound waves, in order to be transmitted over long distances, must in turn be "translated" into something else, for instance, electrical currents (in telephony) or electromagnetic waves (in radio). His problem is the accurate reproduction of sounds first encoded into something else, then decoded into sounds again. The larger communication problem is that of extending the analysis of events backward to their origin in the brain of the speaker and forward to their final destination, the brain of the hearer. How can this be done?

It is hopeless to start at either end of the communication chain, that is, to examine the actual physiological events (brain activity) associated with specific ideas. We simply do not have the observation techniques necessary to relate the enormously complex activity of billions of brain cells to the production of ideas (in the sense of "ideas" as images, logical relations, etc.). Nevertheless, we can examine the pattern of events called language.

As has been said (cf. p. 22), we can examine these events on various levels. We can analyze the *structure* of language, that is, see how shorter events are put together to form longer events called utterances. We can inquire into how these events are related to nonlanguage, that is, to things and events about which utterances are supposed to communicate. Also we can examine the way language utterances are related to the *behavior* of the speaker and of the hearer. The behavioral relationship is, of course, the most important and most interesting one for someone concerned with the role of language in determining the human condition. Clearly, however, we shall not get very far in understanding the effect of language on the language user if we do not take into account what he is talking about, or, better said, what he thinks he is talking about. So much will be readily conceded. Reasons for studying the structure of language are less obvious.

Ideally the structure of language could be studied without any reference to meaning. From the point of view of understanding the function of language, this may seem to be a waste of time. Yet some acquaintance with the structure of language, independent of meaning, is necessary for understanding how a language "works," quite in the same way that a knowledge of anatomy is necessary for understanding how the organs of the body function, without regard to their importance.

Elementally, viewing symbolic language as the production of strings of symbols, we find three levels of language analysis:

1. *Syntactics*: the study of the relations that symbols have to each other without connection to any relations that the symbols may have to other things (their referents).
2. *Semantics*: the study of the relations between symbols and their referents.
3. *Pragmatics or psycholinguistics*: the study of the relations between language and behavior.[1]

Structural linguists are primarily concerned with syntactics, the branch of language science that somewhat resembles chemistry. It is a study of how the smallest language units (analogous to atoms) are put together to form larger ones; these, to form still larger ones; and so on. Phonetics, phonemics, morphology, and syntax are branches of syntactics.

In phonetics the *sounds* of human speech are studied. Its methods are linked to those of physiology and physics. For instance, how a sound is determined by the position and action of the speech organs is a question that falls within the scope of phonetics; so does the physical analysis of speech sounds. Modern instrumentation has greatly ex-

---

1. The terms "syntactics," "semantics," and "pragmatics" were used by Charles Morris to denote three aspects of "semiotic," as he called the general theory of signs. (Cf. his *Foundations of the Theory of Signs*, International Encyclopedia of Unified Science, vol. 1, no. 2 [Chicago: University of Chicago Press, 1938].)

tended the range of techniques available to phonetics. Sound patterns can now be "translated" into light patterns so that the investigator can study the photograph of a sound at his leisure instead of depending on a short-lived sound event. Phoneticians are learning to read voice prints, that is, to identify sounds and even whole words from photographs. It is even possible to identify the speaker by his voice prints, as it is possible to identify a person by his fingerprints. In fact, whether or not voice prints are admissible as evidence in criminal cases was questioned recently in an American court.[2]

Methods of psychology are also applied in the study of phonetics but only on the physiological level, as in the study of the extent to which the human ear can distinguish variations in the sounds of speech.

Phonemics identifies *differences* in sound units that "make a difference" in language. For example, the sounds of "b" and of "p" are produced by the speech organs in almost the same way except that "b" is voiced and "p" is not. The difference—voiced-unvoiced—makes a difference in English: take "bin" and "pin," two different words.

There are, however, other differences in sound units that "do not make a difference" in a language. For example, the "p" in "pin" and the "p" in "spin" are actually different sounds. This can be shown by a simple experiment. Hold a small strip of tissue paper in front of your mouth and say first "pin" and then "spin." You will find that the "p" in "pin" is accompanied by a puff of air that blows the paper away, but that the "p" in "spin" is not (or at any rate the puff is weaker). The "p" in "pin" is called an aspirated "p," sometimes written "p'" to distinguish it from the unaspirated "p" in "spin." The difference between the aspirated and the unaspirated "p" is a *phonetic* difference in English, not a *phonemic* difference because there is no pair of words in English distinguished *only* by a different "p" sound (as "bin" and "pin" are distinguished by the voiced-unvoiced difference). In another language, however, the difference between "p" and "p'" may be a phonemic difference. Speakers of such languages will distinguish between "p" and "p'" better than we do.[3] Contrarily, in

2. Ross E. Steinhauer, "Voice Prints. A New Aid in Detecting Criminals," *Saturday Review* (September 6, 1969). See also Aleksandr Solzhenitzyn's novel *The First Circle* (New York: Harper & Row, 1968, Chapter 13), where the plot centers on the identification of the speaker by a taped telephone conversation.
3. I found it difficult to distinguish the two kinds of "t" in Bengali (cf. p. 36) because the difference between them, while phonemic in Bengali, is not phonemic in English.

Arabic the difference between "b" and "p" is not a phonemic distinction. This linguistic fact is illustrated in the following joke.

"How do you spell 'Peter'?" asks one Arab of another.

"B-e-t-e-r," say the other.

" 'B' as in what?"

" 'B' as in 'Bombay.' "

" 'Bombay, India,' or 'Bombay, Italy'?"

Speakers of Yiddish have difficulty distinguishing between the "a" in "bad" and the "e" in "bed" because there is no corresponding phonemic distinction in Yiddish. Nor does Yiddish have a "w" sound. For this reason Hyman Kaplan thinks that "vast" is a point of the compass.[4]

Morphology studies the way words are put together from phonemes and the way words are modified in different grammatical contexts.

Syntax studies the way words are combined into larger units such as phrases, clauses, and sentences.

While structural linguistics does not go beyond the analysis of the sentence, the method of syntactics can be extended beyond the sentence. For instance, logic can be viewed as a study of the way sentences are put together in chains of deduction. We shall have a great deal to say about this matter in Chapters 13 and 15.

The structural linguist tries to construct as much as possible of his science without recourse to a theory of meaning. The *concept* of meaning must, of course, enter his theory quite early, already on the level of phonemics. Recall that a phonemic difference is one that distinguishes between different words, hence between different meanings. However, the structural linguist tries to bring as little of meaning as he can into his investigations. For example, it is sufficient for him to determine the fact that "bin" and "pin" are two different words and presumably carriers of two different meanings; on the phonemic level he does not need to know, nor does he care, to what the words refer outside of language.

Since *semantics* is concerned with meaning, and semantics is the subject of this book, we shall be mostly concerned with meaning. To begin our discussion of meaning, we shall keep as close as possible to the subject matter of structural linguistics. Since our topic is broader than the focus of structural linguistics, however, I shall not hesitate to cross from linguistics to psychology—but the crossing will be post-

4. Leo Rosten, *The Education of* H*Y*M*A*N K*A*P*L*A*N (New York: Harcourt, Brace and Company, 1937).

poned as long as possible. When it occurs, we shall find ourselves in a badly charted territory where structural linguistics is of little help in getting our bearings. We shall then backtrack in search of an area where a "pure" semantics can be constructed, where the meaning of an utterance resides entirely in the referent—and the psychology of the language user can be excluded. This is the realm of science. We shall see, however, that even in the area of science (where meanings are strictly delineated by apparently exact definitions), we shall have to take into account the role of the scientist who, as observer, becomes the language user. And so, even in the exact sciences, it is necessary to clarify the relation between meaning and action—in this case between semantics and pragmatics, two levels of language analysis. Here we shall follow the principle of "building the bridge when we come to it."

To be honest with ourselves, we should wonder how communication between human beings is possible at all by means of ordinary language with its confused, at times "pathological," semantics. Questions will be raised as to what extent "effective communication" is a help or a hindrance to man as a social animal and as to whether or not man is making proper use of the survival mechanism we have posited language to be. Armed with the insights that have crystallized in the "pure" semantics of science and those gradually taking shape in the psychology of language, we shall attempt to answer some of these questions. The theme of the concluding chapters is that semantics, which in its broad sense must include pragmatics, may point the way to self-knowledge wherein "self" refers not alone to an individual human being but to man as a species.

APPLICATIONS

I. Recently there has been a popular fascination with something called "body language" (your body talks without your being aware of it), and Edward Hall's *The Hidden Dimension* (an expansion of Chapter 10 of his previous book *The Silent Language*) has attempted to apply certain linguistic principles formulated by Benjamin Lee Whorf to all culture. The arguments of these books boil down to a banality: one should not imagine that one can understand everything going on in a person's mind through his words alone; his body "language" and the way he relates his body to space are very significant in conveying information.

Is it possible to make a good argument that "body language" and "the silent language" are little more than a pattern or set of *signals*? What is the difference between the kind of *signals* discussed at the beginning of this chapter and the more elaborate form of signals known as "body language" and "the silent language"?

II. Ludwig Wittgenstein, often regarded as one of the fathers of the philosophical movement known as "logical positivism," said: "When I think in language, there aren't 'meanings' going through my mind in addition to the verbal expression: the language is the vehicle of thought." This statement implies that one can only think the kinds of thoughts that his language allows him to think. Do you agree with this statement? If so, do you think this is a limitation that dooms "the total act of communication"? What thoughts, if any, do you have that cannot be expressed in language?

III. In *The Raw and The Cooked*, Claude Lévi-Strauss says: "I therefore claim to show not how men think in myths, but how myths operate in men's minds without their being aware of it."

1) What myths operate in the minds of others (your parents, your friends, your teachers) without their knowing about them?
2) What myths operate in the minds of both men and women in regard to sex roles?
3) How do "black liberation" and "women's liberation" movements relate to Lévi-Strauss's assertion?
4) What, if anything, is bad about having myths operate in your head without your being aware of them?
5) According to the author himself, *The Waste Land* (T. S. Eliot) is about the kinds of myths Lévi-Strauss is speaking about. Read the poem and show the truth of Eliot's statement.
6) To what extent does language contribute to the "unconscious" nature of our dominant myths?

IV. A cryptogram is a message written in secret characters. Each letter of the cryptogram stands for another letter—the same letter each time it appears. Groups of letters stand for words and form a sentence. Try to break the following code by using your knowledge of English grammar. Then explain how you did it. Some hints: Which three-letter words are common? Do you see letter combinations suggesting affixes or suffixes? What kind of word contains only two letters?

CEPF EKX CWSS MJKH BL HOJ OWSS HORJJ
POJJRA YTR HOJ
MOWHJ EKX USBJ

1) Now invent a code of your own. See if your classmates can break it.

/II
SYMBOL
AND
MEANING

4/meaningfulness

You are looking now at a page of written (printed) English. In becoming an accomplished reader, you train your eyes (unbeknown to you) to make minute movements so as to focus on linear groups of letters just long enough to take in enough of the text to gather a "meaning." In all likelihood these groups are larger than words (only beginners read word by word); but, unless you are an exceptionally accomplished reader, they are shorter than sentences. As you read, you keep these "chunks of meaning" in your memory and add successive chunks until what you have read "makes sense."

Stop reading now and see whether you can repeat to yourself "in your own words" what you have just read from the first paragraph of this chapter. Check it by reading the passage again. If it "checks," I have communicated to you an idea of how one reads (at least I hope so).

To an illiterate person, even more to a person reared in a culture where reading is unknown, the process may seem miraculous. If such a person speaks English, he can whisper something into my ear; I can write what he has whispered on a piece of paper and hand it to you; and you can repeat exactly what he said. It will seem to him that I have made a piece of paper "talk."

We are so accustomed to communication through writing (and reading) that the process seems no more miraculous to us than communication by talking. Actually we should say that communication by talking is no *less* miraculous than communication by writing for only familiarity makes communication of any kind seem a commonplace event. When we try to analyze just what happens as "ideas are transmitted from mind to mind," we begin to see the enormous complexity of this process. Instead of wondering why on many occasions "communication fails," we should, as mentioned, wonder that it can take place at all. Although we still understand very little about what does take place " in the mind" as signals in the form of sounds or black marks on paper are "processed" into meanings, we do understand somewhat more about how combinations of sounds or marks on paper become "meaningful."

Imagine that you are illiterate. Now the printed page "says" nothing to you. You see only black marks on paper, Nevertheless, examining more closely what you see, you notice that the black marks are grouped so that empty spaces appear between the groups. You notice also that not all the marks are different; certain shapes keep recurring. To save time, let someone call your attention to the nature of these black marks. He can point out that there are only fifty-two different shapes, and, to fix ideas, he will tell you that the marks are called "letters" and that really there are only twenty-six of these, the other twenty-six (capitals) being only variants of the same. For the time being, he will say, you can disregard the extra marks such as "." and ";" and so forth. He will tell you that practically everything that can be said in English can be represented by combinations of these twenty-six letters; that, if you are of ordinary intelligence, you can get these black marks to "talk" to you in only a few weeks or months; that if you can understand anything spoken in English, you will be able to understand the same thing through these black marks.

Spoken language, like written language, is essentially the totality of possible sequences of discrete speech units. These units (which linguists call *phonemes*) are considerably harder to identify than are letters of an alphabet. For one thing, letters are inventions and are fixed; phonemes evolve with language.[1] For another, while letters stay put on a page, phonemes are fleeting: we can "detect" them only as they occur in the course of speech. Besides, spoken phonemes blend together; the divisions between them are not sharp. Worse, different speakers having different speech habits, pronunciations vary from person to person. The task of identifying all the phonemes of a given

---

1. Actually, letters also evolve. For instance, most Roman letters evolved from the Greek; these, in turn, from Phoenician. However, because written language is fixed while spoken language is fluid, the evolution of letters is on the whole considerably slower than that of phonemes.

language is a major one, and linguists are justifiably proud of having developed techniques for accomplishing this task. Letters of an alphabet (especially English) correspond only very roughly to the phonemes: several letters frequently represent the same phoneme, and the same letter may represent entirely different phonemes. For this reason, linguists tend to deny to letters the status of being important units of speech.

I believe that this denigration of the alphabet stems from the conviction of most linguists that spoken language is the more fundamental means of communication—that written language is only an auxiliary form. This conviction is reinforced by the circumstance that for the last several decades the languages of preliterate peoples have been a fertile field for linguistic investigations. Clearly these languages can be studied only in their spoken form. Assuming that spoken language is the primary material of language science, linguists may regard written forms as distortions of the spoken forms. In written forms the nuances and variations of pronunciation are suppressed. Written language often is, in fact, a source of gross misconceptions about how a language is actually spoken.[2]

I, for one, fail to see why written language cannot be made an object of study in its own right. Extinct languages are known to us only in written form. They present as much challenge to linguists, even if many questions about these languages, of central interest to linguists, must forever remain unanswered for lack of evidence (living speech). Analysis of language or of human communication can begin, however, on many different levels. The linguist often prefers to begin by analyzing the way the sounds of speech are produced. Here his science is linked to physics and to physiology, that is, to the study of actual physical events. It is a long, long way from there to "meaning," and so "meaning" usually becomes the border to which the structural linguist carries his investigations, beyond which typically he does not venture because his methods cannot carry him further. Oppositely,

2. Mispronunciation of foreign names can be traced directly to their spelling. For example, a Russian pronounces Einstein's name as Aynshtayn because the Russian letters corresponding to "e" and "i" are pronounced "ay" (as in "hay"). Curiously, the substitution of the equivalent of "sh" for "s" reproduces the German sound more exactly. Possibly, when Russians first began to transliterate German names, they were more influenced by sounds than by spelling. Russians also pronounced Hoover as Goover and Hitler as Gitler because there is no "h" in the Russian alphabet. The Ukrainian letter corresponding to the Russian "g" is pronounced as "h," so the Russians use it to transliterate "h," pronouncing it as a hard "g."

early scholars of language (philologists) began at the other end with the study of the literature of a language. Their methods did not reach down to the more elementary components of meaning. Nor could their investigations be linked to "actual events" with which science, as traditionally understood, is supposed to be concerned.

In this book we shall take an intermediate position between a "strictly scientific" linguistics and the study of the "large" meanings with which the humanities are concerned. Written language (with an alphabet) will be taken as given. The problem of identifying the "atoms" is then a trivial one: the atoms of a *written* language are the letters of the alphabet. These are really and truly "atoms," that is, indivisible units. Break a letter into its constituent strokes or curlicues and nothing is left that has any relation to language. Yet a letter is already a symbol: it stands for a sound, albeit not unambiguously; concatenations of letters form larger language units, and so on. In this way, our definition of language as sequences of symbols is valid "all the way down." Even its atoms are symbols.

Does a single letter have a meaning? A letter being a symbol, by agreement it stands for something else. It stands (more or less definitely) for a sound. In a way, therefore, the sound that the letter stands for can be said to be the "meaning" of the letter. However, by "meaning" in language we ordinarily understand something more. Generally speaking, we do not think of letters as having linguistic meaning. Words, on the other hand, usually are said to have meanings. Why? Because, many will say, words stand for something *outside* of language. Words stand for things. We know, however, that this is not always so. Words like "the," "of," "or," etc., do not stand for anything, even if under "things" we admit also qualities, actions, and so on. Do words like "of," "the," "because," etc., then have meanings? We like to think so, and therefore must extend the notion of meaning beyond the relation of words to "things."

We find, further, that parts of words may also have meanings of sorts. For example, the suffix "ness" in "blackness," "happiness," and "business" seems to have a meaning, but it is not easy to capture it. We can, of course, explain the occurrence of the suffix on *grammatical* grounds: it serves to make nouns from adjectives ("black," "happy," "busy"). The fact that we have to resort to grammatical categories in order to explain meaning (if we admit that suffixes like "ness" have a meaning) already extends the notion of meaning beyond the referents of words, as these are commonly pictured (things, properties, qualities, actions, etc.). So we have extended the notion of meaning to relations of words to words—*syntactic* (or grammatical) meaning.

Other possible meanings of meaning will be examined later in Chapters 8 and 9. For the time being, let us discuss *meaningfulness*. I shall not define meaningfulness precisely because I do not believe it can be done. There are *degrees* of meaningfulness; no sharp boundaries separate what is meaningful from what is meaningless. We can say that meaningfulness is related simply to intuitively felt familiarity and explain the rest by examples.

To begin the exercise, compare the two combinations of letters: "bird" and "ptak." The first combination makes an English word; the second does not. It makes sense to say that the first combination is more meaningful than the second to an English reader. The second combination, however, is more meaningful to a Polish reader because it makes a Polish word (meaning "bird") while the first does not. Here meaningfulness seems to depend on whether a combination of letters makes a *familiar* word or not.

Consider now another combination of letters: "birt." This combination does not make an English word, but it looks somewhat more familiar than "ptak." That is, it resembles an English word; may, in fact, be a misprint for "bird" or for "dirt" or for "birth." If we dispense with a rigorous criterion for meaningfulness, we may agree that in a sense the combination "birt" is more meaningful to us (English readers) than "ptak." This is so even though "ptak" could be a misprint for "peak," a common English word. If you agree, let us see how the difference comes about. "Ptak" looks strange to us because the sequence of letters "pt" does not occur in the beginning of English words. The sequence violates some rule of combining letters into English words (of which we may not have been aware before we inquired into the matter).

Continuing along these lines, consider the following sequence of letters: XFOML RXKHRJFFJUJ ZLPWCFWKCYJ FFJEYVKCQSGHYD QPAAMKBZAACIBZHJQD.[3] A more "meaningless" sequence is hard to imagine. We feel strongly that this cannot be "English" because it

---

3. This and the following examples are taken from Claude E. Shannon and Warren Weaver, *The Mathematical Theory of Communication* (Urbana: University of Illinois Press, 1949).

bristles with letters that occur only infrequently in an English text—
"X," "Q," "Z," etc. Next, the "words" are too long. Finally, the
sequences seem bizarre because there are too many consecutive consonants.

This sort of sequence is called a "zero-order letter approximation
to English." It was obtained by choosing the successive letters (including "space") by chance, with each of the twenty-seven symbols
(the twenty-six letters plus "space") having an equal probability of
occurrence. Consequently "space," having only one chance in twenty-
seven to occur, occurred too infrequently, and the "words" became
too long. Also, since there are twenty-one consonants and only five
vowels, too many consonants were chosen. No attention was paid to
the rules of combination typical in English. Consequently "bizarre"
sequences of letters like "XF," "RX," "FFJ," "MKB," etc., appeared,
precluding any resemblance to an English text.

Now examine a so-called "first-order letter approximation to English." Here the letters were chosen in accordance with the actual
frequencies of their appearance in an English text. That is, the letter
"e" had the greatest chance of being chosen since this letter appears
with the greatest frequency in English; the letter "t" was chosen with
the next greatest probability, and so on. OCRO HLI RGWR NMIELWIS EU
LL NBESEBYA TH EEI ALHENHTTPA OOBTTVA NAH BRL. The "text" still
looks bizarre, but somewhat less so than the first example. The
"words" are about the right length (because "space" was chosen with
a probability appropriate to it in English). The "rare" letters ("Q,"
"X," "Z,") are altogether absent. In a longer text they would, of
course, occur, but with a "decent" frequency. Still, the resemblance
to English is remote because strange combinations such as "HL,"
"RGW," and so on, occur.

These combinations can be eliminated if we take into account not
only the frequencies with which individual letters occur in English
but also the frequencies with which *pairs* of letters occur. When we
do so, we get a "second-order letter approximation to English." Here
is an example: ON IE ANTSOUTINYS ARE INCTORE ST BE S DEAMY ACHIN
D ILONASIVE TUCOOWE AT TEASONARE FUSO TIZIN ANDY TOBE SEACE
CTISBE. Now the "text" begins to look like English. We even get some
real English words such as "ON," "ARE," and "BE." We also get "words"
that look tantalizingly close to English: "DEAMY," "ACHIN," "ILON-
ASIVE."

Can we say that as we progress to "higher order approximations to

English" the text becomes "more meaningful"? Certainly not, if we stick to a definition of meaningfulness that places a severe demand on utterances: to be meaningful, an utterance must "say" something. In fact, we shall impose just this demand when we speak of meaningfulness in the sense of the "pure" semantics of science. The point to be made here is that this criterion of meaningfulness, that an utterance must "say" something, is not usually applied in ordinary communication. There being degrees of meaningfulness, the degree of meaningfulness of any utterance is closely related to its familiarity and need not be related to a correspondence between the utterance and "reality." For example, "Eenie-meenie-minie-mo" is not related to any "reality"; it does not "inform" us of anything. Yet it is more "meaningful" than "bavy-tavy-kavy-resh" simply because the former appears in speech (that of children playing) while the latter does not.

A case in point is Lewis Carroll's poem "Jabberwocky."

> 'Twas brillig, and the slithy toves
>   Did gyre and gimble in the wabe:
> All mimsy were the borogoves,
>   And the mome raths outgrabe.
>
> . . . .
>
> He left it dead, and with its head
>   He went galumphing back.[4]

The poem contains nonwords such as "brillig," "slithy," "toves," "outgrabe." Yet who but a pedant would say that the poem is completely devoid of meaning? Possibly adult speech sounds like "Jabberwocky" to very young children: it has an "almost" meaning, enough to fix their attention on it. Real semantic meaning emerges gradually and only as the sounds of speech become associated with events and experiences. First, however, the sounds of speech must become familiar. They acquire meaningfulness (not yet meaning) from their familiarity.

To continue our examination of "approximations to English," note that approximations can be made on the level of words as well as on the level of letters.

The following is an example of a first-order word approximation

4. From Lewis Carroll, *Alice's Adventures in Wonderland* (New York: Heritage Press, 1941), pp. 23–25. See also Richard E. Young, Alton Becker, and Kenneth Pike, *Rhetoric: Discovery and Change* (New York: Harcourt, Brace & World, 1970), p. 304.

to English. That is, words were selected with probabilities corresponding to the frequency of occurrence of the words in an English text but with no regard for the frequencies of sequences of words. REPRESENTING AND SPEEDILY IS AN GOOD APT OR COME CAN DIFFERENT NATURAL HERE HE THE A IN COME THE TO OF TO EXPERT GRAY COME TO FURNISHES THE LINE MESSAGE HAD BE THESE.

Note the conspicuous frequency of articles and prepositions. These are the most frequently occurring words, but, since no attention was paid to word sequences, they make no grammatical sense. In contrast, examine the following second-order word approximation. Here, pairs of words were chosen in accordance with their frequency of occurrence. THE HEAD AND IN FRONTAL ATTACK ON AN ENGLISH WRITER THAT THE CHARACTER OF THIS POINT IS THEREFORE ANOTHER METHOD FOR THE LETTERS THAT THE TIME OF WHOEVER TOLD THE PROBLEM FOR AN UNEXPECTED.

The text still does not make semantic sense, but it begins to make much more grammatical sense than the first-order approximation. It reads as if someone is trying to say something but is continually swerving from the path of his thought. To convince yourself further of the difference in the degree of meaningfulness between the last two texts, try reading them aloud. Probably you will find that you read the first text in a monotone, pausing slightly after each word, but that in reading the second text you *group* the words—for example, "frontal attack on an English writer," "that the character of this point," "that the time," and so on. These groups convey "chunks of meaning." It is these chunks that you keep in mind when you read a semantically meaningful text. Chunks of meaning occur in the second-order word approximation, but they do not combine into larger chunks to make semantic sense.

A language can be defined as a totality of utterances, that is, as "everything that can be said in it." Each utterance is essentially a sequence of language units: in the case of the written form, a sequence of letters. Not all sequences of letters are utterances in a given language. For example, none of the samples of approximations to English is an utterance in English. A single English word, however, is an utterance in English, and so is an English phrase like "a frontal attack on an English writer," and, of course, so is an English sentence. In short, a language consists of certain *acceptable* sequences of units to the exclusion of others among all the possible ones.

A set of rules that determines the distinction between acceptable sequences and others is called a *grammar*. In this generalized, technical sense, grammar includes *spelling* (rules governing the composition of words from letters), *grammar* in its textbook sense (rules governing changes in the form of words in different contexts), and *syntax* (rules governing the composition of sentences from words).

What are these rules? We can certainly state some of them. For example, since we know that there is no English word in which a consonant other than "z" follows "z," we can state the following spelling rule: "The letter 'z' must be followed either by a space, a 'y,' a vowel, or another 'z.' " Further, we can say, "Every word must contain either a 'y' or a vowel." Concerning the composition of sentences from words, we can state a rule to the effect that no sentence may end in "the" or may contain a "the" followed by an "a."

These are not the sort of rules we find in school grammar textbooks. The usual rules of spelling are of this sort: "When a word ending in a consonant is extended by a suffix, 'ing' or 'ed,' the consonant is doubled if the syllable is accented, but not otherwise. Examples: sit—sitting, gut—gutted, compel—compelling, but cancel—canceled, level—leveling." Another: "The present perfect form of a verb is used to express completed action. Example: 'I have read this book'."

Note that these rules take a great deal for granted, such as that we know what an "accented syllable" is or what "a completed action" is. However, in trying here to construct the notion of "grammaticalness" (related, as we shall see, to meaningfulness) from the ground up, as it were, we are putting ourselves in a position of complete ignorance with regard to a language, something like the position of a linguist confronted with an inscription in a completely unknown, extinct language. There is no one to tell him the "rules" of that language. He must figure them out from the material on hand.

Actually the linguist is not quite so helpless. In his studies of language structure, he has obtained considerable experience with a variety of languages. There *are* features common to the structures of even very remote languages. The linguist has a language with which to talk and think *about* languages—a "meta-language," as it is sometimes called. The specialist's linguistic awareness not only warns him about trying to apply the concepts derived from the structure of one language to the analysis of another (cf. Chapter 2); it also alerts him to these common features. Besides, he may have some clues as to what he should look for. The site where the inscription was found may suggest to which known languages the unknown language may be related, along with other points of anchorage from which to start the investigation.

Our purpose in trying to build a grammar (of, say, English) "from the ground up" is not to duplicate the experience of a linguist trying to decipher an unknown language, who, after all, has a formidable arsenal of research tools at his disposal. Our purpose is to see how much of the grammar we can reconstruct without recourse to what we already know *intuitively* about a language.

Textbook grammars depend a great deal on this intuitive knowledge. We can learn the grammar of our own language (and of closely related languages) because we *already* know a great deal about it, having spoken it correctly for as long as we can remember. This knowledge, however, is not easy to state in the form of rules. In fact, people who speak their native language correctly may not be able to state a single rule of grammar. Speaking is a natural activity (for man), like walking. We can walk without being able to say anything definite about how we walk—for example, what muscles are contracted and in what order.

That children acquire an intuitive feeling for the rules of grammar is evidenced by their frequent "logical errors." A child sometimes says "I knowed" instead of "I knew," "two sheeps" instead of "two sheep," showing that he learns his language not just by repeating what he hears but by applying rules of grammar, which happen to be violated in these examples by the irregularities of the language.

The clear role of analogy in the process of language acquisition and use offers strong evidence against the view (represented, for example, by B. F. Skinner[5]) that language, like many other forms of behavior, is acquired primarily by operant conditioning, that is, by trial and error where only "correct" utterances are reinforced. A rather devastating critique of these views was undertaken by Noam Chomsky.[6]

Our intuitive knowledge of grammar is reflected in our ability to *recognize* what is acceptable in our language and what is not, even when we do not know the rules of grammar. Anyone speaking English

5. B. F. Skinner, *Verbal Behavior* (New York: Appleton-Century-Crofts, 1957).
6. Noam Chomsky, "A Review of B. F. Skinner's *Verbal Behavior*," *Language* 35, 1 (1959): 26–58.

will recognize that "The bird is in the bush" is an acceptable utterance (technically a *sentence*), while "The bird is in the" or "In bush is the the bird" is not. We recognize the difference even if we know nothing about "subjects," "predicates," or anything else taught in English textbooks. How is a native speaker, unversed in the rules of grammar or syntax, able to distinguish an acceptable utterance from an unacceptable one?

It might be thought that he is able to do this because he matches the utterance with utterances he has heard. But this cannot be so. The number of possible acceptable utterances is so vast (practically unlimited) that no one can be expected to have heard them all. Note that you have in all likelihood never read a sentence exactly like the one you have just read, and yet you recognize it as a sentence. You do this without going through a syntactic analysis requiring you to identify the subject and the predicate, to check the agreement of pronouns with their antecedents, and to follow all the other procedures that supposedly enable you to decide whether an utterance is or is not grammatical. Evidently the native speaker has "internalized" the grammar of his language, as he has internalized many other forms of "knowledge," without being able to state just what he knows, much less how he knows what he knows.

It is in this sense that "grammaticalness" is related to meaningfulness. Acceptable (that is, grammatical) utterances are already meaningful to a degree in that they evoke some sort of mental images that begin to "make sense."

An utterance can make more or less sense. Taking the previous illustration, most people will agree that "The bird is in the bush" makes sense and that it is also a perfectly correct English sentence. They will also agree that "The bird is in the" makes no sense at all and that it is not an English sentence. Now consider "The bird is in." Perhaps the sense of this utterance is not immediately apparent. One might wonder "in what?" Yet "The doctor is in" makes perfect sense.

Is "The doctor is in" an acceptable English sentence? It is not easy to state a rule of English syntax that makes this utterance acceptable, at any rate not as easy as to state the rule that makes "The bird is in the bush" acceptable. In some textbooks we may even find a rule that could be interpreted as rejecting "The doctor is in"—for instance, the rule that forbids (or frowns upon) ending a sentence with a preposition. On the other hand, it would seem pedantic to exclude this utterance from acceptable English sentences. No matter how thoroughly the cultured young lady receptionist has been trained in "correct English," she will not readily plead guilty to "bad English" every time she says "The doctor is in. Please be seated."

It is, of course, possible to resolve the alleged contradiction between the rule against ending English sentences with prepositions and the bona fide credentials of "The doctor is in" as an English sentence. It can be argued that the preposition "in" in "The doctor is in" is really an abbreviation for the prepositional phrase "in his office." But this amounts to interpreting usage in a way that allows the vindication of the rule rather than judging an utterance by a fixed rule. Let us, however, accept the explanation. We now ask, when are abbreviations of this sort permissible?

Imagine a pigeon fancier waiting for the return of his favorite bird, which finally does return, and the man says "The bird is in." Not many would quarrel with the grammar of this utterance, but how far can we carry it? From a purely grammatical point of view (speaking now of conventional grammar as it is taught in textbooks), the sentence has the following structure:

Article (the), noun (doctor, bird), copula (is), preposition (in).

Is this sequence always acceptable? Let us keep the article, the copula, and the preposition constant while varying the nouns, the point being to see which nouns can properly play the same role in this sentence as "doctor" and "bird."

The table is in.
The chair is in.
The window is in.
The dinner is in.
The banquet is in.
The miniskirt is in.
The freckles are in.
The crimes are in.
The galaxies are in.
The hazards are in.
The election returns are in.

Most people will agree that the majority of these sentences do not seem quite right. One of them is definitely proper, namely "The election returns are in." If we are liberal about colloquial expressions, we shall also accept "The miniskirt is in" (meaning "in fashion"). A case can be made for the window that has just been installed. The remaining utterances are more difficult to justify, although with a stretch of the imagination, it can be done in the case of some. For example, "The dinner is in" may be an eccentric person's way of saying that he has just eaten his dinner. "The freckles are in" is marred by the article "the," which, if omitted, would make the utterance semantically (though not grammatically) analogous to "The miniskirt is in."

Evidently our feelings about whether or not an utterance is grammatical depend strongly on the ease with which we can draw an *analogy* between a particular utterance and other utterances of the same grammatical form and which, without question, suggest imaginable situations.

To illustrate the point further, consider the following example:[7]

"Colorless green ideas sleep furiously." The utterance is nonsensical, but its grammatical form is perfect: adjective—adjective—noun—intransitive verb—adverb. By making substitutions (adjectives for adjectives, noun for noun, adverb for adverb), we can turn this utterance into "Healthy young children sleep soundly," which, of course, makes perfect sense.

Are we to conclude that if words in the same grammatical category are substituted for a nonsense sentence, thereby making it a sensible one, then the sentence is grammatical? If so, we are in difficulty. For then we would have to say that "The doctor is at" is grammatical because "at" is a preposition that was substituted for "in." In fact, other prepositions can be substituted for "in" in "The doctor is in," and the sentences will still make sense:

The doctor is on (meaning the doctor is on the air, making a speech).

The doctor is through (meaning the doctor has finished examining the patient).

The doctor is out.

If these sentences are acceptable, why not "The doctor is of," "The doctor is to," and so forth?

The only way out is to insist that "in," "on," and "through" are really abbreviations for phrases denoting "in his office," "on the air," "has finished," or the like. If so, then we see that syntactic and grammatical analysis is considerably more complex than it appears when

7. An example given by N. Chomsky.

applied to simple textbook samples with their clear-cut subjects, predicates, adverbial phrases, and so on. Conventional analysis according to clearly stated rules is obviously not adequate either for deciding whether or not a sentence is grammatical or for making all possible grammatical sentences. More is involved; namely, an examination of the *sense* of an utterance. This is semantic analysis. However, semantic analysis alone is not adequate either. "Colorless green ideas sleep furiously" appears to be nonsense, but "Sleep green furiously ideas colorless" makes even *less* sense.

An utterance makes sense *both* through its syntactic structure *and* through its semantic content. If it has an easily recognizable syntactic structure, it gives us a *framework into which* to put a semantic content. Once we put it in (recognizing the meanings of the words), the meaning of the entire sentence is made clear.

Sometimes we must work to supply the syntactic structure with semantic content. For example, if we are intent on making sense of "Colorless green ideas sleep furiously," we can let our imagination roam until a content of sorts is supplied. Thus, we can suppose that by "green" ideas the speaker meant "undeveloped ideas"; further, that by "colorless ideas" he meant uninteresting ideas. How can ideas sleep? Well, by stretching still further, we can concede that an idea is asleep if it goes unnoticed. How can anything or anybody sleep furiously? I suppose a loud snorer can be said to sleep "furiously." But how can a "sleeping idea" snore? Frankly, I don't know. My imagination fails me at this point. Perhaps the reader can do better.[8] The point of this bizarre exercise is to demonstrate that we can at least try to make semantic sense of an utterance that has acceptable syntactic structure. If it does not have the structure, we cannot even begin. We have no *framework* into which to put the meanings.

An utterance, then, is recognized as meaningful if it has become familiar as *itself* or if it has a familiar grammatical structure which allows us to relate it to familiar utterances of similar structure.

"Fire!" is a perfectly meaningful utterance in itself. Its meaningfulness does not depend on grammatical structure. In fact, this utterance has no conventional grammatical structure (subject, predicate, etc.), and it is pedantic to insist that "Fire!" is "actually" an abbreviation of

8. After the manuscript of this book was completed, my attention was called to a poem entitled "You, Noam Chomsky" by Sister Mary Jonathan, O.P., that appeared in *College English*, February 1965, and was reproduced in Young, Becker, and Pike, op. cit., pp. 306–7. It turns out that someone did make poetic sense of this apparently semantically preposterous sentence.

"A fire has broken out." "Fire!" is a meaningful utterance because it is a familiar one. In the same class are other such "announcements." The cry "Gas!" must have become a very meaningful utterance in the trenches during World War I. "Contact!" became a meaningful utterance in the early years of aviation; "Camera!" and "Cut!" in movie-making; "Scalpel!" and "Forceps!" in surgery, and so on. Such one-word utterances come into usage *in situations where no more is needed* to evoke an appropriate image or to initiate appropriate action. Grammatical structure is superfluous to communication in situations of this sort.

Other utterances are meaningful because, although they have never been heard or read before, they are framed in a familiar grammatical structure. Often it requires some "work" on our part to accept them as meaningful. If too much work has to be done, we say the utterances are not meaningful.

You may have heard many times the utterance "I am eating an apple." Probably you have never heard the utterance "I am eating a centipede," but it is unquestionably a meaningful one. Although the idea is not attractive, it is not impossible to imagine someone eating a centipede. With other objects, credulity might be strained ("I am eating a brick," "a sonata," "a ventilator"), but with effort some sort of image can be evoked. If imagination fails us altogether ("I am eating a concert," "a vibration," "an indolence"), we may declare the utterance to be "devoid of meaning." *Formally* such utterances are "grammatical" because the sequence (pronoun—transitive verb—indefinite article—noun) is acceptable in English. *Most* such sequences may be absurd ("I am chopping a pinch," "He repaired a walnut"), but grammar as it is taught cannot draw the line between the commonplace and the absurd. The grammarian, having declared that the sequence "Pronoun—transitive verb—indefinite article—noun" is grammatical, must declare all utterances grammatical in which the slots have been filled by words coming under the appropriate classifications. Conversely, if a grammarian insists (as they once did) that a "sentence" must consist of a subject and a predicate, then he must deny the status of sentencehood to utterances like "Fire!" or "Oh, my goodness!" Nevertheless, the utterances are meaningful because they are familiar.

This presents us with two aspects of meaningfulness of an utterance: grammatical (or syntactic) meaningfulness and semantic meaningfulness. In ordinary language the two are often intertwined so that it is not easy to separate them. There is, however, at least one language in which syntactic meaningfulness can be studied in its "pure form," namely, music. Like ordinary language, music is a succession of sounds, and its written form has an alphabet. The "atoms" of music are tones. In the music of Western countries, there are twelve tones. From about the fifteenth to the twentieth centuries, this music was strictly tonal; that is, in any musical "utterance," seven of these twelve tones were selected to constitute a "key." Tones not belonging to the key were used only occasionally, if at all. The seven tones of a key were selected not arbitrarily but in one of two ways: to form either a major or a minor scale. Music is perceived as combinations of tones occurring simultaneously (harmony), as a succession of tones (melody), and as a recurrence of certain harmonic and melodic patterns (rhythm). As with language, a person accustomed to the idiom of tonal music would consider certain musical utterances to be acceptable ("grammatical") and others unacceptable. As in the case with language, it would be difficult, perhaps impossible, to state all the rules of "musical grammar." However, there are certain rules, analogous to the rules of grammar in ordinary language, that govern the composition of tonal music, many of which are stated explicitly and are taught—the rules of harmony, counterpoint, and musical form. But the explicit rules by no means exhaust the implicit "rules" internalized by composers.

The elusiveness of "musical grammar" is demonstrated by experiments with synthetic music, "composed" by programming a computer with rules for choosing combinations and sequences of tones. "Approximations" similar to the approximations to language (cf. pp. 62–64) can also be programmed. For example, frequencies of certain short sequences can simulate the observed frequencies of these sequences in the works of composers. Thereby "approximations to Mozart" or "approximations to Bach" can be constructed; for example, phonograph recordings made from playbacks of electronic synthesizers.[9]

It is not surprising that high-order approximations to Mozart and Bach sound something like Mozart and Bach because the method of constructing these approximations reproduces short snatches of what actually occurs in the music of the composers. From the standpoint of the psychology of musical perception, it would be interesting to ascertain how high the order of approximation must be before a person with

9. "Switched-on Bach," Carlos, MOOG Synthesizer (Columbia Records, MS 7194, November 1968).

a certain degree of musical literacy can "identify" a sample of synthetic music as Mozart-like or as Bach-like or can distinguish the one from the other. It is clear, however, that synthetic "music" cannot approach in quality the music of the masters. Many a music lover will feel that this finding only confirms a truism: that, of course, it is impossible to reduce the art of music to a set of rules. Actually, however, the finding shows only that it is difficult to "explain" the aesthetic appeal of music by a few easily formulated rules. Moreover, even if this aesthetic quality derives from syntactic principles (relations of tones to tones, not of tones to something outside of music), this can only mean that there are syntactic rules of music internalized by great composers but not uncovered by analysis.

Possibly, of course, the aesthetic quality of music derives from allusions to things outside of music. If so, then the language of music does have a semantics, but one quite unlike the semantics of ordinary language. In all ordinary languages, at least some words are "rigidly" connected to things or situations outside of language and so have concrete *referents*. There is no analogue of such fixed symbol-referent relations in music. While musical utterances do occasionally symbolize concrete references, most "referential" music is trivial, as in pieces composed to make music amusing to children (for example, "The Cat and the Mouse," "Grandfather's Clock"). Some combine light entertainment with substantial musical content (for example, Prokofiev's *Peter and the Wolf*). There is also serious "descriptive music" with concrete references. Best examples are the music dramas of Richard Wagner and the tone poems of Richard Strauss. However, in all these examples, the direct relations between musical symbols and concrete references are established ad hoc, that is, only in the context of a particular composition; they are not incorporated into the language of music as such. Most music is devoid of specific references outside of itself.

Nevertheless, music can be properly called a symbolic language. It certainly has a syntactic structure in the sense of combinations of small units into larger ones and these into still larger ones. Its semantics (if any) depends for the most part (with exceptions noted) not on concrete references but on much more subtle suggestions. These are discussed in Chapters 8 and 9. The point to be made here is that, whatever "meaning" we ascribe to musical utterances, their meaningfulness can be evaluated. The meaningfulness of a musical utterance depends on the listener's familiarity with the syntactic devices used in it, specifically the melodic, harmonic, or contrapuntal, in short, structural, patterns. In this sense the meaningfulness of music is analogous to the grammaticalness of ordinary language.

Meaningfulness precedes meaning. In a way, meaningfulness is a sort of protomeaning, a substratum from which meaning is constructed. Evidence for this relationship was provided by Dr. Jean-Marc-Gaspard Itard in his teaching of Victor, "the wild boy." Victor was found in September 1797 in a forest in France, living the life of an animal. Other cases of children living alone in a wild state were reported from time to time, giving rise to romantic speculations about human babies being suckled and brought up by beasts in the manner of Mowgli in Kipling's *Jungle Books*. More probably, such children were abandoned by their parents at an age when they could survive by foraging for food. In the case of Victor, there was reason to suppose that he was abandoned at about the age of seven. He seemed to be about twelve years old when he was found.

The discovery of Victor created a sensation. Believers in the theory of "the noble savage," man in his "natural state," expected Victor to be a paragon of virtue. There were even those who wondered, like Frederick the Great, whether Victor would speak Hebrew or Greek (cf. p. 34). Needless to say, all these people were disappointed. Victor could not speak at all and gave no evidence of "nobility." He behaved like any captured wild animal, scared and hostile, given to biting and scratching.

At first the boy was put in a cage and exhibited. A prominent psychiatrist examined him and declared him to be a congenital idiot. Dr. Itard, a young physician, thought otherwise and undertook to teach Victor. (He gave him this name.) Itard began by training the boy to recognize the sounds of human speech *without* any reference to meaning. To do this, he devised a game, which Victor apparently enjoyed. The game involved five vowels, each of which was associated with one of the boy's fingers. When Itard pronounced a vowel, Victor was to lift the corresponding finger. Next came *reading* instruction, again without reference to meaning. Victor learned to recognize the shapes of letters, then combinations of letters, so that he could tell whether two words were the same or different. In this way he learned to recognize words as *themselves* before he knew what the words stood for. Only then did Itard begin to teach Victor the connections between words and their referents: at first, of course, objects, later "qualities" (colors, textures), finally relations, such as of size.

Eventually, Victor learned to understand written French. He would obey simple written commands and could use cards with words on them to indicate what he wanted. He did not learn to speak. Indications were that Victor's intellectual capacity was subnormal. Whether he was abandoned for this reason, or whether being deprived of human company impaired his intellect, is an open question. At any rate, Itard probably owed his partial success to an insight that familiarization with symbols and their combinations *as such* is a first step in learning a symbolic language.[10]

Another line of evidence for the way familiarity serves as a framework of meaning is provided by the method used in the attempt to decode the language of gesture. Professor Ray L. Birdwhistell has worked for many years on this problem.[11] There is no question but that in face-to-face communication we make use not only of our voices but also of body movements. Some people, more than others, "talk with their hands," and there are well-drawn cultural differences in this respect, but there is no speech without gesture, whether of body, limbs, or face. It is easy to imagine that an expert in *kinesics* (as Professor Birdwhistell calls the linguistics of gesture) could learn to recognize the nationality of a person by "seeing him speak" (say, in a soundless movie) as easily as a trained linguist can recognize a person's nationality through his accent. Even gait, posture, and so on, may indicate a person's cultural or national background.

Explorations of this sort lead to an intriguing and exciting conjecture that there are gesture languages in parallel with spoken languages, and that kinesics can follow in the footsteps of linguistics, classifying such languages into groups and families, identifying "units" analogous to phonemes, combinations of these units analogous to morphemes, and so forth. Clearly such a language of gesture, if it exists, would be more akin to music than to ordinary language. It might be a sort of paralanguage, accompanying spoken words and imbuing them with

10. For a fuller account of this story and of theoretical issues suggested by it, see Roger Brown, *Words and Things* (Glencoe, Ill.: Free Press, 1958).
11. Ray L. Birdwhistell, "Background to Kinesics," *ETC.: A Review of General Semantics* 13, 1 (Autumn 1955): 10–18.

emotional meanings, somewhat as the music of a song stresses the emotional content of a poem.[12]

Professor Birdwhistell and others working in kinesics obtain their samples of the "language of gesture" by taking movies of people in interaction. They then study these movies, examining the film foot by foot. Their method is to single out recurring gestures to see how these relate to what is being said or, perhaps, to what is *behind* the spoken words.

I have seen several of these movies in connection with lectures on kinesics. As an example, I shall describe a movie made of a psychiatric interview. The patient, a pretty young girl, comes into the office of a psychiatrist, a handsome young man. He says after she is seated, "What can I do for you?" The lecturer concentrates on these few feet of film which take only a few seconds to run. There is a world to be seen in this footage. Both the young man and the young girl go through motions, and these motions are large complexes of component motions. The man has crossed his legs, then moves the top leg toward the girl. His head goes through several movements, his hands move, and each finger moves. Simultaneously, the girl manifests similar complex motions.

The lecturer runs the few feet of film over and over again, at the same time interpreting what is going on. The situation obviously involves flirtation. The lecturer proceeds to analyze what the two say to each other through gesture. Along with the formal "What can I do for you?" there is a wealth of meaning related to the "situation," a young, handsome couple face-to-face for the first time, reacting to each other's attractions.

The lecturer selects a portion of the film where the psychiatrist says "do for you." Hearing the phrase repeated, we become conscious of the stress on the word "do," and at that moment we see the young man's crossed leg in a jerky movement toward the girl. At the same

12. The meaning of certain gestures is clearly bound up with specific language communities. In some speech communities, beckoning is expressed by waving fingers extended upward, in others, by waving fingers extended downward. Some gestures, such as slang expressions, may have only a short life span. For instance, in the United States, a man (but not a woman) examining his fingernails (a preening gesture?) is understood to be expressing conceit and is so mimed in comic strips and in mass entertainment comedy. Students of kinesics are interested less in these clearly stylized, deliberate gestures than in the involuntary, internalized ones.

time, she leans her body in his direction. The frames of these apparently coordinated gestures are run five, ten times in rapid succession. We hear "*do* for you," see the jerk of the leg, see the girl's body apparently "responding," again and again. The "meaning" becomes crystal clear.

Might not all of this be an illusion induced by the repetitions? Consider that in the actual situation the gestures were fleeting. They may have been purely accidental. As we see them repeated, they become familiar, therefore *predictable*. We now *expect* the young man to jerk his leg toward the girl as he says "*do* for you." We *expect* the girl to "respond"; and we see our expectations fulfilled. Familiarity has induced meaningfulness; meaningfulness has induced meaning. Through repetition, the gesture becomes firmly linked to the "situation" and thereby acquires "meaning." Now, if a similar gesture were linked with similar situations in *independent* events, there would be excellent justification for deducing a meaning in it. But here the *same* event is artificially repeated, creating the impression of a constant linkage, hence of meaning. (The scientist would be well advised to keep this possible source of self-deception in mind.)

Utterances become meaningful by repetition regardless of whether they relate to something outside themselves. No one has yet explained the meaning of "galumphing," but familiarity with the word through repeated reading and hearing of "Jabberwocky" has made the word meaningful to lovers of nonsense poetry, and they conjure up a vivid picture of the monster's slayer as he goes "galumphing back." Prayers are memorized by children and become meaningful quite independently of what they "mean."

Hans Reichenbach begins his book *The Rise of Scientific Philosophy* with a quotation that you will find on page 355 (Chapter 19). Reichenbach maintains that the passage is an example of atrocious nonsense, but he points out that if we read the passage repeatedly, we may think that we have fathomed its meaning—especially if we are philosophy students who must read utterances of this kind year-in, year-out. We learn to expect such utterances from philosophers; our expectations are fulfilled, and the language of philosophy becomes meaningful to us. A similar situation prevails in many so-called fields of knowledge that are created and transmitted by language alone.

In summary, the meaningfulness of symbolic utterances is related to the way they fit into our expectations. Meaningful patterns provide us with a framework into which meaning can be put. Often, these meanings are of our own making.

APPLICATIONS

I. "Generally speaking, we do not think of letters as having linguistic meaning." Would you care to argue the point? Do letters have linguistic meaning at a certain time in the school term? A motion picture was made of "Z," a novel written about "O," another by Thomas Pynchon about "V," and one by John Berger called "G." "J" and "M" are authors of books about sex.

What linguistic meaning is associated with the following letters: A, AAA, A1, F, G's, I, K, R, X, XX?

II. One of the most amusing ways to make fun of obscenity and its censors is to use approximations in place of the real word. Gerald Sussman, in *The Official Sex Manual* (Putnam), tells all about the *erroneous zones*, the *vesuvious* and the *plethora*, a "tiny football-shaped object located near the *frunella*, just above the *pomander* tubes." In *Billy and Betty*, a novel by Twiggs Jameson, those who cannot find partners for *clamming* can always *automate* instead, and Jameson illustrates by example how to do so, whether you have an empty *pudarkus* or a full *glander*.

1) W. C. Fields, Lenny Bruce, and other humorists often used a form of approximation known as "double-talk." For examples, see Robert Lewis's biography of W. C. Fields and *The Essential Lenny Bruce*. In the given context, what is the purpose of the "double-talk"?
2) Read the monologues of Dr. Malachi Mulligan in the "Night-town" chapter of James Joyce's *Ulysses*, which purport to be medical diagnoses of Leopold Bloom; the approximation of "The Pledge of Allegiance" in e. e. cummings's *him*; and Lucky's long soliloquy in the middle of Samuel Becket's *Waiting for Godot*. What effect is produced by these approximations? Can you think of any others? Comment on the following passage:

Sir Tristram, violer d'amores, fr'over the short sea, had passencore rearrived from North Amorica on this side the scraggy isthmus of Europe Minor to wielderfight his penisolate war: nor had topsawyer's rocks by the stream Oconee exaggerated themselse to Laurens Countys gorgios while they went doublin their mumper all the time: nor avoice from afire bellowed mishe

mishe to tauftauf thuartpeatrick: not yet, though venisson after, had a kidscad
buttened a bland old isacc: not yet, though all's fair in vanessy, were sosie
sesthers wroth with twone nathandjoe.

3) Select a paragraph of what you regard as pretentious prose and render
it into "double-talk" by using approximations. Legal or academic language lends itself to this treatment when it is overinflated.
4) Sometimes, as in the case of Joyce and Beckett, there is a discursive
message contained in the approximations. Why should the author wish
to disguise the message?

III. Does the following "ungrammatical" passage make sense:

O that awful deepdown torrent O and the sea crimson sometimes like fire and
the glorious sunsets and the figtrees in the Alameda gardens yes and all the
queer little streets and pink and blue and yellow houses and the rosegardens
and the jessamine and geraniums and cactuses and Gibraltar as a girl where I
was a Flower of the mountain yes when I put the rose in my hair like the
Andalusian girl used or shall I wear red yes and how he kissed me under the
Moorish wall and I thought well as well him as another and then I asked him
with my eyes to ask again yes and then he asked me would I yes to say yes my
mountain flower and first I put my arms around him yes and drew him down
to me so he could feel my breast all perfume yes and his heart was going like
mad and yes I said yes I will Yes.

This passage comes from the writings of one who has been regarded as
the most obscure and most difficult author of our time. Does your "intuitive knowledge of grammar" help you to break "the code"? Does this
passage suggest that the author knew grammar very well or that he was
ignorant of the rules of grammar?

IV. "We can . . . try to make semantic sense of an utterance that has
acceptable syntactic structure." Using an approach similar to the one.
employed to analyze "Colorless green ideas sleep furiously," decide which
of the following statements make intelligible sense, which are nonsense.

a) Bronze by gold heard the hoofirons, steelyringing.
b) Somnambulant odors perambulate in golden ambiances.
c) During coginus, the male's vector has to break the hyphen.
d) Altarwise by owl-light in the half-way house/The gentleman lay grave-
ward with his furies.
e) Now curlew cry me down to kiss the mouths of their dust.
f) Majesty of horns sweeps in the stagtide.

g) The seed slips in the galleons of death.
h) Wherefore art thou, Romeo?
i) Wherefore art thou Romeo?
j) Time present and time past,/Are both perhaps present in time future,/And time future contained in time past./If all time is eternally present/All time is unredeemable.

Do you need a context in order to decide?

V. The human voice can now be simulated so exactly that counterintelligence services are afraid to trust tapes allegedly carrying messages from their operators: if the operator has been detected, false information can be conveyed through his simulated voice. Right now, the voice of a popular singer can be simulated so closely that the record companies, using their technology, can produce a record of a Judy Collins "singing" a song that she has actually never sung or perhaps an Enrico Caruso singing rock. This development could pose some interesting problems.

1) In your opinion, would a record company have the moral right to sell "Bach" or "Beethoven" disks of music that neither ever wrote? of lyrics that Bob Dylan has never sung? What factors would determine the moral (and legal) position?
2) Would you accept synthetic Bach, Beethoven, or Bob Dylan? Do you think the listening public would? Would such disks be "manufactured reality"?

VI. If the "semantics of music" depends upon knowledge of melody, harmony, and counterpoint, does it mean that you cannot understand music without such a background? Does it mean that you cannot enjoy music fully?

Some years ago, Walt Disney made a film called *Fantasia*. It provides concrete, visual referents for the structures of several musical compositions. It has been one of the most financially successful films ever made. Can you account for its success in terms of semantics?

In some musical compositions, a "shape" principle is at work. For instance, in a Bach oratorio about Christ, one group of voices will "cross" another group of voices to create an auditory image of the cross. As the composer approaches paradise in his thoughts, the voices will rise. Can you find this "shape" principle at work in other musical compositions?

VII. Does each generation have its own "kinesics"? Can you determine the generation a person belongs to by his gestures and his "body language"?

1) For the next week, observe people who are in their teens, their early twenties, and thirty or older. On what basis do you make judgments as to their ages?

2) Is it really possible to establish a person's *nationality* through "kinesics"? Watch a number of foreign films on television, observe acquaintances who were born abroad, and decide how, if at all, an "expert" can determine the nationality of a person by "seeing him speak."

5/the chemistry
of meaning

There is a striking resemblance between chemistry and semantics. Chemists distinguish between elements and compounds. Molecules of elements consist of only one kind of atom. Molecules of compounds are composed of atoms of two or more kinds. The constituent parts of a molecule of a compound are no longer particles of that compound. For example, the smallest particle of sulfuric acid is a molecule labeled H_2SO_4, to represent two atoms of hydrogen, one of sulfur, and four of oxygen. *Parts* of this molecule are not particles of sulfuric acid but of hydrogen or of sulfur or of oxygen or some combination of these that is not a molecule of sulfuric acid.

To see the parallel between chemistry and language, think of a molecule as a word and of atoms as letters. Let us "spell out" the molecule of sulfuric acid by writing HHSOOOO. It is known that under ordinary circumstances a single atom of hydrogen cannot exist by itself. As a gas, hydrogen consists of molecules, each of which is a pair of hydrogen atoms. This is to say, "H" is not a "chemical word," but "HH" (H_2) is. Further, "HHS" (H_2S) is a chemical word; it stands for a compound called hydrogen sulfide. Next, HHSO and HHSOO are not chemical words: they do not spell any compound. But HHSOOO is a chemical word (sulfurous acid). We have already seen that HHSOOOO is a chemical word (sulfuric acid.)

Now let us build up the word "banking" in the same way. Neither "b" nor "ba" is an English word. But "ban" is an English word, and so is "bank." Further, neither "banki" nor "bankin" is an English word, but "banking" is.

The analogy can be stretched further. Although "ing" is not an

English word, it is a *morpheme*, in this case a carrier of grammatical meaning. It performs the same function in "eating," "seeing," and "going." Similarly, although SO_4 is not a chemical word (that is, it does not spell a compound), it is a frequently occurring "suffix" in chemical words. It occurs in many salts called sulfates, $ZnSO_4$ (zinc sulfate), Na_2SO_4 (sodium sulfate), for example. In fact, in *solution*, SO_4 can exist as an *ion*, that is, a particle carrying a double negative electric charge. Under certain conditions, this ion will combine with metallic ions carrying a double positive electric charge to form salts called sulfates.

Chemists analyze compounds into their constituent elements and study the properties of elements and of compounds, especially their behavior in chemical reactions. In chemical reactions, atoms combine, separate, and recombine so that substances appear to change into other substances. For instance, when hydrogen burns, atoms of hydrogen combine with those of oxygen in the ratio of two-to-one to form molecules of water. Under certain conditions, molecules of water may be made to break up to form hydrogen and oxygen.

Among the most important facts of chemistry is that substances may have properties quite different from those of their constituent elements. For instance, sodium is a soft metal that reacts violently with water. Chlorine at room temperature is a greenish gas which, moreover, is poisonous (it was a principal constituent in World War I poison gases). The combination of sodium and chlorine ($NaCl$ or sodium chloride) is ordinary table salt, which does not react violently with water and is not poisonous.

Language, we have said, consists of combinations of symbols. Morphemes are the smallest symbols that are carriers of grammatical or semantic meaning. Morphemes combine into larger units; these, into still larger ones. The meanings of symbol combinations, however, are not simply the "sums of meanings" of their constituent particles. Larger symbolic units have *emergent* meanings. Knowledge of a language involves an intuitive understanding of how the meanings of larger units (phrases or sentences) emerge from the smaller units (words and morphemes).

Some words themselves are morphemes. They cannot be broken into smaller meaningful units. Many words, however, are composed of two or more morphemes (just as molecules of compounds are composed of atoms).

Consider the words "propose," "depose," "expose." Each of these words has a common part, "pose," which is a word with a meaning of its own, while the prefixes are not words by themselves. However, anyone who knows English can sense a meaning in each of these prefixes. Or else their meanings can sometimes (though not always) be guessed from the meanings of the words in which they appear. Similarly the meaning of "pre" in "precede" can be guessed from words like "preface," "prenatal care," "prescience," and "prefix." It certainly has something to do with "ahead" or "before."

We can dig deeper for meaning into the Latin origins of many English words. The Latin preposition "cum" (English "com") means "with," which fits into the notion of "togetherness," as in "combine" and "community."

Let us examine the "chemistry" of another language, say, Russian. Here are some Russian words, all with one "root," or main part, and each with a different prefix. Unlike English prefixes, Russian prefixes are usually prepositions in their own right: otoiti, podoiti, pereiti, priiti, naiti.

The root "iti" means "to go." The prefixes have the following meanings as prepositions: ot = from; pod = under; pri = at; na = on. The prefix "pere" is not a preposition, but its meaning is very close to that of the English prefix "trans." See now whether the meanings of the words you may have guessed correspond to their actual meanings in Russian. "Otoiti" means "to go away from." "Pereiti" means "to cross" (a street, a bridge, etc.); "priiti" means "to arrive." You may have guessed these, or, if not, you might agree that the composite meanings are not unexpected. Now, "podoiti" means "to come near." Does one "come under" when one "comes near"? Compare it with the English "come over" which has a meaning in some contexts similar to "come near." "Over" and "under" seem to have opposite meanings. How did it come about that Russians use the preposition "under" to express an idea that English speakers express with the preposition "over"? It would be interesting to know (cf. the discussion of the Sapir-Whorf hypothesis, pp. 208–9).

The situation with "naiti" is even more interesting. It means "to find." How did the word meaning "to find" come to be composed of "to go" and "on"? We can only guess, but if we exercise some imagination, we might make sense of it. One goes along the road and *comes on* something: one has found something. The explanation may

seem terribly far-fetched. It may not even be correct. But it is a possible explanation, and it gives us an idea of how the meanings of words
may have been composed by accidental combining of meanings of
smaller units.

English, of course, has similar, no less far-fetched combinations of
meanings. Take "substance." It is composed of the prefix "sub," which
has the general meaning of "under," and "stance," which is related to
standing. Is a "substance" something that "stands under"? The connection seems puzzling. Suppose, however, we look at "lying" instead
of "standing." We have the word "underlie," which has some meaning
connected with a foundation because a foundation lies under a building. It is not hard to connect the idea of substance with the idea of a
foundation. Substance is matter, something of which all things are
made. Substance "lies" under material things, as a foundation lies
under a building. Well, then, if a substance can be imagined as "lying
under" material things, can it not also "stand under," which is what
"sub-stance" suggests?

Now turn "stand under" around. We get "understand," which is
composed of the same units as "substance." We might "justify" the
meaning of "understand" in the same way. The meanings of words
composed of "meaningful" units can sometimes be justified quite obviously. In some cases, however, it takes considerable stretching of the
imagination "to make sense" of the composite meanings on the basis
of what the constituent parts generally mean. *This transmutation of
meanings when units are combined is a most fundamental characteristic of language.*

Sometimes the same morphemes may combine into words with very
different meanings, for instance "substandard" and "substance." The
meaning of a word may also change radically when the order of its
constituents is reversed. Examples:

overdo   — do over
overlook   — look over
undergo   — go under
understand— stand under
income   — come in

The fact that the "words" on the right-hand side are actually pairs
of words is of little semantic importance. It is a consequence of a peculiarity of the English manner of speech (and writing) that when a

preposition combining with a verb precedes the verb, it merges with it (in the sense that the two are pronounced without pause), but when the preposition follows the verb, the two are separated in speaking and in writing. From the point of view of semantics, "do over," "look over," and so on, can be understood as single words since their meanings are given by the combination of the morphemes, rather than by the morphemes separately.

In English, as in other Germanic languages, "nominal compounds" are often formed by simply putting whole words together. Examples: ice cream, housewife, bookcase, bookkeeper, warship, sleepwalker, death sentence, chairman, life insurance policy, Ann Arbor Community Symphony Orchestra.

Note that the constituent words of nominal compounds are sometimes separated, sometimes joined. There is no clear rule that determines whether or not the "compound" is written as a single word. I had to consult a dictionary to find out whether "life buoy" is one or two words. Knowing that "life buoy" is written as two words does not help me to conclude that "lifeboat" and "lifeguard" are written as one word. The compound words function as single words whether they are separated or joined.

Next, we find that the meanings of nominal compounds are often immediately apparent from their constituents, as in "lampshade," but sometimes the emergent meanings are quite different, as in "stool pigeon." Sometimes the history of a word reveals how the compound word acquired its meaning, but often the history is forgotten. I do not know how the thymus gland or the pancreas of a calf came to be called "sweetbread" when prepared as a food.

In German and Danish, the fact that nominal compounds are usually written as single words accounts for the very long words encountered in those languages. Examples: Donaudampfschiffsfahrtgesellschaft (German) = Danube Steam Ship Travel Company; and Statskundskabsteoretikere (Danish) = political science theoreticians.

During World War I, German superpatriots insisted on purging the German language of "foreign" words. Telephone is still often called *"Fernsprecher"* (far-speaker) in Germany, although it is "Telefon" in Austria and in Switzerland. It is said that the Germans called a tank "Schuetzengrabenvernichtungpanzerkraftwagen." "Schuetzen" (to protect) + "Graben" (ditch) = trench; "Vernichtung" = destruction; "Panzer" (armor) + "Kraft" (force) + "Wagen" (car) =

armored motorcar; hence, armored motorcar for destroying trenches.

I cannot vouch for the authenticity of that example. However, the following is from my own experience. When I passed through Germany in 1938 during a time of extreme nationalism, my passport was stamped with "Einundwiederausdurchreisesichtvermerk." "Ein" (in) + "und" (and) + "wieder" (again) + "aus" (out) + "durch" (through) + "Reise" (travel) + "Sicht" (sight) + "Vermerk" (notation) = transit visa.

The language of organic chemistry is especially rich in long compound words. Here, the structure of a word actually corresponds to the structure of the chemical compound designated by it. Example: 3–(4–amino–2–methyl–pyrimidyl–5–methyl)–4–methyl–5 (β–hydroxy–ethyl)–thiaozylium hydrochloride stands for vitamin B_1. The long name is of course quite impractical for spoken communication. Chemists call the compound "thiamine" for short. What the long name does is indicate the way in which the various constituents of thiamine are structurally related to each other. It enables the chemist to draw a picture showing how the atoms are hooked together to form a molecule of the substance. The chemistry of the compound is faithfully reflected in the "chemistry" of its name.

Complex technology is another breeding ground for long nominal compounds. In simple technology we find compound words that designate what tools do—for example, screwdriver, lawn mower, pencil sharpener. The complexity of such words grows with the complexity of the technology.

NASA (National Aeronautics and Space Administration) has given birth to a jargon that abounds in long nominal compounds. Examples:

"Nozzle gas ejection ship attitude control system" (the system that controls attitude of the ship by ejecting gas through nozzles).

"Russian embarrassing module making astronaut orbiting program" (a program that orbits astronaut modules—and embarrasses Russians).

The longest reported nominal compound is mentioned in the *Congressional Record*: "Liquid oxygen liquid hydrogen rocket powered single stage to orbit reversible boost system." It contains a past participle ("powered") and an infinitive ("to orbit"). Nevertheless, taken as a whole, the phrase serves as a noun. It can fill the blank in the sentence: "This ——— is too expensive." [1]

1. David McNeil, "Speaking of Space," *Science* (13 May 1966).

Children's poet T. S. Geisel (Dr. Seuss) often satirizes the practice of promiscuous compounding. Example:

"Three seater zatsit nose patting extensions." [2]

If we now view words as atoms and sentences as molecules, the analogy between chemistry and semantics persists on the level of the sentence.

"Birds" is not a sentence.

"Birds fly" is.

"Birds fly south" is.

"Birds fly south in the" is not.

"Birds fly south in the fall" is.

Certain combinations of words, analogous to certain combinations of letters, serve as standard combining forms (like ions in chemical reactions). For instance, "in the fall," "across the street," "God willing," "which does not seem advisable," "unless you suspect him" are all carriers of partial sentence meanings. These combinations of chunks of meaning, called phrases and clauses, do not have the status of sentences since they do not express "sentence meanings" (do not express "complete thoughts," as is demanded of sentences in textbooks). Nevertheless, they are carriers of partial sentence meanings, as suffixes are carriers of partial word meanings.

In written discourse, sentences are supposed to combine into paragraphs, paragraphs into chapters, chapters into books in such a way that larger and larger "meanings" emerge. The quality of expository writing is judged by the way in which the "meanings" of its paragraphs, chapters, and large units "hang together." However, there are no syntactic rules for judging whether a paragraph is properly a paragraph or a chapter a chapter. This is largely a matter of subjective judgment. In certain kinds of discourse, however, the logic of construction is easier to judge than in others. In mathematics, for example, theorems logically depend on each other and must be presented in a specific order. Literary critics judge the "construction" of novels and plays by the way in which the large meaning of the whole work emerges as one reads the novel or views the play.

From the foregoing, it should be clear that "meaning" appears on several different levels. A mark on paper has "meaning" if it is recognized as a letter in a written language. Its "meaning" is a sound. Com-

2. T. S. Geisel (Dr. Seuss), *On Beyond Zebra* (New York: Random House, 1955).

binations of letters have meaning if they are recognized as morphemes or words. Combinations of words convey meanings on higher levels if they form phrases or clauses. Strings of phrases or clauses acquire meanings as sentences. Sequences of sentences acquire meanings as messages.

The meaning of any linguistic unit depends not only on its level but also on its environment. Linguistic environment is called *context*.

The importance of context is clearly seen even on the level of letters. English spelling is difficult because a letter may stand for very different sounds in different words. Observe the "meanings" of the letter "o" (that is, its sound) in "woman," "women," "hot," "tone," and "moon."

On the level of words, changes of meaning with context are well-known. Words that look or sound entirely alike but which may have different, *unrelated* meanings are called homonyms. The meaning of a homonym is usually clear from its context. Examples: In that novel, the *page* declares his secret love for the queen on *page* 137. Just for a *lark*, he asked the waiter to bring him breast of *lark*. I can't *bear* to see a *bear* suffer. (Needless to say, such sentences are to be avoided. They are used here for illustrative purposes only.)

More often, the different meanings of a word as determined by context *are* related, in which case they are not true homonyms. For example, "hood" in "She put up the *hood* of her raincoat" and in "She lifted the *hood* of her car" denote quite different objects and so have quite different denotative meanings (cf. p. 116). Yet the two contextual meanings of "hood" are related: both emerge from the function of a "hood" as a protective cover.

It is sometimes difficult to decide whether a pair of words are true homonyms or not. The two meanings of "hunch" in "I have a *hunch* that the *hunch* on his back is part of a disguise" seem unrelated. But it is possible that the U.S. colloquial word "hunch," meaning "premonition," was the end product of several extensions of the connotation (cf. p. 125) of "hunch" (protuberance), since forgotten.

Consider the following uses of the word "keep": 1) Farmer Jones *keeps* cows. 2) When faced with danger, Jones *keeps* calm. There is a sort of connection between the two meanings of "keep"; it has something to do with "holding on to." Farmer Jones "holds on to" his cows, considers them his property. Faced with danger, he also "holds on to" his self-control. The connection is admittedly far-fetched, but it is rather typical of the way certain so-called "heavy-duty" words function in a language. These "heavy-duty" words are usually some of the simplest, that is, most familiar, words in a language. Examples in English are "keep," "go," "put," "give," and so on.[3] Scores of different meanings of these words are listed in dictionaries. Many of these meanings become apparent if the words, usually linked with a preposition, are put into an environment (context). Examples: to put on (to don); to put off (to postpone); to put something over (to deceive); to put up with (to endure).

Here, it is actually the combination of "put" with the various prepositions that creates the meaningful unit. In a way, therefore, the prepositions can be considered as suffixes attached to the stem "put."

We have already said that "put on," "put off," and so forth, can be viewed as single words. Nevertheless "put" is a morpheme, a carrier of semantic meaning. The meaning of "put" depends on the preposition that follows it, that is, on its environment. Similarly, prepositionlike prefixes acquire different "meanings," depending on what stems they combine with. Thus "super" means something like "over" in "super-fluous" (literally, "overflowing") and perhaps in "supernatural" ("over and above the natural"), but something like "surface" in "superficial." "In" as part of "inject" means "in"; as part of "indiscrete," it means "not."

From the way the meanings of small units are affected by their environment, we can suppose that the larger units have meanings of their own, and these larger meanings *impose* the specific meanings-in-context on the smaller ones. Let us see to what extent we can justify this supposition.

First, consider phrases composed, say, of an article, an adjective, and a noun. Example: a white horse. To the extent that the phrase evokes a picture in your mind, it has a meaning. Now, since "white"

3. The characteristic brevity of "heavy-duty" words has been offered as evidence of the so-called "principle of least effort" by G. K. Zipf. (See his *Human Behavior and the Principle of Least Effort* [Cambridge, Mass.: Addison-Wesley, 1949]. According to this principle, the more frequently a word is used, that is, the more "load" it carries in communication, the shorter it is likely to be. A more rigorous analysis of this principle was undertaken on the basis of mathematical information theory (cf. B. Mandelbrot, "An informational theory of the statistical structure of language," in *Communication Theory*, ed. W. Jackson [London: Butterworth, 1953]. The inverse relation between the length of a signal and the frequency with which it is used is observed on levels below words. For example, in Morse code the shortest letter signal is "e," denoted by a dot, which is also the most frequently used letter in written English.

and "horse" are separate words in English, we tend to think that the meaning of "a white horse" is a composite of the meanings of "white" and of "horse." On reflection, however, it is difficult to believe that this is so. I doubt that, when you read the phrase, you saw in your mind's eye first a horse, then "whiteness" (or vice versa), and then put them together. Most likely, you "saw" a white horse all at once. Only because "white" and "horse" also appear in other contexts do we tend to think that the meaning of "a white horse" is a composite one. Such an idea might not have occurred to someone speaking a language in which "white horse" is a separate word that contains neither "white" nor "horse" as a part. There is, in fact, a German word "Schimmel," which means "white horse" and is not related either to "horse" or to "white." It is easy enough to find similar words with apparently composite meanings in any language, where the composite nature of the meanings is made apparent only when the words are defined in terms of other words. Examples: puppy (a young dog); pauper (a person without means of subsistence); tank (an armored motor vehicle). I submit that, for most people, these familiar words—"puppy," "pauper," "tank"—immediately evoke simple images, not composite ones. The composite nature of these images is perceived only when we think of the dictionary definitions of these words. The same is true of phrases, even though phrases are combinations of words. "Running water," "a broken home," "a tongue-in-cheek remark," "a jack-in-the-box," "a monthly payment plan," "a fight to the finish," evoke mental pictures no more complex than do single, simple words such as "book," "pipe," "paper," "house," and so on.

Simple sentences are also perceived as wholes rather than as composites of their constituent parts. When someone says "I am cold," you perceive his situation at once. You need not put together the meanings of "I," "am," and "cold." In fact, he might have said simply "Cold" or even "Brrr . . ." and would thereby have conveyed exactly the same meaning. And, as we saw in Chapter 2, in some languages whole sentences are typically expressed as single words. On the other hand, some of *our* single words are actually composites of parts, each with a definite meaning of its own which we do not perceive separately because we only perceive the meaning of the whole. In other words, because of the structure of our language, we have preconceived notions about what constitutes a single meaning. As an example, take the word "preconceived." Four separate "meanings" are combined in that word. The prefix "pre" means something like "before"; the main part "conceive" contains two meaningful particles, "con" and "ceive." Neither stands by itself, but in combination with other particles, it acquires a variety of meanings, all vaguely unified into a general notion. "Con" (already noted to come from Latin "cum") usually denotes togetherness of sorts, as in "concord," "concubine," "convention." The particle "ceive" enters other combinations (for example, "perceive," "deceive," "receive") and has something to do with awareness. Finally, the particle "ed" denotes the past tense. It is a peculiarity of our language, existing in many but not all languages, that the time of occurrence of an event is denoted by a morpheme that has no independent existence as a word.

It is difficult to say how large a combination of symbols can exist and still be recognizable as a whole without being analyzed into its constituent parts. Words can certainly be so recognized, even to the extent that we are not ordinarily aware of their constituent meaningful parts. Short sentences too are typically recognized in this way. Examples: "It is cold." "Please pass the salt." "I love you." Very long sentences cannot be instantaneously understood. They must somehow first be broken up and the meanings of the parts pieced together. The ability to do this constitutes the ability to understand a language. Conversely, the ability to put together meanings of words, phrases, and cases into sentences (synthesis) constitutes the ability to speak or write a language.

The fact that a sentence has its own meaning, which is not simply a composite of the meanings of its separate parts, is seen most clearly in the problem of translation. It is common knowledge that acceptable translations cannot be accomplished by translating every word of a sentence from the source language into a corresponding word in the target language. At best this word-by-word translation results in bizarre expressions, at worst in completely meaningless ones. When a Spaniard pronounces the Spanish words for "no" and "know" in succession, he means "I don't know." The English translation must supply the missing first person pronoun, usually omitted in Spanish, and must express the negative by the auxiliary verb "don't." The German "What gives?" is translated into English as "What's the matter?" If we guess the meaning, it is only because many German idioms have been incorporated into colloquial American. The Russian, when he says

"What's the matter?" says "v chom dyelo," which literally translated says "In what [is the] business?" [4]

We attribute all these peculiarities to differences in idiom. Actually, however, the entire grammar of a language is a generator of idioms. What we call idioms are only those peculiarities of a foreign grammar that are specially far removed from our own.[5] A grammar is essentially a set of rules according to which meanings carried by the smaller units of language—words, morphemes, and phrases—are put together to compose the meanings of the larger units, namely sentences.

Does the meaning of a sentence change with context? It certainly does. In fact, sentences, like words, may be homonyms. Consider the following sentence: "They are flying planes." [6] It can have two different meanings. As an answer to the question "What are those objects?" it can be paraphrased as "Those objects, flying above us, are planes." But in answer to the question "What are those people doing?" the same sentence says in effect "Those people are piloting aircraft."

A rather far-fetched example is the sentence "Time flies." If the rejoinder is "Yes, last year seems like last week," then "Time flies" was understood to say that days, months, or years pass rapidly. But the rejoinder could also be "All right; give me a stop watch." Here "Time flies" was understood as a request to measure the locomotion speed of insects.

A more subtle homonyn is illustrated by a sentence such as "The tall man is the girl's father." At first sight the sentence seems unambiguous. However, it can be understood in two different senses: (1) as an answer to the question "Who is the tall man?" and (2) as an answer to the question "Who is the girl's father?" The different meanings are not distinguished in written English. In spoken English, they may be distinguished by slight changes of emphasis or intonation. In the first case, we are likely to put more stress on "father"; in the second, on "the tall man." In Japanese, the difference in meaning is reflected in the difference between two articles corresponding to "the." If the statement "The geisha is playing the samisen" answers the question "Who

4. The words in brackets are omitted in Russian because the present tense of "to be" is dropped (except when emphasized) and articles do not exist.
5. To be sure, idioms of English are listed also in English grammars, but I suspect that this aspect of grammar was included only when grammarians became aware of the fact that English is a foreign language to non-English speakers.
6. Example given by Noam Chomsky.

is playing the samisen?" then the word for "the" is "ga"; if the same statement answers the question "What is the geisha doing?" the word for "the" is "wa."

Intonation often conveys the meaning of a sentence in a larger context. "He *did* it" says more than that "he did it." The emphasis on "did" indicates that the sentence resolved an uncertainty as to whether or not he would do it. On the other hand, "*He* did it" indicates that the sentence resolved the uncertainty about who did it.

In English, questions are normally indicated by the use of the auxiliary word "do." In some languages, however, questions are indicated by change in intonation. This manner has also crept into colloquial American, probably borrowed from Yiddish. Example: "You call this a bargain?"

Also, in English, because of the absence of distinguishing markers, the grammatical category of a word (the part of speech) may depend on the context. As was noted in Chapter 2, a large number of English words can play the parts of both noun and verb, sometimes also of adjective. Unrestricted interchangeability between nouns and verbs stimulates more and more of these fusions. "To chair a meeting" and "to table a resolution" probably represent comparatively recent uses of old nouns as new verbs.

New situations bring into being new expressions to describe them. In some cases new words are invented. For the most part, however, the expressions are compounded from old words. How they are compounded depends on what sort of combinations are "natural" in a given language and, to a large degree, on the attitudes of the language community to language change. Some language communities are conservative; some are tolerant of far-reaching changes in usage. And, of course, within the same language community, there are people who will gladly experiment with language, guided only by a need to create vivid word forms and expressions to fit new situations, and others who are scandalized by what they see as a bowdlerization of the language. I know people who suffer when they hear words like "finalize" or "hopefully" (used in the sense of "I hope that").

In some cases, the resentment may not be against language change as such but against the occupations or social roles of those who introduce it, particularly when language innovation is associated with unwelcome changes in the institutional structure of society. In the United States, a plethora of new institutions (bureaus, agencies, etc.) appeared during the Roosevelt administration. With them came the widespread practice of compounding names from initial letters. The "alphabet soup" (NRA, WPA, FCC, SEC) sprinkled over the pages of newspapers became a constant reminder of a growing bureaucratization of American life. One might raise the question as to what extent these abbreviations constitute actual language change. This depends on the degree to which the new combinations acquire distinct meanings of their own without reference to the meanings of the words from which they were constructed. At times this is definitely the case. During the era of Nazi terror, who did not recognize "Gestapo" as a word with its own sinister meaning, which had no direct relation to the "geheime Staatspolizei" (secret state police) from which the acronym was constructed? Similarly, in the United States, the word pronounced "eff-bee-eye" has distinct meaning as a word, regardless of the fact that it is written FBI and stands for Federal Bureau of Investigation.

The clumsiness of nominal compounds practically forces the formation of acronyms. These are often constructed with a view toward picturesque effects.

Examples from NASA jargon:[7]

FEAR (failure effect analysis report)
SMASH (special material and special handling)
EGADS (electronic ground automatic destruct sequences)
NASA has a Manpower Utilization Department. Its name is MUD.

The acronyms of the military establishment sometimes reflect a morbid sense of humor.[8] Examples:

BAMBI (Ballistic Antiballistic Missile Boost Intercept)
INFANTS (Iroquois Night Fighter and Night Tracker System)
DEW (Directed Energy Weapon, also Distant Early Warning)
SAINT (Satellite Intercept)

Not only do the acronyms reflect a morbid sense of humor, but often they attempt to euphemize the reality. It is harder perhaps to object to paying taxes for BAMBI and INFANTS than it is for expensive missiles and tracking systems that become obsolete overnight. Those who

7. Donald H. Sears and Henry A. Smith, "A Linguistic Look at Aerospace English," *Word Study* 44, no. 4 (April 1969): 1–8.
8. Paul Dickson, "The Culture of Bureaucracy: Put Them All Together They Spell Mother," *The Washington Monthly* 1, no. 3 (January 1970): 32–36.

deplore the hypertrophy of the military establishment may resent also the characteristic "chemistry" of its language.

For the most part, hybrid words and acronyms, created ad hoc, are short-lived. They do become incorporated into language if the institutions or agencies they designate become more or less permanent fixtures. Thus the Russian words "politbureau," "kolkhoz" (collective farm), "raykom" (regional committee), all hybrid words, are now definitely established in the Russian lexicon. In the United States, the hybrid "gerrymander" has survived.

Once a new principle of word formation is established, combinations made on that principle multiply rapidly. For instance, culinary invention and merchandising initiative spawned the "cheeseburger" as a companion to the traditional hamburger. The cheeseburger became popular, and its name was added to the American lexicon. Inevitably the floodgates were opened to "chiliburgers," "chicken-burgers," and so on. Whether these mongrels will make it into dictionaries or will remain on the fringes of language as awkward, cheap imitations depends on how firmly the concoctions represented by them are incorporated into the American cuisine. In the 1920s a mechanized cafeteria was christened "Automat." The word has remained on the border between a brand name and a common noun. We now have hydromatic cars, coin-o-matic change dispensers, and laundro-mats. The words are jarring to a sensitive ear, probably because of the haphazard, unimaginative way they are put together. Possibly, when the novelty of automation wears off, simpler words will replace them, just as "movies" replaced the "biograph," the "bioscope," and the "cinematograph"—words that emphasized the "scientific" pedi-gree of movies.

The wave of direct-action protests against racial segregation in southern United States began with the so-called "sit-ins." Negroes sat down at lunch counters and, after being refused service, continued to sit until they were forcibly ejected by the police. The word "sit-in" alluded to the "sit-*down*" strikes of the 1930s when striking workers, instead of picketing outside the plants, occupied the premises. The sit-ins eventually broke the solid segregation practices in the South. Five years later, students and faculty members, protesting United States involvement in the Vietnam war, invented the "teach-in," a combination of demonstrations against the war and seminars on the war's historic and political background. "Teach-in" alluded to the "sit-in" and through it to the "sit-down strike," thus partaking in the connotation of a protest action along with occupation of premises. Imitations, of course, soon followed—the "love-in," the "sing-in," the "be-in," and so forth. These latter neologisms are not likely to survive. However, the political impact of sit-down strikes, the sit-ins, and the teach-ins may put these words into dictionaries.

In short, whether a new "synthetic" word lives or dies depends on whether it came into use as a result of a real need or whether it was foisted on the language community to promote something. The automobile came to stay, but all of its fancy names, designed to emphasize the novelty of the invention ("horseless carriage," "quadricycle," even "automobile" itself), were supplanted by the simple "car." On the other hand, the hybrid word "motel" became a respectable international word. There are motels, so named, even in the U.S.S.R.

APPLICATIONS

I. Shakespeare was a master of compounding, and even the most cursory reading of his plays will reveal how he enriched his language through use of this device. Today compounding is one of the ways in which a writer can be linguistically inventive. Used with restraint, compounds add liveliness and color to our prose ("gunslinging outlaw," "earsplitting yell," "gross-booted draymen"). Here are some simple exercises to start you off if you are compound-shy.

1) What would you call someone who steals wallets?
2) How would you characterize a righteous member of your community who is always pointing a finger at the shortcomings of transgressions of others?
3) A baseball player who hits well against fastball pitching?
4) A ranch worker who is expert at subduing horses?
5) A clerical worker who keeps his eye on the clock?
6) A phrase that is difficult to pronounce correctly?
7) An automobile that holds the road very well?
8) Cold weather that makes the mind go numb?
9) Someone who attends church, sings hymns on Sundays, and on Mondays uses unscrupulous business tactics?
10) A "hippie" who dances provocatively?

II. Someone once remarked that a translation is like a woman: either faithful and ugly, or unfaithful and beautiful. Though this may be an exaggeration, it dramatizes one of our statements: "A sentence has its own meaning, which is not simply a composite of the meanings of its separate parts." If this seems mysterious to you, think of this analogy. A living human being is dismembered in an accident; a surgeon sews all of the members together in a skillful professional way, so that there are no signs of surgery or sutures. The only difference between the "before" and the "after" is that the body is no longer alive. The living body had its own meaning or its own life, which could not be restored simply by recomposing it. Often a "faithful" translation will miss the spirit of the original. You can discover this for yourself by comparing two or more translations of a poem by Baudelaire, Mallarmé, Rilke, or Goethe, or by working on the following application:

Assume that you are spending the summer in a European city. How would you translate for a curious citizen of that city the following expressions:

a) "I don't dig that place—it makes me uptight."
b) "Some American tourists are square, some are hip."
c) "I'd like to make out with the blond chick."
d) "She's outasight—like really far-out."
e) "If I weren't so spaced, I'd split."
f) "Well, I reckon I ain't no call to expect no more of him than of his mangrowed brothers."
g) "Just play it straight and don't put him on."
h) "I'll lay ten to one that he runs out of dough before he gets his next allowance."
i) "I liberated some groovy furniture in Macy's."
j) "When I really open up the Mercedes, it hits ninety in third—and it gives you a smooth ride. It really goes."

III. The impulse to create acronyms for organizations with cumbersome names is understandable: aside from the economy, the acronym is a mnemonic device. But what factors seem to determine whether a person or an institution will be reduced to initials? For instance, among our presidents, there were FDR, JFK, and LBJ, but never HST, DDE, or RMN. In politics, there is the GOP and there was OK (Old Kinderhook Party of New York). In England, many titles are abbreviated (O.M., K.G., and M.P.). On the stock exchange, there is AMBAC (American Bosch Arma Company) and NYLIC (New York Life Insurance Company) and, of course, IBM.

1) Compile a list of acronyms and commonly used initial clusters. Can you detect any trend or tendency of a linguistic nature?

2) James Joyce made use of every imaginable rhetorical and linguistic device available. In *Finnegans Wake*, HCE and ALP stand for Humphrey Chimpden Earwicker, an Irish pub-keeper, and his wife, Anna Livia Plurabelle. Both keep changing shape and character, but we recognize them through the initials (Here Comes Everybody, He'll Cheat E'erawan; Annshee lispes privily, Alma Luvia, Pollabella). The initials are *signals*. In *Ulysses*, a sandwich man carrying the initials H.E. L. Y.'S. wanders in and out of the action; Leopold Bloom ponders the meaning of the initials U.P. When Stephen sees the poet A. E. Russell and remembers that he owes him money, he reflects: "A.E. I.O.U." On page 338, Joyce satirizes British pomposity:

... the Duke of Cronwall's [*sic*] light infantry under the general supervision of H.R.H. rear admiral the right honorourable sir Hercules Hannibal Habeas Corpus Anderson K.G., K.P., K.T., P.C., K.C.B., M.P., J.P., M.B., D.S.O., S.O.D., M.F.H., M.R.I.A., B.L. Musc. Doc., P.L.G., F.T.C.D., F.R., U.L., F.R.C.P.I., and F.R.C.S.

One section of the Aeolus chapter is entitled "K.M.R.A." and another "K.M.R.I.A."—instructions about the part of the Royal Irish anatomy on which a kiss is to be bestowed.

What appears to be Joyce's intention in this use of initials? Does the Beatles' hit of a little time ago "Lucy in the Sky with Diamonds" owe anything to Joyce?

IV. Recently, we have been witnessing a new linguistic phenomenon: neologisms replacing neologisms that have grown aged. For example, hardly anyone any longer says, "I'm going by airplane." We travel by *jet* or by 707, and the *international set* has become the *jet set*.

1) Here are some recent neologisms that may have outlived their usefulness. With what words are they being replaced?

television	moving pictures
motel	movies
a depression (economics)	cop
nuts (crazy)	hippie
Mary Jane	chick

2) Can you think of any neologisms current last year that are now on the way out? What words are replacing them?

3) A contemporary writer observed not long ago that "over 30 is not a time or an age, but a place, a country set off from the country of the young." He is, of course, speaking about the so-called "generation gap" in his own metaphor. If you believe in the myth of the "generation gap," to what extent do you think it is the result of language—the differences in the idioms, the slang, the neologisms, and even the syntaxes of two generations? In your opinion, would the study of the "semantics of the generation gap" contribute to greater understanding of the generations? What would you include in such a study?

V.   The people engaged in the space program march to the beat of a different drummer. This is most readily seen in their language, which is made up of strange-sounding words with obscure meanings. For instance, the following event reportedly occurred in *aeropause*, near the *aerothermodynamic border* during an *anomalistic period*: "The Apollo 15 *astronauts* spotted some *unsymmetrical dimethyl hydrazine* during their *space probe*, but *Mission Control* said it was *storable* and *hypergolic*."

1) Can you draw up a list of neologisms as jargon terms associated with a particular field or activity familiar to you? Write a short paper about this special vocabulary. What are the roots of these terms? How have the root meanings been transformed?

6/pedigrees
of meaning

Serious and systematic study of language as a creation of humanity (as distinct from studying specific languages for practical purposes of communication) began in Europe in the eighteenth century. An impetus was provided when scholars recognized that Sanskrit, an ancient language of India, was strikingly similar in many ways to the so-called "classical" languages, Greek and Latin.[1] The discovery gave rise to the idea of language "parentage" and language evolution. The time was evidently ripe for general concepts of evolution, which were already penetrating biology. Accordingly scholars began a systematic classification of languages into large "families" that in turn consisted of smaller subdivisions. Most of the European languages were found to belong to the so-called Indo-European family thought to have derived from Sanskrit and from several "sister" languages which have not "survived." [2] The Indo-European family was in turn subdivided into smaller groups, among them the Germanic, the Romance, and the Slavic. Each of these contains among others, the "living" languages as we usually think of them: English, Swedish, and German belong to the Germanic family; French, Italian, and Spanish, to the Romance; Russian, Polish, Czech, and Serbian, to the Slavic.

1. The name "Sanskrit," meaning "accurately made, polished, refined," was probably given to this language by native grammarians to distinguish it from the "uncultivated" popular dialects. "Sam" is a preposition meaning "together" (cf. German "zusammen," English "same"); "krita" is the past participle of the verb "kar," meaning "to make" (cf. "creation").
2. The first suggestion of the possibility of an original, now extinct, Indo-European language seems to have been made by Sir William Jones (1746–94). Systematic investigation of this hypothesis was begun about 1815.

It is obvious to anyone in contact with "families" of languages that Danish and Swedish are quite similar; that both are rather similar to German but not as much as to each other; that there is more similarity between Swedish and German than between German and French; finally, that all of the Indo-European languages are similar to each other in certain important ways.[3] Even though most of them are not "mutually intelligible," they all contain certain words and especially certain grammatical features not found in other language groups.

Words have an "ancestry." Every good dictionary mentions the pedigree or the *etymology* of a word together with its definition. The ancestry of words often reflects the history of a language community. English, for example, is a "child" of two language strains. The Romans occupied Britain in the first century A.D. and introduced Latin. The Angles, Saxons, and Jutes, who settled in Britain in the fifth century A.D., spoke Germanic languages. In the late eighth century came the Scandinavians, speaking Germanic dialects; also in the eleventh century came the Normans led by William the Conqueror. The Normans were descendants of the Vikings (Scandinavians), but they had lived in France since the middle of the ninth century and spoke French. So the English language became a mixture of Germanic and Romance strains.

It is interesting to observe that in English most of the common words of everyday usage ("earth," "bread," "house," "food," etc.) are of Germanic origin, while words related to "matters of the intellect" are more likely to be of Latin origin. (The reason is not far to seek. Latin continued to be the official language of the church and government long after the Roman Empire disintegrated, and for many centuries Latin was the only written language; thus literate people automatically knew this language and formulated their ideas in it.) Examples can be found on practically every page of a dictionary, such as:

emasculate (to deprive of procreative power), from Latin *emasculatus*: e = away; masculus = male

---

3. In a strikingly similar way, a cat and a puma are more like each other than a cat and a dog; a cat is more closely related to a dog than to a rabbit, more closely related to a rabbit than to a lizard, more closely related to a lizard than to an oyster, more closely related to an oyster than to an orchid. Living things are grouped into species, genera, families, classes, and phyla. The narrower the category to which two organisms belong, the more anatomical and physiological features they have in common.

right (cf. German Recht)
piety, from Latin pietas = dutifulness
testimony (Latin testis = witness)
sea (cf. German See; Danish sø)
cut (cf. Swedish kuta; Norwegian kutta)

Walter Scott's novel *Ivanhoe* deals with the resistance of the older Anglo-Saxon inhabitants of Britain to their French-speaking conquerors. One of the characters makes the astute observation that the names of live domestic animals are of Anglo-Saxon origin while the names of their *meats* are French. Examples:

calf—veal (French veau)
ox—beef (French boeuf)
sheep—mutton (French mouton)
swine—pork (French porc)

This linguistic fact is cited as evidence of the humiliating class distinctions imposed on the Anglo-Saxons by their Norman masters. The former tended the animals; the latter ate their meat.

The pedigree of a word is frequently apparent in its spelling, especially in English, which is noted for its conservative orthography. Thus all the silent *k*'s preceding *n*'s have their origin in older German (often Greek) words where the *k* sound (or the related *g* sound) *was* heard. Examples:

knave (cf. German Knabe—boy)
know (cf. German kennen—to know; also Greek gnos)
knight (cf. German Knecht—serf; then Old English cniht—boy, military
    attendant.) Note the upgrading in status, changing the connotation of
    servility to one of nobility.

The English silent *gh* has its counterpart in the German *ch*, which is pronounced. Examples:

ENGLISH	GERMAN
night	Nacht
naught	nichts
right	Recht
light	Licht

The silent letters are remarkable analogues of so-called vestigial organs in biological evolution. As organisms evolve in the process of adapting to changes in environment, certain structures or organs sometimes become useless. However, they do not disappear all at once but often persist for many generations as anachronistic appendages. The vermiform appendix of the large intestine is a well-known example. Birds that no longer fly, such as ostriches, still have wings. Human beings still have muscles for cocking ears although only few of us can still use them.

These vestiges are found not only in the anatomies of living things but also in their "artifacts." Termites, for example, build huge "cities," great hills with labyrinths of galleries. Some of these galleries have been found to be useless dead ends (like the human appendix). A study of *fossil* termite hills revealed that at one time these galleries were functional. At some later time their function ceased, but the dead-end galleries still appear as "vestiges" in modern termite hills. No better evidence can be marshaled to support the analogy among evolutionary processes than the vestiges of linguistic elements, the anachronisms of language.

Enthusiasts of phonetic spelling have only contempt for these relics. Their opponents ridicule the *fonetik speling kampane by egzhibiding samplez uv inglish speld fonetikalee*. One argument, that the results look bizarre, is not conclusive. Most innovations look bizarre. Opposition to radical reforms of spelling involves more than a reluctance to relearn. A crucial point is that written language has a semantics of its own, internalized by literate people, and that this semantics, derived from the pedigrees of meanings, would be destroyed if words were cut loose from their derivations. As an illustration, consider derivatives from Greek.

One need not know Greek to recognize the meanings of parts of words like hydro (water), pyro (fire), psycho (mental), pneumo (air), photo (light), and so on. These prefixes are not phonetically spelled. [Note phono (sound).] Occurring as they do in written language, it is their *appearance* that immediately suggests their meanings. Phoneticization of spelling would destroy the appearance of these parts of words and with it their suggestiveness.

It can be argued, of course, that we are accustomed to the way these combinations of letters look because we have been taught to spell them. Had we been taught from the start to spell them phonetically, there would be nothing to lose. However, there is another powerful argument in favor of conservatism in spelling: it counteracts the comparatively rapid changes that beset spoken language. These changes divide previously unified languages into dialects. If spelling followed pronunciation, written language would either have to be likewise differentiated or else follow one of the dialects; but in the former case, the dialects would move even further apart, and in the latter case what would be phonetic in one dialect would not be phonetic in another.

The clearest illustration of the unifying role of written language is written Chinese. Written Chinese is not phonetic at all because it is written in ideographs, not in an alphabet. As a consequence, people of China speaking very different dialects (actually different languages because they are not mutually intelligible) can nevertheless all read written Chinese. Even Japanese can read Chinese, although Japanese and Chinese languages are entirely unrelated. The universal use of Arabic numerals is another example. The pronounced names of numbers are quite different in different languages. But everyone can read numerals in whatever language they occur.

The study of word pedigrees can be fascinating. Here are some well-known examples.

Money is derived from the Latin *moneta*, which originally meant "forewarned." According to legend, enemies were preparing to attack Rome at night, but when they penetrated into the city they awoke the sacred (or, perhaps, sacrificial) geese housed in the Temple of Juno. The cackling awoke the guards, and the city was saved. Thereafter the temple was called the Temple of Juno Moneta (forewarned). The mint was next to the temple, and the coins minted there came to be known as *monetae.*

Other words related to money: *Soldier* is derived from *solidus,* a Latin word for a gold coin. (Italian armies in the late Middle Ages consisted largely of mercenaries.) *Salary* is derived from Latin *sal* (salt), which served as pay in ancient times. Gold *bullion* got its name from the fact that cattle once served as money.

Statistics is now a branch of mathematics. The word comes from the same root as "state." Originally statistics was a compilation of data on states, their populations, military forces, resources, and so on. The word "statistics" sometimes is still used this way. But statistics as a branch of mathematics has nothing to do with the specific data with which statistics was originally concerned.

Electricity is derived from the Greek word for "amber" because it was the peculiar behavior of amber (when rubbed with fur or wool) that first attracted attention to electrical phenomena.

Journal is derived from the French word *jour* (day). Ordinarily journals appear as weeklies or monthlies, rather than dailies; but journal also means "diary," a record of the day's events (as the word "diary" suggests). It was the *record of events* that connected the meanings of "journal" and "newspaper."

Companion is derived from Latin *panis,* meaning bread. Hence companion—someone with whom ("com") one eats bread.

Husband is an amusing example of how "original meanings" turn out to make ironic comments on modern life. Etymologically related to "housebound," husband once meant farmer (cf. husbandry); farmers were once serfs "bound" to their domiciles.

At times a word is coined, that is, makes a sudden appearance and thereafter becomes incorporated into the language. These dramatic births (called *neologisms*) are sometimes associated with names of persons who became sensationally famous, or, more often, notorious. Examples:

Boycott (Captain Charles C.) was a land agent in County Mayo, Ireland. To thwart his practice of swindling indebted farmers out of their land, the people of that county in 1880 agreed among themselves that no one of them would speak to him, do business with him, or in any way include him in their affairs. The word came into the language to mean a concerted ostracism, either social or economic, to express disapproval of an offender or to induce redress, such as has been employed by various protest movements, trade unions, and so forth.

Quisling was a Norwegian politician who became the puppet of the Germans in occupied Norway during World War II. His name has become associated with the special kind of treason he represented.

Mesmer was an eighteenth-century physician who used hypnosis as a therapeutic technique; hence, "mesmerize"—to hold spellbound.

Guillotine was a French physician who in 1789, the period of the French Revolution, first proposed the use of a mechanical blade, instead of the hand-wielded axe, for executing persons by beheading.

Closely related to this type of derivation are words whose origins are particular events that later acquired important social significance. Example: Workers, enraged because they were replaced by machinery, hurled their wooden shoes (sabots) into the machines to wreck them. Hence, *sabotage*—deliberate wrecking of machinery or, more generally, a plan of disruptive action, usually for political ends.

A common symptom of linguistic innocence is the notion that the "real" meaning of a word resides in its pedigree. Supposedly the Latin or Greek ancestor of a word carried its "original" meaning, which has since been corrupted or perverted. The loquacious high school principal in Belle Kaufman's satirical novel *Up the Down Staircase* believes that he is saying something profound about pedagogy when he insists that "education" is derived from Latin *educo*, meaning "I lead out of." It is said that when Freud first reported his observations on symptoms of hysteria in men, some learned physicians scoffed at the idea. "How could men possibly suffer from hysteria," they asked, "when any literate person knows that 'hysteria' is derived from the Greek word meaning 'womb'?"

In one stormy session of the United Nations, a Greek delegate berated a Ukrainian delegate for misusing the word "democracy," protesting that "democracy" was a Greek word and therefore no one understood the meaning of democracy better than the Greeks.

I once discussed Middle East politics with a Moslem who assured me that Arabs could not possibly have aggressive intentions against anyone because they professed the Islamic faith, and Islam means "peace" in Arabic.

If anything is to be learned about the meanings of words from their origins, it is that meanings usually change more rapidly than do the words. That is, the old words remain in usage long after the underlying meanings have been radically modified, often beyond recognition. In fact, the original meanings of words can be seriously misleading. Malaria is now known to be a disease induced by an amoebic parasite transmitted to man by the bite of a mosquito. Since mosquitoes abound in marshy places, malaria was endemic in those localities. Consequently the disease was attributed to the marshes, specifically to vapors emanating from the swamps. Hence the derivation of "malaria": mal + aria = "bad air." That eventually malaria could be controlled was a consequence of the recognition of its entirely different origin. Control of a disease depends on the understanding of its *etiology*, not of the *etymology* of its name.

Though the often odd ancestry of words may be interesting and historically instructive, the pedigree of a word has no more relation to its contemporary usage than does the remote ancestry of individuals to their present character or social roles.

Words "borrowed" directly from other languages are found in all languages. Borrowings occur when no suitable words exist in the language of a people coming in contact with new objects or situations. The origin of the borrowed word is a reminder of the origin of the referent. "Tea" is an anglicized Chinese word. "Spaghetti" is, of course, Italian, a diminutive of *spago*, a thin cord; "fillet" is French, "borscht" is Russian, "sauerkraut" is German. Names of animals are frequently borrowed from languages of people who knew the animals before the word borrowers did. "Orangutan" (Malaya), "koala" (Australia), "kangaroo" (Australia) are examples.

In English, many words relating to fashion are borrowed from French. In Russian, many words related to navigation are borrowed from Dutch, many related to sports are borrowed from English, and many military terms have been borrowed from German. The Tartar domination of Russia (thirteenth to fifteenth centuries) left its mark on the language. For example, the Russian word for "horse" (*loshad'*) is of Tartar origin. There is no similar sounding word for horse in any Slavic language.

One of the most important as well as the most fascinating problems of comparative linguistics is that of tracing the paths of language evolution. Since languages are known to evolve like organic species, the classification of languages into groups, families, and so on, can be based on the "degree of kinship." Related languages are those descended from a common one.

As we noted earlier, French, Spanish, Italian, and Portuguese are closely related languages, all having a common ancestor, namely Latin, from which they sprang less than a millennium and a half ago. The Germanic languages (German, Swedish, Dutch) also have a common ancestor and are of about the same "age" as the Romance languages. Traced backward, the common ancestors of Romance and Germanic languages have an older common ancestor from which the Slavic languages, Persian, and many languages of India also sprang. This original language is much older than, say, Latin. Since it existed before the invention of writing, there are no material traces of it. Nevertheless linguists are able to "reconstruct" it (Proto-Indo-European) because there are certain regularities in the way the sounds of languages change, and knowledge of these regularities provides linguists with guidelines of reconstruction.

One principal guideline is the comparison of *cognates*, words in related languages that have come down from the same word in the language that is the common ancestor of both. Examples:

	FRENCH	SPANISH	LATIN (common ancestor)
mother:	mère	madre	mater
father:	père	padre	pater

	LATIN	GREEK	SANSKRIT (common ancestor)
god:	deus	theos	devas

Cognates are recognized by their similarity. However, similarity between two words in two languages is not alone conclusive evidence that they are genuine cognates. The word may have been borrowed by one language from another. In some cases the borrowing is obvious, as in the Japanese words "besubolu" and "bifuteku." Clearly these are borrowings from English, not cognates of "baseball" and "beefsteak."

Acquaintance with cognates and some knowledge of the way words change in evolving languages are frequently of considerable help in learning a language related to one's own. Consider the following pairs of cognates:

ENGLISH	GERMAN
day	Tag
yesterday	gestern
may	mag
say	sagen

A "g" in German becomes a "y" in English. Knowledge of this transformation makes it easier to recognize the English cognates of German words. Another well-known regularity is the addition in Spanish of an initial "e" to Latin words beginning with "sp" or "st". Examples:

	LATIN	SPANISH
state:	status	estado
hope:	spes	esperanza

In French, the "s" frequently disappears, leaving only a residue in the form of an "acute accent" on the "e," as in "état" (state).

We have already mentioned "vestigial parts" of words apparent in the silent letters occurring frequently in languages with nonphonetic spelling. Above, we traced some of these vestigial letters in English words to their German or Old English cognates. Carrying the tracing further reveals relations that may be unsuspected. For instance, "know," "agnostic," and "ignorance" have a common origin in the Greek word *gignoskein* (to know). The silent "k" in "know" stems from the "g" in "*gignos*" ("g" and "k" are the voiced and the unvoiced variants of the same sound). The prefix "a" stems from the Greek prefix *a* meaning "not" (cf. "amoral," "atonal," "asymmetric"). The prefix "*i*" in "ignorant" is a contraction of "in," which in English also signifies negation (cf. "invincible," "indivisible"). Thus both "agnostic" and "ignorant" mean "not knowing." But "agnostic" means specifically "one who does not know whether God exists," whereas "ignorant" means "not knowing" generally.

In summary, the pedigree of a word provides clues to deciphering the chemistry of meaning by calling attention to the time dimension. Not only is the emergent meaning of a word often far removed from a simple sum of the meanings of its constituent parts: the meanings of the parts may be vestiges of ancient meanings.

Legitimately, the study of etymology puts language in the perspective of evolution. Everything that has an identity has a history, whether it be a person, an institution, a nation, a species, or the life process as a whole. Language is no exception. To understand an *organic* system (as distinct from a mechanical system), we must know something about its history. To understand the actions and predispositions of a person or a state, we must know something about how the actions and predispositions evolved. Again language is no exception, for it too is an organic system. However, we must keep in mind just *how* knowledge of the history of a word or a language helps us to understand it.

The present meaning of a word is not a "corrupted" version of its original, presumably "correct" meaning. The present meaning of a word resides in the way it is used; the way it is used is determined by the way it serves the user—to inform, to express, to persuade, to control, or to deceive. However, since the word may carry vestiges of old meanings, knowing what these are helps us to realize how meanings of words change with the uses to which they are put. Once again, the analogy with biological evolution is instructive. The wing of a bat, the leg of a horse, and my arm have the same "ancestor" in the forelimb of our common ancestor, an early vertebrate. The *uses* to which this appendage has been put—flying, running, embracing—have nothing in common. Understanding their common origin is of no help in understanding these later uses, but it raises a host of important questions as to how it came about that the "same" anatomical structure was adapted to such diverse uses. Also it leads to an important insight: anatomy is more "conservative" than the way of life. That is to say, organisms change their ways of life but, in doing so, they utilize the anatomical structures already available, adapting them to new uses. Similarly, language is more conservative than the meanings it carries. As our condition changes, so do meanings. But we usually adapt the language already available to serve new meanings.

APPLICATIONS

I.   Shakespeare is reputed to have coined more new words than any other writer in English. If you care to investigate the methods modern linguists and philologists use in determining these matters, take a play such as *Hamlet* and in any given scene decide which words must have been neologisms in Shakespeare's time and which of them in particular he invented.

1) Many latter-day neologisms have been derived from the names of men associated with the activity described by the word. In addition to those cited in the text, the following people have been immortalized in permanent neologisms. Can you provide the word and define it?

a) Marquis de Sade   f) Thomas Bowdler
b) Leopold von Sacher-Masoch   g) Graf von Zeppelin
c) Lord Cardigan   h) Julius Caesar
d) Plato   i) Oedipus
e) Queen Victoria   j) George F. Babbitt

   Add other name neologisms. Can you find any pattern in this process?
2) Like the names of people, place-names yield new words by the process of "de-capitalization." What words have the following places fathered?

a) Frankfort   h) Mecca
b) Champagne   i) Macao (very tricky)
c) Limousin   j) Chartres
d) Hamburg   k) Scotland
e) Bologna   l) Madeira
f) Parma   m) Shanghai
g) Kashmir   n) Camembert

Can you think of any others? To what kind of activity do most of these words refer?

II.   There are other synonym clusters that can be understood better in terms of the "meat on the hoof—meat on the table" relationship. Try to account for the presence of similar words like those in the following sets. Can you make distinctions among the terms in each set (use a thesaurus if necessary):

a) climb—mount—ascend
b) speak—declare—utter
c) backside—rear—dorsum
d) love—amour—charity
e) earthly—mundane—global
f) friendly—amiable—companionable
g) holy—sacred—spiritual

III.   The so-called "youth culture" or "counterculture" has contributed a number of words to common currency: "LSD," "a bad trip," "it's groovy," "joint," "grass," "smack," "ball," "swing," "SDS," "pigs," "trash," "hooker," "john," "the pill," "dope," "rip off," "the Man," "Charlie," "hype," and so on.

Develop a lexicon (dictionary) of terms that have entered the common language (if the word is used on television or in films, it is part of the common language) in the past ten years, largely through the agency of the college generation. Can you draw any conclusions from your lexicon? For example, do the terms tend to be concrete or abstract? Do they draw largely upon English or upon other languages? Do they tend to be "picturesque"?

IV.   In discussing language, one cannot leave the subject of "pedigree" without examining, however briefly, the meaning of "obscenity." Obscenity is of two types: pornography and scatology. Pornography means writing about amateur or professional whores and is properly applied to bedroom words, while scatology applies to bathroom words. Some people regard both as vulgar, while others find one obscene but not the other. One might infer from what has been said that obscenity is a matter of artificial rules, but it may have much deeper psychological roots than that.

1) Ponder for a moment the words that you would not use in front of your mother. Do you associate them with a period in your life?
2) Now think of their equivalents in a language you learned after you were

ten years old. Do these words retain their potency in the other language? Is it possible to say words like *merde, Scheiss, fourrer, vögeln, cul,* or *Schwanz* without embarrassment? Are they more or less abstract than their English equivalents? Are most obscene words associated with specific senses, such as smell and taste?

V.   Using dictionaries, trace the changes over the years in the meanings of the following words. In particular, note the instances of widening or narrowing of meaning and the gain or loss of respectability in meaning. The *Oxford English Dictionary* is excellent on word histories because it was compiled from a historical point of view, but *Webster's International* will serve for this exercise:

marshall	steward
onion	virtue
disease	person
fellow	wench
nice	rape
injury	power
magazine	glamour

7/ meanings
of meaning

In the preceding chapters we have discussed "meaning" without specifying what the word itself means, relying instead on the reader's intuitive notions. To define "meaning" amounts to writing a book on semantics. In fact, *The Meaning of Meaning* is the title of a famous and influential book on semantics by C. K. Ogden and I. A. Richards that first appeared in 1924. In this chapter we shall take the ideas of those authors as one point of departure.

In Chapter IX of their book, also entitled "The Meaning of Meaning," Ogden and Richards list different definitions of "meaning." Some of the definitions, apparently paraphrasing disquisitions of philosophers, are anything but informative. What, for example, are we to make of a definition of meaning as a "unique unanalyzable Relation to other things" or as "the Place of anything in a system"? To be sure, these are abbreviated definitions, elucidated by further discussion. But philosophical discussions of the "meaning of meaning" are seldom illuminating, as anyone can convince himself by honestly facing the question of whether he understands more after having read the philosophical disquisitions on the subject.

In Chapter 3 we discussed three levels of language analysis: syntactics (the relation of language units to other language units), semantics (the relation of language units to things or situations in the world, that is, to referents), and pragmatics (the relation of language to the users of language). These aspects are reflected in the various definitions listed by Ogden and Richards. For instance, one definition of meaning reads "The other words attached to a word in a Dictionary." Clearly this definition is in the "syntactic mode" since it relates a symbol (the word defined) to other symbols (the words of the dictionary definitions). Another definition reads "That to which the user of a symbol actually refers." This definition of meaning is in the "semantic mode." The user is mentioned, to be sure, but the meaning is said to reside in the *referent* of the symbol. Still another definition identifies meaning with "an event intended." Later this definition is illustrated by the usage of the verb "to mean" in expressions like "They meant no harm," "He means well," "I meant to go," "What I meant was what I said," and so on. Here the reference to meaning is in the "pragmatic mode." It relates symbols (or acts) to the intentions of the users of the symbols or to actors. Similarly, the definition "That to which the user of a symbol believes himself to be referring" is also in the pragmatic mode; the meaning is supposed to reside in the user of the symbol rather than in a referent.[1]

In this chapter, for the most part, we shall discuss meaning in its syntactic and semantic aspects. The pragmatic or psycholinguistic aspects of meaning will be discussed more fully in Chapter 11.

If we do not know the meaning of a word, we usually reach for a dictionary. We also usually depend on a dictionary when we are confronted with a foreign word. In dictionaries we find two kinds of information about words. We find "attached to the words defined" other words that have approximately the same meanings as those being defined. Examples: grime: dirt; lenitive: soothing. We shall call these definitions *synonymic*: they convey the meaning of a word by listing some of its synonyms.[2]

Other dictionary definitions are more formal. They follow the prescript of Aristotle which says that a proper definition should put the word defined in a class of similar things and then say what distinguishes the thing defined from other things in the same class.

Example: Lens: A piece of glass or other transparent substance, bounded by two curved surfaces or by one curved and one plane surface, by which rays of light are made to converge or diverge.[3]

1. C. K. Ogden and I. A. Richards, *The Meaning of Meaning*, 2d ed. rev. (New York: Harcourt, Brace and Company, 1927).
2. Linguists call words that have the same or approximately the same meanings *synonyms*; words that sound alike but have different meanings are *homonyms*.
3. Funk and Wagnalls, *Standard College Dictionary* (New York: Funk and Wagnalls, 1968).

In this definition a lens is first identified as a piece of glass (or other transparent substance) and then distinguished from other pieces of glass by a certain shape and by the use to which it is put. Meaning conveyed in this manner will be called the *connotative* meaning of a word. (Caution: We shall use the words "connotative" and "connotation" in two different senses to be explained below.)

Sometimes pictures of things defined appear alongside dictionary definitions—pictures of animals, musical instruments, architectural features, and so forth. This way of conveying meaning clearly simulates the act of *pointing* to the thing defined or of displaying an example of it. We shall call this sort of meaning the *denotative* meaning of a word.

To summarize, meaning may be conveyed by a synonym, simply another *word* that has approximately the same meaning; by connotation, that is, by listing the *properties* of the thing defined; and by denotation, that is, by calling attention to an *actual example* of the thing defined. Each way of conveying meaning has its advantages and its shortcomings.

Definition by synonym is most useful in explaining the meaning of a foreign word. We can look up "ptak" in a Polish-English dictionary to find that the English word "bird" corresponds to it. Usually this is all we wanted to know, and we are satisfied that now we know the "meaning" of "ptak." There is no escaping the fact, however, that the synonymic definition did nothing but refer the meaning of one word to that of another. If we are inclined to delve deeper into the meaning of words, we ask ourselves what the meaning of "bird" may be, even though we know what the word refers to in the ordinary sense of "meaning." Clearly, continuing to use the dictionary "all the way" will not do. A good dictionary may well "define" every word that we are likely to encounter. But, except for occasional pictures of things, it must do so by reference to other words, either synonyms or formal definitions. Since the total number of words in even the largest dictionary is finite, eventually we shall come upon words in the definitions that have already been used. In a cheap pocket dictionary, we may find "freedom" as a synonym for "liberty." As we look up "freedom," we may find "liberty" as *its* synonym. Thus verbal definitions can never get us *out* of a language for a dictionary in a language totally unknown to us would be completely useless.

A denotative definition tries to get around this difficulty by exhibit-

ing an example of the thing defined. To convey the meaning of
"chisel," we can show a chisel and, perhaps, also the way in which it
is used. To explain the meaning of "bird," we can point to one that
happens to be around, and so on.

Still, definitions by denotation have two essential shortcomings.
First, not everything can be exhibited or pointed to. In a satirical story,
Mark Twain describes the perplexity of the young reporter who came
to interview him. To play a joke on the young man, Mark Twain
reaches for a dictionary and, after paging through it, asks the reporter
how to spell "interview."

"What do you want to spell it for?" the reporter asks.

"I don't want to spell it. I want to see what it means. . . . I was
hoping I might tree her among the pictures. But it's a very old edition."

"Why, my friend, they wouldn't have a *picture* of it even in the
latest ed. . . . " [4] In short, it is difficult to "point" to an interview

Second, even if the thing defined can be exhibited, there is no
guarantee that a denotative definition will enable us to recognize *every*
instance of the thing defined. Chairs and cats come in all shapes, sizes,
and colors. When we "define" a chair or a cat by pointing to one, we
hope that this will enable the inquirer to distinguish a chair from a
table or a cat from a lion.

When Victor (cf. p. 74) was learning the meanings of words, it
took him a long time to learn that "book" meant any book, not just
the book pointed to. Afterward he carried generalization too far:
magazines and sheafs of paper were also "books" to him.

In the course of acquiring language, most children somehow learn
to make correct generalizations and distinctions. At first only the
family cat may be "kitty." Later the child may call every furry animal
or toy "kitty." Eventually he will distinguish kitties from doggies.
Partly, we assume, language learning proceeds as the child associates
different names with different *classes* of things. Still we do not know
how the notion of the class to which a word properly applies becomes
internalized. No child has seen all cats and all dogs, nor are the differences between cats and dogs usually explained to him. Yet, by the
age of three, the child usually recognizes a dog as a dog, even though
dogs may range from Chihuahuas to Saint Bernards. Moreover a
young child will recognize that a cat looks more like a panther than

4. Mark Twain, "An Encounter with an Interviewer," in *The Writings of Mark
Twain*, vol. 20 (New York: Harper & Brothers, 1917), pp. 378–79.

like a terrier despite the fact that the cat and the terrier are more similar in size.

It seems therefore that meanings, originally acquired by associating names with single examples of what they denote, are eventually extended to the *ranges* of denotation.

To see how denotative definitions can fail to convey meaning (in the sense of defining *properly* the range of denotation), let us extend the method of denotative definition to the *listing* of the members of the class to which a word properly applies. This method of definition is called the *extensional*[5] method, or *definition by extension*. For example, we can define "spices" by enumerating them: cloves, bay leaf, pepper, ginger, and so on. Similarly we can define "the countries of Europe" by enumerating them: France, Spain, Poland, Yugoslavia, and so on.

Now, if we have not included onions on our list of "spices," someone may be at a loss to decide whether or not onions are a spice. From our list he might have deduced that "spices" are ingredients added to food to enhance flavor. Onions are added for that purpose, so onions might be a spice. On the other hand, he may have concluded that spices are "fancy" ingredients, and onions, to his way of thinking, may not meet this specification.

Similarly, examining our partial list of "the countries of Europe," someone may wonder whether Denmark, Turkey, and the U.S.S.R. should be on that list. Most of their territories are not in Europe, but the capitals of Denmark and the U.S.S.R. are, and so is Turkey's largest city.

There is only one way in which an extensional definition can delineate the range of denotation of a word, namely by listing *all* of the members of the class that constitute the range. It is easy to do this, of course, if the class has only one member. Words that denote classes having only one member are often called *proper nouns*.

The range of denotation of "Mr. Smith" is Mr. Smith. Of course, we think of "Smith" as a proper noun and write it accordingly with a capital "S." *Semantically* speaking, however, "Smith" is a proper noun only if it refers to a single specified Smith. In fact, if "Smith" as a proper noun applies to two or more persons, then "Smith" and "Smith" are *homonyms*, words that sound and look alike but have different meanings, like "page" and "page" (cf. p. 89). The word

5. Cf. Note 1, Chapter 8.

"cat" can also refer to more than one cat. But "cat" and "cat" are not homonyms because "cat" is *meant* to apply to all cats and is therefore a common noun. If "Smith" is meant to apply to all Smiths, it is, semantically speaking, a common noun like cat. It is a name common to all Smiths, the name of a class.

In learning to speak, we probably learn proper nouns first. In particular, "mama" serves the baby as a proper noun, since its denotation is a unique person. "Daddy," or equivalent, and the names of siblings are also among the first words learned. Recall Piaget's experiment in which a little boy with one brother denies that his brother has a brother. To him "brother" is still a proper noun: "Brother" is one of his brother's names. It is not his own name, and so he does not think of himself as "brother."

Returning to the extensional definition, we see that its semantic function is discharged if the range of denotation of a word is not too large to be *completely* enumerated. "The spices" can probably be completely enumerated, and so can "the countries of Europe." After the countries have been named, there should be no question as to whether Denmark, the U.S.S.R., or Turkey is or is not a "country of Europe." If any of them has been included in the list, it is; otherwise, not. Similarly, if "onions" were included in the list of "spices," then onions are a spice; if not, not.

Supposed now we have included Turkey among "the countries of Europe" and someone raises an objection. "Turkey is not a country of Europe," he insists, "because its capital is not in Europe." If an argument arises, it is not about Turkey but about the propriety of the definition. The objection implicitly favors another definition of "a country of Europe" that admits only countries whose capitals are in Europe. Such a definition would be not a denotative one but a *connotative* one. (The nature of a connotative definition will be explained presently.)

The most useful feature of denotative definitions is that they delineate *exactly* the range of application of a word. For this reason these definitions are often used in legal documents, where the range of application of words should be clear. For example, my contract with the publishers of this book reads:

... Agreement made ... between Anatol Rapoport ... (hereinafter called the "Author") and Thomas Y. Crowell Company ... (hereinafter called the "Publisher"). ...

In this context, Author and Publisher are proper nouns. Each refers to a specific person or company.

People may argue about the meaning of "close relative." In matters involving the law (for instance, matters pertaining to obligations of support, marriage, income tax exemptions, etc.), it is desirable to avoid such arguments. Therefore laws involving "close relatives" usually define "close relatives" extensionally. For example: "In the context of this statute, 'close relative' shall mean mother, father, son, daughter, brother, or sister . . ." naming all those and only those to whom the words "close relative" shall apply.

The denotative or extensional definition follows the semantic rule laid down by Humpty Dumpty: "When *I* use a word, it means exactly what I *choose* it to mean—neither more nor less."

Whether the range of denotation given to a word by a denotative or extensional definition *ought* to be what it turns out to be is often a legitimate question. For instance, the range of denotation may be different from that ordinarily ascribed to the word in common usage, or the range of denotation may introduce undesirable associations in people's minds. Such objections should not be ignored under the pretext that "all definitions are arbitrary," but they should be considered separately. For the purpose of a specific discussion or communication, all that is needed is an *agreement* on the range of denotation of a word. This agreement can be easily reached by the use of a denotative or extensional definition.

When a referent of a word cannot be pointed out or exhibited, the denotative method of definition cannot be used. When a class is too large to enumerate, the extensional definition cannot exactly establish the range of denotation. The *connotative*, or *intensional*, method of definition gets around these restrictions. This method follows Aristotle's formula already mentioned: name a class to which the thing to be defined belongs; then state the properties that distinguish it from other members of the same class (cf. p. 4).

Example: Interview: A conversation conducted by a reporter, writer, radio or television commentator, etc., with a person from whom information is sought.[6]

The class of things to which an interview belongs is "conversation."

6. Funk and Wagnalls, *Standard College Dictionary*.

An interview, however, is defined as a special kind of conversation, namely one in which a reporter, etc., seeks information from the person with whom he converses. Note that within this intensional definition of "interview" is an implicit extensional definition of the class of persons to which one party belongs: reporter, writer, radio commentator, etc. The "etc." indicates that the class has not been exhausted by the examples named.

Example: Button: A knob or disk sewn to a garment, etc., serving as a fastening when passed through a narrow opening or buttonhole.[7]

A button belongs to a class of disklike objects. However, a button is distinguished from a coin because a coin is not sewn on a garment, etc.

Example: Grace (Theol.): The divine influence operating in man to regenerate, sanctify, or strengthen him.[8]

Here the *context* is supplied in which a particular meaning of "grace" applies, namely in theological discourse.

If the purpose of a definition is to convey the meaning of a word and if we understand "meaning" in its semantic sense (a relation between a word and something in the world), then one of the purposes of a definition is to enable us to tell whether something is or is not in the range of denotation of a word. Let us see how each of the definitions cited accomplishes this purpose.

There seems to be no difficulty with "button." If we know what "a garment" means, that is, can distinguish garments from non-garments, and if we can determine whether the object in question performs the function of "fastening," we can tell a button from a non-button.

With "interview," the matter may be somewhat more complicated. We may have no difficulty recognizing a "conversation" when we witness one. We may also be able to decide whether one of the parties to the conversation is "a reporter, writer, etc." There may, however, be some ambiguity about the purpose of the conversation. Is the purpose indeed that of eliciting information? How can we tell? Does the

7. Ibid.
8. Ibid.

fact that one of the parties asks questions and the other answers them establish that the purpose of the conversation is to elicit information? There may be instances in which this is not the case: some "interviews" are arranged for publicity purposes; some, in order to provide a political figure with a sounding board for his views; and so on. How long must an exchange of questions and answers be to qualify as a "conversation"? When is an "interview" not an interview?

With "grace," the matter is still more complicated. It is not at all easy to decide in the light of the definition whether a particular person is "in the state of grace" (as theologians say) because criteria are not indicated by means of which we can decide whether a "divine influence" is or is not operating in a particular person. Nor is it easy to tell whether a man is being "regenerated, sanctified, or strengthened."

One might suppose that such criteria are known to specialists (here theologians) in somewhat the same way as criteria of health and disease are known to specialists in these matters (physicians). Clearly, however, "the state of grace" cannot be recognized in the same way as a state of tuberculosis or freedom from it.

The chief limitation of intensional (connotative) definitions is that these sometimes vast differences in precision which presumably establish the range of denotation of a word cannot be estimated from the definition itself. The form of such definitions is exactly the same whether a "button" or "the state of grace" is being defined. Nor are degrees of precision generally recognized. Dictionary definitions *look* precise, and a dictionary is generally accepted as an authoritative source on the "meanings" of words. Accordingly, people feel that they have fathomed the meaning of a word when they have read a formal (intensional) definition of the word in a dictionary.

Webster's New International Dictionary, Second Edition, defines love as "A feeling of strong personal attachment induced by that which delights or commands admiration by sympathetic understanding, or by ties of kinship, ardent affection, as the love of brothers and sisters."

In what sense does a definition of this sort convey the "meaning" of love? Is the meaning of the word "love" clearer to someone who has read this definition? A definition can sometimes make the meaning of a word clearer by annexing to the word defined other words that are more commonly used, whose meaning, therefore, can be assumed to be known. Thus, when "trisdekaphobia" is explained as "the fear of the number thirteen," the definition performs its function. This is certainly not the case with the above definition of love. "Attachment," "admiration," and "sympathetic understanding" are not more familiar words than "love." Why, then, are such common words as "love" defined at all if it takes less common words to define them? The reason is that a dictionary must be substantially complete. If a word is likely to be encountered in a sample of a language, it must become an entry in a dictionary and a "definition" must be supplied for it no matter how ludicrous it may appear and no matter how useless it may be.

The definition of "love" in *Webster's* is useless as a definition because it is hardly possible that one who has read it is thereby enabled to tell love from non-love better than one who has not. It appears ludicrous (at least it appears so to me) because it attempts to convey, by means of words, a meaning that cannot be conveyed by means of words. This is clear from the definition itself. Love is correctly classified as a *feeling*, and the meaning of feelings can be gained only by having the feelings. In this way, love is similar to a toothache or to the smell of ammonia. If you have had a toothache, you understand the meaning of the word in a way that enables you to tell a toothache from a non-toothache. If you have ever smelled ammonia, you understand the meaning of the smell in a way that will enable you to distinguish that smell from other smells. If you have never felt love or had a toothache or smelled ammonia, no verbal definition will convey to you the meaning of these words (relate them to referents). In these cases, therefore, denotative definitions, that is, putting the person directly in contact with the referent or pointing out to him that he is in contact with the referent when he is, are the only ones that can convey meanings.

In traditional education, great emphasis was placed on verbal knowledge. The successful scholar was someone who could absorb, and show that he had absorbed, what had been written in books. Knowledge of grammar was identified with the ability to repeat that "A noun is a name of a person, place, or thing." Knowledge of geography meant knowing that "An island is a body of land completely surrounded by water" and that "A peninsula is a body of land *almost* surrounded by water" and being able to identify a yellow spot on a map as "Persia." Knowledge of history was exhibited by naming kings, battles, and their dates. Knowledge of religion was tested by the ability of the student to match answers to questions in the catechism.

Changes in the philosophy and theory of education have, of course, eliminated much of this nonsense. However, in the realm of language, the notion still persists that meanings of words reside in their verbal definitions and, especially, that a dictionary is the authoritative source of the "true" meanings of words.

Frequently controversies arise regarding the "true" meaning of a word, especially of words related to moral qualities (decency, justice, courage, hypocrisy, etc.) or concepts central to political convictions (tyranny, freedom, patriotism, democracy, etc.).

Example: Mr. Alpha insists that a novel by Henry Miller is pornographic. Mr. Beta denies this. They may agree to consult a dictionary in order to ascertain the "true" meaning of pornography. They read:
Pornography: Obscene literature or art.[9]

It seems to each of them that the dictionary has confirmed his view. Mr. Alpha now argues that the novel is pornographic because it is clearly obscene. Mr. Beta argues that it is not pornographic because it is not obscene. The next step is clearly indicated. Look up "obscene." They read:

Obscene 1. Offensive or abhorrent to prevailing concepts of morality or decency; indecent; lewd.[10]

Again it seems to both Mr. Alpha and Mr. Beta that the dictionary has confirmed his view. They still disagree. They may want to go on and look up "offensive," "prevailing," "decency," and so forth. However, it is not likely that their quest will settle their controversy. It might if a dictionary definition provided them with a method of referring to a *criterion* on which they could agree. However, even when such criteria are provided, the controversy may go on.

For example, Mr. Gamma may insist that charging 12 percent interest on a loan is "usury," and Mr. Delta may deny it. Their dic-

9. Ibid.
10. Ibid.

tionary defines "usury" as "the act or practice of exacting a rate of interest beyond what is allowed by law." [11] Here a way of settling the argument seems clear: look up the law governing the rate of interest on loans. If 12 percent is legal, it is not usury. Mr. Delta, however, may not yield so easily. He notes another meaning of "usury": "2. The lending of money at interest." [12] He is astonished. Not only 12 percent, but *any* rate of interest is usury according to this definition. Nevertheless, since 12 percent is obviously "usury" according to this definition, he can point to *this* definition as proving his case. His triumph is short-lived because Mr. Gamma calls his attention to the *Obs.* *Obs.* stands for "obsolete." Consequently, if Mr. Delta insists that any rate of interest on loans is "usury," he is behind the times. To this Mr. Delta replies that the *original*, hence the "true," meaning of usury is *any* rate of interest.

As has been pointed out in Chapters 1 and 2, the conviction that words have "true" meanings is a mark of linguistic innocence. It is akin to the belief of some souls that astronomers discover the true names of stars.

To what extent, then, are dictionaries sources of authoritative information on the meanings of words? There are two opposite views on the subject. For clarity, we shall state both in their extreme forms. One view has it that dictionaries give (or should give) the "correct" meanings of words. We should not suppose that the proponents of this view believe that these true meanings are forever welded to the words. Rather, the proponents of this *prescriptive* function of dictionaries are linguistic conservatives. They want to preserve meanings of words for as long as possible. They insist that "to lie" means "to be in a reclining position" and "to lay" means "to *place* in a reclining position." They deplore the use of "lay" in place of "lie," regardless of how general this usage becomes. To be consistent, these people should insist that "lady" refers properly only to "a woman showing the refinement, gentility, and tact associated with the upper ranks of society," and not just to any woman. They should insist that "paddy" refers to "rice in the husk," not to the field where rice grows.

Opposing these views are people who insist that the function of dictionaries is only a *descriptive* one. The dictionary should give

11. Ibid.
12. Ibid.

meanings of words as these words are actually used at a given time. In American folk language any woman is called "lady." In newspaper accounts of war in Southeast Asia, "paddy" came to mean the rice field, not the rice husk. People say they have "mutual interests" or "mutual friends" when they mean they have interests or friends in common. When I went to school, my English teacher took pains to explain that the title of Dickens's novel *Our Mutual Friend* was an expression of an uneducated Englishman who did not know that "mutual" means "two-sided" (as in "mutual aid"), not "possessed in common."

The proponents of descriptive dictionaries insist that the meanings which have attained common usage should be given citizenship on a par with older usage. They say that it is not the purpose of a dictionary to tell people how they should speak or write but merely to *record* how people do speak or write, in particular in what senses they happen to be using words or phrases.

The descriptionists support their arguments by pointing out how dictionaries are made. A large staff goes through millions of printed words. They *infer* the definitions from the contexts in which these words are used. The very process of making the dictionary, then, insures that the definitions *reflect* usage rather than prescribe it.

The prescriptionists also have a case. They point out that most people, when they look up a word in the dictionary, want to know how to use it *correctly*. Correct usage cannot be simply current usage. If we accepted the principle that however a word was used, that was correct usage, how far would we go? Would we say that, if an individual chose to use a word in a certain way, henceforth that would be its meaning? If not, why not? If the idiosyncratic use of a word by a single individual does not change its meaning, how many individuals would it take to change the meaning of a word or, say, to introduce a grammatical form?

The case of "ain't" is perhaps the most salient manifestation of this issue. *Webster's New International Dictionary, Third Edition*, finally admitted "ain't" without labeling it "substandard" (except as a contraction of "has not"). In this way the dictionary proclaimed its militantly descriptive outlook. The controversy about *Webster's Third Edition*, which verged on bitterness, attested to the importance people attach to the proper function of a dictionary.

The difficulty in defending the prescriptive function of a dictionary stems from the necessity of facing social change. In the nineteenth century (in fact, up to World War I), the class structure of all societies in the Western world was clearly recognized, and there was no doubt as to who the "better" classes were. "Correct" usage was therefore identified with the usage prevalent among the "better" classes. This is not necessarily to say that all the members of the "better" classes always adhered to what was prescribed as correct usage. But they did accept the idea that among the "better" people there were the "best" people, and that these were the natural arbiters of usage. Recall that in England good English was called the king's English. (Similarly, when the first attempts were made to standardize units of length, the king's foot or arm was used as a standard.)

Different "quality" of the different social classes being accepted as a fact of life, the "lower" classes aspired to the manners and style of the "better" classes. Education has always been associated with an opportunity to raise one's social status. Consequently, if a person used the dictionary at all, he expected from it an indication of how a word was used "correctly," that is, by the "better classes," regardless of how it happened to have been "perverted" by plebeians.

As the claims of the "better classes" to higher culture, better manners, and so on weakened in the course of this century, the descriptionists gained ground together with the linguists who denied that any classical language (such as Latin or Greek) was a perfect model. This was essentially a democratization process.

It is possible to make a case for a prescriptive role for a dictionary without appealing to class distinctions. There is a certain value in slowing down language change and in counteracting the tendency of languages to split into dialects. Prescription of standard usage helps to do this. To be sure, the fracturing of languages into dialects has been somewhat arrested by the mass media, which tend to "homogenize" language. However, language change has been greatly accelerated by ever more rapid social change. Technocracy and bureaucracy have influenced language considerably. The competence of engineers is rooted in technical knowledge rather than in the traditionally respected language skills. Administrators often come from the business world. Technocrats and administrators have brought with them special jargons—to the dismay of language purists. The descriptionists, however, insist that language is not a monument to be preserved but an instrument to be used. They readily admit words like "finalize" and "publicity-wise," which the purists view as a debauching of language.

So far we have used the term "connotation" only in the sense of the range of application of a word established by some properties of the thing defined. There is also another sense in which the word "connotation" is used, namely, that which is called to mind by a word. This is the *psychological* aspect of connotation. The psychological connotation of a word may be different for different individuals. For instance, the word "sheep" may evoke some things in my mind and other things in your mind. Or else the psychological connotation of a word may have been fixed in the language; it is then the same for everyone in the language community. Thus many names of animals evoke certain personality characteristics:

sheep — conformity
mouse — timidity
  rat — treachery
  ass — stupidity
 lark — happiness
 bee — industry

Psychological connotation should be distinguished from logical connotation. Two words may have the same logical connotations; that is, the range of denotation of the two words may be the same. Yet their psychological connotations may be different in the sense that they evoke quite different attitudes. The choice of the "right word" or expression in speaking and in writing is often a matter of choosing a word with culturally accepted psychological connotations appropriate for the occasion. For instance, the denotation of "that man," "that gentleman," and "that character" may be the same person. But the three phrases have widely different psychological connotations. They reflect different attitudes of the speaker toward the referent and may evoke different attitudes in the hearer.

Examples:
"A salary of $10,000 per annum" and "wages of $200 per week" denote about the same rate of compensation. However, the connotation of "salary" is that of compensation associated with a position, while the connotation

of "wages" is that of pay that goes with the job. Note that the phrases "associated with a position" and "goes with the job" also have different connotations.

An enlisted man goes on a furlough; an officer goes on a leave. A cabinet minister is asked to resign; a factory worker is fired. A contractor builds houses, which the real estate agent sells as homes.

A game, said to have been invented by Bertrand Russell, is called "Conjugating Adjectives." It is played by mentioning three adjectives having the same denotation but different connotations. Example: I am thrifty; you are tight; he is stingy.

The denotation of all three adjectives is an actually observed trait of character, namely, a reluctance to spend more money than necessary. The different connotations of "thrifty," "tight," and "stingy" are obvious. Other examples: I am outspoken; you are tactless; he is brutal. I am cautious; you are timid; he is cowardly. I am bold; you are rash; he is reckless. I am firm; you are rigid; he is obstinate.

Of course, other parts of speech can be "conjugated" in the same way. Examples: I am a statesman; you are a politician. I am an intelligence officer; you are a spy. I am a sportsman; you are a gambler. I am a patriot; you are a chauvinist. I have an interest in that business; you have a finger in that pie.

EUPHEMISMS

Euphemisms are words chosen as substitutes for words that evoke connotations that the speaker wishes to avoid. In our grandparents' day, direct names of certain parts of the body were avoided. In polite conversation, legs became "limbs," breasts became a "bosom." (In our own day, direct names of certain other parts of the body are still avoided.) Pregnant women became "expectant mothers." A woman was "compromised" if she "committed an indiscretion." In our own day, certain rooms are called "bathrooms" even if they contain no bath. They are sometimes called more frankly "toilets," but "toilet" itself was once a euphemism: it originally meant "grooming," "hairdressing," and so forth. Hence the contemporary euphemism for a euphemism: "powder room."

We have already mentioned the avoidance of the names of deities.

The synonyms for God and Devil in Christian countries are numerous. God is "The Lord," "The Creator." The Devil is " The Tempter," "The Evil One."

Of special political significance are euphemisms related to large-scale instances of violence, as in war and in punitive actions against rebelling populations. People killed and crippled in battle are called "casualties." In czarist Russia, detachments sent to punish striking workers were called "pacifying detachments" (an echo of this terminology entered the language of the United States military during the Vietnam war). The Nazis called the extermination of the Jews "the final solution of the Jewish problem." In Russia, after the revolution, massive killings of people accused of obstructing the regime were called "liquidations," a word previously meaning the disbanding of business enterprise. Torture during interrogations was called "applying physical pressure." In the United States, the beating of prisoners during interrogation is euphemized as "the third degree."

If euphemisms associated with gruesome situations serve any purpose at all, their function is short-lived. Eventually the euphemism absorbs the grim connotation appropriate to its denotation. Thus, "liquidate," "the final solution," "the third degree," and so on, evoke as much, if not more, revulsion or fear as the more direct designations. The same is true of the circumlocutions used in military communiques to camouflage reverses and defeats. During World War II, people very soon came to understand the events behind expressions like "adjustments of the front" (retreat) and "breaking off contact with the enemy" (flight).

Institutions where the mentally ill were confined used to be called madhouses. Later, to avoid the insulting connotation, the institutions came to be called "insane asylums." Today we do not think of "insane" as a euphemism, but it served once as a euphemism for "mad." When the euphemistic varnish of "insane" wore off, another euphemism was invented: "mentally ill." Modern madhouses are called "mental hospitals." If they cater to people of means (another euphemism for "rich people") they are called "sanatoria," "rehabilitation centers," or "Esalen."

Children who failed to acquire skills expected at their age used to be called "dull." Later they were called "retarded." Now they are called "exceptional."

People without cities, machines, or a written language, wearing

scanty clothes, used to be called "savages," then "primitive." Now
they are called "preliterate." Their countries, called only yesterday
"underdeveloped," are now called "developing." [13]

National and ethnic minorities who are legally, or as a consequence
of prejudice, assigned to a low social level are often designated by
words intended to be insulting. These so-called "terms of oppro-
brium" are essentially antieuphemisms. It is important to note that
even well-meaning words may *acquire* insulting connotations. For
example, in the United States, the word that denoted persons of
African descent had two variants, one in the southern dialect, one in
the northern. Eventually the southern variant became an insulting
designation. Southerners who wanted to avoid the insulting connotation resorted to the euphemism "colored." They avoided the northern
variant "Negro" because of the associations of this word with those
people's aspirations for social equality. In the last years of the 1960s,
at the insistence of militant leaders of the civil rights movement, the
word "blacks" came into use as the polite designation of people of
African descent. Ironically, the descendants of the indigenous population of South Africa are called "blacks" by the dominant white
minority whose attitude strongly resembles that of American racists.

In Poland "zyd" (pronounced zhid), a cognate of the Yiddish word
"Yid," is a neutral word meaning "Jew." In Russia, however, the
same word is a profoundly insulting one (the polite word is "yevrei,"
a cognate of "Hebrew"). Russian-speaking Jews find it extremely
difficult to avoid spontaneous emotional reactions to the Polish word.
Clearly, in this case, the "insult" is in the mind of the hearer.

To summarize, the main components of meaning (as it is understood in semantics) are *denotation* and *connotation*. Denotation has to
do with the referents of words, what the words stand for. Connotation has two meanings: in one sense connotation has to do with the
characteristics that define the range of denotation of a word; in another sense connotation has to do with what the word calls to mind
besides the distinguishing features that fix the range of denotation;
for example, emotions and attitudes associated with the use of a word.
In short, the psychologically *connotative* meaning of a word resides

13. Social movements of the "underprivileged" (a euphemism) sometimes bring back
the "frank meanings" that had been long camouflaged by euphemisms. In the United
States, militant organizers of the ghetto dwellers insisted on calling them "the poor"
instead of "the underprivileged" or "the disadvantaged" or "people in low income
brackets."

in the mind of the speaker or hearer. Thus psychological connotation is a link between semantics and pragmatics.

Does every word have a denotative meaning? Not if we define denotative meaning in terms of referents that can be exhibited. If witches do not exist (as I believe they do not), then the word "witch" " has no referent "in the world." One might say that it has a referent in the minds of people who believe that witches exist. In this book, however, "referent" will mean something that exists *outside* people's minds. The "something" does not, of course, need to be an object. The word "red" (adjective) has a referent—that which all objects that reflect light of a certain wavelength have in common. Names of "abstractions" like love, justice, and so on, may have referents if we can describe events, circumstances, or conditions to which the word applies. Verbs have referents if they designate demonstrable actions or conditions. The important thing about referents is not how "concrete" they are but how *demonstrable* they are. Some referents are of course much more precisely defined by the denotations of words than are others, but we shall say that a word has a referent if it can be related to *something* outside people's minds, no matter how difficult it may be to delineate that "something" precisely.

APPLICATIONS

I. During the invasion of Cambodia by American troops, the *New York Times* published a "Webster's New American Dictionary" compiled by Anthony Lewis. Below are some typical definitions:

humiliation: what the United States avoids by widening the war in Indochina, alienating her oldest friends abroad, and shattering the social peace at home.
character what the United States demonstrates by invading Cambodia.
reckless game: shooting at American reconnaissance planes that fly over North Vietnam. Americans do not shoot at North Vietnamese planes over South Vietnam since there are none.
negotiation: process leading to confirmation of the Thieu-Ky government in Saigon.
bums: college students who think there is something to protest about in the United States.

1) In the sense of the chapter you have just read, describe the technique that Mr. Lewis is using to formulate his definitions.
2) Provide your own definitions for the entries above and also define these

from Mr. Lewis's lexicon: *provocation, violation of neutrality, aggression, warning, threat, pretext, credibility, patriot, soft-headed liberal, effete snobs.*

II. Because three customers felt that the denotative meaning of the term "chopped meat" was very shifty, twenty-one supermarkets in southern California were sued for $40 million in damages by three Beverly Hills attorneys and their wives in August of 1971.

The plaintiffs alleged that the markets did not actually use chuck, round, and sirloin in the ground beef sold under those names but that the beef was the same in all categories. The lawyers maintained that they had "absolute proof" of the mislabeling of the ground beef—scientific tests and testimony that indicated the fat content exceeded the 30 percent permitted by law. E. V. Walsh, the president of Ralphs Grocery Company, one of the defendants, said "This lawsuit has hit us on something we have been trying to solve." Can you offer any helpful suggestions to Mr. Walsh?

III. As equally difficult to define as "love" is "life." In *Studies in Words* (1967 edition), C. S. Lewis devotes a chapter to defining "life" on a deeper level than the "lexical and the historical." (He also deals with nature, wit, free, sense, conscience, conscious, and world.) Lewis discerns more than the obvious senses of "life"—the "concrete, the chronological, the qualitative, and life as the common lot"—and he observes that "life" has taken on a "semantic halo," a mystique of positive associations. In twentieth century usage, "life" has transcended the bounds of a logical, abstract, universal term to become a kind of modern Platonic ideal. Lewis points out that the halo around the word "life" has begun to confuse us and that we overlook the fact that life is no more inexhaustible than death; indeed life is defined only by death. "The one will keep on occurring as long as the other, and no longer." Similarly pursue a word with a "semantic halo" to the deeper issues it raises, even if it means the risk of stepping on "the corns of a giant." Examples: *simple, education, travel, law, radical,* and so on.

IV. You can perform a simple experiment by yourself that may help to clarify the descriptionist-prescriptionist argument.

1) Draw up a list of "controversial" terms; that is, terms that might be given a usage label in a standard dictionary. Among them might be: *cool* (imperturbable): *heavy* (intellectually deep); *he don't; contact* (as a verb); *enthused; due to* (as an adverb); and so on. Approach friends and people in three categories: those who need language in earning their livelihood; those who have moderate need of it; and those

who do not need language to earn their livelihood. Ask these questions of each. Would you use the word in conversation without embarrassment? Would you use it in a speech? Would you use it in writing? Tabulate your results, draw conclusions, and compare them with those of a recently revised dictionary. Is the dictionary "conservative" or "liberal" by the standards of the people you interviewed?

2) Keep track of your reading to note how often these "controversial" terms occur in print and in what context. Can you draw any conclusions?

V. Present-day linguists regard the speech patterns of American black people as a unique dialect, something like a southern or New England dialect. They do not label the speech of blacks as "substandard" but as "dialect," exactly as they would classify the expression, "If I had my druthers."

What are the implications of this view in our school system, where from an early age students are required to speak "correct" English. What advice would you give an English teacher or a speech teacher faced with a student who habitually says, "You my teacher?"

VI. Do you believe there is such a thing as a "black dialect"? Try to characterize it—the diction, the syntax, the rhythm. You may find useful J. Haskins and H. F. Butts, *The Psychology of Black Language* (New York: Barnes and Noble, 1972).

VII. "Psychological connotation should be distinguished from logical connotation. Two words may have the same logical connotations . . . yet their psychological connotations may be different in the sense that they evoke quite different attitudes."

(*New York Times*, 5 April 1970.)

"When a white man calls a black man 'crazy,' it may be his way of objecting to the color of his skin, not the state of his mind, a Syracuse psychiatrist suggested."

"According to Dr. Thomas Szasz, whites and blacks alike are increasingly using psychiatric epithets to imply racial slurs."

"By rejecting people as 'mad' when they really mean racially 'bad,' Dr. Szasz said, whites or blacks can 'exalt their own race and disparage other races without having to consider themselves 'racists.' "

Dr. Szasz, writing in the Spring 1970 issue of the Yale *Review*, goes on to say that whites, in particular, are practicing what he terms "psychiatric repression" of blacks.

1) Do you support Dr. Szasz's contention that to white Americans blackness and madness have been traditionally symbols of evil, whiteness and sanity symbols of good?
2) Literature often reflects the attitudes of a society. Using among others the following books, write a paper supporting or opposing the above contention: Nathaniel Hawthorne, *The Scarlet Letter*; Herman Melville, *Moby Dick* and *Benito Cereno*; Mark Twain, *Huckleberry Finn*; Richard Wright, *Native Son*; William Faulkner, *Light in August*; Ken Kesey, *One Flew Over the Cuckoo's Nest*; and Jacqueline Susann, *The Love Machine*.
3) Dr. Szasz also said that the trend toward substituting the vocabulary of mental illness for "plain English" was harmful because it debased the language: "We have seen how, in Nazi Germany, the debasing of language went hand in hand with the debauchment of morals and conduct." Do you believe there is such a correlation between language and morals? Do you see any signs that English is being "debased"? What about rock lyrics and Madison Avenue advertisements? If you believe there is such debasement going on, is there anything you, as a private individual, can do to oppose it?

VIII.   James Dickey, the poet-novelist, says that one of the great blows to "the spirit of America" has been our exposure to what advertising research people say are more than 50,000 "messages" a day. It is for this reason that poetry is important, he believes—"it is the last resort of nonmanipulative language" ("Firing Line," Channel 28, August 25, 1971). Do you agree with his statement? Does this have any bearing on the distrust of words that many young people profess today?

8/figurative meanings

Heraclitus (c535–c475 B.C.) said that one cannot step into the same river twice. A disciple supposedly commented that one cannot step into the same river even once because the river changes at the time one is stepping into it. On reflection not only rivers but everything about us appears to be in a state of constant flux. The surface of a lake on a still day looks deceptively motionless, but molecules of water are always escaping from it as vapor. Boulders, mountains, and trees appear to be solid, but they too are composed of tiny particles in constant motion. When x-ray pictures are taken of your body, the rays pass unimpeded through your tissues, through the swarm of atoms that are "you." Hardly any of the physical particles that constitute your body today were there a year ago or will be there a year hence.

If we were always aware that nothing stays put, we would hardly bother to name anything, for in naming a thing, we attribute an "identity" to it. We name individual mountains, people, buildings, animals, sometimes even individual trees, if they are notable. We do not name individual clouds, waves, or flashes of lightning, but we do name *classes* of these occurrences, as well as classes of things, properties, actions, situations, and relations. By doing so, we call attention to their similarities and disregard their differences. We give proper names only to things that are recognizable as "themselves" in order to fixate them in our memory, as a moving train is "fixed" on a photograph. To help us discriminate likenesses and similarities, we give common names to things that are recognizable as members of classes. In both cases, *constancy* is involved: in the case of proper names, constancy of identity in time; in the case of common names, constancy of characteristics among the members of the class.

In Chapter 7, I said that the denotation of a word relates the word to specific recognizable things, actions, or situations. The range of *denotation* includes all the items to which that word can be properly applied. The *connotation* of a word is the totality of the properties that each specific thing in the range of denotation has in common with every other thing in the same range. Connotation, then, is a set of *abstracted* features, or properties, of the thing named.

"Jellycuddles" is a (proper) name of a specific cat. Although this specific cat changes every moment, we disregard these changes; having named him, we have given him an identity. And though each cat is different from every other cat, to the extent that we recognize certain features common to Jellycuddles and all his fellow cats, a cat is a cat. The word "cat" fixes the category Cat, which implies that there are such common, recognizable features in all cats. These features constitute the intensional (connotative) definition of the category, the kind of definition usually found in dictionaries.[1]

Now, the greater the number of features that can be included in an intensional definition of a cat (or any thing), the smaller is the category defined because fewer individual creatures will exhibit the criteria of "catness" required to satisfy the definition. For instance, if along with other properties of a cat, we include "weighing less than twenty pounds," then lions, tigers, and leopards will not be included in the category Cat. On the other hand, if weight (or size) is not a criterion, then lions, tigers, and leopards may be included, assuming that they satisfy the other catlike features included in the definition. (In fact, circus people, zoo attendants, and others in regular contact with lions, tigers, and leopards do call them "cats.") The range of denotation of the category Cat can thus be extended, say, from the species *Felis catus* to the genus *Felis* or to the family *Felidae*.

Suppose further that instead of considering only the biological characteristics of Cat we concentrate on supposed psychological features. These supposed features of the cat's "character" need not be accurate

---

1. "Intensional," spelled with an "s," is not related to in*tent* but to "internal." It is opposed to "extensional," related to "external." Thus an intensional definition is one that lists the properties of the thing defined; an extensional definition lists the things to which the word defined refers (cf. pp. 116–21).

in any sense; they may simply reflect impressions that humans have of a cat's psychology. Then people (women especially) who give the impression of possessing these traits of character will also be called "cats." In that case the range of *denotation* of "cat" is further extended, be it noted, through the *connotations* of the word (the supposed features common to cats).

Take another example. The intensional definition of a newspaper may include a variety of criteria, such as "printed on paper," "reporting the news," "appearing regularly," and the like. Supposing we settle for only the criterion of reporting the news periodically, news broadcasts can also be called "newspapers," as in "newspapers of the air"; the "paper" part of the word then becomes an anomaly, a vestigial part (cf. pp. 103–4) that can be disregarded in perceiving the meaning of "newspaper" in this broadened sense. Similarly, while a "theater of the air" seems to be an "illogical" designation to someone who thinks that a building is essential to the concept of a "theater," to those who think that only the performance is essential, the meaning of "the theater of the air" is clear.

Compare "theaters of the air" and "castles in the air." In some contexts, "theater" and "castle" refer to a building. "Air" usually refers either to atmosphere or to the space aboveground. Neither "theaters of the air" nor "castles in the air" denotes buildings suspended aboveground. The former designates regular broadcasts of plays; the latter, unrealistic dreams. Both illustrate so-called *figurative* meanings of words.

Ordinarily we distinguish figurative from literal meanings by relating the latter to objects, actions, properties, or situations more directly perceived by the senses. Literal meanings are probably the older ones. Words acquire figurative meanings when their denotations are broadened by dropping the connotations associated only with concrete meanings.

For example, literally, "cutting" denotes the act of breaking the continuity, say of a string, by a sharp edge. The meaning becomes figurative if we omit "the sharp edge," leaving only "breaking the continuity." Hence in "Cut the string," "cut" carries its literal meaning, while in "Cut the comedy," it carries its figurative meaning.

In its literal meaning, "running" refers to locomotion by moving one's legs. If we ignore legs, we can speak about running trains, clocks, water, and, by analogy with the latter, even running noses.

The king is dead in the literal sense. In the figurative sense, the engine is dead, a town is dead, one's (figuratively) "burning" passion is dead.

Other examples:

LITERAL MEANING	FIGURATIVE MEANING
A moving train.	A moving speech.
I live in a house.	The drinks are on the house.
I hear music.	This news is music to my ears.
The streets were icy.	Her greeting was icy.
I am sitting on a chair.	I am addressing the Chair.
The Kremlin was built in the fifteenth century.	The ambassador is awaiting instructions from the Kremlin.

Names of buildings and of larger cities frequently acquire figurative meanings associated with activities or centers of control for which they are famous. In addition to the Kremlin, we have the White House, the Pentagon, 10 Downing Street, the Vatican, Hollywood, Wall Street, the City (London, once the banking center of the world), Broadway, even Off-Broadway, and so on.

In Europe, names of months often refer to the political events that occurred in those months. In France, Thermidor (as August was renamed in 1793) now refers to the overthrow of the Jacobins in 1794. In Russia, the Decembrists were the participants in an aborted revolution in December 1825, and October is a synonym for the Bolshevik Revolution of 1917. In Mexico City, several streets are named after specific historical dates: May 5, September 16, and so forth. All these designations have acquired figurative meanings.

Figurative meanings of words are so common that ordinarily we do not think of them as such. This is especially true with respect to "heavy-duty words," discussed in Chapter 5. To illustrate, I shall take a book from my shelf at random. I open the book haphazardly and read from the first complete sentence on the page:

The program for breaking up the Zaibatsu, the great combined vertical and horizontal trusts, was put in the icebox.[2]

"Program" means literally a sequence of performed events to be

2. Owen Lattimore, *The Situation in Asia* (Boston: Little, Brown, 1949), p. 116.

seen or heard, or a sheet of paper on which the titles of the events are displayed. Figuratively, a program means any planned sequence of actions.

We break a thing literally when we impair its wholeness as an object. An organization is figuratively "broken up" when it can no longer function as an organization.

"Vertical" and "horizontal" refer literally to directions respectively toward or away from the surface of the earth and parallel to it. Figuratively, a vertical organization is one comprising different "levels" of units. (Here "levels" is also used figuratively. Observe how difficult it is to avoid figurative uses of words!) A horizontal organization is composed of units on the same level. In the 1930s, for example, the organizing of "vertical" and "horizontal" unions was an issue in the policies of the American labor movement. "Vertical" unions were those that included all the occupations in an industry, such as the automobile industry, the oil industry, and so forth. "Horizontal" unions were those that covered specific occupations ("levels") in various industries: carpenters, electricians, lathe operators, and so on.

The literal meaning of "trust" refers to confidence in someone's honesty or good intentions. In business, a trust is an amalgam of parallel enterprises. The relation of the two meanings is far-fetched, but if you want to take the trouble, you can probably trace the emergence of the figurative meaning from the literal one.

All of the above figurative meanings will be found in any dictionary. The specific expression "was put in the icebox" will not, although something close to it is included in Funk and Wagnalls *Standard College Dictionary* under the entry "ice" (on ice: U.S. slang. Set aside; in reserve).

When a word is used in a figurative sense that is not included among the dictionary definitions of the word, we have an instance of *metaphor*. In textbooks, metaphors are listed among different types of "figures of speech," which include also similes, personifications, hyperboles, and allegories, each carefully distinguished—and students are expected to "diagnose" all of them. A simile involves a specific comparison, which in a metaphor is only implicit. A personification attributes human characteristics to abstractions or inanimate objects. A hyperbole is a poetic exaggeration. An allegory is a story involving personifications, and so on.

For our purposes, the word "metaphor" shall refer to any figure of speech. The essential distinguishing feature of metaphor is that the figurative meaning carried by it must be inferred by the exercise of the imagination since it cannot be looked up in a dictionary. Poetry is especially rich in metaphors. For this reason, appreciation of a poem sometimes requires a considerable amount of "work," that is, exercise of imagination on the part of the reader. Perhaps this is why some people like to read poetry and some do not. Examples:

> *Geysers of doom upsprout*
> (Robert W. Service, ON THE WIRE)

> *And winking Mary-buds begin to ope their golden eyes*
> (Shakespeare, AUBADE)

> *All the world's a stage*
> *And all the men and women merely players*
> (Shakespeare, AS YOU LIKE IT)

> *Seeking the bubble reputation* (Ibid.)
> *Swift horses of fear or of love . . .*
> *. . . the meadows of memory . . .*
> *the highlands of hope . . .*
> (A. C. Swinburne, HESPERIA)

> *Sooty retainer to the vine*
> *Bacchus' black servant, negro fine*
> *Sorcerer, that maks't us dote upon*
> *Thy begrimed complexion*
> (Charles Lamb, A FAREWELL TO TOBACCO)

The emotional impact of a metaphor emanates from its originality and its aptness. Originality implies that the comparison expressed by the metaphor, or the imagery it carries, has not occurred to anyone before. Aptness implies that the analogy is remarkably appropriate or that the imagery is remarkably vivid. To put it in another way, a good metaphor evokes a feeling of both inevitability and surprise, as of an inspired solution to a tantalizing problem suddenly seeming perfectly obvious. Such a feeling is akin to *insight*.

Since originality is lost in repetition, a metaphor does not have much of an impact after it has been used. Resorting to a metaphor invented

by someone else is considered a mild form of plagiarism, especially if
the metaphor is serious, powerful, or elegant. Metaphors carry a sort
of implicit copyright.

Nevertheless, metaphors are borrowed and repeated, frequently
being incorporated into a language as special expressions. They then
become "public property." Sources of these "embedded" metaphors
often are great literary works. Some are the common heritage of
numerous language communities (the Bible being the most famous
example); some are cherished possessions of specific language communities, as for example, the works of Shakespeare and those of Goethe.
Note that, *as literature*, both Shakespeare and Goethe have become the
heritage of the entire Western world, and beyond. However, as a
treasury of *language*, the metaphors of Shakespeare are enshrined
mainly by English-speaking people, those of Goethe by German-
speaking people. Examples of embedded metaphors:

from the Bible:
   A house divided against itself
   An eye for an eye; a tooth for a tooth
   To cast the first stone
   My brother's keeper
   By the skin of our teeth
from Shakespeare:
   The world's mine oyster (*Merry Wives of Windsor*)
   A rose by any other name (*Romeo and Juliet*)
   My kingdom for a horse (*Richard III*)
   A horse of that [or another] color (*Twelfth Night*)
from Homer:
   Between Scylla and Charybdis
from Aesop:
   Sour grapes

Typically, the original expressions were initially used literally.
Later, someone used them metaphorically and, through repetition, they
became embedded metaphors based on the figurative sense of the
words used at first in the literal sense. For instance, "to cast the first
stone" refers to the inappropriateness of making a damning moral
judgment if one's own conscience is not clear. The origin of the
expression is attributed to Jesus' challenge to whoever was "without

sin" to begin stoning a confessed adulteress, as prescribed by Mosaic law. (No one dared.) "An eye for an eye; a tooth for a tooth" originally meant just that. Now it means "retribution in kind." Scylla and Charybdis were monsters guarding the opposite shores of the Straits of Messina. The expression came to designate the dilemma of avoiding two opposite, equally onerous perils. (Cf. "between the devil and the deep blue sea.")

The Russian language is richly pervaded by quotations from two authors, Griboyedov and Krylov, neither of whom is well known outside of Russia. Krylov adapted the fables of Aesop and La Fontaine into Russian. He used the rich, vivid language of the peasant, thus breaching the barrier between literature and folk speech. Griboyedov wrote an eminently successful comedy in which the troglodytes of the day, the smug landed gentry, were exposed to merciless, glaring light. Expressions from Krylov's fables and from Griboyedov's comedy *Woe from Wit* entered the Russian language as embedded metaphors. Familiarity with these expressions is necessary to an understanding of numerous allusions in Russian journalism, literary criticism, and political speeches. Khrushchev[3] frequently used these allusions (along with folk expressions and proverbs), sometimes with telling effect. Obversely, in Alexander Kuprin's story *Captain Rybnikov*, a spy arouses suspicion by *too* frequent use of such expressions.

The proverb is also a form of embedded metaphor. Examples: A bird in the hand is worth two in the bush. (It is wiser to realize an immediate advantage than to miss the opportunity in the hope of a larger gain.)

Too many cooks spoil the broth. (Committees are ineffectual.)

It is noteworthy that proverbs often come in pairs expressing opposite principles. "Penny wise, pound foolish" can be construed as a counterweight to "A bird in the hand is worth two in the bush"; "Look before you leap" to "He who hesitates is lost"; "Two heads are better than one" to "Too many cooks spoil the broth."

Related to proverbs are the kinds of embedded metaphors that call to mind characters or situations, making them "come to life" by evoking concrete images. Examples: A bull in a china shop (a very awkward person insensitive to his surroundings). A snake in the grass (a treacherous person).

3. Nikita S. Khrushchev, Chairman of the Council of Ministers of the U.S.S.R., 1955–64.

Many metaphorical expressions originate in the unique terminology of specialized occupations. Examples: Full steam ahead (seafaring); A knockout (pugilism); Two strikes against him (baseball); Just marking time (military training); His stock went up (finance).

Slang is essentially a collection of vivid metaphors in the speech of the less educated who, as a rule, do not write. Whether these "non-literary metaphors" enter the "standard" language depends on whether they reflect a genuine expressive need or merely strive for novelty. The latter case is exemplified in passing-fad expressions, especially among teen-age groups. Words and phrases appear, spread rapidly among the "ins," and disappear as their novelty wears off or as they are supplanted by other picturesque expressions. In the former case, slang terms enter the language identified as slang but with a permanent place assured. Examples: guy, O.K., broke, flush, dumb, buck, big shot.

Much of technical slang is incorporated into standard terminology. For example, in American engineering circles, technical difficulties are called "bugs." Now, eliminating errors in a computer program is called "debugging," an exceedingly inelegant term by literary standards but a firmly established one. "Payoff," common underworld patois, was appropriated by John von Neumann and Oscar Morgenstern as a term in their formidable and abstruse mathematical theory of games and economic behavior.

The political cartoon with its personification of States, War, "Isms," and so on, is the modern version of the *allegory*.

A *parable* is a simple story, like an allegory or fable, that illustrates a moral principle by means of a concrete situation. The stories told by Jesus, as given in the New Testament, are so exemplary of the form that in most of Western culture the denotation of parable is associated with Jesus' stories. Examples: Behold, a sower went forth to sow: And when he sowed, some seeds fell by the wayside, and the fowls came and devoured them up. Some fell upon stony places, where they had not much earth; and forthwith they sprung up, because they had no deepness of earth: And when the sun was up, they were scorched; and because they had no root, they withered away.

And some fell among thorns; and the thorns sprung up and choked them: But others fell into good ground, and brought forth fruit, some a hundredfold, some sixtyfold, some thirtyfold.

Who hath ears to hear, let him hear.

The meaning is successfully conveyed if the hearer, or reader, is made aware of the broader connotations of the concrete referents. The communicative (or pedagogical) purpose is to make abstract meanings vivid by linking them to meanings associated with more direct, pedestrian experiences. Jesus understood this principle of concretization and explained it to his disciples:

"Why speakest thou unto them in parables?" they asked him. "Because it is given unto you to know the mysteries of the kingdom of heaven, but to them it is not given." [4]

Jesus' intent is clear: the common people of Judea are not likely to understand high-order abstractions: The "mysteries" must be translated for them into the everyday language of concrete experience.

Abstract language often carries a tone of detachment; concrete language, of involvement. Winston Churchill in a famous speech told the British people that they would have to work hard, suffer many casualties, and bear personal sorrows. (The occasion was Britain's almost hopeless position during World War II after the disaster at Dunkirk in the spring of 1940.) Had he said this as I have, it is unlikely that he would have inspired anybody. Instead, Churchill resorted to words with concrete meanings—common, sensuous words denoting bodily secretions: blood, sweat, and tears. It was the juxtaposition of the three monosyllabic, experiential words and their spoken rhythm that made the phrase unforgettable.

Eventually, an embedded metaphor loses its metaphorical character completely. It then becomes an idiom. Example: "How do you do?" The meaning of this "question" cannot be inferred either from the literal meanings of the words or from a metaphorical allusion. Originally it was a question about a person's state of health or, more generally, about his situation. Now it is simply a formula to say upon being introduced. The meaning of the words has disappeared. Only the whole expression has a meaning, something like "I acknowledge having made your acquaintance."

There is no sharp dividing line between an embedded metaphor and an idiom. Example: "I was cooling my heels in the reception room." Clearly, the temperature of the heels is entirely irrelevant

4. Matthew 13.

to the meaning of the sentence. The real meaning is "I was made to wait." But someone who does not know this would not guess it.

Idioms illustrate better than any other linguistic units the difficulties of translation when parts of equivalent expressions in different languages do not correspond. Specifically, idiomatic differences are those that cannot be inferred from syntactic or semantic rules; "idiom" relates to "idiosyncrasy" (eccentricity) and to "idiot" (an eccentric person). The meaning of the English expression "Put it in your pipe and smoke it" and of the Russian expression "Wind this around your mustache" is approximately the same: "Remember this well and guide your actions accordingly." However, equivalences of this sort are anything but visible. They must be dug out and learned separately in each instance, further complicating the task of learning a foreign language.

This is another illustration of a fundamental principle of language chemistry: the meaning of the whole cannot be expected to be correctly inferred from the meanings of the parts.

APPLICATIONS

I.   Psychological "features" attributed to animals often appear in our common vocabulary. For instance, we speak about a "cool cat," a "catty woman," a "cat-and-mouse game," "agile as a cat," a "cathouse"; we say a person leads a "dog's life" or he is "in the doghouse" or that he has a "hangdog look"; we call a person a "cur" or a "hound dog" and bemoan our "doggone" luck. We also may call an enemy a "rat" or a docile person a "mouse."

The three animals mentioned above probably are the ones referred to most frequently in our language. Do you see any reason for this pattern? Can you develop a principle of vocabulary formation from this observation?

II.   I. A. Richards, the critic and semanticist, believes that education on the higher level is the process of mastering what he calls "verbal shift"; that is, the ability to shift from the knowledge that "cat" refers to the species *Felis catus* (in childhood) to genus *Felis* (at the zoo age) to a person (high school age) to an irritating female (maturity). Another way to say it would be: "Education is the process of mastering metaphor."

Can you illustrate this thesis by using the language or the jargon of your own generation? Begin with words like "trip" and "heavy." Do you regard a colleague as educated if he has not learned the "verbal shift" these words have undergone?

III. As pointed out in the text, the names of buildings, streets, cities, and even countries frequently acquire figurative meanings associated with activities or events for which they are famous.

1) What figurative meaning is associated with the following:

a) Alamo	**i**) Pearl Harbor
b) Bastille	**j**) Bay of Pigs
c) Berlin Wall	**k**) Prague
d) Haight-Ashbury	**l**) Chicago
e) Madison Avenue	**m**) Bohemia
f) Street Called Straight	**n**) Las Vegas
g) Wailing Wall	**o**) Guernica
h) Village	**p**) Watergate

2) Extend this list with your own suggestions. How many of these words do you think will achieve a permanent place in our language?

IV. A good part of our everyday language is composed of what is called "dead metaphor" or "embedded metaphor." A "dead metaphor" is simply what the term implies: a word which once had striking figurative force but which through repeated use has been worn down toward denotative meaning. For instance, in the sentence "He hurled an insult at him," the verb was once highly figurative in that it was intended to conjure up the image of a spear-thrower releasing a deadly weapon after an enemy or a Polyphemus throwing a missile after the figure of the fleeing Odysseus. At present it means little more than "uttered vigorously." It has become so commonplace that the original image is not likely to be conjured up, although it may be for a child who first encounters the word in this context—the child soon learns the less pictorial meaning of "hurl" through "verbal shift."

1) Examine a page of prose from your favorite author. Underline the words which sound as though they are "dead metaphors." Are there many of them? Do you detect any "principle" at work in the conversion process?
2) Does a good writer avoid "dead metaphor"? Cliches? For what reasons?
3) What is the difference between "dead metaphor" and idiom?

V. Which of the linguistic features discussed in the text do you find in the following passages?

1) "The opportunities for options in life distinguishes the affluent from the disadvantaged. Perhaps through better motivation the upper levels of the poor could be tempted onto the option track. But most important is motivating such people close to the breakthrough level in income because they are closest to getting a foot on the option ladder."—magazine article by an advertising executive, quoted in *Newsweek*, 8 June 1964.

2) "A shortfall from our projections seems to indicate a disappointing trend not quite up to seasonal expectations, but calculations on the basis of the latest balance sheets point towards a remarkably stable upward trend."—release from a financial advisory service.

3) "People do not recognize 'mental illness' as a behavioral condition, but infer it instead from the association of the subject with the stigmatizing officials. This will illustrate that just as the ordinary man in the Middle Ages had no way of knowing who was a witch, and recognized her only from her identification by inquisitors—so, in our day, the ordinary man has no way of knowing who is a madman, and recognizes him only from his identification by mental health workers."—Thomas Szasz, *The Manufacture of Madness: A Comparative Study of the Inquisition and the Mental Health Movement* (New York: Harper & Row, 1970).

4) "The person who cannot perform sexually unconsciously attributes his failure to genital mutilation (castration), the anticipated parental punishment for his sexual transgressions, real or imagined. He then generalizes this castration fantasy to include all failures of performance, nonsexual as well as sexual. Thus, to put it conversely, the penis becomes the symbol not only of successful sexual performance, but also of mastery in all other areas of behavior; that is, the penis becomes the symbol of total adaptive capacity. Once this has occurred, the person unconsciously conceives of any adaptive failure in terms of injury to his penis. A symbolic reflection of this idea is concern with penis size: success is equated with a large penis, failure with a small one."—Lionel Ovesey, *Homosexuality and Pseudohomosexuality* (New York: Science House, 1969).

5) ". . . I feel that since women have an inborn aptitude for—and naturally get gratification from—understanding and helping people and creating beauty, and since most of them are going to spend fifteen or twenty-five years of their lives primarily raising their children, it would be fairer to them if they were brought up at home and educated at school and college in such a spirit that they would enjoy,

feel proud of, and be fascinated by child rearing rather than frustrated by it."—Benjamin Spock, "Decent and Indecent," *McCall's* (July 1970).

6) "We have seen how the literatures of freedom and dignity, with their concern for autonomous man, have perpetuated the use of punishment and condoned the use of weak nonpunitive techniques. It is not difficult to demonstrate a connection between the unlimited right of the individual to pursue happiness and the catastrophes threatened by unchecked breeding, the unrestrained affluence that exhausts resources and pollutes the environment, and the imminence of a nuclear war."—B. F. Skinner, *Beyond Freedom and Dignity* (New York: Alfred A. Knopf, 1971).

7) "Untrained group leaders . . . operate from abstract theories of social order. By Procrustean manipulation they shape the participants to match the group leader's requirements. Along these lines, it has been suggested that the encounter culture has launched a campaign to exorcise the superego of modern man. Sometimes skillfully, often unwittingly, core values and attitudes which society has deemed essential to a regulated society are being reshaped, cavalierly disregarded, or brutally removed by means of group pressure, and identification with the 'guilt-liberated' group leader."—Carl Goldberg, "Encounter Group Leadership," *Psychiatry and Social Science Review* (15 September 1970).

8) "Cancer is one of the umbrella words. It covers a number of disease conditions, some less dangerous than others. But they all have this in common, that they are associated with the growth of tissue by successive division of cells in which each cell divides to form two daughter cells, and so on. Growth occurs in this way almost throughout the plant and animal kingdom. In higher organisms it appears to cease in adult life. But this is only true for certain tissues; in many parts of the body, e.g., in the roots of the hair, repair and replenishment take place continuously by cell growth and cell division, and almost all tissues do in fact retain the power to proliferate, as can be seen during the normal healing of wounds. The behavior of cancer cells must be looked at against this background of the general phenomenon of tissue growth. This is the problem: is there any aspect of their behavior which can be regarded as characteristic of their growth? There is one—their lack of organization. This is most important, and it is the aspect I should like to consider.

Let me define what I mean by organization in this instance. Suppose I have a bunch of marbles in my hand. . . ."—E. J. Ambrose, "Cancer: A Problem of Cell Organization," *The Listener* (8 August 1957).

9) "The next dimension of psychology, the step that may take us beyond a primitive mind/body empiricism, could well be semantic. . . . It may

be that human speech is in some way a counterpart to that decoding and translating of the neurochemical idiom which defines and perpetuates our biological existence."—George Steiner, *Extraterritorial* (New York: Atheneum, 1971).

10) "The reality principle is about over

Thought as work can be buried in machines and computers
the work left to be done is to bury thought; quite a job
To put thought underground
                    as communication-network, sewage system, power-lines
So that wildness can come above ground
Technical rationality can be put to sleep
so that something else can awaken in the human mind
something like the god Dionysius
something which cannot be programmed."

—Norman O. Brown, "From Politics to Metapolitics," the Frederick William Atherton lecture, Harvard University, 20 March 1967, in *A Caterpillar Anthology*, ed. Clayton Eshelman (Garden City, N. Y.: Doubleday Anchor, 1971).

11) "Sure, some kids had bad trips, but considering the state of the world, it's a wonder the mental wards are not fuller than they are."— Timothy Leary, in an interview (UPI) on his role as "high priest of the drug cult," 28 August 1971.

For further reading, see Ernst Cassirer, "The Power of Metaphor" in *Language and Myth* (New York: Dover, 1946).

9/internal meanings

Bertrand Russell's game "Conjugating Adjectives" (cf. p. 129) is an ironic comment on a well-known human foible: the same situation evokes one connotative meaning for me and another for you. When I am reluctant to spend money, I say I am thrifty; you say I am stingy. The two words have in this case the same *denotation*: my apparent reluctance to spend money. But we use different words to describe it, the words reflecting our different attitudes by their different connotations.

A good dictionary frequently points out the psychological connotations of words, or it may include them in the definitions. In *Webster's Third New International Dictionary*, we read:

stingy . . . . reluctant to deal out, grant, or part with something; not generous.
thrifty . . . . characterized by economy and good management.

The dictionary also records usage. Hence, the definitions of "thrifty" and "stingy" imply that the two words are generally used to denote different situations. The "Conjugation of Adjectives" game suggests that words with different connotative meanings may be used by different people to denote the *same* situation. It follows that a dictionary, no matter how descriptive it purports to be, cannot give account of *all* instances of usage. The dictionary must confine itself to a least common denominator of usage.

What, then, shall we say about connotative meanings that reflect the personal attitudes of individual speakers? If two speakers designate the same situation by two different words with different connotations, shall we say that at least one of them is using a wrong word?

In the case of logical connotation, we certainly can. If Mr. Epsilon calls a certain animal a "dog," while Mr. Zeta calls it a "wolf," we can agree that one or both of them must be mistaken. The question should be decided by people whose business it is to distinguish those animals properly called "dogs" from those properly called "wolves." The situation is different if Mr. Theta, observing an instance of my behavior, says that I am thrifty, while Mr. Eta, observing the same instance, says I am stingy. Evidently Mr. Theta and Mr. Eta have attributed different motives to my behavior or, perhaps, the words they use reflect their different attitudes toward my behavior or even toward me personally. Here "experts" will be of no help in deciding which of the two, if either, is right.

Consider another situation. Mr. Iota is bound, blindfolded, and shot. Mr. Kappa calls the act an "execution." Mr. Lambda calls it "murder." In common usage, "execution" refers to killing a person by order of a legitimate authority as punishment for a crime. "Murder" refers to killing (usually premeditated) without sanction of legitimate authority. To decide whether Mr. Iota was executed or murdered, we must decide whether those who ordered the killing represented "legitimate authority." Here usage will not help us because some people may refer to the same "authority" as a "government," while others may refer to it as a "criminal conspiracy." In diplomacy, a government is usually understood as an authority that exercises effective control of a country. But governments, insurgent groups, guerrilla bands, and so on, all at times exercise control over territories and people. All of them sometimes resort to violence in exercising control. To decide whether a group that imposes control over a territory or a population is a "government" or not, we must decide whether the territory is a "country" or not and sometimes whether their power to control was obtained "legitimately" or not. These questions hinge on the meaning of a "country" and of "legitimacy." Again, common usage will not help us because different people use different criteria to decide whether a territory is a country or whether a power-wielding authority obtained its power legitimately.

There was a time when the eldest son of a deceased monarch was, by definition of legitimacy, the legitimate ruler of the realm. However, while we now say "by definition," the monarchs said that legitimacy was conferred on them "by grace of God." In 1776 some Americans declared that the government of the British king was no longer legitimate in the thirteen colonies. In fact, the insurgents changed the definition of legitimacy so as to stipulate that legitimacy is conferred on a government by the people governed, not by God.

Now, the student of comparative semantics will note this historical change in the range of denotation of "legitimacy." The lexicographer will, perhaps, record it in a dictionary. The psychologist is interested in how the word came to mean something different to people, and the social scientist is concerned with the social consequences of the change.

In short, meaning resides not only in a connection between a situation and the symbols that designate it, but it also resides in the *users* of the symbols, their perceptions, evaluations, memories, and attitudes. Several of the definitions of meaning listed by Ogden and Richards[1] point to this *internal* component of meaning.

Examples: "That to which the user of a symbol Believes himself to be referring." "The Mnemic[2] effects of a stimulus. Associations acquired." "The event Intended."

Apparently, then, we can distinguish between *external* and *internal* meanings. Synonymy, denotation, and logical connotation bring out external meanings. Synonymy refers a word to other words; denotation relates a word to referents; logical connotation lists criteria which supposedly enable us to recognize the thing defined. In all these contexts, meaning can be examined and discussed without reference to what goes on in the mind of a *particular* speaker or hearer. On the other hand, psychological connotation and intent bring out internal meanings, and these are bound up with what goes on in the mind of a particular speaker or hearer, the mental images or attitudes evoked, desires felt, acts intended, intentions inferred, and so on.

Some semanticists insist that internal meanings are implied in all cases. Thus, Ogden and Richards schematize denotative meaning in their so-called Triangle of Reference, shown in Figure 2.

According to this scheme, if a symbol has meaning, it is supposed to evoke in someone's mind a thought (a *reference*), and the thought refers to a referent, that for which the symbol is supposed to stand. Thus there is a causal connection between the symbol and the reference (the symbol evokes a thought) and a causal connection between

1. C. K. Ogden and I. A. Richards, *The Meaning of Meaning*, 2d rev. ed. (New York: Harcourt, Brace and Company, 1927), pp. 186–87.
2. Mnemic: pertaining to persistent or recurring past experiences in the memory of an individual or of a race.

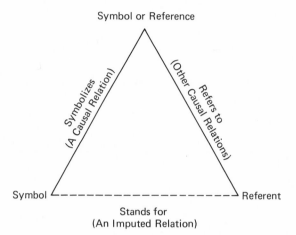

Figure 2

the reference and the referent (the thought is directed to the referent), but there is no direct causal relation between the symbol and the referent. The relation between them must be *mediated* by a process in somebody's mind.

Internal meanings of words and of other linguistic units are a central object of interest in psycholinguistics. Psycholinguists and psychologists have developed several methods to study internal meanings and their relation to behavior. We shall examine some of these in this chapter and the next.

A way of inferring something about the associations evoked by a word is through a so-called word association experiment. In such an experiment, the participant (called subject) is usually presented with a word, called the stimulus word. He is then asked to respond with some other word that comes to his mind. For the sake of developing such experiments in a systematic manner, subjects may be variously instructed. In a completely free association experiment, the subject may be simply asked to respond with any word that comes to his mind. In some experiments, the range of responses may be restricted. For example, the subject may be asked to respond with a *superordinate* word, one that has a larger range of denotation than the stimulus word. Thus a superordinate response to "fork" might be "silverware" or "utensil"; to "limousine," it might be "car" or "vehicle," and so on. Or the subject might be asked to give a *subordinate* response, a word that is more specific than the stimulus word. Such a response to "dog" might be "collie"; to "car," "sedan" or "convertible" or "my Chevy," and so forth.

Other types of responses called for are *opposites*, such as "darkness" to "light" or "wisdom" to "foolishness"; *verbs* in response to nouns, such as "smoke" or "play" to "pipe"; *adjectives* to nouns, such as "pretty" to "girl," and so on.

As would be expected, some words elicit highly stereotyped responses. In free association, more people respond with "woman" to "man" than with any other word. Responses to other words are much more varied. A linguist might be interested in the range of responses elicited by different words or kinds of words. A psychologist, on the other hand, might be interested in the range of responses elicited by a given population of subjects.

For instance, Carole J. Quarterman and Klaus F. Riegel[3] compared the results of word association experiments obtained from nine-year-old and fifteen-year-old children. Several different restrictions were used. We shall discuss here the results obtained under the restriction of "similarity"; that is, the children were asked to respond to the stimulus word with a word "most similar in meaning." The experimenters present their data as shown in Table 1.

The first column is a list of all the response words that were given more than once by the entire population of children, fifty in each group. The next two columns show the number of children in each group who gave each of the words. At the bottom are listed the numbers of words that were given only once (that is, by only one child) and the numbers of children in each group who failed to respond to the stimulus word.

The simplest comparison is a quantitative one. If the responses of a population can be described by some *numerical index*, the populations can be quantitatively compared with respect to that index. One index frequently used in word association tests is the so-called *type-token ratio*. Suppose a population of subjects produces 100 responses to a single stimulus word and 50 of these responses are *different* words. The 100 responses are 100 *tokens*; the 50 different words are 50 *types*. The type-token ratio in this case is $50/100 = .5$. In a way, the type-token ratio is a measure of the *range of association* of the stimulus word among the population in question.

Another measure is the *uncertainty* of the response. Suppose we

3. Carole J. Quarterman and Klaus F. Riegel, "Restricted Associations of 9, 12, and 15 Year Old Americans" (unpublished), Report No. 28, *Development of Language Functions* (Ann Arbor, Mich.: Center for Human Growth and Development, University of Michigan, December 29, 1967).

Table 1 *Responses of 9-year-old and 15-year-old Americans to some stimulus words* (After Quarterman and Riegel)

Stimulus word: ANGER	Number of responses by		Stimulus word: SEX	Number of responses by		Stimulus word: SOCIALISM	Number of responses by	
Response words	9-year-olds	15-year-olds	*Response words*	9-year-olds	15-year-olds	*Response words*	9-year-olds	15-year-olds
happy	1	3	age	2	—	communism	—	5
hate	—	1	appeal	—	1	friend	2	—
mad	34	22	boy	2	—	friendly	1	6
madness	4	1	female	1	—	history	2	—
mean	2	2	gamete	—	2	person	—	4
temper	—	4	girl	2	3	society	2	—
			love	1	9	togetherness	2	—
Singles	5	3	male	4	5			
No response	3	3	man	3	3	Singles	7	13
			person	1	4	No response	36	18
			pretty	2	—			
			yourself	2	—			
			Singles	11	12			
			No response	20	10			

know the responses given by a group of subjects to a certain word. How likely is it that we can guess the response to a given word from an arbitrarily selected subject? Certainly we would be more likely to guess correctly if most of the subjects gave some one response than if each of the responses were given by an equal number of subjects. A method used in the mathematical theory of communication provides a convenient measure of "response uncertainty." [4] Roughly, the more "bunched" the responses are, the smaller is the response uncertainty;

4. The "uncertainty" of response is calculated as follows. The probability of a particular response type is estimated from the relative frequency with which it was observed among all the given responses. Thus, if among 50 responses (tokens), a particular response type was observed 14 times, the probability of the response type is taken as $14/50 = .28$. Call the probabilities of the occurring types $p_1, p_2, \ldots, p_k$. These probabilities are multiplied respectively by their logarithms. The sum of these products with a minus sign attached is the uncertainty of the response. In symbols,
$$\text{H (the uncertainty)} = -(p_1 \log p_1 + p_2 \log p_2 + \ldots + p_k \log p_k).$$
If the base of the logarithms is 2, H is measured in "bits." In our calculations, it was more convenient to use the so-called "natural" base, approximately 2.718. In this case, the uncertainty is measured in "nats." What we call stereotypy is the inverse of the uncertainty; that is, $1/H$.

the more evenly spread the responses are, the larger is the response uncertainty. Clearly, if the response uncertainty is small, we can also say that the *stereotypy* of response is large. In the extreme case, if all the children respond with the same word to the stimulus word, the responses are completely stereotyped. Thus, we can use the reciprocal of the response uncertainty as a measure of stereotypy.

Table 2 shows the type-token ratios (t/T) and the stereotypy measures calculated from data obtained from Quarterman and Riegel.

Table 2 *t/T: type-token ratio, the number of* different *words, elicited as responses to the stimulus word, divided by the total number of responses elicited.*
S: "stereotypy," the reciprocal of the uncertainty of the response.

Response word		9-year-olds	15-year-olds
Anger	t/T	.20	.43
	S	.87	.46
Bird	t/T	.45	.59
	S	.40	.38
Butterfly	t/T	.21	.40
	S	.60	.45
Sex	t/T	.70	.47
	S	.44	.39
Socialism	t/T	.71	.53
	S	.84	.44

In general, the type-token ratio is larger in fifteen-year-olds than in nine-year-olds, and the stereotype index is smaller—a result easily explainable by the larger vocabulary of the adolescents.[5] No less notable, however, are the *reversals* observed in the stimulus words "sex" and "socialism." Here there is more "concentration" on fewer associates in the older children. One can suppose that the meanings of these words have become "sharper" for them. Examining the actual responses to "sex," we see that in nine-year-olds the most frequent response was given only 4 times, and (significantly) no response at all was given in 20 instances out of 50. In fifteen-year-olds, the most frequent response was given 9 times. No response was given in 10 instances out of 50. The response given 4 times by the nine-year-olds was "male"; that given 9 times by the fifteen-year-olds was "love."

5. This result was observed in the responses to a large majority of the 40 stimulus words in the Quarterman-Riegel study. Exceptions are noted in the text.

The data on "socialism" are equally interesting. No response was given more than twice by the population of nine-year-olds. Thus, if we view the response as a spontaneously expressed "meaning" of the stimulus word, there was hardly any agreement among the younger children on the "meaning" of "socialism." The fifteen-year-olds responded 5 times with "communism" and 6 times with "friendly" (evidently confusing "socialism" with "sociable"). This word elicited no response from nine-year-olds in 36 instances and from fifteen-year-olds in 18 instances. This accounts for the large "stereotypy" in the nine-year-olds since "no response" was coded as the same response in calculating this measure.

In an experiment conducted by Elliot J. Stern and Klaus F. Riegel, a population of schizophrenic patients was compared with twenty-four subjects recruited from the hospital staff. The same list of stimulus words was used on each population. It turned out in the free association test that the type-token ratio of the list of responses from schizophrenics was 0.65, while that from "normals" was only 0.50. That is, on the average, the range of words elicited by the stimulus words used in the experiment was larger in the population of schizophrenics than in the population of "normals." [6]

It is interesting to observe that the type-token ratio of schizophrenics was larger than the corresponding type-token ratios of the "normals" in every one of the association tasks used in the experiment. The results are shown in Figure 3.

From the figure we see also that, although the graph of the type-token ratio of schizophrenics always stays above the corresponding graph of normals, it goes up and down with the tasks in about the same way as that of the "normals." This means that in tasks where the type-token ratio is larger in "normals" it is also larger in schizophrenics, and vice versa. The difference is only in the overall type-token ratio.

One should, of course, be extremely wary of drawing unwarranted conclusions from such results. The data do not necessarily support the tempting conclusion that "schizophrenics are 'more disorganized' in their thinking than normals because they 'wander' more in their as-

6. Elliot J. Stern and Klaus F. Riegel, "Comparisons of the Restricted Associations of Chronic Schizophrenic and Normal Control Subjects," *Journal of Abnormal Psychology* 75, no. 2 (April 1970): 164–71.

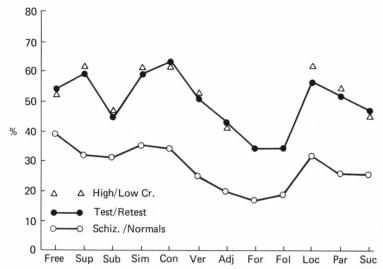

Figure 3 *Minimum Group Overlaps (MGO) for twelve tasks of restricted associations and three pairs of groups.*

sociations." Equally possible is the conclusion that the responses of the schizophrenics are less stereotyped than those of normals, perhaps because schizophrenics are more "creative" in their thinking. It may well be that if we compare a population of poets with a population of nonpoets we would observe the same difference: a higher type-token ratio among the poets. But surely we could not conclude from this that poets resemble schizophrenics. All that we learn from the above experiment is that *if* the associative processes in schizophrenics are "disorganized" the type-token ratio reflects one possible aspect of the disorganization.

More direct evidence of "disorganization" of the word association process in schizophrenics is seen from the specific responses of schizophrenic subjects to stimulus words. The following data were collected by G. H. Kent and A. J. Rosanoff.[7] Among the responses of two schizophrenic patients, we notice the following types:

1. Conventional responses, of the sort observed in most "normal" subjects. Examples:

7. G. H. Kent and A. J. Rosanoff, "A Study of Associations in Insanity," *American Journal of Insanity* 67 (1910): 37–96.

Stimulus	Response
dark	black
music	sweet
man	boy
mutton	beef
woman	girl
eating	pie

2.   Unusual responses, reflecting associations that are difficult to trace, of the sort seldom observed in "normal" subjects. Some of them, however, may indicate a rich imagination rather than "disorganization." Examples:

Stimulus	Response
sickness	monk (via priest administering last rites?)
deep	lesson (profound lesson?)
river	cast (as in fishing?)
red	Roman (a cardinal in his red robes?)
window	crow
command	cork
earth	bell (both associated with a funeral?)
dark	gone (images gone?)
fruit	narrow
white	Andes (unusual, but clear!)
girl	call (also clear in our day, hardly in 1910 when the data were collected)
soldier	gas (gas was not yet used in war in 1910)

3.   Neologisms, that is, nonwords. Frequent use of these is a typical characteristic of schizophrenic speech. Examples:

Stimulus	Response
music	caffa
eating	formble
mountain	gair
woman	hummery
slow	bemper
river	bumper
beautiful	gimper
citizen	humper
needle	himper
sour	imper
working	gumpip

Examining the successive responses of one patient, we can almost see how the association process goes into some sort of spin. He (or she) begins with ordinary responses but, after a few of these, starts giving neologisms, at first of different kinds, finally entering the compulsive chain of humper, gumper, gimper, and so on. Neologisms abound also in the second patient's responses, although compulsive repetitions are not as evident.

Now let us examine some samples of schizophrenic writing.[8]

SAMPLE 1.

If things turn by rotation of agriculture or levels in regards and "timed" to everything; I am re-fering to a previous document when I made some marks that were facts also tested and there is another that concerns my daughter she has a lobed bottom right ear, her name being Mary Lou. . . . Much of abstraction has been left unsaid and undone in this product/milk syrup, and others due to economics, differentials, subsidies, bankruptcy, tools, buildings, bonds, national stocks, foundation craps, weather, trades, government in levels of breakages and fuses in electronic too all formerly "stated" not necessarily factuated.

SAMPLE 2.

The players and boundaries have been of different colors in terms of black and white and I do not intend that the futuramas of supersonic fixtures will ever be in my life again because I believe that all known factors that would have its effect on me even the chemical reaction of ameno [sic] acids as they are in the process of combustronability are known to me.

Note the striking resemblance of these samples to the second-order word approximation to English shown on page 64. We catch glimpses of "chunks" of meaning that bind a few words together but then dissolve. Similarity of products may be indicative of similarity of underlying processes. Therefore let us examine the process that we *know*, the process of constructing an approximation to English.

A second-order word approximation to English, such as the sample

8. From B. A. Maher, *Principles of Psychopathology* (New York: McGraw-Hill, 1966). For further discussion, see Harold S. Vetter, *Language Behavior and Psychopathology* (Chicago: Rand McNally, 1969).

on page 64, can be constructed as follows. Take a sample of written English and choose any two consecutive words. Then read the text until you come to the next occurrence of the same two words. Add the word that follows them. Read on until the last two words are again encountered. Add the word following and continue in the same manner.

The resemblance of such an approximation to schizophrenic writing may be a reflection of a similar process in the mind of the schizophrenic. He starts out to express a thought, which a "normal" person would do by writing a complete sentence, but, before finishing the sentence, the schizophrenic is diverted by the stimulus of some word or group of words he has written. The writer puts down the word evoked by the association. This starts a new train of thought, which is again interrupted, and so on. Note how, in Sample 1 above, an association chain got started with single words as links: "economics," "differentials," "subsidies," "bankruptcy," "tools," "national stocks." . . .

It seems as if the schizophrenic's verbal output is guided by a more or less freewheeling stream of association, where the words he himself says or writes serve as stimulus words.

Neologisms, too, strongly resemble approximations to English, namely letter approximations. Compare the neologisms produced by schizophrenics with the "near words" of the second-order letter approximations (cf. p. 64), such as "deamy," "teasonare," and so on. Perhaps they are likewise produced by sudden switches in the association process, resulting in new combinations of letters. Note that although the neologisms are not English words they nevertheless look like English words, an indication that the new combinations are still governed by the speech habits of the individual who produced them.

It may well be that freewheeling association processes go on in all of us at least part of the time and that when we speak or write "coherently" we exercise control which the schizophrenic is not able to exercise. James Joyce, in his two famous novels *Ulysses* and *Finnegans Wake*, captured this freewheeling association process, the so-called "stream of consciousness." In a way, those novels reveal what *actually* goes on in our minds—at least when we relax control over our thought processes.

What we can learn about thought processes, hence about internal meanings, from word association experiments depends a great deal on the ingenuity of the researchers. The advantage of the method is that it yields clear data—easily recorded, processed, and quantified. Moreover, large masses of data from large numbers of subjects can be gathered quickly. The problem is how to penetrate deeply enough to where internal meanings are manufactured. In general, the more controls used in the experiment (that is, the more restrictions placed on the responses), the easier it is to systematize and to interpret the results, but also the more difficult it is to tap the most psychologically interesting mechanisms of association. In a minimally structured situation, as in hearing someone's "stream of consciousness," we must depend a great deal on our own imagination and intuition to draw conclusions from what we hear and so stand in danger of falling victim to delusions stemming from our own "free associations."

This trade-off between the objectivity of findings and the depth of their meaning characterizes a great deal of psychological (in particular, psycholinguistic) research.

Let us turn to another technique designed to ferret out internal meanings. The method was developed by Charles E. Osgood, G. J. Suci, and P. H. Tannenbaum, and is applied in a wide range of psycholinguistic research.[9] This instrument is called the *semantic differential*. The subject is asked to respond to a stimulus word with a mark on a scale whose extremes are labeled by two opposite adjectives. For instance, the stimulus word might be "father" and the scale might be "hard . . . soft." The scale is graduated into seven intervals. A mark in the interval next to "hard" would indicate that the subject thought of "father" as "very hard"; the next interval designates "quite hard," the next "rather hard," the next "neither hard nor soft," the next "rather soft," and so on. The subject is asked to associate the stimulus word with a position on several such scales, that is, "happy . . . sad," "slow . . . fast," and so forth.

It turns out that the subjects' evaluations of the stimulus words on the various scales are often closely related. Consider the two scales "slow . . . fast" and "active . . . passive." If a subject associates a stimulus word, say "father," with the extreme "fast" end of the first scale, he is likely to associate the same stimulus word with the extreme "active" end of the second scale. Similarly, if he associates "father" with a position toward the "hard" end of the "hard . . . soft" scale, he

9. Charles E. Osgood, George J. Suci, and Percy H. Tannenbaum, *The Measurement of Meaning* (Urbana, Ill.: University of Illinois Press, 1957).

is likely also to associate "father" with a position toward the "strong" end of the "strong . . . weak" scale.

By means of a mathematical technique called *factor analysis*, the many scales can be "collapsed" into a few. To see how this is done, look at an analogous situation in geography. Suppose we record the several distances of a given city from several other cities. Actually three such distances would usually fix the position of the city on the earth's surface. Suppose we are told that a certain city is 350 air miles from Chicago and 1,230 air miles from Atlanta. We draw one circle with Chicago as center and with a radius of 350 miles and another circle with Atlanta as center and a radius of 1,230 miles. These two circles will intersect at two points. Our city must be at one of them. If we are told also that the city is 710 miles from New York, we draw a circle with New York as center and with a radius of 710 miles. This circle must pass through the city, therefore through at least one of the two points. Its position will then be fixed.[10]

We know further that the position of a city on the earth's surface can be completely determined by just two numbers, latitude and longitude. If we are told the distances between every pair of, say 10 cities, we are given 55 numbers, for there are 55 pairs of cities among the 10. We know that these 55 numbers can be "collapsed" on just 20, namely a latitude and a longitude of each city. The 20 numbers will give the same amount of information as the 55.

Factor analysis uses the same principle in "collapsing" many measurements into just a few. (In actual application of factor analysis, this cannot be done exactly because the data to which factor analysis is usually applied are subject to random fluctuations). These few fundamental measurements are called dimensions, analogous to latitude and longitude, or distances along three axes in space. It turns out that a measurement on three dimensions approximately accounts for a subject's evaluations of a stimulus word on a much larger number of scales.

These three dimensions can be represented respectively on an *evaluative* scale (roughly "good . . . bad"), on a *potency* scale (roughly "big . . . little"), and on an *activity* scale (roughly "active . . . passive").

10. In the very special case when the third circle passes through *both* points of intersection of the first two circles, we still do not know at which of the two points the city is located In that case, we must choose some other cities as reference points.

Thus, for each subject, each stimulus word occupies a position in a "three-dimensional semantic space." For example, "father" may be for one subject "good, big and active" (with an appropriate gradation in each dimension), for another, "bad, big, and passive" and so forth.

An interesting application of the semantic differential was made in 1954 by Charles E. Osgood and Zella Luria.[11] About that time two clinical psychologists, C. H. Thigpen and H. M. Cleckley, submitted a paper to a journal wherein they described a case of "split personality."[12] The case was unusual because *three* completely distinct personalities were involved. Apparently the patient passed suddenly from one to the other and led three distinct modes of life. (Cases of this sort are occasionally described, lending credence to Robert Louis Stevenson's famous story of Dr. Jekyll and Mr. Hyde.) The editor of the journal suggested to the authors that it would be interesting to collect data for a semantic differential analysis from the three "persons" living in the patient. The idea was to see whether the differences among the three personalities, apparent to the psychologists through overall impressions, would be reflected also in an analysis undertaken on the basis of data gathered by means of an "objective" instrument, the semantic differential.

Certain precautions had to be taken. First, the analysis based on the semantic differential data had to be done "blind," that is, in ignorance of the impressions of these personalities already gathered. Second, the semantic differential data had to be taken more than once from each personality, to see whether the "pictures" so obtained differed more from each other when they were constructed on the basis of data obtained from different personalities than when they were constructed on the basis of data obtained from the same personality.

These precautions were taken. At intervals of about two or three months, Drs. Thigpen and Cleckley twice administered semantic differential tests on each of the three personalities. The data were then sent to Osgood and Luria, who constructed a "semantic space" for each set of data. They knew only that they were dealing with a "triple personality," labeled respectively "Eve White," "Eve Black,"

11. Charles E. Osgood and Zella Luria, " A Blind Analysis of a Case of Multiple Personality Using the Semantic Differential," *Journal of Abnormal and Social Psychology* 49 (1954): 579–91.
12. C. H. Thigpen and H. M. Cleckley, "A Case of Multiple Personality," *Journal of Abnormal and Social Psychology* 49 (1954): 135–51.

and "Jane," and some facts about the patient such as that she was married, had a child, and was working outside the home.

As has been said, if the several adjective scales used in an experiment are collapsed into three, a model of a "semantic space" is three-dimensional. Each stimulus word occupies a position in that space. The coordinates represent the "value" of the stimulus word on each of the three dimensions. Such a model can be represented physically by a number of balls connected by rods, in the same way that organic chemists construct the spatial structure of a complex molecule where the balls represent the atoms. A two-dimensional picture of such a model is less than satisfactory, but when we communicate by symbols printed on flat paper, we have no choice.

Figures 4–6 show respectively the "semantic spaces" of Eve White, Eve Black, and Jane. The similarity between the pairs of pictures

Figure 4   *Semantic Space for Eve White.*

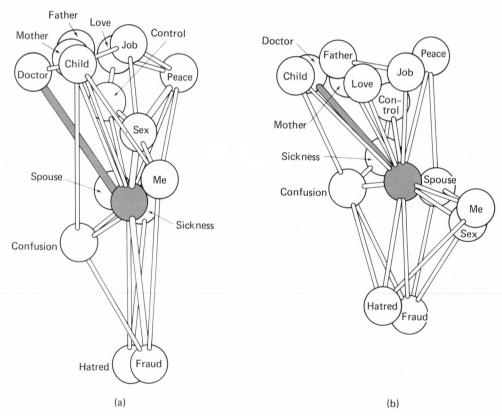

(a)   (b)

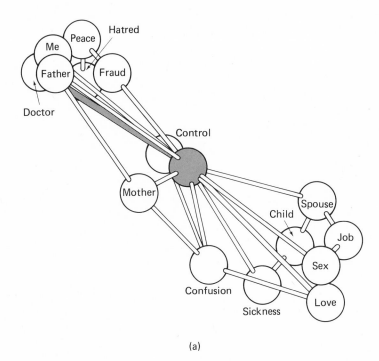

(a)

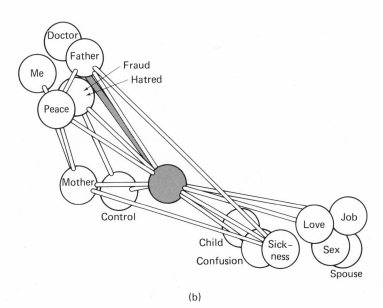

(b)

Figure 5 _Semantic Space for Eve Black._

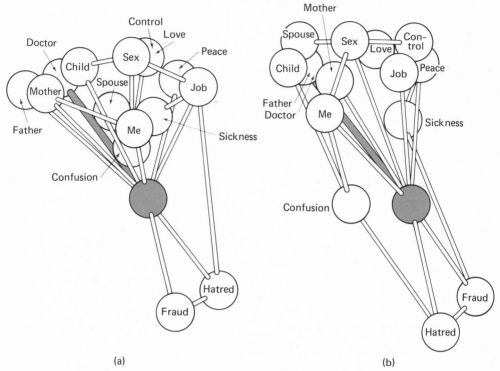

Figure 6   *Semantic Space for Jane.*

representing the same personality as well as the contrasts among the pictures representing different personalities are immediately apparent.

In the pictures, the directions up and down the page represent the evaluative dimension (up = good); left and right, the activity dimension (left = active); toward the viewer and away from the viewer, the potency dimension (toward = weak). The black circle is the neutral point. The stimulus words are shown as labels on the circles.

From these models, Osgood and Luria ventured to "read off" the three personalities. Their descriptions can be compared with those of the psychologists who were in direct contact with the woman. The extent to which the descriptions are similar, even though they were made independently, speaks for the usefulness of the semantic differential as an instrument in the study of personality through the internal meanings of words.

Osgood and Luria write this about Eve White:[13]

She is aware of both the demands of society and of her own inadequacies in meeting with them. She is concerned and ambivalent about her child, but apparently is not aware of her own ambivalent attitudes toward her mother. Those psychoanalytically inclined may wish to identify Eve White with dominance of the superego: certainly, the superego seems to view the world from the eyes of Eve White, accepting the mores or values of others (particularly her mother) but continuously criticizing and punishing herself.

Thigpen and Cleckley write about Eve White:

Mrs. White admits difficulty in her relation with her mother, and her performance on the Rorschach and drawings indicate conflict and resulting anxiety in her role as a wife and mother. . . . Demure, retiring, in some respects almost saintly. . . . Voice always softly modulated, always influenced by specifically feminine restraint. . . . An industrious and able worker. . . . Limited in spontaneity. . . . Consistently uncritical of others.

Osgood and Luria describe Eve Black in these terms:

Eve Black is clearly the most out of contact with social reality and simultaneously the most self-assured. She sees herself as a dominant, active wonder woman and is in no way self-critical. Those psychoanalytically inclined could say that the id looks out at the world through the eyes of Eve Black. Like a completely selfish infant, this personality is entirely oriented around the assumption of its own perfection. . . .

Here are the impressions of Thigpen and Cleckley:

Eve Black's career has been traced back to early childhood. She herself freely tells us of episodes when she emerged, usually to engage in acts of mischief or disobedience. She lies glibly and without compunction, so her account alone can never be taken as reliable evidence. . . . Obviously a party girl. Shrewd, childishly vain, and egocentric. . . . Voice a little coarsened, "discultured," with echoes of implications of mirth and teasing. Speech richly vernacular and liberally seasoned with spontaneous word and gesture.

13. The following excerpts are cited in Osgood, Suci, and Tannenbaum, *The Measurement of Meaning*, pp. 264–71.

Osgood's and Luria's comments on Jane:

Superficially, Jane is a very healthy personality—"all's well with the
world, and day by day I'm getting better and better." Her spouse is becoming more like the noble doctor all the time, and she is coming to perceive herself, even, as a pleasant and reasonably active (if somewhat weak
and submissive) person.
But all this is a little too rosy, a little too pat. We note that Jane is becoming more and more "simple-minded"—all of her judgments tending to
fall along a single factor: good-strong vs. bad-weak. . . . Those psychoanalytically inclined may wish to view this personality as representing
dominance of a self-deceptive ego which has woven a web of repression as
to the state of reality; or, they may wish to view Jane as an essentially
strong, healthy, and improving ego-dominated personality.

Thigpen and Cleckley:

It is easy to sense in her a capacity for accomplishment and fulfillment
far beyond that of the sweet and retiring Eve White, who, beside this
genuinely impressive newcomer, appears colorless and limited. In her are
indications of initiative and powerful resources never shown by the other.

Apparently Thigpen and Cleckley do not share the skepticism of
Osgood and Luria with regard to the genuineness of Jane's positive
traits. In spite of occasional discrepancies, however, an outsider would
probably have no difficulty in matching the independent evaluations
of Osgood and Luria with those of Thigpen and Cleckley that refer
to the same personality.

Like the general word association test, the semantic differential may
be used either as an instrument for differentiating persons or for differentiating words. In particular, it can be applied in studying what
we have called the chemistry of meaning (cf. Chapter 5). To illustrate, suppose we determine the semantic space coordinates of a noun,
taking the average values of these coordinates from the responses of
a large population of subjects. Next, we do the same with an adjective.
Can we say anything about the resulting coordinates of the combination of the adjective with the noun?

Osgood, Suci, and Tannenbaum report the coordinates so obtained
of the word "secretary" (noun), of "shy" (adjective), and of "shy
secretary." The position of "secretary" on the evaluative scale is quite
high (6+), a little above neutral on the potency scale (4+), and

rather high on the activity scale (5.5). The position of "shy" is neutral on the evaluative scale (4), rather low on the strong-weak scale (3—), and still lower on the activity scale. The position of "shy secretary" is intermediate between the other two on all three scales but characteristically much closer to the position of the adjective than to that of the noun. The authors point out that this dominance of the adjectival component in adjective-noun phrases is a typical observation.

In a way, it is not surprising that coordinates constructed on the basis of adjective responses are influenced more by the adjective than by the noun in adjective-noun stimulus phrases. It would be interesting to gather data where combinations of adjectives and nouns elicit responses *not* intermediate between those elicited separately, indicating a reversal of evaluations. Suppose, for instance, that both "female" and "executive" appear high on the good-bad scale. It may well happen that "female executive" will rate low on the same scale because of possible unfavorable connotations suggested by the combination that are not suggested by the components.

Finally, it should be clear that the semantic spaces suggested by the semantic differential method are purely *connotative* spaces (connotative being here understood in its strictly psychological, not logical, sense). Thus, although two stimuli words might practically coincide in someone's semantic space, the *referents* of these words are not necessarily connected in the mind of that person.

Osgood and Luria come close to risking an unwarranted conclusion when they write, describing Jane's semantic space, ". . . Love and sex (quite unlike Eve White) are both favorable and quite closely identified. Her spouse is becoming more like the noble doctor all the time." If this is so, the model of semantic space provides evidence for it; but *because* the doctor and the husband are close in the connotative space does not warrant the conclusion that the two are "identified."

A case in point is an application of the semantic differential in analyzing the responses of a sample of voters during the U.S. presidential campaign of 1952.[14] The stimulus words included names of candidates (not yet nominated): Taft, Eisenhower, Stevenson, etc., and such words as "socialism," etc. It turned out that, in the semantic space of voters who announced their intention to vote for the Democratic candidate, "Taft" and "socialism" were closer to each other than

14. Ibid., pp. 104–16.

"Eisenhower" and "socialism." From this, we can by no means conclude that those voters thought that Taft, the more conservative of
the two, was more inclined toward socialism than Eisenhower. An
alternative explanation easily suggests itself. The sample of voters was
taken from rural Illinois. Their predominant attitude toward "socialism" was probably negative, whether they were Republicans or
Democrats. Now, Democrats could be expected to like Eisenhower
more than they liked Taft because Eisenhower was more "liberal."
Consequently Taft would rate lower than Eisenhower on the evaluative scale and so closer to "socialism," which was also rated low on
the same scale.

The range of application of word association experiments in all
their variants is very large, but it is advisable to proceed with caution
in applying these tools, as with any other tools that are supposed to
tap events going on deep within the skins of people and to make these
manifest as "objective data." The extent to which such experiments
may help us infer something about internal meanings of words and
how they are related depends much on the suitability of the instrument to the research task selected.

Laboratory experiments are designed to obtain objective data. Quantitative data are the most objective. For this reason, the results of
laboratory experiments involving human behavior are often presented
statistically so that individual responses of individual subjects are
"washed out." This makes for a gain in objectivity and precision but
also for a loss in depth. To restore depth to the analysis of internal
meanings, the investigator must engage his intuitive knowledge of
language and sometimes of the language user; he must act more like
an artist than a scientist. Humanistic studies require expertise of this
sort.

Comparative semantics offers a sort of middle ground between
science and art. As remarked earlier, many words have a concrete
"core" of literal denotation along with a "penumbra" of figurative
meaning involving a metaphorical extension. By comparing the degree
of overlap of these metaphorical meanings of words in several languages, the comparative semanticist often can make inferences about
the internal meanings associated with these words. It is difficult to
support such inferences by "hard" experimental evidence, but there is
no reason on that account to exclude them from psycholinguistic
theory.

In English, several "dimensions" of metaphorical extension can be discerned.

From object to function

Bureau: a piece of furniture used for writing on becomes an administrative unit.

The White House: a building acquires the meaning of executive authority because of its occupant.

Chain: a device used for linking or suspending acquires the meaning of a sequence of connections because of the way it is constructed.

Analogies with parts of bodies

The mouth of a river.
The muzzle of a revolver.
An arm of the sea.
A leg of a journey.
The head of a family.
The brain of an organization.
A law with teeth in it.
The main artery of a city.

Paths

Outlet, entry, channel, gate, obstacle, road, detour, shortcut—all have to do with getting from here to there but not necessarily by moving through space.

Extensions of mechanical concepts

A breakdown of negotiations.
Support of a policy.
Nail down to a commitment.
Balance of power.
Punch a hole in an argument.
The wheels of progress.

Transformed modalities of sensation

Sounds can be sharp, piercing, dull, high, low.
Relations between people can be warm, cold, or frigid.
A contradiction can be glaring; an example can be shining; a solution can be brilliant.
Truth can be bitter; humor, salty or spicy.

Metaphorical use of shapes
The circle of friends, the social pyramid, the love triangle.
Straight and square mean honest; crooked means dishonest.

The task of comparative semantics would be to examine analogous extensions in various languages with the view of estimating the richness or paucity of particular dimensions of imagery. Are some languages richer than others in sensual images or in mechanical images or in images of motion? If so, does this reflect in any sense the dominant life style of the language users?

Another possible approach to internal meanings, as yet comparatively unexplored, is through musical aesthetics. Aside from aesthetic appeal through its syntactic structure (cf. pp. 73–74), music almost certainly evokes internal meanings. However, excepting the referents of explicitly descriptive music, these meanings are for the most part difficult to capture. To be sure, there are obvious allusions to energy in rapidly moving musical patterns and to repose in slowly moving ones. Still, the way in which musical modes evoke different moods is largely a mystery. The Greeks wrote extensively about the emotional qualities of their several modes—the Ionian, the Dorian, the Phrygian, and so on.[15] In Western music, two principal modes in use since the Renaissance are the major and the minor. Musically literate people in the Western world generally agree that major is for the most part associated with optimistic moods and minor with pessimistic ones. To what extent these associations are universal is not known. Nor is it

15. Medieval musicologists used the same nomenclature, but the names of the medieval modes do not correspond to the names used by the Greeks. The following names of modes were used by the Swiss monk-musicologist Henry of Glarus (1488-1563). Each mode is obtained from the C-major scale by shifting the keynote to the corresponding tone:

Name of Mode	Keynote
Ionian	C
Dorian	D
Phrygian	E
Lydian	F
Mixolydian	G
Aeolian	A

Two facts relevant to our discussion of the semantics of music are worth noting. First, Henry of Glarus rejected the last of the possible modes (the Locrian) with B as the keynote on the grounds that the last three steps, F–B, were all whole tones, a succession that medieval musicologists called *diabolus in musica*. Second, the first and last of Glarus's six modes, corresponding to our major and minor, had been rejected by the church authorities, the former on the grounds that it was the *modus lascivus*, characteristic of vulgar (folk) music.

known whether the associations are psychologically inherent or culturally conditioned. That they are psychologically inherent might be conjectured from the fact that children sensitive to music report these associations ("glad" and "sad") at a very early age, but the evidence is not conclusive: they may be responding to subtle cues from adults. And even if this is not so, the associations may still be culturally conditioned in the sense that the intonations of speech in, say Indo-European languages may correspond to characteristic features of the one or the other mode, depending on what is said. For example, the minor scale tends to "gravitate downward" because of the lowered third and sixth steps, and so also may the voice when something "sad" is uttered. There are, however, exceptions to the minor-sad–major-glad rule. Many "sad" songs are in major keys, and many lively dances in minor ones. Whether these exceptions belie the generally accepted connotation, or whether they express subtle mixtures of gladness and sadness, is difficult to say.

Western music, more so than the music of any other culture, has incorporated so-called "architectural principles." The large musical forms (fugues, sonatas, symphonies, tone poems, and operas since Wagner) are constructed on the principle of thematic development. A theme acquires "meaning" only by being juxtaposed to other themes and by appearing in different musical contexts in the course of the development of the large composition. It thereby acquires an "identity." The listener follows its transformations, departures, and arrivals as he would an actor's in a play, except that concrete meaning has been distilled out of the plot and only a diffuse abstract "meaningfulness" remains.

The nineteenth-century romanticists, particularly Berlioz, Liszt, and Wagner, injected semantic meaning into the framework of abstract "meaningfulness" by associating persons or situations with particular themes, called *leitmotifs*. Wagner went especially far in adapting the leitmotif technique to the music drama (as he called his operas). Not only the action on the stage but also the thoughts of the characters are reflected in his orchestrations. The orchestra in Wagner's operas takes on the role of the chorus in the Greek tragedy, that of commenting on the meaning of the dramatic action, uttering these "comments" via musical imagery instead of in words.

The harmonic and contrapuntal richness of Western music gives it the power to "say" several things at once. In the famous finale of *The*

Valkyr, the god Wotan, having surrounded his sleeping daughter with fire, pronounces the invocation "Whoever fears my spear shall never pass through the fire." The leitmotifs denoting "sleep" and "fire" are combined as the orchestral accompaniment of Wotan's words, while the invocation itself is intoned as the leitmotif that in the next opera of the tetralogy (*The Ring of the Nibelung*) will denote the fearless hero, Siegfried, for whom neither Wotan's spear nor Loki's fire have meaning.

In this way Wagner realized his conception of art as an evocation of internal meaning through several parallel "inputs," as the contemporary communication engineer would say. The viewer sees myth come to life, the sleeping demigoddess surrounded by a raging fire and, silhouetted on a cliff, the tragic figure of a god destined to lose his power. The listener hears the endless recurring sleep motif, suggesting eternity, and, through the sudden appearance of the new (Siegfried) motif, is told something that even a god does not know—the coming of a man bound neither by fear, custom, conscience, nor obligations.

Music is a language with its own system of meanings. In order to grasp what is being expressed in a concerto, a symphony, or an instrument solo, the listener must acquaint himself with "the metalanguage" of music. It is not absolutely necessary that one have a technical training in music to understand what is happening, but one must be willing to expend the effort required to familiarize himself with the "semantics" of that art.

APPLICATIONS

I. George Steiner believes that internal (or private) associations with words have been reduced by the events of the twentieth century. He points out that, in public life, totalitarianism has corrupted language by "unspeaking" the actual past and conjugating verbs in the "depersonalized present" and in the "utopian future." Studies of urban telephone calls indicate that there has been a drastic diminution and standardization of vocabulary and syntax. Madison Avenue advertising has regularized and controlled the "free associations" linked to words.

Do you agree with these generalizations about the state of linguistic "crisis"? You can do a little test of your own. Using the word list of the Kent-Rosanoff experiment (p. 160), ask a number of your friends (or the members of your class) to respond with internal associations. Compare the results and decide on that basis whether there is a tendency toward standardization. Write a paper interpreting the results as you see them.

II. Browse through the articles in one or two of the magazines devoted to motorcycling as a sport. "Bike" riders, it will soon become apparent to you, have their own language (jargon).

1) Does the jargon of the "biker" seem to be richer in images of motion than everyday English? Assemble evidence.
2) If so, do these images reflect the dominant life style of the "bikers"?
3) Read Ernest Hemingway's "The Short Happy Life of Francis Macomber." Analyze the passage in which he describes the charge of the rhinoceros while Macomber tries to pick him off with his Mannlicher. Note and describe the kind of imagery Hemingway uses (pay particular attention to the verbs and the verbals—words ending in "–ing"). What is the effect of this imagery?
4) Repeat this analysis with page 47 in James Joyce's *Ulysses* (New York, Modern Library) ("A woman and a man. I see her skirties."). Can you deduce any useful principles about writing from this kind of analysis?

III. André Gide's beautiful little novel *Strait Is the Gate* may seem to be simple and uncomplicated until you associate the imagery with one of the dimensions of "metaphorical extension" (pp. 173–74)—the class labeled *paths*.

1) How can the discursive meaning of the novel be discerned from the metaphorical language?
2) The study of a novel's imagery or metaphorical language almost always reveals whether a writer knows how to use this powerful instrument to reinforce his "meaning" or whether he dissipates his meaning by using imagery and metaphor randomly. Apply this approach to the last novel you have read and comment on your conclusions.

IV. If you are interested in the "semantics of music," you can do an exercise that may throw light on moods associated with major and minor scales. Play excerpts from ten or fifteen pieces of classical music to a friend and ask him (her) to describe in two or three words the mood the music induces. Try this with several people. Then check their responses with the composers' notations.

V. In literature, "leitmotif" is called "theme" as a rule (though Thomas Mann preferred to use the term "leitmotif" with its overtones of musical meaning when discussing his own work, such as *The Magic Mountain*). The meaning of "theme" can be formulated as follows: a theme is an idea—thus an abstraction—that recurs in a piece of fiction. It is represented in the fiction itself by all the concrete utterances, each a linguistic fact, that refer to it and bring it to the reader's attention. In François Mauriac's *Thérèse Desqueyroux*, the references to walls, bars, grills, cages, enclosed places, caged animals, and so on, are images or "motifs" attached to the theme of captivity, which Mauriac identifies in the opening passages as the dominant one of the book. Thus, in Mauriac's opening equation of Thérèse with a caged beast, he presents both in a state of capacity. *Captivity* is the theme of this particular image and, as we learn from observation, the theme of the book. At the same time, each later mention of caged animals or of cages is established as a "motif" since it recalls the theme to the reader's mind.

1) Using any novel that you have read recently, try the following exercise: each time an image occurs more than twice, write down the image and the "motif" you associate with the image. These are your "linguistic facts" or your extensional connotations. Index cards might simplify this operation.

2) After you have assembled your data, infer what the theme of the novel is.

3) This exercise diverts attention from the novel as an individual work of art and focuses it on the novel as material for the study of the creative mind. What does this exercise reveal to you about the psychology of creation?

4) Apply this approach to William Faulkner's *The Sound and the Fury*. As you do so, keep in mind the dilemma Marcel Proust points out in *Contre Sainte-Beuve*: that the private personality that produces the great book is not identical with the public one accessible to biographical study.

VI. Try roughly the same experiment with the next film you see, noting images that do not seem to be part of the narrative itself. Do these non-discursive images contribute to the meaning?

10/content analysis

Content analysis comprises systematic methods aimed at "distilling" internal meanings from verbal outputs. Frequently these internal meanings suggest not so much the intent of the speaker or writer as they reflect his state of mind, over which he may have no control and of which he may even be unaware. Seen from this angle, content analysis appears to be based on the same principle as stylistic analysis. Since stylistic analysis is simpler, it will be useful to make a short digression to examine its underlying principles.

As has been said, any utterance is a sequence of unit symbols. In the case of a written text, the smallest of these units are clearly identifiable: they are the letters of the alphabet. If we count the occurrence of each letter in a large "corpus" (that is, a long text) of, say, the size of an average book (about a half million letters), we shall find that each of the letters appears with a frequency characteristic of the language in which it is written, regardless of the content of the particular book. We have already mentioned these frequencies in connection with the first-order letter approximation to English (cf. p. 62). Thus, of the total number of letters in an English text, .105 of the occurrences will be the letter "e," .072 will be the letter "t," and so on. Newspaper linotypists used to fill space with the "words" "etaoin shrdlu," the letters of the alphabet in order of the frequency of their occurrence.

As I write this, I am unaware of these frequencies; I produce them "automatically" because I am writing in English. Moreover, there is not much I can do about these frequencies unless I really put my mind to it, say, by selecting special words, which would seriously constrict the content of what I write. Without such selective effort, I am *bound* to reproduce the letter frequencies of the language in which I am writing. For this reason, if a corpus produced by me (say this book) were compared with a corpus produced by someone else, the two corpora would be indistinguishable with regard to letter frequencies. It follows that the author of the corpus could not be identified in this manner.

Instead of letters, we can take larger units, say, words, as our units of statistical analysis. Here there will be marked differences. For example, the proper name "Bloom" appears more frequently in James Joyce's *Ulysses* than in almost any other corpus because Bloom is the name of the hero of that novel. The word "semantics" occurs in this book more frequently than in many other books because the subject of this book is semantics. Word frequency analysis may reveal something about the content of a corpus but it will not necessarily identify the author. Thus, if we did not know that Joyce was the author of *Ulysses*, we could not infer the authorship from the fact that "Bloom" occurs in that book with an unusually large frequency because, clearly, Joyce might have chosen some other name for his hero. There are, however, methods of statistical analysis that help to identify the author of a corpus. Several different statistical measures together can present a profile of a corpus that may be as characteristic of an individual as is his voice, his handwriting, or his fingerprints.

Sentence length is an example of a statistical measure that varies, sometimes widely, from author to author. L. A. Sherman compared the average sentence length in corpora of several English authors and obtained the following results.[1]

Author	Average number of words per sentence
Fabyan	63.02
Spencer	49.82
Hooker	41.40
Macaulay (essays)	22.45

That sentence length is a stylistic feature of an author can be seen by comparing different samples of the same author's output. Sherman calculated the average sentence length in four samples of 10,000

---

1. L. A. Sherman, *Analytics of Literature*, in C. Herdan, *Type-Token Mathematics* (London, The Hague, and Paris: Mouton and Company, 1960), p. 55.

sentences, each from Macaulay's *History of England*, and found them to be respectively 23.33, 23.18, 22.32, and 23.73—all close to 22.45, the average sentence length in the 500-sentence sample taken from the same author's *Essays*.

By itself, neither average sentence length nor any other statistical measure is a reliable indicator of authorship because the statistical aspects of any given author's style may vary with the subject on which he is writing and also generally in the course of his life. However, if several different statistical measures are examined, the author's stylistic "profile" emerges and may identify him.

A famous case of disputed authorship arose in connection with a medieval work entitled *Imitatio Christi*. The question was whether the book came from the pen of Thomas à Kempis (c1379–1471) or was the work of Jean Charlier de Gerson (1363–1429). G. U. Yule compared frequencies of occurrences of words in *Imitatio* with those in other known works of Thomas à Kempis and of Gerson.[2] He also compared the works of the two authors with each other. For each comparison, Yule obtained an index of similarity (called the *coefficient of correlation*). It turned out to be .9 between *Imitatio* and Kempis, .81 between *Imitatio* and Gerson, and .84 between Kempis and Gerson. This means, roughly, that Gerson is about "as far" from Kempis as he is from *Imitatio*, but that Kempis is considerably closer to *Imitatio* than he is to Gerson; also that Kempis is closer to *Imitatio* than is Gerson. On this basis, the authorship is attributed to Kempis.[3]

It goes without saying that the reliability of the method is checked by applying it to works of *known* authorship to see whether it attributes authorship correctly.

Content analysis extends these methods to include semantic factors. The aim of content analysis is focused on the problem of inferring the state of mind of the author who produced the corpus, the subject of his concern, his attitudes, the purposes for which the corpus was produced, and the like. Some of these questions can be answered, of course, without applying any systematic techniques, simply by reading what has been written. However, different people may read

2. G. U. Yule, *The Statistical Study of Literary Vocabulary*, quoted in C. Herdan, *The Advanced Theory of Language as Choice and Chance* (Berlin, Heidelberg, and New York: Springer-Verlag, 1966), pp. 161–63.
3. The meaning of "correlation" in its technical sense is more fully explained in Chapter 17 (cf. pp. 313–15).

different meanings *into* what they read or hear. The techniques of content analysis serve to establish *objective* evidence for our impressions and possibly to bring out features of the corpus that may have escaped the "naked eye."

The "author" of a corpus subjected to content analysis may be not a single person but a whole group. For example, a government-controlled press usually reflects the preoccupations, the attitudes, sometimes the intentions of the ruling circles of a country. Some of these preoccupations, attitudes, or intentions may "shine through" the verbal output whether the "collective author" has intended to display them or not. Propaganda analysts are naturally interested in these internal meanings. During a war or a period of intense hostility between nations, each keeps a watchful eye on sources that may give indications of the "state of mind" of the other. During World War II and the period of the cold war that followed it, content analysis in one form or another became a principal tool of the intelligence agencies of rival powers.[4]

The simplest indicator of the degree to which an author or a "collective author" is preoccupied with any subject is the frequency of allusions to it. It is hardly surprising that, in times when events of prime political concern occur in some part of the world, the press will allude to those areas with increasing frequency. The same is true of allusions to political figures, "issues," and so forth, that come into prominence. A quantitative analysis may place these fluctuations under a greater resolving power and bring out certain features of the process not otherwise immediately apparent. For instance, if we plot a curve showing the frequency of allusion to an item against time, we can get a picture of the rate at which a situation becomes of increasing concern, whether the concern builds up gradually or "flares up," the size and sharpness of the peak, the rate of decline, and so on. We can superimpose two or more such curves taken, say, from the "prestige papers" of two or more major powers and in this way see "leads" or "lags" if they occur; that is, which "collective mind" became focused on the issue first and how long it took for the attention of the other "collective mind" to turn to the same issue.

4. In the United States, "Kremlinology" refers to studies purporting to reveal the internal politics of the Soviet hierarchy. The studies make extensive use of content analysis. Cf. Michel Tatu, *Power in the Kremlin: From Khrushchev to Kosygin* (New York: Viking Press, 1969).

"Collective mind" as used here is not a mystical concept. It is a *theoretical* concept. If there *were* such a thing, it would manifest itself in some way. The gross statistical indices of large verbal outputs representing a set of policies, attitudes, concerns, and so on, *are* such manifestations and justify the assumption that such "collective minds" exist.

Figure 7 is a simple illustration of what may be a manifestation of a "collective mind." [5] The dotted line is a plot of the number of

Figure 7

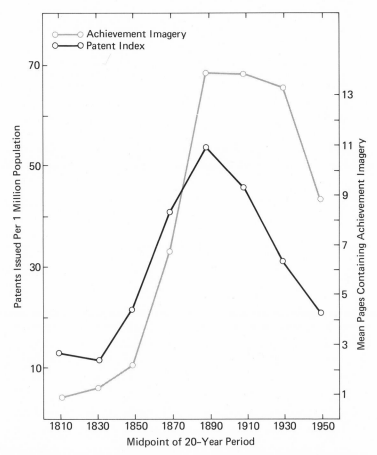

5. Eugene Webb and Karlene H. Roberts, "Unconventional Uses of Content Analysis in Social Science," in *The Analysis of Communication Content*, eds. George Gerbner, Ole R. Holsti, Klaus Krippendorff, William J. Paisley, and Philip J. Stone (New York: John Wiley and Sons, 1969).

patents per year per million population issued in the United States from 1810 to 1950. Note the peak in 1870, soon after the Civil War, when the country reached the "takeoff point" of industrialization. The solid line represents data obtained by content analysis. It is a plot of frequencies with which words denoting or connoting initiative, self-reliance, drive for achievement, success, and so on, occurred in children's readers. Note the similarity of the curves.

The early American inventor was an adventurer, a pioneer of technology. Typically, he worked alone in a homemade laboratory. He represented the well-known American virtues of industry, practicality, ingenuity, independence, and perseverance. The number of patents issued per million population can be taken as an index of the degree to which the career of the inventor attracted Americans and the intensity with which they pursued it. Reasonably, the index of achievement imagery in children's readers can be taken as a measure of the intensity with which ideas conducive to such a career were inculcated in young minds.

More refined analysis shows that the strongest correlation (cf. p. 314) between the two sets of data is obtained when the patent index is matched with the achievement index of about *twenty years* before. It is tempting to conclude that the content of the school readers had an impact on the young generation's subsequent choice of career and on the energy with which they pursued it.

No less noteworthy than the sudden upsurge of both curves is their subsequent gradual decline. On the one hand, the growth of large industrial combines institutionalized technological innovations. The early freewheeling, individually initiated, and personally conducted technological research was progressively replaced by systematized, organized team research, ordered and supported by corporations. As a result, the number of individual patents per million population started to decline. At the same time, the frontier was pushed to the limits of the continent and the economic role of the individual entrepreneur diminished. The relative weight of initiative and independence as ingredients of "success" declined too. This also is reflected in the "collective mind," the downward trend of the achievement imagery curve. It would be interesting to see whether a similar achievement imagery index, obtained by a content analysis of popular magazine stories, dime novels, and so forth, would show a similar rise and decline.

Content analysis may be of varying degrees of "hardness." It is "hard" to the extent that the interpretations are directly related to the data and are free of improvised conjectures. Suppose we look to content analysis for a confirmation or a refutation of the following hypothesis: The intuitively perceived increase of hostility between China and the U.S.S.R. from 1958 to 1962 is reflected in the frequency and intensity of pejorative adjectives that the press of one side applied to the leaders or policies of the other side. Having set up certain criteria (specifying pejorative adjectives, measures of their intensity, etc.), we proceed to collect data and to process them in accordance with these criteria. Note that in order to test the hypothesis we must state it *in advance*. That is, before we process the data, we must state specifically *what sort of evidence* will be interpreted as a confirmation of the hypothesis and what sort will be regarded as a refutation. (Compare this procedure with a similar one in a simpler situation described on p. 308.)

It is important to note that the "hardness" of the analysis depends not so much on the self-evident relevance of the data to the hypothesis as on the clarity with which the criteria to be examined are defined. In the example relating "achievement imagery" to the number of patents, the point at issue is not whether the relation of "achievement imagery" to subsequent choice of career can be directly demonstrated but whether the manifestations of "achievement imagery" are sufficiently clearly defined for the purpose of the analysis. In a "hard" analysis, the analyst would have to state explicitly and in advance how the index of "achievement imagery" is to be constructed—by how frequently certain specified words occur or the like. A definitive test of "hardness" is whether or not the task of collecting the data can be entrusted to a clerk who knows nothing about content analysis or the purpose to which it is put.

In some cases this ideal cannot be achieved. For instance, the intensity of "achievement imagery" may be expected to be reflected not so much in frequencies of specific *words* as in frequencies of recurring themes dealing with success, self-reliance, and so forth. Recognition of such themes requires a "feeling" for the subject matter and so involves subjective impressions. Analysis of this sort can be "hardened" by using several *independent* evaluators. If they agree on their ratings of samples with regard to the degree of emphasis on "achievement imagery," their agreement can be taken as evidence that the index is based on something objective, something other than the impressions of a particular evaluator.

A great deal of work in content analysis is devoted to the development of techniques for distilling as much of internal meanings as possible while keeping the criteria of evaluation as objective as possible.

Modern data-recording and data-processing equipment makes it possible to record and to process vast amounts of data, provided the items can be clearly categorized. The task of the content analyst is to select categories readily recognizable and relevant to the purpose of the analysis.

Ole R. Holsti described a program for a systematic recording of data gathered from corpora relevant to the study of international relations (speeches and writings of statesmen, diplomats, delegates to the United Nations, etc.).[6] The program includes a "semantic differential dictionary." Recall that the semantic differential singles out three principal dimensions of psychological connotations of words: the evaluative, the potency, and the activity dimensions (cf. Chapter 9). Key words occurring in the corpora can be accordingly *coded* by triples of numbers. The "semantic differential dictionary" is a list of such coded words. For instance, the word "accost" is coded $(-3,2,2)$ to indicate that it is at the extreme negative end on the evaluative dimension (here the seven intervals range from -3 to $+3$), has next to the largest value on the potency dimension, and the same on the activity dimension.

Clearly the coding of individual words is not sufficient. Meaning emerges only in context. Context is coded in terms of categories indicating roughly "who said what about who did what how to whom." Specifically, the symbols for marking a running text include

The author of the document
The perceiver when other than the author
The agent (or an action) and modifiers
The action and modifiers
The direct object of the action (when target is the indirect object)
The target action and modifiers

6. Ole R. Holsti, "A Computer Content-Analysis Program for Analyzing Attitudes: The Measurement of Qualities of Performance," in *Analysis of Communication*, eds. G. Gerbner, *et al.*

Consider the following sentence:

"During the years since my last report, the wealthy nuclear powers have not provided enough vital economic aid to the many poor underdeveloped, noncommitted nations." Besides the author of the statement, who in this case is also the perceiver, we have

The agent—"the nuclear powers"
Modifier of the agent—"wealthy"
The action—"provided"
Modifier of the action—"not enough"
The direct object—"economic aid"
Modifiers of the target—"poor, noncommitted"

From the mass of data so coded and recorded, one can recover information—specifically, from the coded sentence above, one can recover the information that Mr. So-and-so, representing a country So-and-so, on such-and-such a day perceived the underdeveloped countries as "poor" and "noncommitted," the nuclear powers as "wealthy," and the economic aid provided by the latter to the former as "not enough."

So far no more information has been recovered than was put in. However, massive content analysis is concerned not so much with specific items of information as with what emerges from a great many items. The larger the corpus, the more "stable" become the gross emergent meanings, emphases, and attitudes because the less important become the idiosyncracies and fluctuations of the states of mind of specific authors on specific occasions. The gross characteristics of a large corpus are not subjected to conscious control of individuals. Even when produced by a single individual, a large corpus is less subject to his conscious control than is a specific utterance. The situation resembles that in handwriting. I can, perhaps, disguise my handwriting in a single sentence, but if I have to write several pages rapidly, my handwriting will identify me no less surely than my fingerprints. My muscular habits emerge in it, regardless of what I consciously try to do. In the same way, a "collective mind"—its perceptions, its attitudes, possibly even its intentions—may emerge in a large collectively produced corpus.

Data-recording and data-processing technology makes it possible to record and to process a large number of categories. In addition to the syntactic code mentioned above ("who said what about who did what how to whom"), Holsti mentions several "theme codes" used in his program, such as:

The time element: current, past, future
The mode of expression: indicative, normative, comparative, imperative, probabilistic, interrogative, aspiring
Conditional statements: antecedent (if . . .), subsequent (then . . .)

Which of these may be especially relevant to the task of "distilling meanings" is not known a priori. This can be decided only in the light of ongoing experience with content analysis. Nevertheless the currently used categories make it possible to answer many questions of intrinsic interest, such as:

How do two given corpora compare in their relative emphasis on past, present, and future?
Was there a change in the way country A tended to perceive country B over a given period?
To what extent are reported facts, normative judgments (good, bad, encouraging, alarming), theoretical inferences (if . . . then), aspirations, etc., predominant in a given corpus?
How do two corpora compare in this respect? Are time trends discernible? Etc.

Analysis is "soft" if interpretations of the content of a corpus are offered without advance specification of what was being sought and how the findings would be interpreted. When we read a letter, an editorial, a poem, or what not and declare the meaning we have fathomed from it by "reading between the lines," we are in effect making a "soft" content analysis.

Charles Osgood (who developed the method of the semantic differential, cf. Chapter 9) made an analysis of Goebbels's diaries.[7] He found that whenever Goebbels mentioned infighting within the Nazi party leadership, he referred to Hitler more frequently than in other relevant contexts. A psychologically oriented content analyst might be

7. Paul Joseph Goebbels, Hitler's minister of propaganda (1933–45).

tempted to infer that Goebbels saw Hitler in the role of supreme judge or arbiter of these conflicts.

The analysis was "soft" because the hypothesis (the interpretation of the difference in the frequencies of allusions to Hitler in different contexts) occurred to the author only *after* this difference was discovered. The hypothesis is certainly plausible. It may well have been the case that when Goebbels wrote about internal strifes in the Nazi party he thought of Hitler as the arbiter. However, more is required in the way of *independent* evidence to confirm the hypothesis. Here we have a good example of how the results of a "soft" content analysis can be checked by seeking out corpora similar to Goebbels's diaries and examining them with a view to finding similar linkages between concern with internal strife and the calling to mind of an authority or an arbiter.

Psychoanalysis is a foremost example of "soft" content analysis. In a psychoanalytic session, the patient verbalizes his "stream of consciousness" and the analyst distills internal meanings from what is said. In general, the analyst does not look for anything specific. He takes what happens to come out.

The basis of the psychoanalyst's interpretations is a theory of unconscious determinants of behavior, in particular of verbal behavior. Content analysis of the patient's presumably free associations aims at uncovering those unconscious determinants. It is assumed that, once the patient becomes aware of his "repressed" desires and fears, he will be freed from restraints and compulsions that constitute the basis of his neurosis.

This basic idea has been credited by Sigmund Freud (generally regarded as the founder of psychoanalysis) to Dr. Josef Breuer, a prominent general practitioner. Breuer used hypnosis in the treatment of disorders of psychogenic origin. Freud was particularly impressed by Breuer's account of a case involving a talented and educated young girl who developed several hysteria-type symptoms while nursing her sick father, to whom she was very attached. Breuer hypnotized the girl and urged her to tell him, while under hypnosis, about what oppressed her. The most significant thing about this procedure was that while the girl was under hypnosis she seemed aware of definite connections between her symptoms and certain past experiences, but in the waking state she knew nothing about them. All of these ex-

periences occurred during the time she was nursing her father. Moreover, the connections between the symptoms could be viewed as
symbols of the experiences. The experiences and the associated repressed affects were the *meanings* of the symptoms. The girl's symptoms vanished following Breuer's treatment.

Breuer and Freud published a joint paper entitled "On the Psychic
Mechanisms of Hysterical Phenomena" (1893) and thereby laid the
foundations of the psychoanalytic method. They called their treatment "cathartic" because the process seemed to work by inducing
an emotional purging. Hysteria, said Breuer and Freud, was "a disease
of the past," a sort of "monument" to some traumatic and repressed
episode in the psyche of the sufferer. The patient is aware of the
monument but not of what it commemorates; however, his "unconscious mind" knows.

Freud modified Breuer's technique by abandoning hypnosis in favor
of "free association." For this, there were several reasons. To begin
with, not everyone can be hypnotized. It appeared also that the cures
effected by hypnosis, although frequently dramatic, were of short
duration. Finally, Freud had an aversion to hypnosis on general principles; he was "against the tyranny of suggestion," as he put it.[8]

The substitution of free association for hypnosis probably made the
task of the therapist more difficult. The presumed repressed experiences had to be inferred from whatever happened to come into
the patient's mind, whereas in hypnosis these experiences were
allowed to "surface" by removing the inhibitions imposed by the
conscious mind. Everyone who has undergone psychoanalysis will
testify to how difficult it is to produce genuinely "free" associations,
that is, to eliminate the control exercised by the conscious mind. It is
also difficult to answer the question how the "real meanings" of the
patient's freewheeling verbal output can be distinguished from what
the imagination of the *therapist* happens to suggest. Corroboration by
the patient is not a reliable criterion of validity; the therapist may
unknowingly impose his own interpretations on the patient. It seems
that abandoning formal hypnosis may not have excluded the possibility of mutually reinforcing suggestions between the patient and
the therapist. From these suggestions, a picture may emerge that may
or may not be relevant to the patient's actual problem. Nor is the

8. For fuller discussion, see A A. Brill, *The Basic Writings of Sigmund Freud* (New
York: Modern Library, 1938), pp. 7–10.

patient's "insight" into the nature of his difficulties a satisfactory criterion of the validity of interpretations. The "insight" may well be a camouflage of the true origins of the symptoms, if indeed the origins were embedded in early experiences.

All these dangers are recognized by most psychoanalysts, and precautions against them are said to have been designed. However, a discussion of psychoanalysis as a theory of personality and as a therapeutic technique is not within the scope of this book. On the other hand, the semantic concepts underlying that method are directly relevant to the present discussion. We shall confine ourselves to these.

The following will serve as an example of an extremely "soft" content analysis suggested by psychoanalytic ideas. The case study was cited by Peter F. Ostwald.

"A middle-aged lawyer, whose fortune and professional reputation had crumbled as a result of personal and economic failures, overstressed certain words and word groupings. Most notable were exaggerated or even incorrect stresses in word couples like 'par'-ty pol-itics,' 'pó-lice pró-tection,' 'pos-ible part-nerships.' From other information obtained about this man, it became apparent that he had failed to develop emotionally much further than the sexually ambivalent orientation of early childhood. For instance, in the face of extremely vengeful feelings toward women, he quite generally directed his dependency strivings toward men.

"An analysis of the stress anomaly in his speech showed that the explosive overemphasis was a veiled calling out for his father, whose early death had robbed him of the emotional support needed to cope with a crippled mother and two elderly psychotic sisters. The patient had never given up the infantile babbled form of paternal address, pá-pá, in favor of more adult versions: pápa, papá, father, etc. Now in his unhappy depressed state, energetic mouthing of the aforementioned word couples gave him an illusory way to magically call out for a father. His associations to the overstressed words (e.g., 'pó-lice, part'-nerships') also revealed fantasies in which an omnipresent agent, usually masculine, was to rescue him from distress." [9]

The extreme "softness" of this analysis is evidenced by its ad hoc character: a possible connection is suggested between a peculiarity

9. Peter F. Ostwald, "How the Patient Communicates about Disease with the Doctor," in *Approaches to Semiotics*, ed. Thomas A. Sebeok (London, The Hague, and Paris: Mouton & Company, 1964), p. 25.

in a patient's speech and his troubles; thereupon the peculiarity is promoted to a symbol of the origins underlying the neurosis. The speculation is surely an intriguing one and ought not to be summarily dismissed for lack of more convincing evidence. However, instead of offering the speculation as an "explanation" of what is observed, an investigator seriously concerned with the mechanism of symbolic transformation should make his conjecture the *starting point* of an investigation aimed at finding evidence for (or against) a general hypothesis: at times peculiarities of speech reveal internal meanings related to symbolizing particular psychic stresses. For instance, one could be on the lookout for patients who put exaggerated stress on pairs of words beginning with "m" to see whether a larger than expected number of them suffered an early traumatic separation from their mothers, or something of the sort.

Another example of "soft" content analysis is the interpretation of dreams, also a technique of psychoanalytic therapy. The meaning of dreams has long been a subject of speculation, and, as often happens when methods of validation are lacking, whatever is suggested becomes established as a firm belief. Dreams have been traditionally interpreted as messages from the world of the supernatural sent as promises or warnings to selected people. The Bible tells of how Joseph interpreted Pharaoh's dreams about the seven fat and seven lean cows (portending seven bountiful years followed by seven years of famine) and how this foreknowledge enabled Pharaoh to hoard grain, to be sold at high prices during the lean years.

Psychoanalytic theory views dreams as symbolic manifestations of unconscious processes. As such, they can be interpreted as "visual metaphors." Recall that a metaphor abstracts some element in the connotation of a word that is especially salient. Objects and situations that play a prominent part in dreams are often interpreted as symbols of objects which, because of cultural or emotional inhibitions, cannot be visualized explicitly. Most frequently, dreams are interpreted in the psychoanalytic settings as symbolic manifestations of repressed sexual desires. For instance, Freud interpreted Joseph's dream of the seven sheaves of wheat to mean that his brothers were bowing to his sexual superiority—Joseph's sheaf remained standing upright. It must be admitted that the symbolism of some dreams is entirely obvious, especially against the background of the dreamer's specific difficulties. Still, the assumption that *every* dream has a significance relative to the therapeutic situation may lead both the therapist and the patient astray. Again, validation techniques are lacking, and attempts to develop such techniques have been neither numerous nor systematic. This is a pity because the idea that dreams are a "symbolic language" is both plausible and intriguing. Languages of some birds and insects have been deciphered in great detail and have become rich sources of insight into animal behavior. There is no reason why the same could not be attempted with the dreams of human beings.

Some psychoanalysts resist the idea of conducting systematic, "hard" investigations of phenomena with which they are concerned on the grounds that each individual is unique and generalizations are unwarranted. To be sure, it would be futile to compile a dictionary of dream symbols akin to those used by fortunetellers. On the other hand, it is by no means true that the "uniqueness of the individual" precludes the discovery of general principles. Each of us is "unique" in many different ways, anatomically, physiologically, and psychologically; nevertheless, some general principles of human anatomy, human physiology, and human psychology have been discovered. There is no reason why certain regularities governing the deeper psychic phenomena cannot also be discovered.

Recall that "hard" content analysis requires the researcher to formulate a specific hypothesis and to search for confirmation or refutation of the hypothesis. Assuming that dreams relate to the emotional life of the individual, we can formulate hypotheses. For instance, in psychoanalytic theory, the so-called Oedipus complex plays a central role. The male child, it is said, sees his father as a rival in his erotic strivings for his mother, and as such, the father becomes an object of repressed resentment. It can be expected that the father will play a prominent part in the child's dreams, and often he does. It happens, however, that at least in Western culture the father is also the dispenser of punishment and so possibly an object of resentment on that account. The question naturally arises as to whether the father dominates dreams (if he does) because he is the mother's lover or because he is the dispenser of punishment. Also, Malinowski showed that in the Trobriand Islands, where there are mother-surrogates, children did not show excessive attachment to the mother. Freud may have been overly impressed by the structure of middle-class Jewish life in an unpredictable culture regarding the Jew, and hence mothers may have been overprotective.

Now, there are some cultures in the South Pacific where the authority figure is not the father but an uncle (mother's brother). Here the two roles of the father are separated. It would be interesting to know which of the two, the father or the uncle, figures most frequently, if at all, and in what roles in the dreams of the children.

I was once told of a most interesting experiment designed to put to a test the symbolic significance of dreams. A girl suffering from enuresis was hypnotized and told under hypnosis that she was dreaming and that at the end of the dream she would wet her bed. She was then asked to relate her dream (as she was having it under hypnosis), and her story was taped. Responding to the hypnotic suggestion, she exclaimed as she woke up that she wet her bed. The tape was then taken to another girl also suffering from enuresis and unacquainted with the first. She was put under hypnosis and was told that she would be dreaming what she heard. The recorded dream was then played to her. Although it contained no explicit mention of the accident, the girl nevertheless exclaimed at the end of the dream that she wet her bed.

If this story is true, it may portend a momentous discovery: a physiological disorder "symbolized" in a dream may be triggered in another sufferer via the "symbol," something in the way malaria is transmitted from one person to another by a mosquito. Unfortunately, the evidence offered for this phenomenon is far from conclusive. It would have been more convincing if the experiment included a control. For example, a dream could have been induced in the first girl *without* the suggestion of the accident. If this "control" dream did *not* trigger bed-wetting in the second girl, this might have been interpreted as evidence that the symbolism of the dream induced by the suggestion of bed-wetting was indeed related to the symbolism of enuresis.

"Soft" content analysis is found also in literary criticism; in fact, much of contemporary literary criticism has been strongly influenced by psychoanalysis. Accordingly we find literary criticism centered around a psychoanalysis of major figures in fiction and drama. The hero of Sophocles' *Oedipus Rex* was psychoanalyzed by Freud himself. Since then most of Shakespeare's heroes have been put on the couch, as well as the heroes and heroines of Flaubert, Dostoevsky, Melville, Ibsen, and many others. Needless to say, the degree to which we accept analyses of this sort depends almost entirely on our own perceptions and dispositions. If the distilled "meanings" of what the figures say and do are meaningful to us, we accept them; otherwise, we reject them.

Occasionally, however, inferences about an author's state of mind, made on the basis of impressions, seem exceedingly plausible. This is so when the evidence marshaled in support of the inference is not likely to have accumulated by sheer chance.

As a first example, take the conjecture that Samuel Clemens was obsessed by the idea of a split personality. The following evidence is offered in support.

1. *The Prince and the Pauper* revolves around the theme of mistaken identity.
2. *Pudd'nhead Wilson* revolves around the theme of mistaken identity.
3. The Italian twins in *Pudd'nhead Wilson* appear in another (unpublished) story as a two-headed monster.
4. Mixed up twins occur in *Tom Sawyer Detective.*
5. During an interview in which Clemens was pulling the interviewer's leg (cf. p. 117), he declared that he had a twin brother, that they were mixed up in the bathtub, that one of them drowned, and that it was actually he, Samuel, who drowned, and that consequently he was really his twin brother.
6. He chose the pen name *Twain.*

Another example of convincing "soft" content analysis in the service of literary criticism is the analysis of popular literature, represented in the United States by the "private eye" adventure story, the stories found in large circulation magazines such as *True Confessions*, the pulps, and so forth. Being produced as salable commodities, these stories adhere to certain conventional models both in their characters and in their plots.

Practically all private detectives are bachelors; they are all tough and cynical; they live in a dog-eat-dog world of gamblers, nightclub operators, and business tycoons; they operate one-man businesses; they are on the side of the law but, unlike the police and the authorities, they are not constrained by the law; they can search apartments without warrants, buy information for money, punish transgressors who are not convicted, and so on. The plots of these stories are also strikingly similar. All action is a matter of matching wits and nerves, eluding the enemy and pursuing him, following hunches, which usually, and always finally, turn out to be right, proving that the lone operator is a more effective instrument of justice than "institutions." Typically, the adventures and escapades are interspersed with consumption of alcohol and sex. In one series of private eye books, I counted, on the average, one drink per page.

At times, specific restraints are explicitly imposed on the content of stories by editors of popular fiction publications. For instance, no romance in which the woman is significantly older than the man may be depicted; death of principal characters is taboo in many publications, and so on. The self-imposed codes of the various branches of the entertainment industry are, of course, instances of the same sort of censorship, although these codes show signs of breaking down under the influence of commercially successful "porno."

In short, the content analysis of mass-produced and mass-consumed fiction can be viewed as the deciphering of a code. The characters, the actions, the situations are symbols. The meanings behind the symbols may be the desires, fears, aspirations, wish-fulfillment fantasies, and ethical prescripts of the population for whom these vast verbal outputs are produced. The recurrence of almost identical symbols makes the task of deciphering the code relatively easy.

The situation is different when an author undertakes to deliver a specific message in "code," for example, with the view of eluding censorship. The satires of Jonathan Swift, Voltaire, and other social critics are well-known examples. The novelist Alberto Moravia used an indirect, oblique style to evade the censor during the dictatorship of Benito Mussolini in his satirical novel *The Masked Ball*, whose protagonist resembles the dictator himself. A recent dramatic example of deciphering a skillfully camouflaged message was the analysis by Edmund Wilson of Boris Pasternak's novel *Doctor Zhivago*. He writes:

One becomes more and more aware that Pasternak's book is studded with the symbolism of the Orthodox Church. The five barless windows of the house in Siberia are the five wounds of Jesus. (The number five elsewhere appears, and always with sinister significance: the five o'clock train from which the older Zhivago throws himself, the five conspirators who try to murder the partisan leader.) . . . Since "Yuri" [Zhivago's Christian name—A. R.] is the Russian equivalent of George, the Russian reader will have guessed by this time that Zhivago is St. George, the martyr, who is supposed to have paid with his life for his audacity in arguing Christianity with Diocletian. [The poem written by Zhivago about St. George's battle with the dragon confirms this conjecure.—A. R.] (One suspects that the legends of St. Larisa [Larisa, Zhivago's beloved—A. R.] and St. Eugraphos [Evgraph is Zhivago's mysterious half brother.—A. R.] . . . would reveal further connections between the characters and the hagiography of the Orthodox Church.)[10]

Thomas Mann's novel *The Magic Mountain* is permeated with references to the number seven. The names of major characters have seven letters: Castorp, Joachim, Clavdia, Behrens, Naphtha. Settembrini's name does not have seven letters, but the name itself is derived from the Italian word for "seven." The Dutchman's name Peeperkorn looks like another exception, but his name is always preceded by the honorific Mynheer (seven letters). The hero stays at the sanatorium for seven years, and there are seven tables in the dining room. The number of the hero's room is 34 ($3 + 4 = 7$). The consistency is too striking to be accidental. Unfortunately, the meaning behind this obsession with "seven" is not clear.

In summary, the methods of content analysis range from routine counting operations that can be fully automated to the fullest use of perceptive intuition. The aim of content analysis is to penetrate through the overt manifestations of language behavior (the verbal output) to the internal meanings that have instigated it. At times these internal meanings reveal themselves regardless of the author's intentions; at times they are obscured by the author's idiosyncratic language habits (as in abstruse poetry); at times they are camouflaged for one reason or another. Content analysis is essentially a decoding operation of the symbols in which internal meanings are coded, either wittingly or unwittingly by the writer or the speaker. Content analysis might be called "the semantics of the subliminal," and those who carry it out are working with a principle laid down by Freud as the basis of greater human enlightenment: "Where there was Id, let there be Ego!"

10. Edmund Wilson, "Doctor Life and His Guardian Angel," *The New Yorker* (November 15, 1955): pp. 213–38.

APPLICATIONS

I. In William Faulkner's *The Sound and the Fury*, three brothers each give an account of the same set of events (roughly). Though this is not the same thing as the triune personality, there are enough similarities to warrant a semantic analysis by those students interested in fresh approaches to literary criticism.

1) How would you briefly describe the character or personality of each of the brothers?
2) Which ten (or twenty) words occur most frequently in the Benjie section? in the Quentin section? in the Jason section? What kind of personality "pattern" would you associate with each of these frequencies, without regard for their Faulknerian context?
3) Does your association coincide with your perception of the character's personality in (1)?
4) This approach may be applied to almost any piece of fiction. It is a useful way of determining whether the author is capable of "discriminating" among his characters, whether he endows them with the foibles and eccentricities of expression that constitute the chief means for a writer to create plausible people in his work. If all of the characters speak in the same "voice" ("voice" is determined by vocabulary, idiom, syntax, imagery, etc.), then the writer has failed. In what other areas can semantic analysis be put to use? Try it in analyzing election speeches of political candidates.

II. Read a short story by Ernest Hemingway and one by Henry James. Do a word count on the sentences. Does it seem to you that sentence length is one distinguishing mark of each?

1) Do the same with three or four pages of William Faulkner, D. H. Lawrence, James Joyce, Samuel Johnson, and two articles from the *New York Times*. What inferences can you draw?
2) Now analyze four or five pages from two books written for young adolescents. Compare your results to those in (1). What are your conclusions, if any?
3) Next, analyze material from books written for preschool children. Again, any conclusions?

III. Return for a moment to Application I for Chapter 9. If you agree that there is a growing "standardization" of vocabulary (you need not— the proliferation of jargon and neologisms might be considered as evidence to the contrary), would you consider this tendency as an indication of a "collective mind"?

IV. Examine a number of children's books for their achievement imagery index, using a technique similar to the one suggested in Application V for Chapter 9.

1) Does the index compiled from present-day books support or deny the thesis that the curve of the index is declining?
2) Are there other imagery indices that seem to be more dominant? From these indices, what would you predict about the future of the young people exposed to these books? Granted that this is "soft" information, consider the possibility of conducting a research project with a "team" of your classmates.

V. Recently, in both films and fiction, we were treated to the spectacle of a "detective" (or government agent) who achieved an unparalleled following. He was James Bond, the creation of Ian Fleming. In almost every matter, Bond fits the description of the mystery-adventure hero given on pages 195–96.

1) If the formula for these stories was so familiar, how do you account for the enormous success of the James Bond figure? In what ways is he different from Mike Hammer or Nero Wolfe?
2) Do a content analysis of the Western "horse opera." Write it out so that you have it on hand for reference. When a Western film is shown at the local movie house, make a point of seeing it. Does it confirm your "soft" analysis? What is the "code" for the Western cowboy story?
3) Try to create "codes" for other genres of film or fiction (the soap opera, porno fiction, the domestic romance, etc.). What, if anything, do these "codes" tell you about our culture? That is, do they reveal anything about the unconscious or unspoken assumptions we live by but often cannot articulate to ourselves? For two excellent studies in this mode, see D. H. Lawrence's *Studies in Classic American Literature* and Leslie Fiedler's *Love and Death in the American Novel*.
4) What parts of these formulas have been adapted by the makers of the recent spate of black detective films?

11/pragmatics

Once we include the language user in the analysis of meaning, we are in the realm of pragmatics. We have departed from linguistics proper (the study of language as a self-contained phenomenon) and entered the area between linguistics and psychology, sometimes called psycholinguistics. The psycholinguist is concerned with internal meanings, those inside the language user. Having no direct access to what goes on in the language user's head, psycholinguists attempt to infer internal meanings by studying language behavior and the bearing it has on the way people reason, express themselves, and relate to each other. Here the center of interest is psychology rather than language in its own right. Pragmatics being a study of how language functions, it stands in relation to linguistics somewhat as physiology (the study of organic functions) stands in relation to anatomy (the study of organic structure).

To what extent language influences our perceptions is perhaps the most important question of pragmatics. That behavior certainly can be directly influenced by words is common knowledge and is hardly occasion for surprise since the biological function of language, including animal languages, is to induce behavior appropriate to corresponding signals. In the course of ordinary social interaction, we comply with each other's requests, answer each other's questions, and so on; in organized work activity, subordinates follow instructions of superiors; laws (strings of words) direct and prohibit specific acts. In short, language affects people's behavior at every turn. However, there is a very important difference between affecting *behavior* and affecting *perceptions*. In complying with verbal requests and even commands, we still retain a measure of autonomy, that is, a feeling of having a choice between complying and refusing to comply, even if the latter leads to undesirable consequences. Again, when we are given information, we may believe it or not, and if we are skeptical, we can check what we are told with what others say or with our own experience.

The situation is quite different if language can change perceptions for then it is possible to make us not only obey commands as a matter of choosing between compliance and consequences but also to make us *want* to obey commands, that is, to induce a feeling in us that we are obeying of our own free will. If language can change perceptions, we can be made to see things in such a way that we actually believe what someone else wants us to believe and desire what someone else wants us to desire. Schopenhauer, calling attention to a limitation on human freedom, once said: "Man can do what he will; but he cannot will what he will." If what we "will" depends on how we perceive the world, and if our perceptions can be manipulated by language, our autonomy is indeed in danger because we can be made to *will* what someone else wills.

In hypnosis, we have the clearest instance of manipulation of perception by language. A hypnotized person can be made to "see" a stick as a snake, a cigar box as a coffin, or what not. The subject can be "made" to perform senseless acts, not by threat but by inducing in him a compulsion, an irresistible desire to perform the act.

Mild forms of hypnosis can be seen to pervade many interactions between language and behavior, as illustrated by the following experiment.

Three groups of subjects are shown the same sequence of simple line drawings. In one group the drawings are associated with one set of names; in another no names are associated with the drawings; in the third the same drawings are given different names from those mentioned to the first group. For instance, the drawing shown in Figure 8 is labeled "eyeglasses" for the first group, is not labeled for the second group, and is labeled "dumbbells" for the third group. Afterward subjects are asked to reproduce the drawings from memory. Their drawings are then compared with the originals and distortions are noted. Some of the distortions can be easily accounted for as influenced by the name the experimenter suggested. Thus, if the drawing in Figure 8 is reproduced as in Figure 9, the influence of the

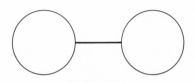

Figure 8

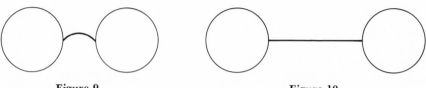

Figure 9   Figure 10

label "eyeglasses" is apparent; if it is reproduced as in Figure 10, the influence of "dumbbells" is apparent. Most of the subjects' reproductions are distorted, and the distortions tend to reflect the particular label suggested. Where no label was suggested, distortions were also observed, but with no bias one way or another. It seems as if the labeling of the drawing "pulls" the subject's perception from the shape depicted in the drawing to the shape suggested by the label.[1]

All of us know of cases where people "talk themselves into" believing or even perceiving things that are not so.

It seems there are three ways in which language can influence behavior.

1. *By giving information.*

Examples: To get to the post office in a strange city, I ask and receive directions. The information influences my behavior (the route I take). Here my autonomy is intact. I use the information to achieve my own original goal—to get to the post office.

At a lunch counter, my neighbor asks me to pass the mustard. Formally, this is a request, but it is semantically equivalent to giving

1. David T. Herman, Richard A. Lawless, and Richard W. Marshall, "Variables in the Effect of Language on the Reproduction of Visually Perceived Forms," in *Psycholinguistics,* ed. Sol Saporta (New York: Holt, Rinehart and Winston, 1961), pp. 537–51.

information. My neighbor has called my attention to the fact that the mustard is within my reach and not within his, and that he wants it. I have been trained in the observance of certain social amenities (manners) which include an obligation to render assistance in such situations. I discharge the obligation voluntarily and so still maintain my autonomy, even though my behavior is influenced by words.

I am told that a lake is polluted so I avoid swimming in it. My original goal (to swim) has been thwarted, but I still maintain autonomy. I weigh the goal I had in my mind against possible consequences of swimming in a polluted lake and make my own choice.

2. By threat of sanctions.

Example: I am confronted by a robber who commands me to give him my wallet and watch. In obeying, I am said to be acting under compulsion, that is, no longer voluntarily. Nevertheless I still retain a certain measure of autonomy since I do have a choice between obeying and resisting. Admittedly the choice is heavily weighted in one direction, but the fact that I *realize* that I am acting "against my will" in handing over my wallet and watch is evidence of the autonomy I retain.

3. By persuasion.

Example: I vacillate between deciding to buy a high-priced or a low-priced suit. I have already examined both for the quality of the fabric, the workmanship, the style, and so on, and I am inclined to buy the cheaper suit, feeling that the other one is not worth the price. In convincing me to buy the more expensive suit, the salesman may give me additional information, for instance, that this suit will wear longer. But he may also use other ploys. He may play on my vanity; he may arouse feelings of sympathy by his ingratiating manner. In this way he may change my perceptions by turning my attention to features of the more expensive suit, to his pleasant manner, and away from the difference in price. In this case my autonomy has been impaired: I am made to believe that I am making my own decision, whereas I would not have made it without the persuasive effort of the salesman.

Categorizing the influence of language on behavior is, like any other taxonomy, an idealization, for in actual practice the influence of language on behavior is mixed. Also, the three categories singled out here are themselves not pure. For instance, the robber who threatens sanctions if I do not obey may be also giving me explicit or implicit information of what will happen if I do not surrender the wallet and watch. The salesman can be said to be invoking implicit sanctions such as the prospect of my feeling regret if I do not buy the expensive suit. While these ambivalences are readily granted, the point to be made is that there is a marked gradation associated with different kinds of communication with respect to the effect on autonomy. At one extreme is the purely informative communication given by someone who has no control over behavior. At the other extreme is hypnosis, which controls behavior through a direct manipulation of perceptions and desires.

The relation between communication and the autonomy of the receiver touches upon grave ethical questions concerning the uses and abuses of language. There is no simple relation between the degree of autonomy of the receiver left intact by a communication and the ethical justification for the purposive use of language.

Modern views of education and upbringing stress the importance of respecting a child's autonomy, or, as is often admonished, encouraging the development of the child's own potential for "self-fulfillment." It is clear, however, that if education or upbringing is confined to purely informative communication, it would not accomplish the purpose intended. Mental and spiritual growth necessarily involve the changing of perceptions and perspectives. What the proponents of child-centered education and upbringing are saying is that *motivation* for these changes ought to originate in the child. Still, even if upbringing and education are directed at stimulating self-motivation, they nonetheless make an impact on the child's perceptions. Even "providing opportunities" for autonomous growth involves directing the child's attention to selected events, relations, or questions. It is difficult to establish a clean-cut boundary between encouraging autonomy and influencing perceptions.

The ethical questions raised by the persuasive mode of communication can be brought into sharper focus if the goals of the persuasive effort are kept in mind. In this way exploitative and nonexploitative goals can often be distinguished or, better said, while nonexploitative goals may be difficult to establish as such, exploitative goals are often conspicuous. The salesman who takes pride in his ability to sell refrigerators to Eskimos is clearly boasting of persuasive prowess put to exploitative purpose.

The vast persuasion industry, including large sectors of consumer advertising, public relations, and political lobbying, specializes in techniques of persuasion that are primarily exploitative. The purpose is explicit to the extent that the "product" of the industry is communication designed to manipulate perceptions so as to induce people to buy advertised products, to vote for announced candidates, to accept policies promoting the interests of special groups, and so forth.

A great deal has been said and written on this subject. The defenders of mass persuasion, especially in advertising, argue that the purpose of such communication is not to *create* desires for consumer goods, which allegedly already exist, but merely to inform the public of what is available and to aid competition, indispensable in a free enterprise economy. Cigarette manufacturers, for example, accused of increasing or maintaining the demand for a demonstrably harmful product, insist that cigarette advertising serves merely to lure smokers away from one brand to another. This claim would be better substantiated if it could be shown that a moratorium on cigarette advertising would not result in an appreciable decline in sales. However, cigarette manufacturers are understandably reluctant to agree to this experiment. Other arguments in defense of mass advertising of consumer goods are to the effect that advertising *does* increase demand, but that increased demand is in the public interest since an expanding economy depends on it.

The various functions and effects of mass advertising are difficult to separate. The crucial criterion of whether any persuasive effort is exploitative or not is whether the *interests of the targets* of the effort are or are not taken into account. Clearly the salesman who sells refrigerators to Eskimos does not have the interests of Eskimos in mind. A lobby promoting a piece of legislation does so primarily in the interests of a special group, not in the interests of those who are the targets of the pressure. The public relations firm promoting a candidate for office usually does so as a paid-for service to the candidate, not necessarily because the members of the firm are convinced that the candidate's election is in the public interest. That this is so is evidenced by the fact that such firms will usually contract to work for almost any candidate, and they do so with energy commensurate with the funds expended, not with the quality of the candidate.

In a society where competitive endeavor is viewed as a normal, justifiable activity, most people do not see that exploitative persuasion raises any ethical problems. Such persuasion is even considered to be an indispensable component in the ethics of certain professions. In civil cases, an attorney is obligated to use his persuasive skill in the interest of his client; in criminal cases, the prosecuting and defense attorneys are duty bound to make their respective cases as strong as possible, regardless of the doubts they may have about the guilt or innocence of the defendant. On the level of international relations, representatives of rival powers are obligated to make their nations appear just and peaceloving regardless of what they do, even to the extent of repeating and defending falsehoods.

The ethical problem arises when we examine the relation between the uses of exploitative communication and the role of language as man's principal mechanism of survival. If the proper functioning of this mechanism depends on its proper use as a tool of cognition, then any use that tends to blur the distinction between truth and falsehood, and so perverts this function, raises ethical questions. Again, if the proper functioning of symbolic language widens the cooperative sphere in human relations, then its use in pursuing unilateral advantages in conflicts impairs the cooperative function by emphasizing competition as the more fundamental aspect of social life.

It would seem that the persuasive power of words could be used to resolve or to exacerbate conflicts. On the whole, however, interest in pragmatics is stimulated more by the "practical" uses of persuasion. The Greeks took great interest and developed great skill in *rhetoric*, essentially the art of the persuasive use of language. Through the Middle Ages, rhetoric was the subject matter of the sophomore year in the standard four-year curriculum (freshmen studied grammar, juniors philosophy, and seniors theology). Today rhetoric is taught in the context of the "language arts," which sometimes includes *forensics*, the art of debating.

In the persuasion industry, skillful manipulation of symbols is highly valued. Special emphasis is put on associative (psychological) connotations of words. Brand names are selected for their evocative power. The brand names of soaps and detergents are supposed to suggest cleanliness; of breakfast foods, cheer and energy; of cosmetics, daintiness and glamour. Names of beer often sound German and are even displayed in Gothic letters because "good" beer is associated with Germany. Research of sorts is done on possibilities of tapping "deeper" internal meanings of symbols. Attempts are made to play on fears, anxieties, sexual frustrations, suppressed appetites.

When advertisers of motorcars got the idea that the automobile is a symbol of aggression, many cars were christened with names of wild beasts. Even a gasoline was advertised as a "tiger in the tank."

The history of election slogans in the United States reflects the attempts of political parties to elicit spontaneous enthusiasm from the voters ("Full Dinner Pail," "Sound Money," "Square Deal," "The Great Society") and, at times, hostility toward political rivals. After the Civil War, for example, the Republicans called the Democrats a party of "Rome, Rum, and Rebellion" because the Democrats depended for much of their support on Catholics, antiprohibitionists, and southerners. In 1952, the Republicans campaigned under the slogan "Twenty Years of Treason," alluding to Communist sympathizers in the Democratic administration.

The secret of the demagogue's success, as Adolf Hitler astutely pointed out, is to seize upon a single, simple, image-evoking idea and to keep hammering away at it without any variation. The technique amounts to the practice of mass hypnosis. If the idea connects with some deep-felt fear, hatred, or longing in the masses, the masses are moved to action. The simplest action is easiest—following a leader, fighting an enemy, shouting down opposition, and the like. These are precisely the sorts of actions the demagogue needs.

Much of mass advertising and political image-peddling follows the same formula and for the same reason. The action wanted is simple: buy a certain brand of product, vote for a particular candidate. Above all, the object of demagogy is to paralyze critical thought. Persistent repetition of slogans or brand names robs them of their meaning as elements of a symbolic language (since this meaning, as we have seen, must be flexible so as to change with context). The slogans become *signals* eliciting immediate, automatic responses, in the manner of signals that constitute animal languages.

Language is also used persuasively, although not necessarily exploitatively, for the purposes of social control. Social life imposes certain obligations on every member of a society. Laws, contracts, marriage vows, oaths of witnesses in court, oaths of office, etc., are typically couched in a peculiarly solemn style, sometimes archaic, to emphasize the permanence of the social institutions that enforce agreements, to pledge performance or restraint in certain acts, to tell the truth, and so forth.

Examples: "Hear ye! Hear ye!" "With this ring I thee wed." "So help me God!" "Know ye all by these presents. . . ." "On this 21st day of August, in the year of our Lord, 1970." Legislators vote with "Aye" instead of "Yes." "Legalese," the jargon of legal documents, is used not only to insure precision (cf. Chapter 4) but also to remind the reader of the enforcing authority.

These all are instances of persuasion because they affect behavior, not merely by providing information or by limiting choice in the face of threatened sanctions, but by putting people into a particular frame of mind induced by certain words, hence, by affecting their perceptions. No society can exist without effective persuasion via induced perceptions because no laws, rules, or regulations can be enforced by sanctions alone. No government has available enough coercive power to make everyone obey. People obey laws largely because they want to obey them. The process of socialization, essential in every human group, is that of inculcating certain perceptions and beliefs.

In addition to the three ways already mentioned by which language affects behavior, there is a fourth way that has attracted increasing attention in the past thirty or forty years and is especially relevant to pragmatics: Language may affect our perceptions, hence behavior, simply by "doing our thinking for us." This aspect of language was especially strongly emphasized by Edward Sapir and Benjamin Lee Whorf. Anthropologists and psycholinguists sometimes refer to the ideas advanced by these scholars as the Sapir-Whorf hypothesis. We shall give a brief account of Whorf's version.[2]

Whorf was an amateur linguist who became interested in the languages of preliterate people, particularly the languages of the North American Indians which were beginning to attract the attention of American anthropologists. He was impressed by both the lexical and the structural differences between these languages and the well-known ones, such as those of the Indo-European group. One expects, of course, that any language will lack words denoting referents that do not present themselves to the speakers. People who have no typewriters, teapots, or trumpets have no words for these objects. When they acquire the objects, they either invent words to denote them or

2. Benjamin Lee Whorf, "Linguistic Relativity and the Relation of Linguistic Processes to Perception and Cognition," in *Language, Thought, and Reality*, ed. J. Caroll (Cambridge, Mass.: The Technology Press and John Wiley and Sons, 1956), pp. 207–19. See also B. L. Whorf, *Four Articles on Metalinguistics* (Washington, D.C.: Foreign Service Institute, 1950).

borrow the words from other languages, just as we borrowed "kangaroo" and "boomerang" from the Australian aborigines. However, there may be lexical differences of another kind, having to do with the *distinctions* made in different languages. For instance, the Eskimos have three different words for snow, to designate falling snow, snow on the ground, and snow packed into blocks to be used for building igloos. On the other hand, in the Hopi language, the same word is used to designate all flying things except birds, such as airplanes, aviators, dragonflies, and so on. Whorf wondered whether the Eskimos "see" distinctions between different kinds of snow that we do not see, that is, whether the lexicon of a language affects the speakers' perceptions.

On the face of it, this idea of Whorf's does not seem to be very convincing. One would expect that the Eskimo, in whose life snow plays a more important part than in the Englishman's, would make finer distinctions in *speaking* about snow without necessarily *seeing* snow in a way different from the way we see snow. In fact, we have no difficulty in distinguishing the Eskimo's three kinds of snow and can express the differences, if we have to, by appropriate phrases: "falling snow," "snow blocks," and so forth. Nevertheless it may make a difference whether we see a distinction only after it has been pointed out or whether the distinction is incorporated in our language. In the latter case, we may pay more attention to the distinctions, and this may affect our perceptions.

English, for example, is rich in denoting different ways of locomotion. We walk, run, hop, skip, jump, leap, saunter, stroll, etc. These lexical distinctions may enable us to draw conclusions about the feelings or intentions of the person who moves in each of the different ways. Certain Polynesian languages are said to be rich in denoting different ways of looking. Perhaps that is why the language of the eyes (glances) plays a more important part in the social intercourse of Polynesians. It is reasonable to suppose that the existence of corresponding distinctions in their language facilitates learning the "meanings" of the various eye gestures and also the use of them.

Languages far removed from each other on the taxonomic tree may also differ radically in structure. Take the English sentence "I clean it (the gun) with a ramrod." The important carriers of meaning are "clean" (suggesting the result of the operation), "with" (suggesting instrumentality), and "ramrod" (denoting the specific instrument). The corresponding "sentence" in Shawnee is a single word "nipek-walakha," which can be analyzed into the following components: "pekw" (dry space), "alak" (interior of a hole), and "h" (by motion of a tool).

Whorf examined the differences in the uses to which "parts of speech" are put. In Indo-European languages, for example, verbs are said to denote "actions," while nouns are said to denote "things." On reflection, however, this interpretation is less than satisfactory because the definitions are circular. If something is denoted by a noun, we *think* of it as a "thing" even though it is quite unlike material things; for example, "conscience." Likewise, because something is denoted by a verb, we think of it as an action although it is quite unlike ordinary actions; for example, "to consist of." Another way of interpreting the difference between nouns and verbs is to say that verbs denote short-lived events, while nouns denote long-lived events. But then it is difficult to explain why "fist," "spark," and "wave" are nouns, while "remain" and "exist" are verbs.

The grammarian, of course, distinguishes nouns and verbs on structural, not on semantic grounds. "Spasm" is certainly a short-lived event, yet it is a noun simply because it can be preceded by an article, varies in number but not in tense, and so on. A spasm is surely not a thing, but it may suggest "thingness" just *because* it is a noun. This is Whorf's point. In the Hopi language, events are actually classified *grammatically* into short-lived ones and long-lived ones. Thus, in Hopi, "lightning," "meteor," and "wave" belong to one "part of speech," while "man" and "house" belong to another. In the Nootka language, on the other hand, most words are "verbs." In Nootka, one cannot say "the house." One says something like "It houses" (or a house occurs), analogous to the way we say "It rains" or "It burns." In English, some names of colors may be verbs, as in "She blushes" and "A paper yellowed with age." In Russian, most colors can be verbs. One says, for example, "A sail 'whitens' in the distance" for "A white sail is seen in the distance"; "Between the clouds the sky is 'bluing'" for "The blue sky is seen between the clouds"; and "He 'greened' with envy" for "He became green with envy."

The question raised by the Sapir-Whorf hypothesis is whether these often surprising differences among lexicons and grammars actually induce differences in the way people in different language communities perceive the world. If so, this should be of the greatest interest to psychologists, social scientists, and philosophers. For then language itself is revealed as a source of "persuasion," hence of restriction on autonomy, more powerful than efforts of people who use it deliberately to persuade. Such aims at persuasion can in principle be detected, and so resistance against exploitative impairment of autonomy can be mobilized. But the limitations placed on cognition by one's own language are inescapable except by transcending the framework of thought imposed by that language. Such escape is difficult and requires sustained intellectual effort. If the Sapir-Whorf hypothesis is valid, a thorough revision of linguistics, especially of pragmatics, or psychology, and of epistemology (the theory of knowledge) is called for.

Evidence for or against the Whorf hypothesis is hard to come by. It is not the sort of hypothesis that can be put to a test in a few well-chosen situations. In fact it is not a scientific hypothesis at all in the sense to be discussed in Chapter 17. It is rather an outlook on language. Nevertheless the ideas of Sapir-Whorf have *suggested* specific hypotheses that can be put to a test. The difficulty is in deciding whether or not these testable hypotheses actually go to the heart of the matter.

To formulate a specific hypothesis about the relation of language to perception, we must select a specific lexical or structural difference between two languages and find some correlate of it in the perceptions or world outlooks of the respective peoples.

To see the difficulties encountered in the process, let us select a grammatical difference at random and try to draw hypothetical conclusions from it. In English we say "He teaches arithmetic to children." Here "arithmetic" is the direct object of "teaches," and "children" is the indirect object. Our grammar seems to imply that the teacher teaches the *subject*, bringing it, as it were, to the children. The Russian, on the contrary, says "He teaches children (to) arithmetic." The "to" in parenthesis indicates that "arithmetic" is put in the dative case, hence is the indirect object of "teaches." "Children" appears in the accusative case in the Russian sentence. The implication seems to be that the teacher teaches *children*, brings them, as it were, to the subject.

Does this difference suggest anything about different philosophies of pedagogy in Russian- and in English-speaking countries? There is an ongoing controversy in pedagogical circles about whether one should teach the subject or the child. Is this controversy related to the fact that in English "children" can be *both* a direct and an indirect object of "to teach," while in Russian "children" is always the direct object of "to teach" and the subject taught is always the indirect object? Further, in Russian, if the subject taught is put in the accusative case, then the word that in the former case meant "to teach" changes its meaning and becomes "to study." In the sentence "He studies arithmetic," "arithmetic" is in the accusative, and "studies" is the same word as "teaches" (*uchit*) in the sentence "He teaches children."

Can we, in the face of these linguistic facts, hypothesize that more emphasis is put on "teaching the subject" in traditional pedagogic methods in English-speaking countries, whereas more emphasis is put on "teaching the child" in Russian?

To answer this question, we must examine the attitudes of pedagogues, but these are much more difficult to single out and identify than are grammatical facts. Moreover, even if we find a difference of emphasis on "teaching the subject" or "teaching the child," we must be extremely careful not to confuse these emphases with other pedagogical attitudes that have sometimes been associated with them. As noted above, proponents of child-centered pedagogy see it as preserving the autonomy of the child, supposedly because it takes into account the needs and motivations of the particular child. But cannot one also argue the opposite, that "teaching the child" involves manipulating the child, "bringing him to the subject," while teaching the subject suggests "bringing the subject to the child," hence leaving the child's autonomy more intact?

The difficulties attending such speculations are apparent. The gap between a simple grammatical difference and a whole outlook is too large. We must look elsewhere for corroborations or refutations of the Sapir-Whorf hypothesis.

To pursue these investigations, some psychologists have selected simple, clear-cut lexical facts, apparently directly related to perception. The names of colors define a suitable area of psycholinguistic experiments. In English, certain colors have simple, short names: "blue," "green," "red," "brown," and so on. Other names of colors are compounded: "bluish-green," "light gray," "dark red." Still others are derived from nouns: "emerald green," "chocolate brown." The number of colors that can be discriminated by a person with normal vision is very much larger than the number of available names.

The color spectrum is actually continuous. Certain positions on this spectrum are identified as "pure red," "pure blue," and so on. It turns out that these "pure" colors are the ones to which the short, common names are applied most appropriately. That is to say, more people will respond with just "red" or "blue" when asked to name these colors than others. The names used for other colors are more varied; some people will call "bluish-green" what others will call "greenish-blue." Also it takes a shorter time for people to respond when naming the "pure" colors. These differences permit the experimenter to assign a measure of "codability" to the different colors. The pure colors are the most "codable": they elicit the quickest, shortest, and most uniform responses.

It also turns out that the most codable colors are also the ones most easily recognized. When a subject is presented with "pure blue" and is later asked to pick out the same color from among several similar colors, he does so more accurately and more rapidly than when he is presented with something he calls "light greenish-blue." In short, codability seems to be related to discriminability at least in the context of color vision. This can be taken as evidence in support of the Sapir-Whorf hypothesis, even if in a very narrow context. It indicates that the existence of commonly used words facilitates recognition, hence is reflected in perception.[3]

Similar experiments can be easily designed. Trained musicians readily discriminate among different harmonies. Triads are classified as major, minor, augmented, and diminished; there are several named varieties of seventh chords, and so on. A person untrained in music but with a good ear can be taught to discriminate harmonies. Suppose we take two groups of subjects, unversed in musical terminology, and teach them to distinguish harmonies. One group will be taught without using the names of the chords, say, by associating different harmonies with different fingers, the way Victor was taught to recognize spoken vowels (cf. pp. 74–75). The second group will be given the names of the chords. Since the named chords will become presumably more "codable," the second group should be expected to learn faster. Note that by "codable" we mean *linguistically* codable because the first group also has a "code," namely, a finger for each chord. In this way we shall be testing the facilitation of discrimination *specifically by language*, an implication of the Whorf hypothesis.

More conclusive evidence for or against the hypothesis could be

3 Roger W. Brown and Eric H. Lenneberg, "A Study in Language and Cognition," in *Psycholinguistics*, ed. Saporta.

obtained from an experiment, which, to my knowledge, has not yet been performed. In the Yakut language (in Siberia), blue and green are named by the same word. This may mean that, for the Yakuts, the most codable color in that part of the spectrum is neither what we call "pure blue" nor what we call "pure green" but rather the color about halfway between these two. If the Yakuts recognize this "blue-green" more readily than our "blue" and "green" (in contrast to us), this would provide rather strong evidence in favor of the hypothesis. It should be pointed out that the corroboration would rest on the assumption that there is no essential difference in the physiology of color vision between us and the Yakuts, probably a safe assumption. I have read recently that also in the Uzbek language (in Central Asia) blue and green are denoted by the same word. At the same time many Uzbeks speak Russian as a second language, and their perceptions may have been affected accordingly. This difficulty could be avoided by comparing Uzbeks who are facile in Russian with those who are monolingual.

The influence of language on perception can be seen more clearly in the special "languages" developed in various spheres of human activity. There is a language of science, a language of politics, a language of religious experience. These are further divided into sublanguages of various specialties, schools of thought, and outlooks. Each of these develops in the context of specialized experiences and shared perceptions. To be sure, the question always looms as to whether the experiences stimulate the development of the special languages or whether the languages organize perceptions so as to facilitate the corresponding experiences. The most likely answer is that the influence goes both ways.

In Part III we shall examine the language of science and its influence on cognition. This is a comparatively new language that has been developing for the last three or four centuries. In the language of science, one can assert a fact, a general statement summarizing many facts, or a conclusion drawn as a consequence of other statements, but one cannot persuade, either by threatening sanctions or by appealing to desires or fears. The only means of persuasion at the disposal of the scientist speaking the language of science is demonstrating the truth of what he says.

Everyone knows that science has radically transformed human life. Until recently, most people living in societies transformed by science assumed that these changes portended a glorious future for humanity, freed from the necessity of life-consuming toil, from diseases, from superstition, and from irrational fears of hostile forces of nature. Lately this vision of the future has been dimmed by some of the uses to which scientific knowledge is put, particularly in the burgeoning weapons systems and ecology-damaging industries, which, if unchecked, can destroy the fruits of science, if not humanity itself.

Even nonmilitary technology is now increasingly seen as a mixed blessing. Industrial societies with their mobile populations and huge metropolises are said to have destroyed man's sense of community. The industrial process is reputed to have deprived men of satisfactions derived from pride in craftsmanship. The hypergrowth of technology is also held responsible for accelerating depletion of the world's resources and for the pollution of air, water, and soil.

It is frequently argued that these unfortunate by-products of science are the results of a lag between the scientific view of nature and the obsolete outlooks prevailing in human affairs, particularly in politics. In this connection, it is also frequently asserted that if man brought to bear the scientific mode of cognition and communication on his view of himself and the societies in which he lives, his perceptions would change, and the broad disparity between the rationality of science and the irrationality in the conduct of human affairs would disappear.

Even if this were so, merely asserting it does not solve the problems emerging from man's growing power of destruction and, concomitantly, his failure to direct science toward the acquisition of wisdom as well as of power. "Let's apply science to solve social problems" is only a slogan. To make it a program of action, one must acquaint oneself both with the sources of power in the scientific outlook and with its limitations, especially with the obstacles in the way of "applying science" in human affairs. These matters will be taken up in Parts III and IV.

APPLICATIONS

I. How does the "vast persuasion industry" differ from the teaching profession which tries to persuade people to like books, films, law, order, and so on? Isn't it true that we are all in reality trying to sell things to one another and that we simply put different labels on the "con job"? If you disagree, state your reasons.

II. Read chapter 21 on the work of Ivan Pavlov, and then return to this chapter. What connection is there between the theory that Pavlov constructed about conditioned behavior and the efforts of demagogues and advertising executives to channel our behavior?

III.
"The Lapps of the arctic regions have no general term for 'snow,' only a number of special names for each state and form of it: snow is so important a factor in their lives that they have to specify its various aspects."—Stephen Ullman, "The Prism of Language," *The Listener* (22 July 1954).

1) How many forms of snow can you perceive? If the Lapps perceive six or seven forms of it and have six or seven words for snow, does it suggest that your perception may be limited by your vocabulary?
2) The Lapps may have special names for each state and form of snow, but the fact remains that they apparently have failed to take the next step, that of subordinating these aspects to the more general concept of *snow*. What are some of the disadvantages of this overconcrete vocabulary?

IV. Some modern thinkers are haunted by the fear that many problems of philosophy are pseudoproblems generated by the structure of our language ("If Aristotle had spoken Chinese, he would have had to adopt an entirely different logic"). How could you support or refute the contention that linguistic *structure* can influence philosophical *structure*?

V. On the other hand, the characteristic structure of a language may tell us a great deal about national *psychology*. Particularly instructive are the habitual patterns of word order which determine the channels along which thought will flow.

1) What is the pattern of most English sentences? of most French sentences? Do the two languages differ in their "inherent logic"?
2) In an inflected language like German, there will be a wider margin of departure from the pattern that governs both English and French, especially in the elaborate constructions known as "encapsulating" (for example, a prefix will be detached from its verb and placed at the end of the sentence, or the verbs will pile up at the end). Does this structure suggest a unique national habit of mind?
3) You have no doubt been given many reasons for studying a foreign language in school. Does the material in this application and in this chapter suggest others to you?

/III
FROM
MEANING
TO
KNOWLEDGE

12/propositions and terms

In scientific discourse, utterances on the level of sentences in the indicative mode are called *propositions*. In ordinary language, we have seen that a sentence in the indicative mode may be semantically equivalent to a question or a command or a request; moreover, it is not always easy to decide whether an utterance purporting to inform does inform about something in the outside world or about the world inside the speaker's head. A proposition always informs about something in the world outside the speaker. It may inform correctly or incorrectly. We can therefore define a proposition as an utterance to which a *value*[1] "true" or "false" can be ascribed. We shall see later (cf. Chapter 15) that "intermediate" truth values can also be ascribed to propositions, as in "true with a certain degree of probability." For the time being, we shall assume that only one of the two extreme truth values (true or false) can be ascribed to each proposition. For instance, we shall regard "Cats are mammals" as a true proposition and "It snowed in Chicago on July 4, 1973" as a false proposition.

One task of science is to discover whether propositions are true or false. Clearly, for a task to be manageable, we must have some general rules or criteria for making such decisions. There are such rules in science. Before we discuss them, however, let us see what rules are

---

1. Here "value" is not used in the sense of "worth" but only in the sense of assigning a meaning. For instance, in mathematics, the symbol x often stands for a quantity that can assume any of several different "values," that is, $0, -5, 1/3, 2$, and so on. Similarly, we may at first not know whether a proposition informs correctly or incorrectly. We say, then, that a proposition can assume either of two values, "true" or "false." Later we shall symbolize "true" by 1 and "false" by 0.

often applied in ordinary discourse to test the truth of an utterance.

One such rule would be to submit every utterance to an arbiter. If he says the utterance is true, it is true; it is false if he says it is false. Boxer, a character in George Orwell's *Animal Farm*, resorts to this rule when he says "If Comrade Napoleon says it is so, it must be so." Devout Catholics in matters of faith accept as truth everything that the Pope says *ex cathedra*. And in American law, the utterance "Mr. Mu is not guilty" is accepted as true if the jury says so.

To be sure, in each of these cases, the pronouncement of the authority is backed by an implicit justification of the authority qua authority. The Pope is supposed to be inspired by God; the foreman of the jury reports the consensus of twelve people's judgment of the evidence, and so on. Nevertheless the pronouncement by an authority, however arrived at in each case, is held to be final.

Another way we sometimes decide the truth of an utterance is by examining our own feelings about it. We are likely to apply this criterion to most value judgments like "Honesty is the best policy" or "Gershwin was a great composer." Closely related to such utterances are those involving belief. "Mr. Nu will succeed (or fail) in his enterprise." "There will be (or will not be) a war between Neptunia and Plutonia." Utterances expressing beliefs or judgments are generally called opinions. To say that something is a matter of opinion is, in effect, to admit that a personal, introspective test has established the "truth" of an utterance for the person concerned.

Still another way of establishing truth is by deduction. Suppose we are "told" by a library catalog that a book, if available, must be on a certain shelf; if we do not find it on the shelf, we may deduce that it is charged out.

A commonly accepted method of establishing the truth of an utterance is by making an observation. We say the utterance "It is raining" is true if we see that it is raining. We say "This cat has four legs" is true if we count the cat's legs and find four of them.

Finally, we establish truths by induction. Having observed that every cat we have ever seen had four legs, we believe it to be true that every normal cat has four legs.

Now, although all of these ways of establishing truth are clearly different, they are interrelated and often intertwined. For example, if we establish the truth of the utterance "It is raining" by the fact that someone said so, we seem to be relying on authority, but implicitly we are relying also on an observation because we usually assume that the person asked has made an observation. If we establish our belief that it will rain tomorrow by consulting a barometer, we are relying not only on observation but also on deduction, even though we may not be aware of it. We are, in fact, making use of a typically linked chain of utterances: "If a barometer registers low atmospheric pressure, the chances are that it will rain; this barometer is registering low pressure; therefore it will probably rain." Even a direct observation depends on introspection because we know what we have observed only by consulting our impressions. "Seeing is believing" means actually "I believe what *I* see" and what I see is, in the last analysis, directly known only to me. Moreover, in the deduction beginning with "If a barometer registers low atmospheric pressure . . . ," we are also relying on authority: we assume there is a connection between barometer reading and weather because someone told us about it or because we read about it.

In scientific discourse, only three of these five methods of establishing truth are allowed: observation, induction, and deduction. Moreover, outside of mathematics, induction and deduction are permitted in establishing only tentative truths subject to verification by observation, which is the last court of appeal. Further, observation does not establish the truth of general propositions, only of specific ones; general propositions remain *forever* tentative. In mathematics, on the other hand, only one method of arriving at true propositions is allowed, namely, deduction. Induction and observation are not admitted as evidence in proving a mathematical proposition.

We have advisedly used the word "utterance" to denote what is said in ordinary discourse, reserving "propositions" for what is said in scientific discourse. To discover the reason for this distinction, let us see what it takes to establish the truth of an utterance by observation.

Take the utterance "Peter is richer than Paul." How would we go about testing its truth by observation? Several procedures suggest themselves. We can compare Peter's and Paul's ways of life, the appearances of their houses, their clothes, the cars they drive, and so on. We can make inquiries about their bank accounts, the securities they own, if any, etc. None of these procedures will give us a definitive answer because objections can still be raised against either conclusion (that the utterance is true or false). If we conclude that

Peter is richer because he owns a more expensive car, someone can point out that Peter has bought a car beyond his means. If we conclude that Peter is richer because he has more money in the bank, someone may object that we did not take into account Paul's larger income. And so on. Clearly, in order to reach a definitive conclusion, we must specify what we *mean* by the word "richer." How, then, can we specify what we mean by that word?

Why should we want to specify the meaning of such a commonplace word as "richer"? Clearly the need for specification arises just because a controversy may ensue as to how we can establish the truth of the utterance "Peter is richer than Paul" if we wish to establish it by observation. And if we want to avoid a controversy about *what to observe* in order to establish the truth of the utterance, we must *agree* on what to observe. Having agreed on this matter, we have essentially agreed on the meaning of the word "richer" *for the purpose we have in mind*, namely, to establish (or refute) the truth of the utterance "Peter is richer than Paul."

To recapitulate, the discussion may go something like this:

> **MR. XI:** Peter is richer than Paul.
>
> **MR. OMICRON:** I doubt it.
>
> **MR. XI:** Well, I think this is true because Peter drives a new Cadillac, whereas Paul just pawned his watch.
>
> **MR. OMICRON:** But I happen to know that Peter has embezzled money, whereas Paul is doing research on pawn shops.

The argument may continue in a desultory fashion until Mr. Xi and Mr. Omicron agree on what observation they *both* can make in order to settle the controversy. To do so, they may appeal to authority, that is agree to accept a criterion usually employed by people who are professionally interested in matters pertaining to solvency, say, accountants. An accountant might tell them that, while he does not in his professional work use expressions such as "rich" and "poor," he does use certain measures related to these, such as "total worth" (calculated by subtracting liabilities from assets or whatever). Mr. Xi and Mr. Omicron may then engage the services of an accountant, and, provided he can obtain access to relevant data, they can reduce the utterance in question to "Peter's total worth is larger than Paul's." The truth of this utterance can be tested by comparing two numbers.

As a rule, no controversy arises about which of two given numbers is larger.

It should be noted that Mr. Xi and Mr. Omicron need not resort to such an elaborate procedure. They may, if they wish, agree on a simpler criterion, such as the size of a bank account or a salary or whatever they wish. If they do, this means that *for the purpose of their discussion* they have agreed on the *meaning* of "richer." The only restriction on their agreement is that it should really serve the purpose of their inquiry, namely, to establish or to refute the utterance "Peter is richer than Paul." The agreement they seek should enable them to say: "Let us make the following observation (specified), which can have only one of two results. If one result is observed, we shall agree that 'Peter is richer than Paul' is a true utterance; if the other is observed, we shall agree that the utterance is false."

In this way the meaning of a word will be directly related not just to observations but to agreements about *what* specific observations to make. It should be pointed out that, even in the most commonplace situations, agreements on what observations to make become necessary as soon as controversies arise if the truth of an utterance is to be established by observation. It seems a simple matter to test the proposition "It is raining" by looking out of the window. But this is only if people agree on relating what they observe to the word "raining." Here, too, ambiguities may arise. The line between "raining" and "sleeting" or between "raining" and "mist" may be hard to draw. If it is important to decide on the truth of the utterance in these borderline cases, more refined observations are called for, along with an agreement on just what they should be.

A word whose range of denotation in a particular context is clear and unambiguous, and is not changed without notice, is called a *term*. *Propositions* are sentences in the indicative mood that contain only terms and logical connectives to indicate relations among the terms.

From the foregoing examples, we have seen that words seeming to have clear and unambiguous meanings turned out to have a variety of possible meanings. Thus the word "richer," before its meaning in the context was fixed, could have meant "has a larger bank account," "gets a larger salary," and so on. As long as this ambiguity existed, the utterance "Peter is richer than Paul" was not a proposition. It was a *propositional function*. A truth value cannot be ascribed to a propositional function. The simplest way to illustrate this principle is by an analogy with a mathematical equation. Consider the mathematical "utterance" $x + 3 = 5$. Is it true or false? It is neither, of course. It *becomes* true if the value "2" is substituted for x, and it *becomes* false if any other value is substituted for x. It is neither true nor false as it stands. In the same way, "Peter is richer than Paul" is neither true nor false until a particular unambiguous meaning has been substituted for "richer." *Then* it becomes true or false. For instance, it may turn out that, if we substitute "has more money in the bank" for "richer," the resulting proposition is true; if we substitute "gets a larger salary" for "richer," the proposition is false.

The most commonplace utterances are, generally speaking, propositional functions rather than propositions. Take the trite utterance "Grass is green." If the denotation of grass is what grows on the hillsides of Vermont in May, the utterance turns into a true proposition. But if the denotation of "grass" is what grows on the hillsides of California in July, the utterance turns into a false proposition. Strictly speaking, "green" too has a variety of meanings. But the purpose of distinguishing propositions from propositional functions is not pedantic hair-splitting for its own sake; rather it is to make meaning as clear as the particular context demands. If an argument arose about what we mean by "green," we would have to specify it more exactly, say, by specifying the wavelengths of light reflected[2] or something of that sort.

And so, we have delineated the range of scientific discourse: it consists of propositions, which are utterances consisting of terms and indicated relations among them to which truth values can be ascribed. The rules for ascertaining the truth of propositions are just three: observation, induction, and deduction. Ultimately, observation is the last court of appeal.

No less important in this definition of scientific discourse is the *exclusion* of other commonly used ways of ascertaining truth. Specifically, appeal to authority as a final arbiter is categorically excluded. Our internal convictions, feelings, hunches, and so on, are also excluded. Scientific truth is public, not private.

Science is often defined as a body of reliable knowledge. In this context, "reliable" means that the ultimate appeal of all controversies

---

2. Light is a certain form of energy propagated by electromagnetic vibrations. The color we see depends on the length of the waves of these vibrations. For instance, the wavelength of "red" is about .000065 centimeters, of "green" about .000052 centimeters, of "violet" about .000041 centimeters, and so forth.

about truths of propositions are the results of observations made by *independent* and *impartial* observers. An observer is independent if he is not influenced by another observer in making the observations. An observer is impartial if he does not allow his personal convictions, prejudices, or desires to influence his observations.

Confining the last appeal to objectively verifiable observations is in no sense to proclaim that "scientific truth" is necessarily more important than other conceptions of truth, such as "truth" purported to be discovered by religious experience or in poetic expression. We are merely *defining* scientific truth in the way it is usually defined so as to make sure of what we are talking about.

In short, to establish a scientific truth, two questions must be satisfactorily answered:

1. What do you mean?
2. How do you know?

The answer to the first question must establish precisely the range of denotation of the terms used in the propositions. These denotations must indicate what we are to observe in order to recognize the referents of the symbols. The second question must be answered in a way that ultimately relates what is asserted to objectively verifiable observations. Thus, answers to *both* questions must indicate observations. The answer to "What do you mean" relates *that about which an assertion is made* to observations. The answer to "How do you know?" relates *that which is asserted* to observations.

In acquiring and adding to the body of reliable knowledge that we call science, scientists have developed and refined certain *techniques* of observation, induction, and deduction. The techniques of observation are the well-known paraphernalia of science: telescopes, microscopes, spectroscopes, thermometers, barometers, voltmeters, and so on—essentially extensions of our sensory apparatus. Discussion of these aids to observation and how they work falls outside the scope of this book. On the other hand, techniques of deduction and induction are intimately connected with the cognitive foundation of language and so to our subject of concern. In the following chapters, we shall discuss these techniques.

APPLICATIONS

I. "Science is often defined as a body of reliable knowledge. In this context, 'reliable' means that the ultimate appeal of all controversies about truths of propositions are the results of observations made by *independent* and *impartial* observers." (pp. 224–25).

In the following instances, certain propositions are put before a group of scientists who promise not to allow their personal convictions, prejudices, or desires to influence their judgments. The letter a) refers to the proposition; b) to the scientist's observation; c) to the rebuttal by the person or group uttering the proposition. Decide whether you support position b or c and explain why.

1) a) "When people have illnesses, the 'penumbra' surrounding the body changes color according to the illness: from white to blue for respiratory, from white to red for circulatory, etc."

   b) "With all of the scientific instruments at our disposal, we could detect no 'penumbra.' Hence, we say that the proposition is not supported by evidence."

   c) "Only people with 'extrasensory perception' are able to detect the 'penumbra' and hence make such diagnoses."

2) a) "Certain people have ESP; this sense enables them to read with a higher percentage of accuracy than guesswork the number on cards held face away from them."

   b) "When we were present, the subject scored no higher than 1 out of 13 with a deck of playing cards. Since this is the statistical norm of pure guessing, we must assume that the subject did not have special powers of the kind claimed."

   c) "The presence of unconsciously unsympathetic observers always inhibits the operation of ESP and, therefore, the test proved nothing."

3) a) "That there is life on other planets is demonstrated by the recurrent appearance of space saucers which many people testify they have seen."

   b) "There may or may not be life on other planets; there have been no such saucers observed by trained scientists; the people who say they have observed them have seen flying objects of some sort, but there is no evidence that they come from outer space."

   c) "Are you trying to say that I am lying?"

4) a) "In acupuncture the forces of Yang and Yin flow through the twelve 'meridians' of the body, and there are 365 points at which the insertion of a needle will have a physiological effect by balancing Yang (good) and Yin (bad). Where there is too much Yin, you jab a selected point with a Yang needle."

   b) "We have not been able to locate the twelve 'meridians' of the body clearly, and in the experiments with Western patients, the needle caused some pain but apparently did little or nothing to cure the condition the patient complained of. Of course acupuncture may be a brand of psychosomatic medicine in which the patient's self-hypnosis plays an important part."

c) "There's nothing miraculous about acupuncture. It's pragmatic medicine, based on thousands of years of application. One certainty is that for many patients, acupuncture helps."

5) a) "It's a myth that cigarette-smoking causes lung cancer. Too many smokers don't get it."

b) "Statistical evidence on hand suggests very strongly that cigarette smoke causes edema of the alveoli in the lungs and promotes a condition that leads to lung cancer. This happens in a significant enough segment of smokers to make cigarettes dangerous to many people over a period of years if the intake is heavy."

c) "If that's the case, why do so many doctors and scientists smoke? They know that it's air pollution that's doing the damage, but the cigarette companies are convenient scapegoats."

II. In *Language in Thought and Action*, S. I. Hayakawa advises the reader to distinguish at least four senses of the word "true."

1) Some mushrooms are poisonous. (If we call this "true," we mean that it is a *report that can be and has been verified.*)
2) Sally is the sweetest girl in the world. (If we call this "true," we mean that *we feel the same way* toward Sally.)
3) All men are created equal. (If we call this "true," we mean that this is a *directive which we believe should be obeyed.*)
4) $(x + y)^2 = x^2 + 2xy + y^2$. (If we call this "true," we mean that this statement is *consistent with the system of statements possible to be made in the language called algebra.*)*

Give three or four instances of your own of each sense of "true." Where would ethics be classified? poetry? a company balance sheet? a medical diagnosis?

---

* Application 4 is a direct quotation from S. I. Hayakawa, *Language in Thought and Action*, 3d ed. (New York: Harcourt Brace Jovanovich, 1972), p. 259. Italicized section would more accurately read: "consistent with a set of fundamental premises (called axioms) in the language called algebra." [A.R.]

13/syllogisms

Logic rests on a set of rules that allows us to deduce the truth of propositions from the truth of other propositions or combinations of propositions. Thus, to reason logically means to use deductions in arriving at truths.

One rule of deduction is stated as follows. If "All A are B" is a true proposition, and "All B are C" is a true proposition, then "All A are C" is also a true proposition. Rules of this sort, applied to certain triples of four-word propositions, are called rules of *syllogistic reasoning*. The first of the four words in each proposition is always "all" or "no" or "some." The second is a symbol (A, B, X, Y, or the like) that can stand for any class of things (that is to say, the range of denotation of a word). The third word is either "are" or "are not" (or in some cases, "is" or "is not," if English grammar so prescribes). The last word is again a symbol that stands for a class. In this way, we can form six types of such four-word propositions:

1. All A are B.
2. No A is B.
3. Some A are B.
4. Some A are not B.
5. All A are not B.
6. No A is not B.

These are now propositional functions rather than propositions (cf. pp. 223–24) because A and B can stand for practically anything as long as their ranges of denotation are not specified. The four-word sentence becomes a proposition when A and B acquire denotative meanings. However, for convenience in the following discussion, we shall refer to these utterances as "propositions" even when they are propositional functions.

"Not" in propositions 4, 5, and 6 is understood as negating B. For example, if A stands for "bachelors" and B for "married," proposition 5 says "All bachelors are unmarried," not "All bachelors are not married," which is equivalent to "Not all bachelors are married." Now "Not all bachelors are married" is equivalent to "Some bachelors are not married." Similarly, "No bachelor is unmarried" is equivalent to "All bachelors are married." (Note that the *factual* truth of the propositions is irrelevant in this context.) Therefore the six types of propositions can be reduced to four:

1. All A are B.
2. No A is B.
3. Some A are B.
4. Some A are not B.

A syllogism consists of a triple of such propositions. If the first contains the symbols A and B, the second must contain symbols B and C in that order. (Of course, any three symbols will do, but the second symbol in the first proposition must be the first in the second proposition.) The first two propositions are called *premises*. The last, called the *conclusion*, must contain A and C in that order.[1]

Let us see how many different triples we can form. We can choose any of the four types 1–4 for each proposition in the triple. In consequence $4 \times 4 \times 4 = 64$ different triples are possible. They are all shown in Table 3.

We shall now establish the "rules of syllogism" by designating the conclusion in each of the 64 triples as "V" for "valid," "F" for "false," or "I" for "invalid." The syllogisms are the triples in which the conclusion is labeled "V" for "valid." An invalid conclusion is

1. The symbol B contained in the two premises is called a *distributed term*. The corresponding assertion must be either "All B are . . ." or "No B is . . ." In textbooks on logic, one of the premises is called the *major premise*, the other the *minor premise*. We shall not make this distinction. Nor is the order of premises important. The essential thing is that the distributed term should appear in both premises and that the conclusion should be distinguished from the premises.

aAB 1	aAB 2	aAB 3	aAB 4	aAB 5	aAB 6	aAB 7	aAB 8
aBC	aBC	aBC	aBC	nBC	nBC	nBC	nBC
aAC V	nAC F	sAC V	sAnC F	aAC F	nAC V	sAC F	sAnC V

aAB 9	aAB 10	aAB 11	aAB 12	aAB 13	aAB 14	aAB 15	aAB 16
sBC	sBC	sBC	sBC	sBnC	sBnC	sBnC	sBnC
aAC I	nAC I	sAC I	sAnC I	aAC I	nAC I	sAC I	sAnC I

nAB 17	nAB 18	nAB 19	nAB 20	nAB 21	nAB 22	nAB 23	nAB 24
aBC	aBC	aBC	aBC	nBC	nBC	nBC	nBC
aAC I	nAC I	sAC I	sAnC I	aAC I	nAC I	sAC I	sAnC I

nAB 25	nAB 26	nAB 27	nAB 28	nAB 29	nAB 30	nAB 31	nAB 32
sBC	sBC	sBC	sBC	sBnC	sBnC	sBnC	sBnC
aAC I	nAC I	sAC I	sAnC I	aAC I	nAC I	sAC I	sAnC I

sAB 33	sAB 34	sAB 35	sAB 36	sAB 37	sAB 38	sAB 39	sAB 40
aBC	aBC	aBC	aBC	nBC	nBC	nBC	nBC
aAC I	nAC F	sAC V	sAnC I	aAC F	nAC I	sAC I	sAnC V

sAB 41	sAB 42	sAB 43	sAB 44	sAB 45	sAB 46	sAB 47	sAB 48
sBC	sBC	sBC	sBC	sBnC	sBnC	sBnC	sBnC
aAC I	nAC I	sAC I	sAnC I	aAC I	nAC I	sAC I	sAnC I

sAnC 49	sAnC 50	sAnC 51	sAnC 52	sAnC 53	sAnC 54	sAnC 55	sAnC 56
aBC	aBC	aBC	aBC	nBC	nBC	nBC	nBC
aAC I	nAC I	sAC I	sAnC I	aAC I	nAC I	sAC I	sAnC I

sAnC 57	sAnC 58	sAnC 59	sAnC 60	sAnC 61	sAnC 62	sAnC 63	sAnC 64
sBC	sBC	sBC	sBC	sBnC	sBnC	sBnC	sBnC
aAC I	nAC I	sAC I	sAnC I	aAC I	nAC I	sAC I	sAnC I

Table 3 *Read aAB as "all A are B," sAnB as "some A are not B," etc. Of the 64 possible triples of the four-word propositions, those marked "V" have valid conclusions, necessarily true if the premises are true; those marked "F" have false conclusions, necessarily false if the premises are true. In the remaining ones marked "I," the conclusions are invalid; they could be either true or false. The triples marked "V" are syllogisms.*

one that may be either true or false. From the table, we see that among the 64 triples, Nos. 1, 3, 6, 8, 35, and 40 have been distinguished as syllogisms.

On what basis did we make these distinctions, establishing whether or not an inference is valid? For the moment, we shall pretend that we have selected the syllogisms arbitrarily, the way one invents the rules of a game. We could argue that the rules of games are arbitrary. There is no compelling reason why a king should rate higher than a ten, as it does in bridge. This will be readily conceded by anyone who plays pinochle, where the ten is rated higher than the king. Or we could argue that, in selecting the syllogisms among the triples, we were setting up the rules of a grammar, as it were, which are also arbitrary. (Syntax sets up rules for putting words together into sentences.) We have set up rules for putting triples of propositions together into syllogisms. The rules specify that after we have uttered the first two propositions of a syllogism, that is, the premises, we must utter the third proposition, the conclusion. If the first two propositions were not the premises of a syllogism, the rules of our grammar say that we cannot utter the conclusion.

To see the analogy with grammar, consider a "microlanguage," actually a very small portion of English. Say the entire vocabulary of this microlanguage consists of just thirteen words: the, a, an, old, good, man, men, woman, women, speak, speaks, sleep, sleeps.

The grammar of this microlanguage prescribes that every sentence contain exactly four words combined according to the rules of English grammar. First, let us see how many such four-word sentences could be formed with this thirteen-word vocabulary if there were no restraints whatsoever on how they were to be put together. Since we have thirteen choices for each of the four words, we can make $13^4 = 28,561$ quadruples. When we impose the rules of English grammar, our choices become severely restricted. In fact, we can easily see that if we are to make a four-word English sentence, we must begin it with either "the" or "a" or "an." If we started our sentence with "the," our next word must be either "old" or "good." If we started our sentence with "an," we must continue with "old." Next if we started with "the," the third word must be either "man" or "men" or "woman" or "women." If we started with "a" or "an," the third word must be "man" or "woman." Finally, if the third word was either "man" or "woman," the last word must be either "speaks" or "sleeps";

if the third word was either "men" or "women," the last word must be either "speak or "sleep." The entire scheme is shown in Figure 11.

Only twenty-four of the 28,561 possible four-word utterances are English sentences. Now it so happens that, in English, the verb must agree in number with its subject. Also, unlike most nouns, the *singular* verb form (in the third person) ends in "s." It certainly

Figure 11 *Each of the twenty-four paths along the branches from left to right represents an English sentence. Exactly twenty-four four-word sentences can be constructed from the thirteen-word vocabulary.*

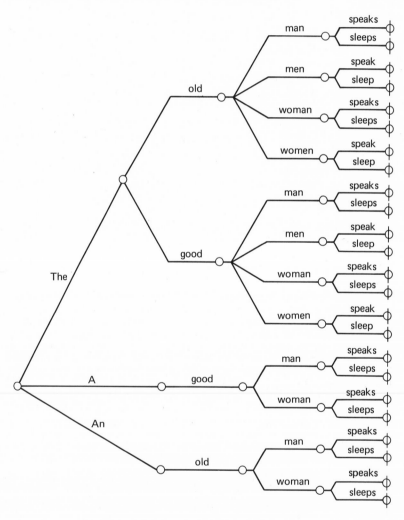

could have been the other way around. Verbs could just as easily (perhaps even somewhat more logically) form the third person plural the way most nouns form plurals—by adding "s." If we imposed this rule on our microlanguage, leaving the other rules of English as before, we would get twenty-four entirely different quadruples out of the possible 28,561 as "sentences." For example, we would have to say "The good man sleep" instead of "The good man sleeps," and so on. Thus a different grammar would single out different quadruples as sentences.

In short, imposing a grammar on a vocabulary amounts to designating utterances composed of words in the vocabulary that are acceptable in the language, a point that we discussed in Chapter 4. If the vocabulary is very small, we can, instead of stating the rules for composing acceptable utterances, simply enumerate the acceptable utterances. This is just what we did when we designated syllogisms— we enumerated acceptable strings of propositions (syllogisms). In this way the rules of syllogism are analogous to the rules of grammar.

Serious objections can be made against the view that the rules of logic are "nothing but" rules of grammar governing the formation of strings of propositions. Let us examine more closely the syllogisms that we designated V, F, and I in Table 3. As examples, take Nos. 1, 4, and 43.

If we supply meanings for our symbols, it will be clear that the designation of the conclusion in No. 1 as "valid" is by no means arbitrary. If every X is Y, and every Y is Z, the conclusion that every X is Z seems inescapable. For instance, if X stands for "men," Y for "mammals," and Z for "vertebrates," the syllogism becomes

All men are mammals.
All mammals are vertebrates.
(therefore) All men are vertebrates.

And *if* all men are mammals *and if* all mammals are vertebrates, then we cannot possibly deny that all men are vertebrates. On the same grounds, if the two premises are true, then the conclusion in No. 4 ("Some men are not vertebrates") must be false because it contradicts the valid conclusion that all men are vertebrates. Finally, in No. 43, after some reflection, we must concede that just because *some* X are Y and *some* Y are Z, the conclusion that some X are Z does not follow. To see this, let X stand for "babies," Y for "females," and Z for "mothers." The proposition "Some babies are females" is true. Also the proposition "some females are mothers" is also true. But we cannot on that basis conclude that "Some babies are mothers" is a true proposition.

As we examine the conclusions in all 64 triples, we can convince ourselves that the conclusions in the V triples are indeed compelling; that those in the F triples are indeed false, since they are denials of the valid conclusions deduced from the same premises; and that the conclusions in the I triples may be either true or false, and therefore not compelling conclusions.

Using our intuitive notions of what conclusions are "compelling," we can reduce the number of syllogisms still further. For instance, the conclusion of syllogism No. 1 contains the conclusion of syllogism No. 3, since if *all* X are Z, then certainly *some* X are Z. Next, syllogism No. 8 says the same thing as syllogism No. 6, since if *no* X is Z, then *some* X are not Z.

Eliminating the redundant syllogisms, we are left with only four. We reproduce them here together with the nicknames they were given by medieval logicians.[2]

No. 1. Mode "Barbara":   All X areY.
                               All Y are Z.
                               Therefore All X are Z.
No. 6. Mode "Celarent":   All X are Y.
                               No Y is Z.
                               Therefore no X is Z.
No. 35. Mode "Darii":   Some X are Y.
                               All Y are Z.
                               Therefore some X are Z.
No. 40. Mode "Ferio":   Some X are Y.
                               No Y is Z.
                               Therefore some X are not Z.

2. The three vowels of these nicknames designate the "quality and quantity" of the propositions: "a" denotes universal affirmative (all . . . are . . .); "e," universal negative (no . . . is . . .); "i," particular affirmative (some . . . are . . .); "o," particular negative (some . . . are not . . .). Thus "Ferio," following the order of the vowels, would read: "No Y is Z; Some X are Y; Therefore some X are not Z." The order here is changed so that B is always the distributed term.

Each of these four syllogisms can be represented by a diagram (see Figures 12–15).

In Figure 12 all the points of circle X are shown inside circle Y, and all the points of circle Y are inside circle Z. Therefore all the points inside X must also be inside Z.

In Figure 13 again all the points of X are inside Y, but Y and Z are shown to have no points in common ("no Y is Z"). Consequently X and Z cannot have points in common ("no X is Z").

In Figure 14 X and Y are shown to have some points in common ("some X are Y"), and all the points of Y are shown inside Z. Consequently some points of X (at least those that are in common with Y) must be inside Z.

In Figure 15 X and Y again have points in common; but Z has no points in common with Y. Consequently some points of X (at least those that are in common with Y) cannot be inside Z.

The validity of the syllogisms, and only of the syllogisms among the 64 possible triples, seems so self-evident that logicians from the time of Aristotle until the twentieth century have often said that the "rules of logic" are actually "laws of rational thought" and that logic itself is a science built upon these laws. Some philosophers went further. They pictured logic as a set of "laws" governing all the "necessary" processes of nature. They believed that things happened as they did because they *had* to happen that way, and that this necessity reflected the operation of some "laws of thought," perhaps of a deity. We shall look into this view in Chapter 18. For the moment, let us accept the traditional view that logical rules are "laws of rational thought" and ask whether the Aristotelian syllogism embraces all of these "laws."

To begin with, reasoning by means of diagrams can be deceptive. We have pictured the proposition "All X are Y" by showing a smaller circle X inside a larger one Y. From the diagram we might conclude that "Some Y are X," since some of the points inside the larger circle are also inside the smaller one. If we so conclude, we may substitute "Some Y are X" for "All X are Y" wherever the latter proposition occurs.

Consider now the two propositions:

All X are Y.
All X are Z.

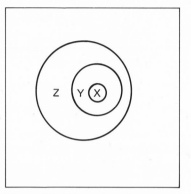

Figure 12 *Diagrammatic repre-*
sentation of mode "Barbara."

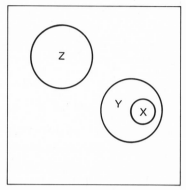

Figure 13 *Diagrammatic repre-*
sentation of mode "Celarent."

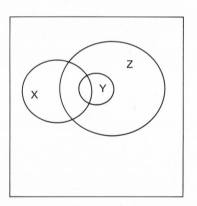

Figure 14 *Diagrammatic repre-*
sentation of mode "Darii."

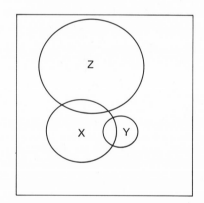

Figure 15 *Diagrammatic repre-*
sentation of mode "Ferio."

Substituting "Some Y are X" for "All X are Y," we get

Some Y are X.
All X are Z.

These two propositions are the premises of the "Darii" mode, except
that the labels X and Y have been interchanged, which clearly does
not matter. We are led to the conclusion "Some Y are Z."
   Thus we are led to another form of apparently valid inference:

All X are Y.
All X are Z.
(Therefore) Some Y are Z.

   Now let X stand for golden mountains, Y for mountains, and Z
for golden (that is, golden objects). Now the proposition "All X are
Y" becomes "All golden mountains are mountains." This proposition
is true by definition: a golden mountain is clearly a mountain.
"All X are Z" becomes "All golden mountains are golden." This
proposition is also true by definition: a golden mountain is clearly
golden. The conclusion becomes "Some mountains are golden" and
certainly does not look like a true proposition.[3] The source of errors
of this sort is revealed by subjecting logical deduction to more careful
scrutiny. We shall return to these matters in Chapter 15.
   Next, let us now see whether all forms of reasoning can be reduced
to syllogisms.
   From everyday usage, we know that propositions from which
other propositions can be deduced are not confined to the four forms
we have examined. We often reason in the following way:

If a piece of metal is held over a flame for five minutes, it becomes
   very hot.
It is dangerous to touch a very hot object.
Therefore it is dangerous to touch a piece of metal that has been held
   over a flame for five minutes.

The grammatical form of these sentences is different from that of

3. Example given by Bertrand Russell.

the propositions in syllogisms. However, we can reduce these sentences to the standard form of syllogistic premises and conclusion. Let X stand for "pieces of metal that have been held over a flame for five minutes." Let Y stand for "very hot objects." Let Z stand for "objects that are dangerous to touch." Then,

"All pieces of metal that have been held over a flame for more than five minutes are very hot objects" becomes "All X are Y."
"All very hot objects are dangerous to touch" becomes "All Y are Z."
"All pieces of metal that have been held over a flame for more than five minutes are dangerous to touch" becomes "All X are Z."

The premises and the conclusion are semantically equivalent to the deduction with which we started. Admittedly the "translation" is clumsy, but the fact that it can be made supports the arguments of the traditional logicians to the effect that all "rational reasoning" can be reduced to syllogisms. However, we are not yet finished with our examination.

Each proposition of a syllogism says one of two things: either things of a certain class belong also to another class or else they do not. We have seen that certain other kinds of propositions can be translated into propositions asserting class inclusion or class exclusion. "If X, then Y" is semantically equivalent to "All X are Y." Each can be translated into the other by making only grammatical adjustments. But can all propositions be put into one of the four forms?

Consider the following: "A human being is either a male or a female." The models of propositions we have so far considered do not provide for "either . . . or." Of course we could say "The class of human beings is included in the class comprising all males and all females." But, to say this, we would have to know what we mean by "comprising both . . . and. . . ." Again there is no proposition among those used in the classical syllogisms into which a proposition involving "comprising both . . . and . . ." can be translated. Yet, propositions involving "either . . . or" and "both . . . and . . ." can be easily combined with other propositions in chains of deduction that seem eminently valid. Example:

1a. All X are either Y or Z or both.   **1b.** Either proposition x or proposition y is true or both.

2a. No X is a Z.

3a. Therefore all X are Y.[4]

2b. If proposition y is true, then proposition z must be false.

3b. Therefore if proposition z is true, proposition x must be true.

Conclusion 3b may not seem as obvious as conclusion 3a, but it can be reasoned out as follows. From 2b we can conclude that if z is true, then y must be false (otherwise z would be false). Next, if y is false, then x must be true, otherwise 1b, which we assumed to be true, would be false.

Deductions of this sort can also be represented diagrammatically, pointing to a connection between logic and a branch of mathematics called the Algebra of Sets. The concepts of that algebra are useful as steppingstones to higher levels of logic (beyond syllogisms) as well as to mathematical reasoning. In fact, the Algebra of Sets is the core of the so-called New Math, introduced in the past few years to the mathematical curricula of American elementary and secondary schools. New Math, which has served to make mathematics more meaningful to youngsters, can be said to deal with the syntactics of mathematics. As in any language, an understanding of its syntactics is a prerequisite to the understanding of its semantics. In turn, an understanding of the semantics of mathematics (that is, the application of mathematical reasoning to science) is a prerequisite for understanding the semantics of science, that is, the connection between meaning and knowledge. In the next chapter we shall examine the essentials of the Algebra of Sets, which will take us naturally into the Algebra of Propositions and probability theory—extensions of syllogistic reasoning. From these we can pass to the syntactics and semantics of mathematics and to the semantics of science, which is the subject of this part of the book.

APPLICATIONS

I. "X is white" is an example of a *propositional function*. As it stands, the statement is neither true nor false. It can turn into a true proposition or a false proposition, depending on what we substitute for X. For instance, if we substitute "snow" for X, we get a true proposition; if we substitute "soot" for X, we get a false proposition.

4. Sometimes deductions involving disjunctions of sets (Y or Z) are included among the syllogisms.

1) Can you argue that "Snow is white" should also be construed as a propositional function? (Think of the different referents of "snow" that can be substituted for the word; also for "white.")
2) What should be substituted for "y" in the propositional function $y + 5 = 13$ to turn it into a true proposition (in the language of algebra, an *identity*)? in "$y - 11 > 11$"? in $y^2 - 5y + 6 = 0$"? in "$y^2 + y - 12 < 0$"? ($>$ means "is greater than"; $<$ "is less than.")

II. Show by actual examples that the third statement of each of the following triples cannot be concluded if the first two are true.

1) Some A are B. Some B are C. Therefore some A are C.
2) No A is B. No B is C. Therefore no A is C.
3) No A is B. No B is C. Therefore some A are not C.
4) Some A are B. No B is C. Therefore some C are not A.
5) It is the case that either p is true or q is false. It is the case that p is true. Therefore q must be true.

14/the algebra
of sets

A set is a well-defined collection, such as the set of all chairs in a room or the set of all blind cats or the set of all whole numbers larger than 11 or of forks or of countries of Europe.

The important thing about a set is that it is well-defined. This is to say, the range of denotation of the name that designates the set is precise so that there can be no ambiguity in deciding whether something does or does not belong to the set. We have already seen how such problems of decision may arise. Without more precise specification, we may not be sure whether a newborn kitten that is "normally" blind is to be counted as a blind cat; whether pitchforks are forks, and so on. All such ambiguities must be resolved if we are going to talk about a set at all in the context of set theory.

Associated with the notion of a set is its *complement*. The complement of a set is the set that contains everything that is *not* in the set in question. We shall denote the complement of the set A by –A.[1]

For the complement to be a well-defined set, it must be defined with respect to some other larger set called the *universal* set. For example, the range of the complement of "All whole numbers larger than 11" would be too vague if we defined it simply as "Everything that is not a whole number larger than 11." If a set is well-defined, its members must be recognized, at least conceptually, as entities. What shall we take as an "entity" if its only qualification is not to be a whole number larger than 11? It will not do to put pianos, piano

1. The complement of a set A is often denoted by Ā. –A is used here for typographical convenience, assuming that the symbol "–" will not be confused with the minus sign of arithmetic.

legs, influenza, steamship lines, cabbages, and kings all on equal footing as "entities" of a set. Therefore, before the complement of a set is defined, a "universal set" is specified. In our example, if we specify the set of "all whole numbers" as the universal set, then the complement of "the set of whole numbers larger than 11" with respect to that universal set will be "the set of all whole numbers not larger than 11." If "musical instruments" is designated as the universal set, then the complement of "the set of all pianos" is "the set of musical instruments that are not pianos." And so on.

A set may have no members. For instance, "the set of all crocodiles in my bedroom" has no members. The set of all triangular circles has no members. The set of all living men more than two hundred years old probably has no members. Sets without members are called *empty sets* or *null sets*.

Distinct sets may have members in common. For instance, the set of all children and the set of all females have "little girls" as members in common.

If every member of set A is a member of set B, we shall say that B includes A, or that A is included in B, and will write A ⊂ B or, equivalently, B ⊃ A.

If A includes B and B includes A, then clearly A and B have exactly the same members and are identical, and so we shall write A = B.

Sets can be "operated on" to give other sets. For instance, we can view the complement of a set (with respect to a given universal set) as the result of an operation called "taking the complement." Similarly, in arithmetic, the number 1/5 may be viewed as the result of an operation on 5—"taking the reciprocal of."

We can also operate on two sets and so get a third. For instance, we can form a set from all the members of two sets that are in both. This operation is called *intersection*. The intersection of sets A and B is written as A ∩ B. For instance, if A is the set of all cities in the United States and B is the set of all cities with more than three million inhabitants, then A ∩ B is the set comprising Chicago and New York.

Union is another operation on two sets. It is performed by calling the members of either set the members of the new set. The union of sets A and B is written A ∪ B. For example, the union of "the set of all little boys in Michigan" and "the set of all little girls in Michigan" is "the set of all children in Michigan."

From the definition of the universal set, we see that every set can be supposed to be contained in some universal set. Once a universal set has been defined, we assume that all the sets to be discussed in a given context are included in it. We shall also introduce the convention that the null set will be considered as included in any set.

From these assumptions, we get the rules of operation involving the universal set (which we designate by I) and the null set (which we designate by $\emptyset$). If A is any set, then

$$I \cap A = A$$
$$I \cup A = I$$
$$\emptyset \cap A = \emptyset$$
$$\emptyset \cup A = A.$$

Note that these rules are almost entirely analogous to rules of arithmetic if I corresponds to 1, $\emptyset$ to 0, A to any number, $\cap$ to multiplication, and $\cup$ to addition. The only exception is $I \cup A = I$. And in general, if $A \supset B$, then $A \cup B = A$; also $A \cap B = B$. Here the analogy with arithmetic breaks down.

Since the complement of a set (with respect to a universal set) is a set and the intersection of two sets is a set and the union of two sets is a set, we can compound the operations. For example, we can form the union of two sets, which is again a set, and then form the intersection of that set with another.

Compound operations in arithmetic are familiar. We can add two numbers, then multiply the *sum* by another number. In this way more than two numbers can be connected by the signs of operations of arithmetic. However, when we connect more than two numbers by signs of operations, we must be careful. By convention established in arithmetic, the multiplication must be performed first, then addition, so that 3 plus 5 times 8 equal 43. But to be sure that this is what we mean, we will do well to *punctuate* the operation thus: $3 + (5 \times 8)$. If we change the "punctuation" and write $(3 + 5) \times 8$, we have indicated that the addition is to be performed first. In that case, we get 64, not 43. The same applies to the Algebra of Sets. In fact, we shall always punctuate set theoretical operations. We shall write $A \cup (B \cap C)$ to indicate that the intersection of B and C is to be formed first and then the union between this intersection with A. We shall write $(A \cup B) \cap C$ to indicate that the union of A and B is to be formed first, then the intersection of that union with C.

In ordinary written language, punctuation frequently serves the same purpose of avoiding ambiguity. For instance, when I write: "I respect the opinion of specialists, who are experienced in this matter," I mean that I respect the opinion of specialists because specialists are experienced in this matter. If, however, I omit the comma and write: "I respect the opinion of specialists who are experienced in this matter," I mean that I respect the opinion of only *those* specialists who are experienced in this matter. The presence or the absence of a comma after "specialists" makes the important difference in meaning. Without punctuation "the heavy artillery officer" might mean either an artillery officer who is overweight or an officer of heavy artillery. Punctuation (in this case, a hyphen: heavy-artillery) could easily distinguish between the two meanings, but in ordinary written language we often rely on context to provide the intended meaning. In speech we rely on short pauses. When we say "the lighthousekeeper," we pause slightly after "light" if we mean a fair-skinned manager of a household, but we pause slightly after "house" if we mean the keeper of a lighthouse.

Sometimes punctuation makes no difference. Thus in arithmetic,

$$(5 + 3) + 8 = 5 + (3 + 8)$$

and in general,

$$(a + b) + c = a + (b + c),$$

where a, b, and c can be any numbers. This is called the *associative law* of addition. There is also an associative law of multiplication, since

$$(a \times b) \times c = a \times (b \times c),$$

where a, b, and c are any three numbers. We can therefore write without ambiguity a + b + c or a × b × c.

Addition and multiplication also obey the *commutative law*, which states that the order in which the numbers to be added or multiplied are written makes no difference. Thus

$$(a + b) = (b + a) \text{ and } (a \times b) = (b \times a).$$

In the Algebra of Sets, the operations of union and intersection also obey both the associative and the commutative laws. Thus

$$A \cup B = B \cup A \text{ and } A \cap B = B \cap A$$

$$(A \cup B) \cup C = A \cup (B \cup C)$$
$$(A \cap B) \cap C = A \cap (B \cap C).$$

In arithmetic, multiplication is *distributive* with respect to addition. That is, we can write

$$a \times (b + c) = a \times b + a \times c$$

or

$$(a + b) \times c = a \times c + b \times c.$$

Similarly, in set theory, intersection is distributive with respect to union, and we can write

$$A \cap (B \cup C) = (A \cap B) \cup (A \cap C)$$

or

$$(A \cup B) \cap C = (A \cap C) \cup (B \cap C).$$

So far the laws of set operations appear as exact analogues to corresponding laws of arithmetic operations. We now come to a fundamental difference. In arithmetic, addition is not distributive with respect to multiplication. Thus we cannot write

$$(a \times b) + c = (a + c) \times (b + c).$$

But in the Algebra of Sets, union (which in the other distributive law is analogous to addition) *is* distributive with respect to intersection, and we can write

$$(A \cap B) \cup C = (A \cup C) \cap (B \cup C).$$

We have mentioned the operation of "taking the complement of a set with respect to a universal set." This operation is applied to single sets (instead of to pairs of sets, as are intersection and union). This operation is, in some respects but not in all, analogous to "subtracting from 1" in arithmetic. Subtraction of sets is defined in the following way: $(A - B)$ is the set comprising elements of A that are not elements of B. Thus $(A - B) = A - (A \cap B) = A \cap (-B)$. If $B \supset A$, then $(A - B) = \phi$. If no element of B is an element of A, then $(A - B) = A$. Since the elements of any set are elements of the universal set, we can write $- B$ as $(I - B)$. The distributive law can be applied to get

$$A \cap (- B) = A \cap (I - B) = (A \cap I) - (A \cap B).$$

But $A \cap I = A$ (cf. p. 242). Therefore $A \cap (- B) = A - (A \cap B)$.

Similarly, in arithmetic

$$a \cdot (1 - b) = a - a \cdot b.^2$$

However, the analogy breaks down in applying "taking the complement of" to intersections and unions of sets. We have

$$-(A \cap B) = (-A) \cup (-B)$$

whereas in arithmetic

$$1 - a \cdot b \neq (1 - a) + (1 - b).$$

Also

$$-(A \cup B) = (-A) \cap (-B)$$

whereas in arithmetic

$$1 - (a + b) \neq (1 - a) \cdot (1 - b) = 1 - a - b + a \cdot b.$$

Again, as in the case of the "rules of logic" applied to the construction of syllogisms, the question arises as to whether the rules governing the operations on sets are like arbitrary rules of grammar or whether they reflect some self-evident truths. The same question occurs with regard to the rules of arithmetic. Some of these rules may appear to us to be compelling. For example, we are convinced that $5 + 3 = 3 + 5$ is a "truth," not just a convention. Other rules, however, do not appear so compelling. It is not obvious to the beginning student of algebra that $-(a \cdot b) = -(a) \cdot (b) = (a) \cdot -(b)$, and it is even less obvious that $(-a) \cdot (-b) = (a) \cdot (b)$. The "reasonableness" of these results, however, can be shown by appeal to certain *interpretations* of negative numbers. For instance, when we compute the total gains or losses in a bank account, we can represent deposits as positive numbers and withdrawals as negative numbers. Next, we can represent a stretch of the future as a positive number and a stretch of the past as a negative number. Now, if a man was withdrawing *a* dollars a month for *b* months, how much more (or less) money did he have *b* months ago? Here the rate of change in his bank account is $(-a)$ because he is withdrawing. Next, we are interested in his bank account *b* months *ago*; then $(-a)$ is to be multiplied by $(-b)$. It is clear that *b* months ago he must have had *ab* dollars *more*. Now the result $(-a) (-b) = ab$ (a positive quantity) appears evident.

2. From now on, we shall write a · b, or simply ab, to denote the product a × b.

On their face, the laws of operations on sets may not appear at all self-evident. However, we can make them appear so by resort to an interpretation represented by a diagram.

In Figure 16 the square represents the universal set, the hatched area some set A. Then the unhatched area, the remainder of the universal set, is —A, the complement of A, that is, the members of the universal set that are not in A.

In Figures 17 and 18 the hatched areas represent respectively the intersection and the union of sets A and B. The "self-evidence" of the commutative laws of union and intersection is clearly apparent. The reader can verify the "self-evidence" of the two associative laws for himself.

To represent the distributive laws, we introduce a third set C. In Figure 19 the union of A and B is hatched horizontally, and C is hatched vertically. Therefore the crosshatched area represents the intersection of C with the union of A and B or C ∩ (A ∪ B). In Figure 20 the intersection of A and C is hatched vertically, and the intersection of B and C is hatched horizontally. The union of these two sets is represented by the area hatched either way or both. We see that the sets obtained in both cases are the same.

Finally, let us see a concrete representation of the result of taking the complement of the union or the intersection of two sets.

In Figure 17 the hatched area represents —(A ∩ B), that is, the complement of the intersection of A and B. In Figure 20 the horizontally hatched area represents the complement of A; the vertically hatched area represents the complement of B; therefore the area hatched either way is the union of the two, which is the same area as the hatched area in Figure 18.

In Figure 19 the hatched area represents the complement of the union of A and B, that is —(A ∪ B). In Figure 20 the horizontally hatched area represents the complement of A; the vertically hatched area represents the complement of B; therefore the crosshatched area represents the intersection between the two. Again we see that the results are the same, and so the complement law has been illustrated.

In short, the Algebra of Sets is quite like the algebra (or arithmetic) that we know, but not exactly. Its rules of operation, however, are entirely self-consistent. Moreover, they are analogous to rules of reasoning, not only in syllogisms, as we have seen, but also in more general contexts, as we shall see in the next chapter.

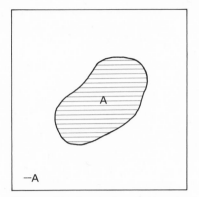

Figure 16 *A set A and its complement.*

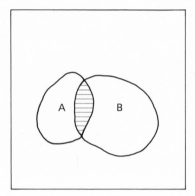

Figure 17 *Sets A and B and their intersection.*

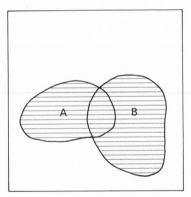

Figure 18 *Sets A and B and their union.*

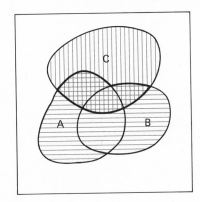

Figure 19 *The crosshatched area is the set* C ∩ (A ∪ B), *also enclosed by the thick border.*

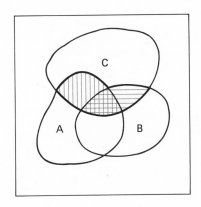

Figure 20 *The set* C ∩ (A ∪ B) *is enclosed by the thick border.*

APPLICATION

Illustrate the validity of the rules of set operations by concrete examples. For instance, let A stand for "males," B for "monkeys," C for "goats." Then A ∩ (B ∪ C) stands for "all male animals that are either monkeys or goats." The equivalent expression (A ∩ B) ∪ (A ∩ C) stands for "all animals that are either male monkeys or male goats," which is the same set. Do the same for all the other set operations listed on pages 244–46.

15/the algebra of propositions

As was discussed in Chapter 13, for over two thousand years logic remained a closed subject in the Western world because it was thought that Aristotle had said everything there was to be said about it. Essentially, what Aristotle said was that logical thought can be reduced to applications of the four types (or modes) of syllogisms listed in Chapter 13:

"Barbara"   All X are Y.
             All Y are Z.
             Therefore all X are Z.

"Celarent"   All X are Y.
             No Y is Z.
             Therefore no X is Z.

"Darii"   Some X are Y.
             All Y are Z.
             Therefore some X are Z.

"Ferio"   Some X are Y
             No Y is Z.
             Therefore some X are not Z.

Variations can be played on this theme. For instance, "All Y are Z" can also be written "No Y is not Z"; "Some X are Z" can be written as "Some Z are X"; therefore, "Darii" can be rewritten as

Some X are Y
No Y is not Z
Therefore some Z are X.

If X stands for "Greeks," Y for "rich," and Z for "having money," we can argue that if some Greeks are rich and if no rich person is without money, it follows that some people with money are Greeks.

Using transformations of this sort, Aristotle extended the number of syllogisms to twelve, and medieval logicians added four more.

The first significant advance in logic did not come until the middle of the nineteenth century, when George Boole published his monograph *The Mathematical Analysis of Logic* and somewhat later *An Investigation of the Laws of Thought*. It was not until the twentieth century, however, that research in logic took off from the launching pad prepared by Boole.

I believe that the long stagnation of logic, compared, say, with the enormous flowering of the natural sciences since the sixteenth century, resulted from the fact that logicians failed to recognize deduction as a process of manipulating symbols according to a set of rules. Instead they thought of logic as a manifestation of immutable "laws of thought," which were "discovered" once and for all by Aristotle. Boole showed that logic could be viewed as a system of symbols together with rules for putting them together; in short, as a symbolic language with a grammar. Once this was recognized, the symbolism of formal logic could be vastly expanded and with it the range of its application. Logic "took off" under precisely the same conditions that enabled mathematics to "take off," that is, when a proper symbolic language was invented for it.

Boole laid the foundations for the Algebra of Propositions. Essentially it is an adaptation of the Algebra of Sets to techniques of deducing propositions from other propositions. The analogy can be seen by comparing the corresponding features of the Algebra of Sets and of the Algebra of Propositions.

Symbols of the Algebra of Sets	*Symbols of the Algebra of Propositions*
Sets: A, B, X, Y, etc.	Propositions: p, q, r, etc.
Complement of a set: —A	Negation of proposition: $\sim p$ (read "not p")
Intersection of two sets: A ∩ B	Conjunction of two propositions: $p \wedge q$ (read "p and q")
Union of two sets: A ∪ B	Disjunction of two propositions: $p \vee q$ (read "p or q")

Set inclusion: $A \subset B$

Set identity: $A = B$

Universal set: I
Null set: $\emptyset$

Rules of Operation on Sets

Intersection is commutative:
$A \cap B = B \cap A$

Union is commutative:
$(A \cup B) = (B \cup A)$

Intersection is associative:
$(A \cap B) \cap C =$
$A \cap (B \cap C)$

Union is associative:
$(A \cup B) \cup C =$
$A \cup (B \cup C)$

Intersection is distributive with
respect to union:
$A \cap (B \cup C) =$
$(A \cap B) \cup (A \cap C)$

Union is distributive with respect
to intersection:
$A \cup (B \cap C)$
$= (A \cup B) \cap (A \cup C)$

Complement of a union:
$-(A \cup B) = (-A) \cap (-B)$

Complement of an intersection:
$-(A \cap B) = (-A) \cup (-B)$

Implication: $p \rightarrow q$ (read "p implies q," or "q is implied by p," or
"if p, then q")

Two-way implication: $p \leftrightarrow p$ (read
"q if and only if p," or "p if and
only if q")

Any true proposition: p, q, etc.
Any false proposition: p, q, etc.

*Rules of Operation on Proposi-
tions*

Conjunction is commutative:
$p \wedge q \leftrightarrow q \wedge p$

Disjunction is commutative:
$(p \vee q) \leftrightarrow (q \vee p)$

Conjunction is associative:
$(p \wedge q) \wedge r \leftrightarrow$
$p \wedge (q \wedge r)$

Disjunction is associative:
$(p \vee q) \vee r \leftrightarrow p$
$\vee (q \vee r)$

Conjunction is distributive with
respect to disjunction:
$p \wedge (q \vee r) \leftrightarrow (p \wedge q) \vee$
$(p \wedge r)$

Disjunction is distributive with respect to conjunction:
$p \vee (q \wedge r) \leftrightarrow (p \vee q) \wedge$
$(p \vee r)$

Negation of disjunction:
$\sim (p \vee q) \leftrightarrow (\sim p) \wedge (\sim q)$

Negation of a conjunction:
$\sim (p \wedge q) \leftrightarrow (\sim p) \vee (\sim q)$

To make the Algebra of Propositions a tool of deduction, we must
symbolize "truth." In two-valued (Aristotelian) logic, every proposition has one of two "truth values": it is either true or false. If a proposition p is true, we write $p = 1$. If it is false, we write $p = 0$.

Negations, conjunctions, and disjunctions of propositions also are propositions and so can also have either of the two truth values, 0 or 1. For example, we can write

$$(p \lor q) = 1.$$

If p stands for "It is raining" and q for "it is snowing," then $(p \lor q)$ = 1 stands for "It is true that it is either raining or snowing." Let us write "It is indeed the case that the boy may have either pudding or pie but not both." Let p stand for "The boy may have pudding." Then $\sim$ p will mean "The boy may not have pudding." Let q stand for "The boy may have pie." Then $\sim$ q will mean "The boy may not have pie." We write

$$(p \land \sim q) \lor (\sim p \land q) = 1.$$

In the first parenthesis, we read "The boy may have pudding but not pie"; in the second, "The boy may have pie but not pudding." The two are connected by "or" ($\lor$). Setting the whole thing equal to 1 marks our proposition as true: "It is indeed the case that. . . ."

Note that in ordinary language the word "or" does not distinguish between "one or the other but not both" and "one or the other or both." [1] Thus the "or" in the proposition "The boy may have pudding or pie" might mean that he could have only one of the desserts; and it might also mean that he could have either or both. The symbol "v" in the Algebra of Propositions always means "one or the other or both." For this reason it would be wrong to write "The boy may have either pudding or pie but not both" as $(p \lor q)$. For the same reason, the previous proposition must be understood as saying "It is raining or snowing or both."

The analogue to truth value "1" in the Algebra of Sets is the Universal Set I. The analogue to truth value "0" is the Null Set $\emptyset$. If the result of operations on sets is the Universal Set, the truth value of the proposition resulting from the analogous operations on propositions is 1. If the result of operations on sets is the Null Set, the truth value of the proposition that results from analogous operations on propositions is 0. This can be seen by comparing the axioms of the

1. In Latin, this distinction is made. "Vel" means "or" in the sense of "either or both"; "aut . . . aut . . ." means "either . . . or . . ., but not both." The symbol "V" in the Algebra of Propositions is derived from "vel."

Algebra of Sets with those of the Algebra of Propositions. Axioms are assertions assumed to be true. They serve as the foundation of the deductive system.[2]

Axioms of Set Theory	*Axioms of the Algebra of Propositions*
	$p \leftrightarrow p$
Axiom 1. A $=$ A	(Any proposition implies and is implied by itself.)
(Any set includes and is included by itself.)	
Axiom 2. A $\cap$ ($-$A) $= \emptyset$	$p \wedge (\sim p) = 0$
The intersection of any set and its complement is the Null Set. This is a direct consequence of the definition of "complement" and of "Null Set."	The conjunction of any proposition with its negation is always false.
Axiom 3. A $\cup$ ($-$A) $=$ I	$p \vee (\sim p) = 1$
The union of any set and its complement is the Universal Set. Again this is a direct consequence of the definition of "complement" and of "Universal Set."	The disjunction of any proposition and its negation is always true.
Axiom 4. A $\subset$ I	If $p = 1$, then $q \rightarrow p$.
Every set is included in the Universal Set.	A true proposition is implied by *any* proposition.
Axiom 5. $\emptyset \subset$ A	If $q = 0$, then $q \rightarrow p$.
The Null Set is included in any set.	A false proposition implies *any* proposition.

The first three of these axioms are the famous three axioms of Aristotelian logic. Axiom 1 is called the Law of Identity. Axiom 2 is

---

2. The axioms of any deductive system can be chosen in many ways. Once chosen, propositions derived from them are called theorems. It is, however, possible to "shift the base" of the system so that some of the theorems are taken as axioms and what had been axioms become theorems. The choice of propositions to serve as axioms is largely a matter of their intuitive "self-evidence" or, at times, a matter of taste. The principle of parsimony (cf. p. 349) demands also that no axiom be redundant, that is, derivable from other axioms; but this is not logically necessary. However, it goes without saying that the axioms must be consistent with each other. Our choice of the axioms of the Algebra of Propositions was guided by convenience in pursuing this exposition.

called the Law of Noncontradiction (a proposition and its negation cannot both be true). Axiom 3 is called the Law of Excluded Middle (either a proposition is true or its negation is true).

These axioms are easily accepted. In fact, most people find it difficult to imagine how it is possible to deny them. We shall see, however (cf. Chapter 19), that in some instances the Law of Excluded Middle may, or even must, be dispensed with. As for the last two axioms, they seem self-evident when stated as principles of set theory but may seem strange in the Algebra of Propositions. What does it mean to say that a true proposition is implied by every other proposition?

Assume that "George Washington was born in 1732" is a true proposition. For an arbitrary proposition, take "Mr. Pi is fond of Welsh rarebit." Axiom 4 says "If Mr. Pi is fond of Welsh rarebit, then Washington was born in 1732." This looks like sheer nonsense because there is no connection between Mr. Pi's fondness for Welsh rarebit and the date of Washington's birth, certainly not if Mr. Pi was born long after Washington died. However, in questioning the application of the fourth axiom in this context, we read too much into the axiom. We may have got the impression that we can *deduce* the date of Washington's birth from Mr. Pi's fondness for Welsh rarebit, which, of course, we cannot. All the axiom says is that if a statement is given as true, we can assert its truth, given any other proposition. Thus, if it *is* true that Washington was born in 1732, then it is true—no matter what we say about Mr. Pi, Welsh rarebit, or anything else.

The meaning of the last axiom is analogous. To say that a false statement implies every other is to say that once a contradiction has been admitted into a logical system, then *anything* can be proved, including every proposition and its negation. Mr. Rho appeals to this principle when he says, "If this is so, then my name is not Rho," meaning that "this" *cannot* be so. Hermann Goering, the chief of the German Air Force during World War II, appealed to the same principle when he declared that if British bombers ever came near Berlin, then his name was Meyer, meaning that it was impossible for British bombers to come near Berlin. When bombings of Berlin by the RAF started, Berliners surreptitiously referred to Field Marshal Goering as "Herr Meyer." Let us translate this story into the Algebra of Propositions. Let p stand for "British bombers come near Berlin,"

and q for "Hermann Goering's name is Meyer." Goering said
"p → q." What he meant was that since p is a false proposition it implies every proposition, even the false proposition q. But p turned out
to be a true proposition. Since a true proposition can imply only a
true proposition, it followed that q was a true proposition, which is
what Berliners asserted when they called Goering "Herr Meyer."

In the light of the same axiom, we can explain the paradoxical conclusion in the apparently valid syllogism (cf. p. 237):

All golden mountains are mountains.
All golden mountains are golden.
Therefore some mountains are golden.

Let p stand for "Something is a golden mountain"; q for "Something is a mountain"; r for "Something is golden." Translated into the
Algebra of Propositions, the syllogism reads:
$$(p \rightarrow q) \land (p \rightarrow r) \rightarrow p.$$
That is, the syllogism says that if $(p \rightarrow q) = 1$ and $(p \rightarrow r) = 1$, we
ought to be able to conclude that $p = 1$. If a golden mountain exists
somewhere, then indeed $p = 1$ ("Something is a golden mountain").
But if there are no golden mountains to begin with, the syllogism does
not help us prove that "Some mountains are golden," for then, even
if $(p \rightarrow q) = 1$ and $(p \rightarrow r) = 1$, we cannot conclude that $p = 1$.
The fifth axiom says that a false proposition implies *every* proposition.
Therefore, from the fact that some proposition implies any number of
other propositions, we cannot infer the truth of that proposition.
If it were false, it would imply every proposition *anyway*. Thus, if no
golden mountains exist, we can write $p \rightarrow x$, where x is any proposition whatsoever including the negation of p. In short, $(p \rightarrow x) = 1$
does not imply $p = 1$.

The situation is quite analogous to the paradoxes obtained from
dividing by zero. If dividing by zero is allowed, we can argue that
since $0 \times 1 = 0 \times 2$, it follows that $1 = 2$. The reason zero cannot
be eliminated from an equation by division is precisely because *any
number* multiplied by zero is zero. Similarly, if $p \rightarrow q$ is true and q is
true, it does not follow that p is true because if p were false, $p \rightarrow q$
would be true anyway.

The rules of operation in the Algebra of Propositions can be
verified diagrammatically if they are first translated into the rules

of operation on sets. For instance, the "negation of a conjunction" was verified in its set-theoretical garb on page 245. Let us see what it says about propositions. The disjunction of p and q says "p or q." If the resulting proposition is true, (p ∨ q) is tantamount to saying that either p is true or q is true or both. To deny this means to assert that both p and q are false, which means that the negation of p and the negation of q are both true. Hence ∼ (p ∨ q) ↔ (∼p ∧ ∼p). Example:

To say that "It is not the case that either Fabius was born under the dog star or he will perish in the sea" is the same as to say "Fabius was neither born under the dog star nor will he perish in the sea."[3]

The rules of operation of the Algebra of Propositions, besides being analogues to rules of operation in the Algebra of Sets, have also near-analogues in the rules of operation of arithmetic. Let p be a true proposition and q a false one. The assignment of truth puts p in correspondence with "1" and q with "0." Now let ∨ correspond to "plus" and ∧ to "times." We can verify by reference to corresponding set operations (interpreting a true proposition as the Universal Set and the false one as the Null Set) that the truth values given in the left-hand column below must be assigned to the several conjunctions and disjunctions.

Truth values of conjunctions and disjunctions, assuming p true and q false.	Operations of arithmetic
p ∧ p is true	$1 \times 1 = 1$
p ∧ q is false	$1 \times 0 = 0$
q ∧ p is false	$0 \times 1 = 0$
q ∧ q is false	$0 \times 0 = 0$
q ∨ q is false	$0 + 0 = 0$
q ∨ p is true	$0 + 1 = 1$
p ∨ q is true	$1 + 0 = 1$
p ∨ p is true	$1 + 1 = 2$

Comparing the two columns, note that the analogy is almost complete. The only exception is the last equation on the right: it has no analogue in the Algebra of Propositions because that language does

3. From Cicero's *De Fato*, in George Boole, *An Investigation of the Laws of Thought* (New York: Dover Publications, 1854), p. 179.

not contain the symbol "2." To make the analogy complete, we would have to write $1 + 1 = 1$. This may look absurd, but only if we think of it as a proposition in the language of ordinary arithmetic. It *is* a true (and sensible) proposition in "Boolean Algebra," as the arithmetic operations analogous to those of the Algebra of Propositions is called. After all, there should be nothing surprising in the fact that utterances in one language look absurd if they are interpreted as utterances in another. We see the importance of recognizing that logic is very much like a grammar. The study of pure logic belongs to *syntactics* rather than to semantics. Correct logical inferences can be deduced without reference to the meanings for which the symbols are supposed to stand.

Boole's great achievement was to show that logical reasoning amounts to manipulation of symbols according to prescribed rules. If, however, we want to connect the inferences to assertions about the world, we must know what we are talking about. Set theory provides symbols for defining *complex* classes, that is, classes compounded of other classes. As an example of a complex class, Boole takes the following definition of "wealth":

Wealth consists of things transferable, limited in supply, and either pro-ductive of pleasure or preventive of pain.[4]

This definition says that wealth is a class of things, the class being *compounded* in a certain way from other classes. Let us see how. Let

W denote the class (set) of things that constitute wealth.
T the cless of transferable things.
S the class of things limited in supply.
P the class of things productive of pleasure.
R the class of things preventive of pain.

Recall that "and" corresponds to conjunction in the Algebra of Propositions and so to intersection in the Algebra of Sets; "or" cor-responds to disjunction in the Algebra of Propositions and to union in the Algebra of Sets. Moreover, the first comma in the above definition of wealth actually stands for "and," which is omitted for

4. Ibid., p. 107.

purely stylistic reasons. We can now rewrite the definition of wealth in the language of set theory:

$$W = S \cap T \cap (P \cup R).$$

We can translate this set equation into a propositional equation if we let propositions denoting class inclusion correspond to the classes. For instance, let the proposition

w stand for "virtue is wealth."
t for "virtue is transferable."
s for "virtue is limited in supply."
p for "virtue is productive of pleasure."
r for "virtue is preventive of pain."

Then we can write (corresponding to the set equation above) the propositional equation

$$w \leftrightarrow s \wedge t \wedge (p \vee r).$$

Suppose now we agree that virtue is limited in supply, is productive of pleasure, and preventive of pain, but is not transferable. Assigning to our propositions truth values that reflect these assumptions, we get

$s = 1$
$t = 0$
$p = 1$
$r = 1.$

Applying the rules of Boolean Algebra to the right side of the propositional equation, we get

$$1 \times 0 \times (1 + 1) = 0.$$

Therefore $w = 0$, or w is a false proposition. Conclusion: virtue is not wealth.

On the other hand, suppose we are convinced that virtue in limited supply *is* transferable, *is* preventive of pain, but *is not* productive of pleasure. Then our "truth equation" would be

$$1 \times 1 \times (0 + 1) = 1.$$

In this case, $w = 1$, and w is a true proposition. Conclusion: virtue is wealth.

It is most important to remember that the Algebra of Propositions provides us with a method of deciding whether a proposition is a true consequence of some other given propositions. It does *not* provide us with a method of deciding whether propositions are *factually* true or false. This is the nature of all purely deductive reasoning.

To take another example, we read in Plato's *Republic*:[5]

SOCRATES:	. . . if we suppose a change in anything, that change must be effected either by the thing itself, or by some other thing?
ADEIMANTUS:	Most certainly.
SOCRATES:	And things which are at their best are also least liable to be altered or discomposed: for example, when healthiest and strongest, the human frame is least liable to be affected by meats and drinks, and the plant which is in the fullest vigor also suffers least from winds or the heat of the sun or any similar causes.
ADEIMANTUS:	Of course.
SOCRATES:	And will not the bravest and wisest soul be least confused or deranged by an external influence?
ADEIMANTUS:	True.
SOCRATES:	And the same principle, as I should suppose, applies to all composite things—furniture, houses, garments: when good and well made, they are least altered by time and circumstances.
ADEIMANTUS:	Very true.
SOCRATES:	Then everything which is good, whether made by art or nature, or both, is least liable to suffer change from without?
ADEIMANTUS:	True.
SOCRATES:	But surely God and the things of God are in every way perfect?
ADEIMANTUS:	Of course they are.
SOCRATES:	Then he can hardly be compelled by external influence to take many shapes?
ADEIMANTUS:	He cannot.

5. Plato, *Five Great Dialogues*, trans. B. Jowett, ed. Louise Ropes Loomis (New York: Walter J. Black, 1942), pp. 283–85.

SOCRATES:	But may he not change and transform himself?
ADEIMANTUS:	Clearly, that must be the case if he is changed at all.
SOCRATES:	And will he then change himself for the better and fairer, or for the worse and more unsightly?
ADEIMANTUS:	If he changes at all, he can only change for the worse, for we cannot suppose him to be deficient either in virtue or beauty.
SOCRATES:	Very true, Adeimantus; but then, would anyone, whether God or man, desire to make himself worse?
ADEIMANTUS:	Impossible.
SOCRATES:	Then it is impossible that God should ever be willing to change; being, as is supposed, the fairest and best that is conceivable, every God remains absolutely and forever in his own form.

From this argument, Boole distills the following *premises* (or "givens").[6]

1. If the Deity suffers change, He is changed either by Himself or by another.
2. If He is in the best state, He is not changed by another.
3. The Deity is in the best state.
4. If the Deity is changed by Himself, He is changed to a worse state.
5. If He acts willingly, He is not changed to a worse state.
6. The Deity acts willingly.

Now let x stand for "The Deity suffers change."

y: "He is changed by himself."
z: "He is changed by another."
s: "He is in the best state."
t: "He is changed to a worse state."
w: "He acts willingly."

Rewriting the premises in the Algebra of Propositions, we get:

1. $x \rightarrow y \lor z$
2. $s \rightarrow \sim z$

6. Boole, *An Investigation of the Laws*, p. 182.

3. $s = 1$
4. $y \rightarrow t$
5. $w \rightarrow \sim t$
6. $w = 1$

Since $s = 1$, $\sim z = 1$, or $z = 0$. (A proposition implied by a true proposition is true, and its negation is false. Note that the negation of a negation of a proposition is the original proposition.) Further, since $t = 0$, $y = 0$. (A false proposition can be implied only by a false proposition.)

Next, if $y = 0$, and $z = 0$, it follows that $y \lor z = 0$ $(0 + 0 = 0)$. Therefore $x = 0$, or $\sim x = 1$.

Conclusion: The Deity does not change ("remains absolutely in the same form").

Again the reader is reminded most emphatically that the factual truth of the conclusion is here not at issue, *nor even the meaning of the conclusion.* Deduction is a symbol-manipulating process and nothing else.

Next, let us solve a "brain teaser" of the sort often published in puzzle collections.

In a certain community, the following propositions are true about all men living in it.

1. If a man likes poetry, he does not play bridge; moreover, if he likes poetry, he is either married or he is not a logician.
2. If a man is not a logician and plays bridge, then he is a married man who dislikes poetry.
3. If a man is a logician or if he does not play bridge, then he likes poetry.
4. A man either plays bridge or he is an unmarried logician.

Mr. Sigma is a member of that community. What can we say about his occupation, his family status, his recreation habits, and his attitude to poetry?

The problem seems difficult because ordinary language obscures the logical relations. It is difficult to keep in mind all the alternatives, implications, negations, and so on. To draw the inferences required, we translate the propositions into the Algebra of Propositions.

Let p be the proposition "A member of the community is a logician."
Similarly, q stands for "He plays bridge."
r stands for "He is married."
s stands for "He likes poetry."
Then $\sim$ p will stand for "He is not a logician," and so on.

Then the formula for the first proposition is

1. $s \rightarrow \sim q \wedge (r \vee \sim p)$.
For the second proposition, we write:
2. $(\sim p \wedge q) \rightarrow (r \wedge \sim s)$.
For the third:
3. $(p \vee \sim q) \rightarrow s$.
And for the fourth:
4. $q \vee (p \wedge \sim r) = 1$.

Now we apply the transformation rules of the Algebra of Proposi-
tions (cf. p. 252). If we negate the right side of formula 1, we get
$q \vee (\sim r \wedge p)$. But according to equation 4, this proposition is true.
Therefore s implies the negation of a true proposition, that is, a false
proposition, and consequently must itself stand for a false proposition.
If s is false, we conclude that no man in the community likes poetry.
Turning to formula 3, we see that $(p \vee \sim q)$ implies a false proposition and therefore must itself be false. If it is false, its negation
must be true. Applying the transformation rule (cf. p. 252), we
write the negation as $(\sim p \wedge q)$, and this negation must be a true
proposition. This tells us that no man in the community is a logician
and moreover that every man in the community plays bridge.
Turning to formula 2, we see that a proposition which we have
established as true, namely $(\sim p \wedge q)$, implies another proposition,
namely $(r \wedge \sim s)$. But a proposition implied by a true proposition
must be true. We conclude that all men in the community are married
and that none of them likes poetry (which we have already established). But Mr. Sigma was *any* man in the community. Therefore
we can say about *every* man in that community, including Mr. Sigma,
that he is not a logician, that he plays bridge, that he is married, and
that he does not like poetry.
It is instructive to see what our conclusion would be if the second

proposition read "If a man is not a logician and plays bridge, then he is a married man and *likes* poetry." Translated into a formula of symbolic logic, the proposition would look like this:

$$(\sim p \wedge q) \rightarrow (r \wedge s).$$

But we have deduced from the other propositions that s = 0. Therefore (r ∧ s) = 0, and (∼ p ∧ q) would have to be false, in contradiction to our conclusion that (∼ p ∧ q) is true. This shows that all four propositions could not be asserted about any man in the community. We would have to conclude that there were no men in that community. If the community exists at all, it must consist exclusively of women and children.

Problems "without an answer" can arise also in mathematics. For instance, if we ask "What number multiplied by zero yields 5," the only "answer" is "no number."

The Algebra of Propositions is part of a larger branch of modern mathematics called *symbolic logic*. Symbolic logic has made a powerful impact on the development of mathematics and its applications. In particular, it made possible the "automation" of reasoning. In an electronic computer, there are elements that "realize" the operations of conjunction, disjunction, and negation. The conjunction element is shown in Figure 21.

The element has two inputs and one output. The number "2" indicates that the "threshold" of the element is 2, that is, the two inputs must both be activated (say, by an electric current) in order for the output to be activated. When the output of an element is activated, the element is said to "fire." Call an activated input or output a "true proposition" and a nonactivated one a "false proposition." Then the element "utters a true proposition" (it fires) if and only if both of its inputs utter a true proposition. In other words, the element performs the operation (p ∧ q) where p and q represent the two in-

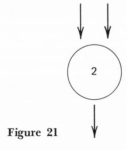

Figure 21

puts, since (p ∧ q) = 1 (the element fires) if and only if p = 1 and q = 1.

The disjunction element is represented in Figure 22. Here the threshold is "1." That is to say, the element fires if *either* (or both) of the inputs is activated. This element, therefore, performs the operation (p ∨ q), since (p ∨ q) = 1 (the element fires) if and only if either p = 1 or q = 1 or both.

Figure 22

The negation element is represented in Figure 23. This element fires if and only if its input is *not* activated. Such an input is called *inhibitory*, designated here by a dotted line.

Figure 23

Elements representing conjunction, disjunction, and negation can be combined in a variety of ways so as to realize any sort of "deduction" that can be represented in the Algebra of Propositions.

Now, one component of "intelligence," as it is generally understood, is the ability to undertake involved chains of reasoning. Problems of the following sort are often included in intelligence tests: "If 5 is larger than 3, cross out the fourth word in this sentence unless 17 is divisible by 4, in which case cross out the seventh word. If you have crossed out either word but not both, or if it is not the case that a yard is longer than a mile, place an x at the end of this sentence."

Complex computations, the retrieval of certain information from records, decisions based on involved contingencies, all require reasoning of this sort. The realization of operations on symbols by means of causally connected electronic events clearly shows that *certain* functions of reasoning can be performed by a machine as well as by "an intelligent being." (Indeed, the electronic computer can perform such logical operations many thousand times faster than a human being.)

The appearance of "intelligent" machines has raised thought-provoking philosophical questions about the "nature of mind" and, as expected, a great deal of controversy, some of it bitter. Arguments continue as to whether a computer "really" thinks or whether the human mind is "nothing but" a complex computer. We shall examine this controversy at the end of this chapter.

Related to the Algebra of Propositions is another very important branch of mathematics called the *theory of probability*. So far we have considered only two possible values of a proposition: "true," designated by "1," and "false," designated by "0." In probability theory, a proposition can have any value between zero and one, the two extremes included. Here the truth value of a proposition is called the *probability* of the proposition. In probability theory, propositions are generally statements that some event will or has occurred (or will not or has not occurred). Therefore we can identify the propositions with the events and speak of the probability of an event.

We shall designate events by A, B, etc., and their probabilities by p(A), p(B), etc. (read "the probability that A occurs," etc.).

The operations of the Algebra of Sets apply to events. For instance, (A ∪ B) stands for "Either event A or event B occurs, or both." (A ∩ B) stands for "Event A and event B both occur." (—A) stands for "Event A does not occur." Then p(A ∪ B), p(A ∩ B), and p(—A) will designate respectively the probabilities of the propositions obtained by disjunction, conjunction, and negation.

Probability theory can be viewed as an "infinite-valued logic," that is, an *extension* of (Aristotelian) two-valued logic to include "fractional" truth values.

Before we compare the operations of two-valued logic with those of infinite-valued logic, we need to define one more concept, that of *conditional* probability. The symbol $p(A \mid B)$ stands for the probability that event A occurs (or will occur) if it is known that B *has* occurred.[7]

In general, $p(A)$ is not equal to $p(A \mid B)$. For instance, let A stand for "A heart is drawn from a shuffled deck of cards." We usually assume that $p(A) = 1/4$, since each of the four suits is thought to have the same chance of being drawn. Now let B stand for the event "The card drawn is red." When we know that the card drawn is red, we think of it as being a heart or a diamond with equal probability. Therefore $(p(A \mid B) = 1/2$.

However, it may happen that $p(A) = p(A \mid B)$. For instance, let A again be the event "A heart is drawn." Now let B stand for the event "The card is drawn on Tuesday." If there is no reason to suppose that the day of the week has any influence on the suit drawn, then $p(A) = p(A \mid B) = 1/4$. In this case we say that A and B are *independent* events.[8]

It may also turn out that $p(A \mid B) = 0$. For instance, if B stands for "The card drawn is black," then the card cannot be a heart. Hence if B occurs, A becomes an impossible event, and $p(A \mid B) = 0$. If $p(B)$ is not zero, but $p(A \mid B) = 0$, we say that A and B are *mutually exclusive events*.

Now we are ready to state the rules of calculating probabilities of events obtained by operating on other events. We have

    1. $p(A \cup B) = p(A) + p(B) - p(A \cap B)$.

    2. $p(A \cap B) = p(A) \times p(B \mid A)$, or

        $p(A \cap B) = p(B) \times p(A \mid B)$.

Assuming that neither A nor B is an impossible event, it can be shown that the right-hand sides of equation 2 are equal:

    3. $p(-A) = 1 - p(A)$.[9]

It is easy to see that these rules are directly analogous to rules that

---

7. Formally, $P(A \mid B)$ is defined as $\dfrac{P(A \cap B)}{P(B)}$, provided $P(B) \neq 0$. Similarly, $P(B \mid A)$ is defined as $\dfrac{P(A \cap B)}{P(A)}$. It follows that we can write either $P(A \cap B) = P(B) \cdot P(A \mid B)$, or $P(A \cap B) = P(A) \cdot P(B \mid A)$.

8. In this case, clearly $P(A \cap B) = P(A) \cdot P(B \mid A)$.

9. Recall that in the Algebra of Sets, $-A = I - A$.

assign truth values to disjunctions, conjunctions, and negations, in the Algebra of Propositions. If we think of A and B as propositions, there are four possibilities.

1. Both A and B are true propositions.
2. A is true, B is false.
3. A is false, B is true.
4. Both A and B are false.

If both A and B are true, $p(A) = 1$, $p(B) = 1$, and $p(A \cap B) = 1$. Thus $p(A) + p(B) - p(A \cap B) = 1 + 1 - 1 = 1$; so that $p(A \cup B) = 1$. In other words, if two propositions are true, their disjunction is true.

Similarly, if only one of the propositions A or B is true, it is easy to see that the disjunction is still true. Only if both propositions are false is the disjunction false, for then $p(A \cup B) = 0 + 0 = 0$.

In the same way, we can verify if the conjunction of A and B is true if and only if *both* propositions are true.

Finally, if A is true, $p(A) = 1$, so that $1 - p(A) = 0$. If A is false, $p(A) = 0$, so that $p(-A) = 1 - p(A) = 1$. In other words, if a proposition is true, its negation is false and vice versa.

In short, the assignment of the extreme truth values (1 or 0) to disjunctions, conjunctions, and negations of probabilistic propositions reduces to the assignment of truth values to disjunctions, conjunctions, and negations of propositions in two-valued logic. Since, however, probability theory covers also intermediate cases, it goes much further than two-valued logic.

For illustration, we shall see how the theory of probability is applied in a game of craps. The game can be viewed as a sequence of "experiments" (throws of the dice). Call the two dice #1 and #2. Each experiment can have one of 36 different *outcomes* because #1 can fall in six different ways, and each can be paired with six different ways in which #2 can fall. If we have no reason to suppose that a die is more likely to fall on one face than on another, we assign equal probabilities to each of these outcomes. An event is any *set* of these outcomes. In particular, the entire set comprising all 36 is also an event. Since this event is certain to occur (the dice must fall one way or another), we assign to it probability 1. Moreover the 36 outcomes are mutually exclusive. That is to say, for any two outcomes A and

B, $p(A \cap B) = 0$. Therefore, according to our formula 1 above, for any two outcomes A and B, we have $p(A \cup B) = p(A) + p(B)$. Therefore the probability of each of the outcomes is $1/36$, since the probabilities of all the 36 mutually exclusive outcomes must sum to 1.

The probability of any event in this game can be calculated by counting the number of outcomes that comprise the event and multiplying this number by $1/36$.

Let us calculate the probability that the sum of the points on the two dice is seven. This event can happen in the following ways and only these:

#1 shows an ace, #2 shows a six.
#1 shows a two, #2 shows a five.
#1 shows a three, #2 shows a four.
#1 shows a four, #2 shows a three.
#1 shows a five, #2 shows a two.
#1 shows a six, #2 shows an ace.

There being six outcomes comprising the event, the probability of a "seven" is $6/36 = 1/6$. On the other hand, the probability of "snake eyes" (two aces) is only $1/36$ because there is only one way in which this event can occur. In fact, the probabilities of the events that "count" in the game of craps (that is, the numbers of points shown) are, starting with two and ending with twelve, respectively, $1/36$, $1/18$, $1/12$, $1/9$, $5/36$, $1/6$, $5/36$, $1/9$, $1/12$, $1/18$, $1/36$.

It is not necessary to resort to counting outcomes in every case. Suppose we want to know the probability that at least one of the two dice will show an ace. Let A stand for the event "#1 shows an ace"; B the event "#2 shows an ace." Then $(A \cap B)$ is the event "Both dice show an ace," and the event that interests us ("Either or both show an ace") is $(A \cup B)$. Now $p(A) = 1/6$; $p(B) = 1/6$; $p(A \cap B) = 1/36$. Applying the formula for $p(A \cup B)$, we get

$$p(A \cup B) = 1/6 + 1/6 - 1/36 = 11/36,$$

which is the probability we seek.

Next, suppose a player shoots an "eight." What interests him is the probability of the event "In subsequent throws, an eight will appear before a seven"; for he wins if that event occurs and loses otherwise. The probability of win will also indicate to onlookers the reasonable odds to give or accept in side bets as to whether the player will "make it." [10]

Here the "experiment" is no longer a single throw of the dice but rather a sequence of repeated throws which ends with the appearance of either an eight or a seven. An outcome of such an experiment is any of the possible sequences of single outcomes ending in an eight or a seven. Of these sequences there is an infinity, and so we cannot count them. Nevertheless the mathematical techniques of probability theory permit us to calculate these probabilities.

The results of such calculations are sometimes surprising. For instance, it can be proved that if 40 people are selected at random, the chances are better than eight to one that at least two of them will have the same birthday. Most people with little experience in these matters find this conclusion difficult to believe. It is nevertheless a logical consequence of rather reasonable assumptions, such as that every day of the year has about the same chance of being an arbitrary person's birthday (that is, about 1/365) and that one person's birthday is not "influenced" by another's.[11]

Skeptics will want to verify the conclusion by experiment. This can be done. Take a table of random numbers (available in any mathematics library). Read off successive triples. Let each triple stand for a day of the year. For example, 028 stands for the twenty-eighth day (January 28); 131 stands for May 11, and so on. Disregard triples larger than 365. In this way you can get successive samples of 40 "days." Examine several such samples to convince yourself that those

---

10. Systematic development of probability theory was inspired by a problem put by Chevalier de Méré, a French gambler, to Pierre de Fermat, a foremost mathematician of the seventeenth century. Essentially, the problem can be paraphrased as follows. Suppose Mr. Tau and Mr. Upsilon match pennies, recording a point for each win. The player who accumulates 100 points first wins the stake. However, for some reason the game is broken off, Mr. Tau having made 90 points and Mr. Upsilon 80. What is a "fair division" of the stake? One could define a "fair division" as one that awards to each of the players a fraction of the stake proportional to the probability that he will reach 100 before the other player. When onlookers make side bets while a player is shooting craps, they are betting on or against the event that the player's number will come up before a seven. The problem of calculating the probability of this event is similar to the problem posed by de Méré.

11. The probability that *no* two people in a crowd of 40 have the same birthday (for simplicity ignoring February 29) is given by

$$\frac{(364)\ (363)\ (362)\ \ldots\ (326)}{(365)\ (365)\ (365)\ \ldots\ (365)} = 1/9 \text{ (approximately)}.$$

Therefore the probability that at least two have the same birthday is $1 - 1/9 = 8/9$.

wherein some days occur more than once are about eight times more numerous than those where all days are different.

Here note again the warning issued earlier: *We are discussing deduction. Deduction establishes only logical consequences, not facts.* Probability theory says nothing about actual birthdays of actual people. It says only this: If you believe that people's birthdays are randomly distributed in the population, and if you believe that a sample of 40 people was assembled without regard to their birthdays (as at an ordinary gathering), then you *also* ought to believe that the chances in favor of at least two coincident birthdays are about eight to one. This conclusion is as compelling as the conclusion that Socrates is mortal if one accepts the premises that all men are mortal and that Socrates is a man. It is a far cry from the nearly obvious conclusions deduced in syllogisms to the sometimes startling conclusions deduced by infinite-valued logic (probability theory). But the two processes have this in common: the truth of the conclusion depends *entirely* on the truth of the premises.

In fact, *all* of mathematical reasoning, being purely deductive reasoning, establishes *only* conclusions of this sort.

We have seen how strict deductive reasoning can be completely "automated" and have mentioned the controversy on the subject of "thinking machines."

It is instructive to analyze arguments of this sort in the same way we analyzed the argument about whether Peter was richer than Paul (cf. chapter 12). Recall that once Mr. Xi and Mr. Omicron agree on what to compare, the argument can be settled if the relevant data are accessible to observation. The difficulty in the present case is that many notions that people associate with "thinking" cannot be translated into observable events. Nevertheless *some* criteria of "thought" can be stated in terms of observable events. If we give someone a problem, say, in arithmetic or in logic, and he solves it, we certainly ascribe to him the ability to think. If we ask a person a question and get a reasonable answer, we do the same. It is possible therefore to argue that, since a computer prints out solutions of many kinds of problems presented to it and gives intelligent answers to many kinds of questions, it gives evidence of "thinking."

A typical objection to this conclusion is that the way the computer "solves problems" or "answers questions" is determined by the way the computer has been put together. On the face of it, the objection does not refute the conclusion, since it stands to reason that the way a human being solves problems and answers questions may also be determined by the way he has been "put together," by the arrangement of connections in his nervous system, for instance. If so, then the only difference between human and electronic "thinking" is that some specialists know exactly what happens in electronic "thought," while no one knows exactly what happens in human thought. But surely our ignorance about the (physiological) details of human thought processes is not a good reason to attribute "thought" to us while denying it to the computer. If it were, we would have to attribute "thought" to a computer if the only people who knew the details of its construction and operation died, and if for some reason it were impossible for others to learn these details.

A more significant difference between natural and artificial "thinking" is the intolerance of the latter to any sort of vagueness. Problems and questions put to a computer must be formulated in a very special language that the computer "understands." These computer languages are all semantically and grammatically perfect. In contrast, meaningful human communication can take place in spite of considerable ambiguity. Much of our understanding of what others are saying is a matter of guesswork guided by past experience, of which we may even be unaware. In particular, we understand analogies and figurative meanings intuitively, and, precisely *because* we do not know how we understand them, we cannot reproduce this "understanding" (cognition) in computers. The limitations on the computer's "thought," then, stem not from the complexity of relations to be discerned (in some ways, computers can discern far more complex relations more quickly than we can) but rather from the computer's dependence on the absolute precision of the language that serves as the instrument of cognition. Typically, a trivial grammatical error in the formulation of a problem will "frustrate" a computer.[12]

This shortcoming in artificial "intelligence," however, could be

12. Similarly, the crucial difficulty in automating translation from one language to another is that no completely formalized grammar of any natural langue has yet been written. Much of our "knowledge" of the grammar of our mother tongue is intuitive—we cannot explain how we know what we know in terms of fixed rules. Grammarians, of course, know a great many details of grammatical structure but not enough to program a computer with a "knowledge" of grammar comparable to that of a human being.

overcome by built-in corrective devices based on matching erroneous communications with correct ones to which they are likely to correspond. This process would be analogous to guessing the meaning of a vague utterance.

Another objection often raised to calling computer operations "thought" is that a computer cannot "think creatively." Again we must face the difficult problem of specifying concretely what we mean by "creative thought." If a novel or unique solution of a problem is evidence of "creative thought," a computer could, in principle, come up with one. It is quite possible to conceive of a computer that can discover a new proof of a mathematical theorem or even prove a theorem that no one has proved before. Chess-playing computers can "improve" their games by comparing their own with others' past performances stored in the computers' memory banks. A chess-playing computer can conceivably become a stronger player than its designer.

Arguments in favor of ascribing thought to computers are dismissed by those who consider that *whatever* the computer does that resembles thought is not "really" thought. Every time some new feat of "intelligence" is performed by the latest "generation" of computers, the deniers of computer-generated thinking tend to redefine thinking in a way that will exclude the performance as evidence of "real thought."

Admittedly, present-day computers can simulate only very special kinds of thought. A vast amount of human mental activity remains outside what it is possible to simulate at present and is consequently ascribed to aspects of human thought forever inaccessible to automation. Yet it would be risky to specify exactly just what a computer will never be able to do. The point is that, once some aspect of mental activity is *sufficiently precisely defined* (in the sense of stating explicitly just what is demanded), it becomes possible in principle to simulate this mental activity via translating logical operations into electronic ones (cf. pp. 264–65). "Imperfect" mental activity, including chance errors, can also be simulated. It is important to keep in mind that the crucial obstacle to simulating so many human mental activities is that they cannot be precisely defined. In other words, the shortcoming is ours, not one that is ascribable to all computers, past, present, and future.

I suspect that the argument about whether or not computers "think" is not an argument about computers but about ourselves. We nurture certain attitudes toward "thinking beings" and other attitudes toward "nonthinking" or "nonsentient" beings. We do not wish to extend to the former our attitude toward the latter, and vice versa. To put it in another way, to deny thought to the computer is to affirm a difference between attitudes we *ought* to have toward machinery, on the one hand, and toward human beings and other living things, on the other. Moreover, the reluctance to attribute "human properties" to the computer stems, I believe, from a feeling that in our civilization empathetic understanding of our fellow human beings has been impaired by increasing dependence on outward manifestations of reality, cut-and-dried criteria of truth and value, and by a denigration of introspection, affect, and so on. This is why many people cling to the internal meaning of thought, derived from direct awareness of their own consciousness. They feel that relinquishing this meaning in favor of objective, externally observable criteria endangers the awareness of distinctions between human life and inert matter.

These misgivings may be amply justified. Unfortunately, they obscure an important issue: to what extent *can* human thought be reducible to the algebra of propositions and hence completely analyzed as a concatenation of elementary logical operations, perhaps manifested in concrete neural events? If it turns out that a large part of what we call "thinking" is so analyzable, the result would be of utmost importance—not necessarily because it would open the way to another flood of new gadgetry but because it would greatly enhance our understanding of our thinking processes, hence of ourselves.

APPLICATIONS

I.

Assume $x = y$.
Then $x^2 = xy$.
Then $x^2 - y^2 = xy - y^2$.
Then $(x + y)(x - y) = y(x - y)$.
Then $x + y = y$.
But $x = y$ (assumed).
Then $y + y = y$.
Then $2y = y$.
Then $2 = 1$.

Find the flaw in the proof.

II.

1) Change some of the assumptions in Plato's dialogue (pp. 260–61). For instance, instead of s → ∼ z, write s → z, or instead of s = 1, write s = 0. See whether and, if so, how the conclusion is altered by each change. Can some combination of changes be made so that the conclusion remains the same? Can any of the assumptions be omitted without changing the conclusion? (Such unneeded assumptions are called *redundant.*)
2) Put yourself in Adeimantus's position and suppose that you do not agree with the conclusion to which Socrates has driven you. Which of the assumptions would you challenge in order to be free to reject the conclusion without violating the rules of deduction?
3) Compose a Socratic dialogue similar to the example given that leads from apparently reasonable assumptions to a dubious conclusion.
4) Can you argue that Socrates' premises are more properly construed as propositional functions than propositions?

III.

1) Compose a brain teaser similar to the one on page 262 and solve it by the Algebra of Propositions. Examine your premises. If one of them implies another, the latter can be dropped from the set of premises (since it can be deduced and that is the solver's job). Did your example contain any such redundant premises?
2) Try to compose a brain teaser without redundant premises.
3) Compose a brain teaser in which one premise contradicts another (but not obviously) and try it on someone who has learned the technique of solving such problems.

IV.   Gather all the information you can on "how computers think" and arrange a serious debate on whether or not what computers do ought to be called "thinking." Take notes on the points made by the debaters to determine if they attach different meanings to "thought" or "thinking." Can the opposite views be reconciled by pointing out that the statement "Computers do (or do not) think" ought to be construed as a propositional function rather than a proposition.

16/mathematics: a language and a tool of deduction

We have seen that the Algebra of Sets, the Algebra of Propositions, and the Algebra of Probabilities could all be viewed as symbolic languages, each with a "grammar." The grammar of the Algebra of Sets is the set of rules that governs operations on sets. Similarly, in the Algebra of Propositions, the operations are on propositions; in the Algebra of Probabilities, they are on events.

In each of these languages, it is possible to make assertions. For example, in the Algebra of Sets, it is possible to say:

Citizens of the United States who are not both male (A) and over 19 (B) are among those who are exempted from the draft (C).

$$\text{In symbols, } -(A \cap B) \subset C.$$

In the Algebra of Propositions, it is possible to say:

It is not the case that either it is night (p) or the moon is not visible ($\sim$q).

$$\text{In symbols, } (p \vee \sim q) = 0.$$

In the Algebra of Probabilities, it is possible to say:

The chances are one in ten that the bill will pass the House (H) and will be either defeated in the Senate (S) or vetoed by the President (P).

$$\text{In symbols, } p[H \cap (S \cup P)] \text{ .1.}$$

Clearly, symbolic languages are much more economical than ordinary ones. The terseness and precision of symbolic languages and the opportunity they present for applying the rules of operation *without regard for the meanings of the assertions* (which frequently get in the way of reasoning) give these languages their deductive power. For example, by applying the rules of operation, we can deduce from $(p \lor \sim q) = 0$ the assertion $(q \rightarrow p) = 0$ which, retranslated into English, says "From the fact that the moon is visible, we cannot conclude that it is night."

Mathematics is a symbolic language. Its function is the same as that of the languages we have examined: (1) to say things tersely and precisely (so that the clumsy grammar and the vague semantics of ordinary language do not get in the way of logical thinking) and (2) to provide an apparatus for making complex deductions. In fact, any symbolic language that has these properties can be considered a branch of mathematics. Many mathematicians feel that logic, too, is a branch of mathematics. Logicians, on the other hand, are more likely to insist that mathematics is a branch of logic. Bertrand Russell, who together with Alfred North Whitehead investigated the foundations of mathematical logic, believed that logic and mathematics are coextensive. "Mathematics," said Russell, "is the totality of all assertions in the form p implies q." We shall not take sides in this matter.

The branch of mathematics familiar to most people is arithmetic. The symbols of arithmetic are numbers. There are four principal operations: addition, subtraction, multiplication, and division, only two of which need to be independently defined—namely, addition and multiplication. Subtraction and division can be defined in terms of these. Addition and multiplication are in many ways analogous to the union and intersection of sets, both being commutative and associative. That is, if a, b, and c are any numbers, then

$$\left. \begin{array}{l} a + b = b + a \\ ab = ba \end{array} \right\} \text{(Commutative Law)}$$

$$\left. \begin{array}{l} (a + b) + c = a + (b + c) \\ (ab)c = a(bc) \end{array} \right\} \text{(Associative Law)}$$

Also multiplication is distributive with respect to addition:

$$a(b + c) = ab + ac.$$

There is no law corresponding to the distributive law of union with respect to intersection (cf. pp. 245–46).

Ordinarily people think of numbers as quantities and readily picture referents of numbers in the real world. Thus "2" can be pictured as that which a pair of shoes, a married couple, twins, and a brace of pheasants have in common. All of us have seen couples, triples, quintuples, etc., and have counted sets of scores of objects. It is more difficult to remember having seen a million of something, much less a trillion. Yet, people accustomed to thinking of numbers have no difficulty in "imagining" any number, however big. Clearly, ideas of such numbers do not come to us from our having experienced them. They are *concepts*, not memories of experience. We can conceive of arbitrarily large numbers because we can imagine the operation of "adding one" continuing indefinitely, and so we can imagine some collection of things growing without bound.

Can we also imagine the reverse—a collection of things diminishing by one indefinitely? Not at first. Children do not immediately conceive the idea of a negative number, since they cannot conceive of anything being "taken away from nothing." Only when we learn to think of operations on numbers without picturing concrete referents (like number of fingers, apples, or sheep) do we breach the barrier that separates simple counting from general mathematical operations. Once the barrier is breached, we can vastly expand our repertoire of mathematical concepts.

Think of subtraction as the inverse of addition. In adding two numbers, we write $a + b = x$, where a and b are two specific (known) numbers, and x is at first an unknown number. After the operation of addition has been performed, the "referent" of x, that is, the number that x stands for, becomes known. If we write $a + x = b$, we ask "What is the number (x) which added to a yields the sum b?" If b is larger than a, we can find x by performing a subtraction $b - a$. But suppose b is smaller than a. If we insist that a number must represent a collection, the operation $b - a$ cannot be performed, and so the equation $a + x = b$ cannot be "solved" for x. However, we need not think of a number as always representing a collection. We can think of a number as a result of an operation. If b is smaller than a, we can still *symbolically* represent the result of the operation $b - a$. Thus -3 is a symbol representing the result of the operation $5 - 8$ or, equivalently, the solution of the equation $8 + x = 5$. Numbers such as -3 can no longer represent collections, but they can represent concepts like the total worth of a man who has no assets but owes three units of money or the distance traveled westward when one has actually gone 3 miles eastward or the "profit" of a transaction that has actually suffered a loss.

Finding referents of numbers and of other mathematical concepts (such as operations) in the real world helps us link these concepts with familiar situations. A mathematician, however, generally does not depend on this sort of concretization. He defines "numbers" and other mathematical objects exclusively in terms of operations. It has taken mathematicians many centuries to learn to define mathematical concepts in this way and so avoid the semantic hangups that plagued the early history of mathematics.

The hangups occurred when certain operations could not be performed with the previously established conceptual scheme. Many of these operations were inverses of operations that *could* be performed. Suppose we begin with the earliest known system of numbers, the so-called *natural* numbers, 1, 2, 3, ... The sum of any two such numbers is again a natural number. So is the product. We can therefore always solve the equations $a + b = x$ and $ab = x$ in terms of natural numbers. Consider, however, the equation $ax = b$, where a and b are natural numbers. This equation has a solution (for x) among the natural numbers only if b is divisible by a. Here the first "hang-up" occurred: how does one divide a certain number of objects among a certain number of people if the division cannot be performed "evenly"? This hurdle was passed comparatively easily because practical situations demanded it. Things that could be broken or cut up (such as plots of land, measures of grain) were broken or cut up into smaller pieces, and so "fractions" were established as numbers. (Note that "fraction" is etymologically related to "break": "fracture".)

It took much longer to grant "citizenship" to negative numbers so as to make the equation $a + x = b$ universally solvable. The concretization of negative numbers (as in banking and credit) involves more sophisticated concepts than cutting up loaves of bread in order to divide 3 among 5.

The inverse of the operation of "raising to a power" presents even graver difficulties. Assume now that we have extended our number system to include fractions. Along with the definition of a fraction, we have adjoined also rules for operating on them. Now we can solve any equation $a^2 = x$, where a is either a natural number or a fraction because squaring a number means multiplying it by itself, and we know how to multiply whole numbers or fractions. The inverse problem now presents itself, namely the equation $x^2 = a$, where a is a known natural number or fraction. The equation reads "What number multiplied by itself gives a?" If $a = 9$, the number is, of course, 3; if $a = 121/25$, $x = 11/5$.[1] So for some values of a we can solve the equation within our number system (in this case, all positive natural numbers and fractions). What if $a = 2$? Clearly, there is no natural number whose square is 2, since $1^2 = 1$, which is too small, and $2^2 = 4$, which is too large. Perhaps there is a fraction between 1 and 2 whose square is 2? It turns out there is not.

A simple proof that there is no such fraction was given by Euclid in the fourth century B.C.[2] The disturbing thing about this result is that it is difficult to imagine how there can be "holes" between fractions inasmuch as between any two fractions, no matter how close together, there is an *infinity* of other fractions. Thus fractions seem to fill the entire interval between any two integers. If we start with 1 and increase the number gradually through *all* the intervening fractions, we will eventually arrive at a fraction whose square is larger than 2—for instance, 3/2, whose square is 9/4. Therefore, we feel, since fractions are "infinitely dense," we must have passed one be-

1. If our number system includes negative numbers, then the question $x^2 = 9$ has two solutions: $x = 3$; $x = -3$ because $(-3)(-3) = 9$, in consequence of the rule for multiplying negative numbers. In general, if a is a square of some positive number, it is also the square of the negative number of the same magnitude.

2. The proof goes as follows. Suppose *a* is a fraction, m/n, where m and n are whole numbers. Now, if m and n were both even, then this fraction would not have been reduced to the lowest terms, since both the numerator and the denominator could be divided by 2. Assume that we have reduced the fraction to lowest terms. Then either m is even and n is odd; or m is odd and n is even; or both m and n are odd. Also, if $a = m/n$, then $a^2 = m^2/n^2$; so if $a^2 = 2$, $m^2/n^2 = 2$ or $m^2 = 2n^2$.

Now we see that m cannot be odd, since if it were, m^2 would also be odd, which is impossible since $2n^2$, being twice a natural number, is even. There remains the possibility that m is even and n is odd. But then m^2 must be divisible by 4, n^2 being odd, $2n^2$ cannot be divisible by 4. Therefore, whatever we assume about the natural numbers m and n, the assumption that $m^2/2n^2 = 2$ leads to a contradiction. Since any proposition that implies a contradiction must be false, the proposition that there exists a fraction whose square is 2 must be false.

All whole numbers and fractions (ratios of whole numbers) are called *rational* numbers. If the equation $x^2 = a$ is to have a solution for all positive numbers a, we must extend our number system to include other than rational numbers. Such numbers have been named "irrational," suggesting that at one time they were thought to be strange or "crazy." Actually, however, "rational" is probably derived from "ratio" (of whole numbers), so that "irrational" numbers are those that are not equal to any ratio of whole numbers.

tween 1 and 2 whose square is 2. Yet Euclid's proof to the effect that there is no such fraction is unshakable.

The "nonexistence" of a fraction whose square is 2 was disturbing to the ancients for still another reason. It was proved (probably by Pythagoras) that the area of a square whose side was the diagonal of a unit square was two square units; therefore the length of the diagonal *must* be a number whose square is 2. It is upsetting to conclude that "there is no such number" because one cannot very well assert that the length of the diagonal of a unit square "does not exist." Only when the number system was extended to include symbols such as $\sqrt{2}$ (the result of performing the operation inverse to that of squaring a number) did the "paradox" disappear.

One more "semantic hangup" in the early history of mathematics is worth mentioning. Faced with an equation such as $x^2 = -1$, what can we say about the solution? It is easy to convince ourselves that this equation "cannot possibly have a solution." If the rules of operation on numbers are to be consistent, the product of two negative numbers must be positive. In particular, the square of a negative number, being a product of a negative number with itself, must be positive. Hence the square of a negative number cannot be negative, and the equation $x^2 = -1$, or equivalently, $x^2 + 1 = 0$, cannot have a solution.

On the basis of this conclusion, we can also argue that many more general quadratic equations can have no roots (solutions). We can write the general quadratic equation as $ax^2 + bx + c = 0$, where a, b, and c are known numbers. It can be shown that the formula for the two roots of this equation is given by

$$x_1 = \frac{-b + \sqrt{b^2 - 4ac}}{2a} \text{ and } x_2 = \frac{-b - \sqrt{b^2 - 4ac}}{2a}$$

Once we have admitted "irrationals" (filling the "holes" between fractions) into our number system, in particular, numbers defined by the operation of taking the square root of a positive number, the operations indicated in the formula can all be carried out, *provided* the number obtained under the radical sign is not negative. If it is negative, and if we deny that square roots of negative numbers "exist," we must conclude that some quadratic equations have no solutions even in the number system that includes irrationals.

This conclusion would not in itself be alarming. Recall the example of a logical problem that had "no solution" (pp. 263–64). It turned out, however, that the solutions of some cubic equations (of the third degree) could be expressed only as sums of two numbers, each of which involved taking the square root of a negative number; and strange to say, these solutions were "real": that is, they were among the numbers already admitted to the number system. What a problem for metaphysicians! Two numbers, neither of which has a "real existence," add up to a number that does have a "real existence"!

As mathematics matured and metaphysical speculations were gradually eased out of the discipline, such paradoxes tended to disappear. Mathematicians learned to define their concepts without reference to concrete magnitudes or to accustomed mental images. Only one thing was demanded of a mathematical system: consistency.[3] Mathematical deduction could not be allowed to lead to a contradiction—"contradiction" understood in a logical, not in a psychological or metaphysical, sense. Thus bizarre conclusions to the effect that "the diagonal of a unit square exists and yet does not exist" or "the square root of a negative quantity is a contradiction in terms" are not really evidence of contradictions. They are only evidence of insufficient precision or of lack of generality of definitions.

To make the long story short, with the growth and maturation of mathematics, the number system had to be constantly enlarged. The

3. For instance, the inclusion of numbers like $\sqrt{-1}$ (a solution of the equation $x^2 + 1 = 0$) extended the number system to the so-called system of *complex* numbers. Every complex number can be represented symbolically in the form $a + bi$, where a and b are *real* numbers, which include both rational and irrational numbers, and i stands for $\sqrt{-1}$. Real numbers can be represented as points on a line extending to infinity in both directions from zero. If we imagine a plane divided into four quadrants by two perpendicular lines intersecting at zero, then the real numbers will be represented by the points of the "horizontal" line, while numbers like bi, called *imaginary*, will be represented by the points of the "vertical" line. The complex number $a + bi$ will be represented by a point on the plane, whose distance (positive or negative) from the vertical line (called the *imaginary axis*) is a and whose distance (positive or negative) from the horizontal line (called the *real axis*) is b. Arithmetic operations on complex numbers can be defined in a way that is consistent with those operations performed on real numbers.

Complex numbers are indispensable in some branches of mathematical physics, for example, electrodynamics. However, as in the case of other extensions of the number concept, the admission of "imaginary" numbers to "citizenship" at first made mathematicians uneasy because they thought of the rule "the square of a negative number is positive" as a "law of thought" or a "fact of nature" instead of as a rule of mathematical grammar. Failure to appreciate the purely *syntactic* nature of mathematical rules made the notion of $\sqrt{-1}$ seem absurd to early mathematicians.

range of the number concept widened and with it the range of the notion of "operation." Various definitions of "number," "operation," and so on, gave rise to different mathematical systems, all of which can be viewed as different languages with different grammars. It should not be surprising, therefore, that assertions that are perfectly justified in one system may look absurd in another.

As an example, take the mathematics of direction. The four points of the compass indicate directions. There are, of course, other directions besides N, S, E, and W, and these are indicated by NW, NE, SW, etc., and in greater detail by NNE, SWS, etc. If we want more precision, further refining in this manner becomes awkward, so we abandon the traditional direction and designate the direction North by 0° and other directions by the angle they make (turning clockwise) with North. Thus NE would be 45°, NWW 292.5°, and so forth. Naturally no direction would be designated by a number larger than 360. In fact, the direction 360° would be identical with 0°.

Let us see what sort of arithmetic we need to deal with these numbers. If a pilot flies north, then turns clockwise 36°, he is heading in the direction of 36°. If he turns in the same direction through 112° more, his final direction is 148°. So ordinary addition of degrees will give the result of successive turns in the clockwise direction. It is easy to see that turns in the counterclockwise direction are tantamount to subtracting the corresponding number of degrees. However, since no direction is associated with a number larger than 360°, it follows that our arithmetic will show some "strange" results. For instance, the result of turning first 270° clockwise, then 120° again clockwise gives the resulting direction of 30°. In our arithmetic, then, we must write $270 + 120 = 30$, which looks absurd in ordinary arithmetic. Nevertheless the arithmetic of adding and subtracting turns through angles is a perfectly consistent one; it is just that some of its rules are different from those of ordinary arithmetic.[4]

Another example of a "strange" but perfectly consistent arithmetic

---

4. Taking the base other than 10 for writing numbers, we also get "strange" results. For instance, if we take 12 as the base, we write $9 + 7 = 14$, meaning one "twelve" and 4 units. In this system of notation, 195 would be written as 143, meaning $1 \times 12^2 + 4 \times 12 + 3$, just as 143 in decimal notation means $1 \times 10^2 + 4 \times 10 + 3$. However, these seeming anomalies arise only because in different systems of notation numbers are "spelled" differently. The rules of operation remain the same regardless of the system of notation. In our example of "direction arithmetic," the rules of operation are different from those of ordinary arithmetic.

is one wherein we are interested in whole numbers only with reference to the remainder they give when divided by 7. Thus in our system all numbers that upon being divided by 7 give the same remainder are equivalent. For example, 3, 10, 17, 24, etc., are all equivalent because they yield the remainder 3. It follows that in this system there are only seven numbers, corresponding to the seven possible remainders, namely 0, 1, 2, 3, 4, 5, 6.

Now, the sum of any two whole numbers is again a whole number, which corresponds to one of the six numbers in our system. Consequently we can write down a complete "addition table" of our new arithmetic. It is shown in Table 4 and can be easily verified. We can also write down the "multiplication table." It is shown in Table 5 and can also be easily verified.

Table 4 *Addition table of "Remainder of Seven" arithmetic. The entries are the sums of numbers designating the corresponding rows and columns.*

	0	1	2	3	4	5	6
0	0	1	2	3	4	5	6
1	1	2	3	4	5	6	0
2	2	3	4	5	6	0	1
3	3	4	5	6	0	1	2
4	4	5	6	0	1	2	3
5	5	6	0	1	2	3	4
6	6	0	1	2	3	4	5

Anyone who feels that these tables are somehow "wrong" or "bizarre" is still in a stage of mathematical innocence analogous to linguistic innocence discussed in Chapter 2. Mathematical maturity comes with the recognition that *mathematical language does not depend on referents and relations found in the external world* (although it may well be inspired by experience with certain relations). Math-

Table 5 *Multiplication table of "Remainder of Seven" arithmetic. The entries are products of numbers designating the corresponding rows and columns.*

	0	1	2	3	4	5	6
0	0	0	0	0	0	0	0
1	0	1	2	3	4	5	6
2	0	2	4	6	1	3	5
3	0	3	6	2	5	1	4
4	0	4	1	5	2	6	3
5	0	5	3	1	6	4	2
6	0	6	5	4	3	2	1

ematics is "pure syntactics." Its rules relate symbols to symbols only and to nothing else. (Although the symbols of mathematics *can* be referred to things and relations in the external world, how this is done, and what it leads to, is a matter outside the scope of mathematics. However, it is within the scope of semantics and will be discussed in Chapter 18.)

Since the language of pure mathematics has only syntactic rules, it follows that mathematical terms can be defined only with reference to other mathematical terms. No referent of a mathematical term can be exhibited the way a typewriter or an ostrich can be exhibited to illustrate the denotative meaning of "typewriter" or "ostrich."

In *teaching* mathematics, especially to children, we do, of course, resort to exhibiting "real world referents" of mathematical objects and operations. Two oranges provide an illustration of "2"; a drawing of a triangle, an illustration of "triangle." Children learn to add by counting objects. Beginning students of geometry learn to prove theorems by referring propositions to visible features of diagrams. But these references are only pedagogical aids to mathematical thinking. Eventually they must be dispensed with if the intellectual barrier between concrete experience and abstract mathematical thought is to be breached, as it must be if progress in learning to think mathematically is not to be impeded. Even arithmetic cannot be learned by someone who cannot be weaned from counting with the aid of fingers and toes.

If, then, definitions of mathematical terms must be made only by referring to other mathematical terms, we must eventually arrive at terms that cannot be further defined; otherwise we would be caught either in circular definitions or in an infinite regress. This has been recognized by mathematicians, and so every mathematical system now contains "primitive" (undefined) terms.

Further, since mathematics is a purely deductive system of reasoning, every mathematical proposition, if it is proved at all, must be proved by reference to other mathematical propositions—not by appeal to experience or observations. Consequently, every mathematical system must contain unproved propositions that are simply assumed to be true. These are called axioms, or the postulates, of the system.

For example, the undefined terms of geometry are "point," "line," "on" (as in "point A is on line L"), "through" (as in "line L goes through point A"), and so on. The postulates of the familiar Euclidean geometry are "Exactly one line goes through two distinct points," "At most one point is on two distinct lines," etc.

Failure to realize the arbitrary nature of the axioms led to an impasse in the history of geometry. The recognition that axioms can be chosen arbitrarily, subject only to internal consistency, led the way out of the impasse. The story is instructive and will be retold here.

When geometry was first shaped into a deductive system by the Greeks, the postulates were viewed as "self-evident" propositions, that is, propositions that any reasonable person could not honestly deny. This sort of "self-evident" truth presented no epistemological problem for a philosopher like Plato, who habitually made "internally perceived truth" the starting point of deductions. (See, for example, the argument on the nature of God reproduced on pp. 260–61.) In the same way, the truth of the axioms of geometry was assumed to be established by introspection. Presumably it is impossible to imagine how more than one straight line can go through two distinct points and, similarly, to deny the other axioms, such as that all right angles are equal and so on.

Now, among the postulates of geometry listed by Euclid in his famous treatise, there was one that gave trouble. It was the fifth in number. It can be stated in different ways. Before choosing one, we shall try to imagine the situation it deals with in order to see the problem it raised.

Imagine a straight line L infinite in extent, and a point A not on it. Next imagine all possible straight lines through A, also infinitely extended, lying on the same plane as L. Some of these lines will eventually intersect L on one side, some will intersect it on the other. The Fifth Postulate says that among all of these possible lines through A there is one and only one that will fail to intersect L on either side, however far it is produced: the line *parallel* to L.

Is this proposition "self-evident"? Appeal to experience is no recourse since we can have no experience with infinitely extended lines. The question is, can we imagine a situation that contradicts the Fifth Postulate? Can we, for example, imagine that there are *two* lines through A that fail to meet L on either side no matter how far they are extended? It might be argued that we cannot because there is only one line that remains equidistant from L at all points. But does the fact that the distance between two lines keeps diminishing on one side imply that the two lines will meet on that side? Suppose that, as the line through A is extended, by a certain stretch its distance from L has been reduced by one half. After extending the line another stretch, the distance will again be cut by one half. But we know that cutting the distance by one half each time will not reduce the distance to zero; so the argument that the distance keeps diminishing does not prove that the lines will eventually intersect. Against this objection one can raise a counter-objection. Having reduced the distance by one half in extending the line through A by a certain stretch, we shall reduce it by the *remaining* half in extending the line by an equal stretch. This proposition, however, remains to be proved. And it turns out that its proof rests on the Fifth Postulate and so leads to a circular argument not allowed in deductive reasoning.

Because the truth of the Fifth Postulate seemed not as "self-evident" as that of other postulates, mathematicians ever since Euclid's time thought that the postulate could be *deduced* from the other postulates in the same way that the theorems of geometry are deduced.

One way of proving a theorem is to assume that its conclusion is false and from that assumption to deduce a conclusion that contradicts one of the postulates. Early in the eighteenth century, an

Italian Jesuit named Saccheri (1667–1733) undertook that task. He started by assuming the truth of all the postulates and by denying the truth of the Fifth. This led him to conclusions that contradicted the conclusions of theorems established in Euclidean geometry. Saccheri thought that this proved the truth of the Fifth Postulate because denying it led to results at variance with what was accepted as true. We see now that this argument is circular. It says in effect: If the Fifth Postulate is not true, some conclusions contradict conclusions previously established. But the previously established conclusions are known to be true; therefore the conclusions that contradict them must be false; hence the assumption that led to the new conclusions (the denial of the Fifth Postulate) must be false. Hence the Fifth Postulate must be true.

The circularity of the argument becomes apparent when we ask "How do we know that the established conclusions of Euclidean geometry are true?" There is only one answer acceptable to the mathematician: they were derived from axioms assumed to be true. But among these was also the Fifth Postulate. Therefore the assumption that the new conclusions are false rests on the assumption that the Fifth Postulate is true, which was what Saccheri set out to *prove*.

Again the hangup is seen to stem from confusing the role of mathematics as a purely deductive system (which *in itself* bears no relation to facts) with the role of mathematics as an instrument of cognition about the real world. It is true, of course, that the propositions of Euclidean geometry can be verified with impressive exactness in the properties of geometric configurations of material objects. For instance, one of the theorems of Euclidean geometry (derived from the postulates, including the Fifth) is that the sum of the angles in any triangle equals 180°. To verify the "actual" truth of this proposition, we must measure the angles of "actual" triangles. Now, as there are no "real" triangles in nature, all we have are configurations that approximate ideal mathematical triangles. To the extent that ink marks are sufficiently thin and sufficiently straight, they can serve as realizations of idealized straight lines. But they are not identical with straight lines because straight lines have no thickness, and perfect "straightness" is only a concept, not a property of some material object. Further, our measurements are exact only within limits. All we can say is that, within the limits of our observation, properties of material triangles seem to confirm the conclusions of Euclidean geometry.

However, it is a far cry from these findings to the conclusion that all space has the properties attributed to it by Euclidean geometry.

To illustrate the fallacy of such a conclusion, imagine beings that live on a very large, perfect sphere. Small portions of the sphere have almost the properties of a plane, in the same way that a small portion of the earth's surface appears flat. The inhabitants of the sphere have constructed a Euclidean geometry, and some are perturbed by doubts concerning the truth of the Fifth Postulate. So they undertake to put the conclusions of the geometry to a test. In particular, they measure the angles of triangles and find that, within the limits of precision that are attainable, the sum of angles of every triangle is indeed 180°. Thereafter extending their observations to larger and larger triangles, eventually they will find that the sum of the three angles of very large triangles exceeds 180° and, moreover, that the excess becomes ever larger as the area of the triangle increases. (You can see this by imagining a triangle formed by a segment of the equator of their sphere and two meridians meeting at a pole: the meridians are both perpendicular to the equator; therefore the sum of the two base angles of that triangle is already $90° + 90° = 180°$. Together with the angle at the pole, the sum is larger than 180°.)

If then these beings could conceive of a "sphere," they might conclude that their world is not really a plane as they assumed, but a sphere—a conclusion analogous to the one we have arrived at regarding the planet we live on. Suppose, instead that the beings themselves are two-dimensional. They then would conceive of space as having only two dimensions and could not visualize a sphere because they had never had an experience with a three-dimensional object. To them "curvature of space" would have no concrete referent. But, supposing further that among those beings are sophisticated mathematicians. *They* could make sense of the observations. They would say something like this: "The space we live in is not Euclidean. That is to say, not all the postulates of Euclidean geometry apply to it. In particular, the Fifth Postulate does not apply. It is not true that through a point external to a given line a line parallel to the given line can be drawn. There are *no* parallel lines: every pair of 'straight lines' must meet. If we replace the Fifth Postulate by the one just stated, we shall obtain a geometry that most accurately describes the space we live in."

Our fictitious two-dimensional mathematician does not refer to a "sphere" in making his point. He does not need to. He can construct a two-dimensional geometry that we three-dimensional beings will recognize as the geometry of the surface of a sphere. "Straight lines" mentioned by the two-dimensional mathematician are put in quotes because, to us, they are not straight lines, since they are drawn on the surface of the sphere. But, to two-dimensional beings, they are straight lines because they have the essential properties of straight lines: they are the shortest paths between pairs of points. There *are* such lines on the surface of a sphere. We call them "arcs of great circles." Given any two points on a sphere, if we cut the sphere by a plane passing through these two points and the center, the plane will intersect the surface in an arc of a great circle, the shortest path between the two points that can be drawn on the surface of the sphere. These are the paths that are usually followed by airliners on long flights. That is why, when you fly from New York to Rome, you first fly northeast, then southeast—not due east—even though the two cities are found on almost the same latitude. Actually, the pilot is following approximately the arc of a great circle, the shortest path between the point of departure and the point of arrival.

Coming back to our own situation, we do not know what would be found if we put the conclusions of Euclidean geometry to a test beyond our immediate spatial neighborhood. In such an undertaking we would confront baffling problems, not only of technical but also of semantic nature. Suppose, for example, we decide to test the truth of Euclidean geometry in outer space by measuring the angles of very large triangles, say, triangles determined by triples of stars, to see whether or not they add up to 180°. Since an actual triangle must be defined in terms of actual straight lines, what shall we take for a physical referent of "straight line"? Obviously we cannot resort to edges of rulers or to taut strings when dealing with configurations in outer space. The path of a beam of light (used also by terrestrial surveyors) seems like a good referent. However, it is now known that beams of light become deflected if they pass in the neighborhood of large masses. So what appears as a "straight line," because we sight along it, may not "really" be a "straight line." This, in turn, brings up a question of semantics. What is a "straight line really"? Questions such as these do not relate to mathematics as a deductive system but rather to the *uses* of mathematics as an instrument of cognition about the world.

The umbilical cord binding mathematics to the world of objects and events was not cut until the nineteenth century. Wolfgang Bolyai (1775–1856) in Hungary and Nikolai Ivanovich Lobachevsky (1793–1856) in Russia derived far-reaching consequences of non-Euclidean geometry in which the Fifth Postulate is replaced by another: Given a straight line L and a point A outside it, *two* lines, L_1 and L_2 (called "parallel to L") can be drawn through A which fail to meet L on either side no matter how far they are extended. The condition is pictured in Figure 24 from which it is easy to see that any line through A contained within the angle made by the two lines "parallel" to L will also fail to meet L. For, to intersect L, any such line must first intersect one of the two parallel lines. This would contradict one of the postulates which non-Euclidean geometry has in common with the Euclidean—namely, that two lines can intersect in at most *one* point.

Like Euclidean geometry, non-Euclidean geometry is a collection of theorems. Some of the theorems (those that do not depend on the truth of the Fifth Postulate) coincide with theorems of Euclidean geometry; others arrive at different conclusions. In particular, in the geometry of Bolyai and Lobachevsky, the sum of the three angles of any triangle is *less* than 180°, the deficiency being the larger, the larger the triangle. Later in the nineteenth century, the German mathematician Georg Riemann developed another sort of non-Euclidean geometry, wherein no parallel lines are possible. The question as to which geometry is "true"—Euclidean, Lobachevskian, or Riemannian —has no meaning for the mathematician since the mathematician recognizes only one criterion of truth: a proposition is true if it is

Figure 24 *The arrows indicate that each line extends indefinitely in either direction. A postulate of "Bolyai-Lobachevsky" geometry states that neither L_1 nor L_2 will ever meet L.*

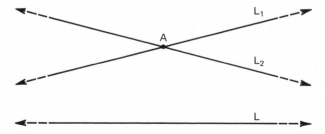

a logical consequence of axioms or of other propositions derived from the axioms. One does not ask whether the axioms are "true" any more than one asks whether an inch is really an inch long.

The breakthrough in geometry eventually led to similar breakthroughs in other areas of mathematics. There is now a plethora of "arithmetics" that rest on foundations other than those of the familiar arithmetic. We have already cited the "arithmetic of directions" and the arithmetic of Boolean Algebra in which $1 + 1 = 1$ and the arithmetic of remainders with its "strange" multiplication table. There are algebras in which multiplication is not commutative, that is, ab is not equal to ba. There is a branch of set theory in which the magnitudes of "transfinite numbers" (numbers beyond "infinity") can be meaningfully compared with each other. And so on.

Nevertheless, the triumphs of modern mathematics, liberated from the necessity of relating propositions to concrete situations, should not blind us to the fact that many of these advances were actually instigated *by* concrete situations. This was not the case with non-Euclidean geometry: its creators did not have an experience incompatible with Euclidean geometry. Rather they were driven by the compulsion of the mathematical profession to draw consequences from a set of postulates. Other branches of "modern" mathematics, however, were clearly inspired by concrete situations or else by problems arising in the practice of mathematics.

As an example, consider the following situation. A cube has six sides and can rest on any one of them. The cube can also have different orientations in space. If we limit these orientations so that the four vertical faces of the cube always face the four points of the compass, it follows that the cube can have 24 distinct orientations. Each of six faces may be on the bottom and, with each of these six orientations, four orientations of the cube with respect to the four cardinal directions (north, east, south, and west) can be combined. The cube can be brought from one orientation to another by rotations. The magnitude of every rotation must be a multiple of 90°. Rotations are possible around each of the three axes of the cube: the north-south axis, the east-west axis, and the up-down axis.

Around each axis, four distinct rotations are possible—namely, 0°, 90°, 180°, and 270° in a given direction.[5] Since rotations around the

5. It may seem strange that we call a rotation of 0° a "rotation." For a mathematician, however, 0 is a magnitude like any other. It is simpler to list 0°, 90°, 180°, and 270° as the possible rotations around an axis than "no rotation, 90°, 180°, and 270°."

three axes can be combined, there are $4 \times 4 \times 4 = 64$ possible rotations around all three axes at once. On the other hand, there are only 24 orientations of the cube. Therefore some of the rotations must be equivalent. If we start with a given orientation of the cube, the application of either of two equivalent rotations will put the cube into the same final orientation. In fact, there are just 24 inequivalent rotations, that is, rotations that bring the cube into each possible position from a given starting position. Consider a mathematical system in which the elements (corresponding to numbers in conventional systems) are the 24 distinct rotations of the cube. Call them R_1, R_2, . . ., R_{24}. Assume that the cube is initially in some "standard" position. If we perform a rotation and then another rotation, we bring the cube into a certain position. Since the 24 positions correspond to the 24 rotations, it should be possible to bring the cube into the same final position by a single rotation (around all three axes). For instance, the result of performing rotation R_1 followed by rotation R_2 may be identical with the result of performing rotation R_7. (See Figure 25.) We can represent this symbolically by writing $R_1 \cdot R_2 = R_7$.

We have used the same symbols that denote multiplication in

Figure 25 *The standard position of the cube is shown in (a). The 6 is on top; the 1 is on bottom; the face opposite 4 is 3; the face opposite 2 is 5.*

R_i is one of the 24 rotations, defined as follows: a turn of 90° away from the reader, followed by a clockwise rotation of 90° around the vertical axis. R_i brings the cube into the position shown in (b).

R_j is another of the 24 rotations, defined as follows: a turn of 90° to the right. R_j following R_i brings the cube into the position shown in (c).

R_k is a third rotation of the 24, defined as follows: a turn of 90° counterclockwise around the vertical axis, followed by a turn of 180° away from the reader. R_k brings the cube into the same position (c) as R_i followed by R_j. This is symbolized by the equation

$$R_i R_j = R_k.$$

The reader can verify that if R_j and R_i are performed in that order, the cube is brought into the position shown in (d), different from that shown in (c). Hence $R_j R_i \neq R_i R_j$.

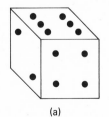 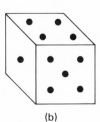 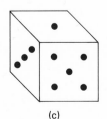 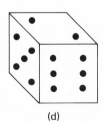

(a)   (b)   (c)   (d)

ordinary algebra. Indeed, the operation of combining sequential rotations will have some of the properties of multiplication, the associative property, for example. Among all the rotations, there will be one that leaves the cube in its original position. We shall symbolize this rotation by "I" and obtain the result that every rotation "multiplied by I" yields the same rotation as the "product," quite as in multiplying by 1 in ordinary algebra.

We shall find, however, that this "multiplication" is in general not commutative. The result of applying two rotations will not always be the same if the order of the rotations is reversed (see legend for Figure 25). Situations of this sort have played an important part in suggesting to mathematicians that self-consistent "algebras" can be constructed with rules of operation different from those in ordinary algebra. As in the case of non-Euclidean geometries, the question "Which is the 'true' algebra" is meaningless.

The strongest impact that experience with real events had on the development of mathematics was in the physical sciences. The world around us is in constant flux. The universality of change impressed some Greek philosophers, notably Heraclitus, mentioned in Chapter 8 ("You cannot step into the same river twice"). Still, the Greeks were not able to develop a mathematical symbolism that captured the essence of *continual* change. Such a symbolism was not developed until the Renaissance.

A prototype of a mathematical expression of change is an equation that connects two or more *variable* quantities; for instance $y = 2x$.

In the language of algebra, the equation says simply that some (unknown) quantity y is twice some other (unknown) quantity x. However, there is another way of reading this equation: *Whatever* value is assumed by x, twice that value is assumed by y. Actually this interpretation implies an *infinity* of different assertions, such as "If x is 1, y is 2; if x is 3, y is 6; if x is 2.75, y is 5.50; if y is -8, x is -16; if x is $\sqrt{2}$, y is $2\sqrt{2}$; and so on." To put it another way, as x *varies*, y varies with it in a manner prescribed by the equation. The somewhat more general equation $y = ax$ states that as x varies, y remains proportional to x. That is, whatever be the values of x and y, both of which vary, the ratio y/x remains constant, that is, remains equal to a certain quantity a, always the same. Here a is called a *constant of proportionality*. Equations of this sort can be assertions about geometry. For example, $c = 2\pi r$ says that the circumference of a circle (c) varies proportionately with the radius of the circle. The constant of proportionality (or the ratio of the circumference to the radius) remains equal to twice π, where π is an irrational number approximately equal to 3.1415926. Similarly, the equation relating the area of a circle to its radius is $A = \pi r^2$, that is, the ratio of the area to the *square* of the radius is π.

Now let t stand for time and s for the distance passed by a freely falling body, starting from rest. Galileo (1564–1642) proposed the following relation: $s = at^2$, which is to say that the distance fallen is proportional to the square of the time elapsed, where a is the constant of proportionality. This constant, Galileo said in effect, remains the same regardless of the material in the body and regardless of the body's weight.[6]

Now, as an assertion about falling bodies, Galileo's formula has denotative meaning; it indicates the *manner* in which bodies fall. Therefore the assertion can be checked against observations. It turns out that in many cases the assertion is false. Raindrops do not fall in the manner described by the formula. The distance fallen by a raindrop when it is already near the ground is approximately proportional to the time elapsed, not to the square of the time; moreover, the constant of proportionality *does* depend on the size of the raindrop—heavier raindrops fall proportionately faster than lighter ones.

Nevertheless, Galileo's formula is in a sense "more true" than Aristotle's suggestion that the speed of a falling body is proportional to its weight. Why this is so touches on important questions in the philosophy of science. These will be discussed in Chapter 18. Here we are interested in the semantic consequences of introducing mathematical symbols that depict continual change.

Assuming for the moment the truth of Galileo's formula (it is approximately true for heavy objects such as cannonballs), we can deduce further consequences from it. For instance, applying rules of

6. Galileo performed his experiments on "falling bodies" by letting cannonballs roll down inclined planes. In this situation, the constant of proportionality depends on the angle of inclination of the plane. If the angle is 90°, the body falls "freely." In that case, if s is measured in feet and t in seconds, a is about 16; 2a is usually denoted by g, called the *acceleration of gravity*. Thus, $g = 32$ (approximately) represents an increase of speed by a freely falling body of about 32 feet per second during each second of fall.

operation stated in the differential calculus,[7] we can deduce that the *instantaneous velocity* (v) of a freely falling body is given by the formula v = 2at. In other words, the instantaneous velocity is proportional to the time elapsed, the constant of proportionality being twice the previous one.

Let us see what is meant by "instantaneous velocity." Owing to our experience with speedometers, we can easily form a conception of instantaneous velocity. As the car in which we are riding gains speed, we watch the pointer of the speedometer. The pointer is moving, showing that the speed of the car keeps changing. However, at a given "moment" the car has a certain speed—the instantaneous velocity at that moment.

In elementary mathematics courses we are taught that "velocity equals distance traveled divided by the time elapsed." More accurately, this ratio is the *average* velocity during the interval of time in question. But if velocity keeps changing, we shall get a different ratio if we divide the distance traveled in one half the time interval by the time elapsed: this ratio will be the average velocity during the half interval. We can take shorter and shorter intervals, getting different ratios each time, but eventually this sequence of ratios will approach a *limiting value.* The shorter the time interval, the closer to the limiting value will be the average velocity associated with it. This limiting value is called the instantaneous velocity. The ratio "becomes equal" to it when both the time interval and the distance traveled have shrunk to zero. We have put "becomes equal" in quotation marks because the ratio 0/0 (zero distance divided by zero time) cannot be defined as such. To ask what 0/0 is "equal to" is to ask what quantity multiplied by 0 gives 0. The answer is "any quantity," and so the symbol 0/0 has no definite meaning. Nevertheless a limiting value can be calculated in specific cases.

As an example, consider the equation

$$y = \frac{x^2 - 4}{x - 2}$$

Like the equations discussed above, this one expresses a relation be-

---

7. The differential calculus is a branch of mathematics concerned with *continuous* change. For instance, if a point is moving along a curved path, the direction of its motion is changing continuously. If certain characteristics of the curve are known, it is possible by means of techniques developed in the differential calculus to determine the direction of motion at a particular instant.

tween two variables, x and y. Given a value of x, a value of y is determined. For example, if $x = 0$, the right side becomes $(0 - 4)/(0 - 2) = -4/-2$, and so $y = 2$. If $x = 3$, the right side becomes $(9 - 4)/(3 - 2)$, and so $y = 5$, and so on. Suppose instead that $x = 2$. The right side becomes $(4 - 4)/(2 - 2) = 0/0$, which cannot be defined. Nevertheless, when x assumes values very close to 2, the expression does assume definite values, and the closer x gets to 2, the closer does the value of the expression (therefore of y) get to 4. For example, if $x = 2.01$, $x^2 = 4.0401$, hence $(x^2 - 4)/(-2) = (4.0401 - 4)/(2.01 - 2) = .0401/.01 = 4.01$, which is close to 4. The value of y becomes *arbitrarily* close to 4 as the value of x gets ever so close to 2. This is what it means to say that y tends to 4 as a limiting value as x tends to 2.

Ideas based on the notion of limits were developed by mathematicians toward the end of the seventeenth century, largely in connection with the new theory of planetary motion proposed by Isaac Newton (1642–1727), one of the inventors of the calculus. *Instantaneous rate of change* is a central idea in the differential calculus. Newton was able to "tame" this concept; that is, make it possible to perform mathematical operations on the symbols that represent it. However, it is not easy to retool the machinery of concepts. Bishop George Berkeley, an outstanding British philosopher (1685–1753), ridiculed the central idea of the differential calculus. That the symbol $0/0$ could not be defined was to Berkeley sufficient reason to dismiss the whole notion of limiting value. To Berkeley's way of thinking, the symbol represented the "ghosts of departed quantities": what was left after both the numerator and the denominator "vanished." Two centuries later, Charles Lutwidge Dodgson (1832–98), better known as Lewis Carroll, satirized the same notion by picturing the grin of the Cheshire Cat, which remained after the cat had vanished.

Attacks on new mathematical ideas from philosophical positions continued throughout the history of mathematics. In all instances the mathematical ideas survived, and the arguments of the philosophers have remained as monuments to mathematical innocence. The lesson to be drawn, in my opinion, is that it is impossible to demolish mathematical logic by nonmathematical reasoning because, if the intellectual battle is joined in the realm of *logic*, mathematics has at its disposal weapons incomparably more powerful than those of conventional language. To be sure, mathematicians have on occasions gotten into intellectual impasses but only because the logical tools then at their disposal were insufficient to deal with the problems. Ways out of the impasses were found when the new mathematical tools became available. These new tools were provided and developed either by mathematicians or by mathematically thinking logicians, never, as far as I know, by philosophers using verbally defined concepts and primitive logical devices.

The language of mathematics performs exactly the same functions as mathematically symbolized logic. First of all, mathematical language cleans up the "pollution" introduced into reasoning by ordinary language. The way this is done can be seen in any elementary problem of algebra. Example:

The area of a field is 407 square rods.
The length is 26 rods longer than the width.
What are the dimensions?

If we continue to think in ordinary language, the problem is difficult. We think of a field, of a rod, and perhaps of things suggested by these words instead of the essential relations to be "disentangled." In antiquity, it took a master mathematician to solve a problem of this sort. Today a high school freshman, equipped with the techniques of algebra, can solve it easily. The length of the field is not known. But it can be *symbolized* by x. If the length is x, the width is $x - 26$. The area is the product of length by width. Therefore $x(x - 26) = 407$. The "grammar" of algebra indicates the operations that can be performed on this equation so as to isolate x on one side and known numbers, connected by operations of arithmetic, on the other. Answer: 37 by 11 rods.

The next example shows how "ordinary logic" can lead to an impasse in trying to solve a very simple problem.

A man contracts to work for a company at a salary that is computed as 10% of the net yearly profit. The net profit is computed by subtracting the man's salary from the gross profit. Assuming that the gross profit is known, what is the man's salary?[8]

8. Example by Lillian Lieber. The reader's attention is called to her several little books (in blank verse) charmingly illustrated by her husband, Hugh. They treat many of the topics discussed in this book, such as non-Euclidean geometry and the theory of probability. *Non-Euclidean Geometry* (Lancaster, Pa.: Science Press, 1940); *The Einstein Theory of Relativity* (New York and Toronto: Farrar and Rinehart, 1945); *The Education of T. C. Mits* (New York: Norton, 1942); *Mits, Wits, and Logic* (New York: Norton, 1947).

It is easy to convince oneself that the problem is "unsolvable," for in order to know the man's salary, we must know the net profit, and in order to know the net profit, we must know the man's salary (which must be subtracted from the gross profit to determine the net profit). This conclusion is, of course, completely unjustified. The problem has a perfectly definite solution; it is left here as an exercise for the reader.

Further, mathematics serves as the most powerful tool of deduction devised by man. The principles embodied in the so-called laws of motion and the law of universal gravitation can be stated in a few words:

Newton's Second Law of Motion (which includes the First Law as a special case): The acceleration suffered by a body is proportional to the force impressed upon it and is in the same direction as the force.

Newton's Third Law: In any isolated mechanical system, total momentum remains constant.

The Law of Gravitation: Every particle attracts every other with a force proportional to the product of the masses and inversely proportional to the square of the distance between the particles.

As long as these principles are stated in words, we are helpless to deduce anything interesting from them. In fact, we may deduce wrong conclusions, such as that, since particles "attract each other," they ought always to approach each other—a conclusion likely suggested by the connotations that the word "attraction" has in ordinary language. In short, the formulation of these laws in ordinary language is all but useless for further development of the theory and may be seriously misleading. But as soon as the principles are stated in the language of mathematics, the rules of mathematical deduction can be applied, and the most unexpected consequences can be deduced; for example, the exact time of an eclipse of the sun many years in the future or the year of return of a comet that was seen only once.

For all its power, however, mathematics by itself is insufficient as an instrument of cognition about the real world. The full potency of *exact (mathematicized) science is realized only in the union of the three methods*: deduction, induction, and observation.

APPLICATION

Read the scene in Plato's *Meno* where Socrates demonstrates to the company that it is possible to lead a person untutored in mathematics to discover a mathematical theorem "by himself." Try Socrates' technique on a child of eight to ten years who has not studied algebra or geometry and see whether or not you can get him or her to discover "by himself/ herself" some simple mathematical theorem, such as $(x + y)(x - y) = x^2 - y^2$ or that the diagonals of a rectangle bisect each other.

Try the same experiment with an adult who has not studied algebra or geometry to discover whether or not the results are the same.

17/induction

A standard syllogism found in logic textbooks throughout the centuries reads:

All men are mortal.
Socrates is a man.
Therefore Socrates is mortal.

If the premises are true, the truth of the conclusion follows. Assume the truth of "Socrates is a man" to be granted. How can the truth of the proposition "All men are mortal" be established? It could be established if all men were observed to die. But then there would be no one left to assert the established truth. Most of us are convinced that every human being, at least those now living, will one day die. What is the source of our conviction? Perhaps the fact that no reliable record exists of any human being having lived more than, say, two hundred years. Even if we accept Genesis as a "reliable record," we must still admit that no human being lived more than 969 years, the reputed age reached by Methuselah. But even Methuselah died, and we can assert without contradiction that no record exists of any human being having lived more than one thousand years. Just what does this prove? That no human being can *possibly* live more than a thousand years? or more than a million years? If so, how is it proved?

If we accept the truth of the assertion "All men are mortal," we must admit that we do so even though it is not *logically* compelling. To put it in another way, we cannot completely dispel doubt about the truth of the assertion. We can, however, accept the assertion as true if we admit another principle of arriving at true propositions. This principle is called induction. Its format is the following: Smith died. Jones died. Schulz, Ivanov, Caruso, Ho Chi-minh, Vijayaragavan, Matsouka, etc., etc., have died. Therefore all men are mortal.

As we have said, the conclusion is not *logically* compelling, but we must accept conclusions of this sort if we are to make use of experience. Practically everything we "know" is based on inductive conclusions. We put a kettle of water over a fire and assume that the water will boil simply because it boiled every time we did the same thing in the past. We take familiar routes to familiar places, assuming that streets and houses stay put because so far they have stayed put. Contrary to the syllogism that deduces an assertion about something particular from something general, induction leads from particular observations to a general conclusion: This crow is black; that crow is black; also this one and that one and that one. . . . All crows are black.

We must distinguish "All crows are black" as an assertion about crows from a tautology. If we choose to include blackness as part of the definition of "crow," we shall not call anything a crow unless it is black. In that case, "All crows are black" will tell us nothing about crows. The utterance tells us of the range of denotation of the *word* "crow." If "All crows are black" is not a tautology, then "crow" must have been defined in some way that is independent of blackness. Assuming that we can recognize a crow when we see one, we can in each new instance verify the proposition "All crows are black." Every time we see a black crow, we shall have an additional confirmation of the truth of the proposition. However, as long as there are more crows to be examined, we shall never know that we may not one day see a crow that is not black. If we actually see a crow that is not black, this single observation will falsify the proposition "All crows are black."

We have seen (cf. p. 238) that the paradigm of a proposition that asserts a scientific finding, "If A, then B," can be translated into "All A are B" by a twist of language. For instance, "If a kettle of water is placed over a fire, it will eventually boil" can be stated "All kettles of water placed over a fire (A) are kettles of eventually boiling water (B)." The difference between the two types of propositions is that in "All A are B," A and B are implicitly understood to be classes of *objects*, while in "If A, then B," A and B are usually *situations*. After some reflection, we must admit that "objects" are also "situations," for, to make a verifiable assertion about an object, we must *recognize* the object. We do so because the sensations that we receive from the object have been previously organized in our nervous system. We see a pattern of colors, a shape, etc., and recognize an apple. We hear a pattern of sounds and say "My sweetheart's voice" or "the cawing of a crow" or "a police siren." In short, we *give names* to frequently recurring situations. In principle, therefore, any situation can be given a name. But, of course, if we did so, the language would become unwieldy. For this reason we must resort to the "If . . ., then" mode. Hearing "if," we expect to hear the description of a situation, sometimes a very complex one, and we listen accordingly. Having "taken it in," we wait for a "then" (or equivalent) and listen for the description of another situation. Logically, however, an "If . . ., then" proposition can be replaced by an "All A and B" proposition where A is the situation described by the "if" clause and B is the one described by the "then" clause.

Since an induction is not logically compelling, it follows that no assertion in the form "If . . ., then" made *about the world* (in contrast to the propositions of mathematics) is logically compelling. If the axioms of mathematics *were* indeed self-evident, and if they *were* propositions about the world, then all of the propositions derived from them would be *certainly* true; moreover, they would be true assertions about the world.

Plato must have been tremendously impressed by the *compelling* quality of mathematical (that is, purely *deductive*) truths. Knowledge based on sensory experience is always subject to error, not only because our senses often deceive us but also because our experience is limited. As stated earlier, no amount of experience with right triangles will establish with certainty the truth of the Pythagorean theorem, but a mathematical proof does, assuming that the axioms and postulates are "self-evident." Since their self-evidence is also apparently independent of external experience—being established by intuitive insight, as it were—it is easy to come to the conclusion that knowledge established by "reason alone," because it is so compelling, is a higher form of knowledge than that which comes to us through the senses.

Plato thought so and based his whole system of philosophy on the primacy of reason over the senses. Realizing that mathematical reasoning applies properly only to idealized mathematical objects, such as perfectly straight lines of no thickness, perfect circles, and so on, Plato held these idealized objects to be more fundamentally "real" than the "imperfect copies" of them in the sensory world. Extending this idea, he supposed also the existence of idealized objects of the sort not commonly examined by mathematicians. For instance, somewhere in the world of ideas, there was supposed to exist a perfect man, possibly a perfect cat, even a perfect bed, or what not. (Cf. remarks about perfectly fashioned furniture, garments, and so on, pp. 260–61). It is knowledge of the properties of these supposed idealized objects that Plato held to be genuine worthwhile knowledge, as distinguished from the often erroneous, irrelevant knowledge of the accidental, material manifestations of the ideals.

To most of us, this view of knowledge appears incongruous. In particular, we do not often associate science with speculations about idealized entities. We see science as preoccupied with investigations of objects and events of our experience with the material world. No one today will take seriously Plato's advice to astronomers to look within themselves rather than at the starry sky if they want to learn the truth about heavenly bodies.

It is easy to dismiss speculations of this sort as irresponsible. On reflection, however, it seems not so easy to draw the line between sensible and nonsensical conclusions based on pure deduction. At any rate, induction was comparatively neglected until the sixteenth century, when Francis Bacon (1561–1626) first expounded the inductive method as the most important method of cognition.

Whereas Plato equated knowledge with wisdom, Bacon equated it with power. The age that produced Bacon was the same age that produced Machiavelli and that ushered in the era of absolute monarchs in Europe. It was also the age of exploration and of rapidly expanding horizons. Actions rather than introspection and speculation characterized the "Man of the Renaissance." Bacon was typical of his age.

If you want to know something about how things are in the world, said Bacon in effect, put the question to nature *directly*. Observe and note what you observe. Collect the results of your observations. Add to the collection. You will then be accumulating knowledge and with it the power to arrange things to suit your needs and your wants.

In our day of burgeoning applied science, we tend to view these observations as belaboring the obvious. However, in a world emerging from the Middle Ages, the idea of "putting direct questions to nature" was a novel one. The influence of Plato, for whom reasoning from intuitively perceived truths was the only true way to genuine knowledge, lasted through many centuries. Moreover the idea of using knowledge to pursue specific goals was not always accepted without reservations. The view that use of knowledge to gain power may be immoral is exemplified in Part II of Goethe's *Faust* which begins with a scene in the imperial court. The empire is on the verge of bankruptcy. Mephistopheles disguised as the jester offers advice: There is gold in nearby mountains. Let's go get it. He is opposed by an ecclesiastical dignitary who gives several weighty reasons why it is wrong to wrest riches from the earth. Ironically, in our own day, we are beginning to have second thoughts about the uninhibited use of knowledge in the service of power. Perhaps Mephistopheles was acting in character (as the Evil One) when he suggested to the emperor what appeared to be an eminently constructive solution of his problem.

After the sixteenth century, Bacon's conception of science prevailed in the Western world, and the age of experimentation began in earnest. An experiment is a "direct question put to nature." The observed result tells us "how it is" in the specific case. Usually, however, we read more into the result. We express our observations in the form of an "If . . ., then" proposition. The tacit assumption underlying such a proposition involves an induction. We assume that if the conditions of the experiment are repeated, the same result will be observed. In fact, without this tacit assumption, there would be no point in performing an experiment. The observation tells us only "how things *were*" at the time of the experiment; but that time is gone forever. What we want to know is "how things are" right now and, how things *will be* in the future because all our contemplated actions are in the future and, if we are going to use knowledge in guiding our actions, we must be sure that the knowledge we have gained will remain valid.

In everyday affairs we do not usually give much thought to these matters. When we "learn by experience," we always assume that under similar conditions similar events will take place. If at times we are mistaken, we assume that the conditions were not altogether similar, and we then look for the difference. The experimenting scientist makes the same assumption. He is careful in setting up specific conditions for the experiment, guarding against extraneous influences and so on. Still, the assumption that under similar conditions the same thing will happen (or that the same causes will produce the same effects) is always at the basis of all experimental science. Since experimental science would make no sense without this assumption, the scientist ordinarily does not give this matter much more thought than does the man in the street.

Philosophers reason otherwise. The quest for *certain* knowledge occupied a great deal of the philosophers' attention, at least in the Western world. The failure of inductive knowledge to meet the criterion of certainty did not escape them.

The "noncompelling" nature of inductive conclusions was most eloquently discussed by David Hume (1711–76) in his *Enquiry Concerning Human Understanding.* In this work Hume undertakes to show that the only meaning to be attributed to *causality* (which is assumed to underlie the connection between the "then" and the "if" in an "If . . ., then" proposition) is that it is a "habit of thought." Having observed that B follows A, we become accustomed to thinking about B whenever A occurs, and that is all that can be said about causality. Hume insisted that no causal relation between two events residing in the nature of things can ever be conclusively proved by a generalization arrived at from repeated observations, that is, by induction. This came to be known in philosophy as "the scandal of induction."

Hume's arguments present a sort of threat to the whole enterprise of science. For if "causality" is nothing but a "habit of thought," in what way can science be said to establish any truths about the world?

We observe that an electric current flows through a wire whenever the wire moves across a magnetic field; this movement through the magnetic field we call the "cause" of the current. We also observe in our town that whenever the campus clock strikes three, an airliner soon passes overhead. While we readily admit the movement of the wire in a magnetic field as the "cause" of the current passing through it, we dismiss the idea that the striking of the clock makes the plane materialize. Hume, however, sees no grounds for making a distinction between the one situation and the other.

Is there a way to demolish Hume's argument and so to save the scientific enterprise from the lowly status implicitly assigned to it by

Hume—that of establishing "habits of thought"? Logically, there is not. But neither is there any need to demolish it, for science, unlike philosophy, is not engaged in quest of *certain* knowledge but only of *reliable* knowledge. Reliability is a matter of degree, and degree of reliability was not considered by Hume.

As the following example indicates, failure to consider degrees of reliability can easily lead to absurd conclusions. Suppose we observe several crows, find all of them to be black, and contemplate the possible inductive conclusion: "All crows are black." We realize that the few observations made are not sufficient to establish the reliability of our conclusion, so we continue to make observations on crows. The proposition "All crows are black" is now a *hypothesis*. Our observations are tests of the hypothesis. We realize that the observation of a single nonblack crow will compel us to abandon the hypothesis because the proposition "There exists a nonblack crow" or, equivalently, "Some crows are not black" contradicts the proposition "All crows are black." We also agree with Hume that no matter how many crows we observe, all black, the hypothesis will remain unproved. Nevertheless, we have *more* confidence in our hypothesis after having observed one thousand crows and found them to be black than we had after observing four black crows. Granted that "confidence" is a subjective matter, it is nevertheless important, or at any rate interesting, to inquire from where this increase of confidence comes. Is it only a matter of establishing a habit by repeated association of "crow" with "blackness," as Hume suggested, or is there a sounder basis for our increased confidence?

Let us perform a logical operation on the proposition "All crows are black" or on the equivalent proposition "If a thing is a crow, it is black." Let p stand for "A thing is a crow" and q for "The thing is black." The hypothesis says $p \rightarrow q$, which is equivalent to $q \vee \sim p$ (cf. Chapter 15), which in turn is equivalent to $\sim q \rightarrow \sim p$. Translated, the last proposition reads: "If a thing is not black, it is not a crow."

To test *this* hypothesis, equivalent to our original one, I pick up the first nonblack object at hand. It happens to be my pipe, which is brown. I note that this nonblack thing is not a crow. "Aha," I say, "another confirmation of my hypothesis that all crows are black." This is silly, you may be thinking, and so it is. But why is it silly? Where is the error? Note that I have seen innumerable nonblack objects which were not crows. So the habit of thinking "If something is not black, it is not a crow" must have been firmly established in my mind. I should be able to assert this proposition with considerable confidence. Why, then, am I not entitled to assert the *logically equivalent* proposition "If something is a crow, it is black" with equal confidence? It seems that "habit of thought" does not provide the entire explanation of our growing confidence in a hypothesis after repeated confirmations.

The scientist's confidence in a hypothesis (which may be derived by induction) is related to the *a priori improbability of the observation that confirms the hypothesis*. Example:

Suppose we are told that there are five balls in a box and that they are either all black or that four are black and one is white. Suppose we assume the hypothesis that all are black and proceed to test this hypothesis by drawing successive balls. We draw one ball and find it to be black. This, of course, does not prove that all five balls are black because we could as well have drawn a black ball if only four of them were black. So, drawing a single black ball is not much of a confirmation of our hypothesis that all five balls are black. The point is that if our hypothesis were false, that is, if there was one white ball in the box, there were four chances out of five to draw a black ball. In other words, the a priori probability of confirming our hypothesis, *supposing it to be false*, was already large, and for this reason we do not consider the fact of drawing a single black ball as strong confirmation of the hypothesis "All five balls are black."

Next,

Suppose we draw two balls and find both to be black. The a priori probability of this result, supposing the box to contain one white ball, is $4/5 \cdot 3/4 = 3/5$, smaller than the previous a priori probability ($4/5$). For this reason our confidence in the hypothesis "all five balls are black" is somewhat stronger if two black balls are drawn. Continuing in this way, we see that the a priori probability of drawing three black balls (assuming that one is white) is $2/5$ and of drawing four black balls is $1/5$. Of course, it is impossible to draw five black balls if one is white.

Our confidence in a hypothesis is the stronger, the less likely is an observed result on the supposition that the hypothesis is false. Now we can see the difference between the procedures used to test the logically equivalent hypotheses "If something is a crow, it is black" and "If something is not a crow, it is not black." Assume we have never seen a crow but know how to recognize one. However, we know nothing about the color of crows. From our past experience, we know that birds come in many different colors. So the a priori probability that a crow is black is not large. The bird could be white or red or gray or multicolored. Therefore, when we see the first crow and find it to be black, we have a considerable confirmation of our hypothesis. If we observe a thousand black crows, we get a strong confirmation because to find a thousand black crows by pure chance (if they happen to come in many colors) is quite improbable. On the other hand, the a priori probability that an arbitrarily selected non-black object is *not* a crow is very large (almost a certainty). And even the probability that none of a thousand arbitrarily selected nonblack objects is *not* a crow is very large (almost a certainty). For this reason our hypothesis is not strongly confirmed in the second case.

In one respect Hume was on the right track. In relating induction to "a habit of thought," he called attention to the subjective component of inductive conclusions. This component is always present. Our acceptance of a conclusion arrived at by induction does involve a measure of belief and therefore a measure of uncertainty. While, for a philosopher in search of "certain" knowledge, this irreducible component of personal belief may be sufficient reason for rejecting induction as a mode of cognition, it is not for a scientist. The scientist has learned to live with uncertainty because he knows that certain knowledge about the world is unattainable. The scientist wants to know *how much* credence he can give to a conclusion arrived at by induction.

The problem of quantifying the degree of confidence in conclusions suggested by observations and experiments is especially keen in the behavioral and social sciences (psychology, sociology, economics, etc.). It is often difficult or altogether impossible to make repeated observations of human behavior under identical conditions if only because the internal states of human beings are usually not subject to the observer's or experimenter's control. For this reason repeated observations, even under apparently similar conditions, give different results. It is possible, however, to note the relative frequency of different results. The paradigm of the scientific proposition "If so, then so" can be replaced by "If apparently so, then probably so." We have seen that probabilities can be quantified. Degrees of confidence in hypotheses are expressed in terms of quantified probabilities.

The mathematical discipline concerned with these matters is called statistics. Applied to the analysis of observations or experimental data, statistical techniques permit the investigator to make *statistical inferences*. Such inferences could also be called "probabilistic induction," although this term is not in common usage. It is important to note that probabilistic induction is the final result of a statistical analysis. In the analysis itself, deduction is used. The logic used in this deduction is the infinite-valued logic of probability theory (cf. pp. 266–67).

Statistical inference is now widely used in medical research. Suppose someone discovers a drug that appears to be effective in treating disease. Discoveries nowadays are usually not accidents but end products of long, systematic research. That the drug is of potential value against the disease may have been suggested by experiments on animals. Eventually the question arises as to whether or not it is effective in humans. The proposition to be checked against facts is "If the drug is administered to a person suffering from the disease, he will get better." The simple paradigm of induction suggests that, if a certain number of patients were helped by the drug to recover from the disease, we may conclude that the drug is effective; that is, the hypothesis is confirmed. But the principle does not tell us how many positive results justify the conclusion, nor what we may conclude if some patients get better and others do not. It certainly will not do to discard the drug even if not everyone is helped by it. For instance, if only 25 percent of people suffering from a hitherto incurable cancer were completely cured by the treatment, the drug would still be a valuable addition to the medical arsenal.

On the other hand, even if every patient taking the drug got better, we could not conclude with certainty that the drug cures the disease. Most diseases are not fatal. People recover from them even if they are not treated. The question we must answer is to what extent the drug was instrumental in effecting recovery if recoveries do occur.

To answer this question, a *controlled* experiment must be performed. The drug is administered to one group of patients—the *experimental group*. Another group, the *control group*, goes without the drug. Results observed in both groups are recorded. A greater incidence of recovery in the experimental group may be evidence but not necessarily a confirmation of even the probabilistic hypothesis "If the drug is administered to a patient, he is more likely to recover than if it is not." For this hypothesis contains the word "likely," which is not a term (cf. p. 223); one must specify comparative likelihoods as probabilities. The fraction of patients that recover does not indicate the probability of recovery; the fraction is only an *estimate* of this probability. The actual *probability* of recovery may be the same in both groups (which would mean that the drug is not effective), and yet the fraction of patients recovered may happen by chance to be larger in one group than in the other. In the same way, ten tosses of a "fair" coin may result in, say, seven heads instead of five because the outcome of each toss is governed by chance. The problem of statistical inference is to calculate the *chances* of confirming the hypothesis that the drug has some effect. This illustrates the principle of induction stated on page 302: the smaller the a priori probability of observing the result that seems to confirm the induction stated as a hypothesis, the larger is our confidence that the induction is justified.

Of course, we have presented a drastically simplified picture of a "controlled experiment." In a controlled experiment, the conditions under which observations are made are controlled. In our case, control is exercised with the aim of keeping as nearly identical as possible the conditions under which observations are made on the two groups. For instance, the control group instead of going without "treatment" entirely might be given a "placebo," that is, something that looks exactly like the drug but has no discernible physical effect, say, a sugar tablet. This precaution is taken to rule out a reaction due to the psychological effect induced by merely "taking a drug." Such precautions are especially important in experiments with drugs used in treating mental diseases, since the experiment itself may be tantamount to a "treatment" regardless of the actual effect of the drug. Further precautions may include the so-called double blind technique. In this procedure not only does the patient not know whether he is taking a drug or the placebo, but also the nurse who administers the pill and the physicians who perform the subsequent observations are kept in ignorance, all in the interest of excluding suggestive and antisuggestive effects.

Controlled experiments in medical research may raise difficult ethical problems. A typical dilemma is depicted by Sinclair Lewis in his novel *Arrowsmith*. The hero, a young physician, goes to a Caribbean island to fight a bubonic plague epidemic. He has with him a new drug (a precursor of antibiotics) to be used as an immunizing agent against the disease. The drug is to be tested in the epidemic. Thus Arrowsmith has two missions: that of a doctor—to help the people of the island—and that of a scientist—to establish the efficacy of the drug.

The young man's mentor, an old German scientist, warns him not to let his humanitarian impulses interfere with the second mission, which is, after all, the important one, since a definitive confirmation of the drug's effectiveness would justify its use in future epidemics. Accordingly, the old man charges Arrowsmith with the responsibility of conducting a properly controlled experiment: the drug is to be given to one half of the inhabitants and withheld from the other half. Arrowsmith promises to carry out the plan, but eventually cannot bear the thought of deliberately denying a possibly lifesaving drug to arbitrarily selected "victims." He finally breaks down and gives the drug to everyone. The epidemic subsides, but the value of the drug remains unknown.

Another type of ethical problem arises in connection with statistical evaluations of diagnostic tests. Assume that a laboratory test has been developed for some disease. As is the case with most tests, it is not one hundred per cent reliable. Four situations can occur in any specific case:

1.   The patient is assumed to have the disease, and in fact he has.
2.   The patient is declared to be free of the disease, but in fact he has it.
3.   The patient is assumed to have the disease, but in fact he has not.
4.   The patient is correctly declared to be free of the disease.

In the first and last of these outcomes, the test clearly serves its purpose; in the second and third, it does not. The second outcome is called a "false negative"; the third is called a "false positive."

Now, the basis of the decision as to whether the disease is present or not is some criterion, say, a quantity, resulting from a measurement. The decision selects a cutting point: if the quantity exceeds some selected critical value, the patient is assumed to have the disease; otherwise, not. Clearly, the critical value can be selected to be so large that it is never exceeded. In this case, there will be no false positives, since everyone will be declared to be free of the disease. Conversely, if the critical value is set too low, there will be no false negatives, since everyone will be assumed to have the disease. Such an approach would make the diagnostic procedure useless. The question, then, is where to set the cutting point. If the accuracy of the test is known, each setting of the cutting point will produce a certain probability of a false positive and a certain probability of a false negative.

In fact, the larger the probability of the one, the smaller the probability of the other. To decide on the "optimum" setting, we must estimate the "costs" of false positives and of false negatives. In the case of a false positive, these costs may involve the trouble and expense of treating a patient who actually does not have the disease. In the case of a false negative, a patient who has the disease does not receive treatment that might have helped him. If numerical values could be assigned to these costs, the best cutting point could be fixed; it is the point at which the average (expected) cost is minimum. But it is often difficult to assign numerical values to costs that involve intangibles, such as failing to treat a sick patient or causing unnecessary worry by the false positive. The assignment of these values does not fall within the scope of the statistical problem. We see, however, how analysis of the statistical problem turns attention to matters involving ethical questions.[1]

Another important clarification introduced by statistical inference is that of the notion of causality. The categorical statement "A causes B" may mean either "A must occur if B is to occur" or "If A occurs, B must occur" or both. Even these meanings do not exhaust the notion of causality. For instance, the assertion "Cigarette smoking is a cause of lung cancer" is believed to be justified in spite of the fact that many

---

1. To take an example, the efficacy of a drug against a given disease and the extent of its possible harmful side effects are principal factors to consider before releasing the drug for general medical use. Now "efficacy" of a drug can be meaningfully represented by a probability that an arbitrarily selected patient will be cured. The extent of its possibly harmful side effects can be represented analogously by a probability. In order to weigh the possible benefit against the possible danger, not only these probabilities must be known but also some numbers must be assigned to the "utility" (benefit) of a cure and the "disutility" (harm) of the side effect. These numbers multiplied by the respective probabilities of the corresponding outcomes represent the *expected utility* of administering the drug. This expected utility can be compared with the expected utility of *not* administering the drug, and a decision can be made on that basis.

However, the decision to release the drug for clinical use involves more. The choice may be between releasing it and delaying release, pending *further* experimentation. The point is that the probabilities of the outcomes are not known exactly. They are estimated from frequencies observed in previous experiments. The more data obtained from experiments, the more confidence we have that the observed frequencies are reasonably close to the "actual" probabilities, hence the more confidence we have in the "rationality" of the decision we shall make. On the other hand, as long as experiments continue (the release of the drug delayed), people may be suffering or dying who *may* have been helped by it. A decision to *postpone* action is also a form of action. Techniques of probabilistic induction (that is, statistical inference) do not help us make a decision, since it is not within the scope of these techniques to assign utilities to outcomes. But the techniques help us to *clarify* the issues by making it *mandatory* to assign numerical utilities to outcomes if a decision is to be defended as rational. In other words, we are forced to assign operational meanings to assertions like "This drug may be of benefit" or "This drug is associated with certain dangers."

cigarette smokers do not succumb to lung cancer and many non-smokers do. What the assertion says is that people who smoke cigarettes are more *likely* to fall victim to lung cancer than people who do not. A statistical index, called the *correlation coefficient*, provides a measure of the "degree of linkage" between cigarette smoking and lung cancer.

Statistical correlation does not establish a causal relation, but it suggests that one may exist, and frequently this is of itself useful information. Specifically, a statistical correlation between two variables tells us how likely we can guess one of them if we are told the value of the other. The stronger the correlation, the more likely we can guess one quantity if we know the other. Example:

We know that people with longer arms are likely to have also longer legs. But we cannot always guess the length of a man's leg if we are told the length of his arm. The question is how close our guess is going to be. Let us take a sample of people and plot the lengths of their legs against the lengths of their arms. Our plot may look like Figure 26.

If all the points fell exactly on a straight line (called the *regression line*) then, knowing the positions of just two points and having been told the length of a man's arm, we could always guess the length of his leg by marking the intersection of the vertical line through the point corresponding to the length of his arm with the regression line. In that case, the two lengths would be perfectly correlated: the coefficient of correlation would be 1.00. Actually the points are scattered. The closer they are to the regression line, the closer to 1 is the magnitude of the correlation coefficient.[2] If the points are scattered hap-

2. The correlation coefficient is calculated as follows. Suppose we have one set of n quantities: $x_1, x_2, \ldots, x_n$; and another, $y_1, y_2, \ldots, y_n$. We wish to know whether the x's are correlated with the y's and to what degree. Form the sum $(x_1y_1 + x_2y_2 + \ldots x_ny_n)$ and call it S_{12}. Call the sum $(x_1 + x_2 + \ldots x_n)$ S_1; the sum $(y_1 + y_2 + \ldots y_n)$ S_2; the sum $(x_1^2 + x_2^2 + \ldots x_n^2)$ $S_1^{(2)}$; and the sum $(y_1^2 + y_2^2 + \ldots y_n^2)$ $S_2^{(2)}$. N.B.: $S_1^{(2)}$ and $S_2^{(2)}$, sums of squares, are not to be confused with S_1^2 and S_2^2, squares of sums. Then the correlation coefficient, r, is given by the formula

$$r = \frac{S_{12} - \dfrac{1}{n} S_1 S_2}{\sqrt{\left(S_1^{(2)} - \dfrac{1}{n} S_1^2\right)\left(S_2^{(2)} - \dfrac{1}{n} S_2^2\right)}}.$$

It ranges in value from -1 to $+1$. A positive value indicates that an increase in x is likely to be associated with an increase in y and vice versa.

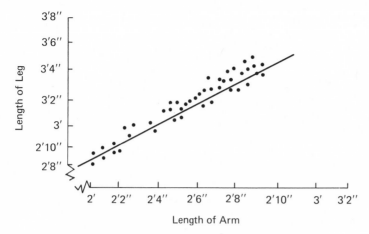

Figure 26 *A hypothetical plot of the lengths of men's legs against the lengths of the corresponding arms. The horizontal coordinate of each point is the length of a man's arm; the vertical coordinate, the length of the same man's leg. The solid line is called the regression line. The clustering of the points near the regression line shows that the correlation between the two variables is high.*

hazardly, not clustering about a straight line, the correlation coefficient is close to zero. The quantities are then said to be uncorrelated. For instance, the length of a man's arm and the number of letters in his full name are probably uncorrelated. A plot of one against the other might look like Figure 27.[3]

Correlation and causality are related, but they are by no means identical. For instance, during the spring months the number of daily traffic fatalities is strongly correlated with the amount of electricity used. The correlation is negative; that is, the more electricity used the fewer fatalities there are likely to be in a given week of March, April, or May. This relation is not causal: if everyone kept his lights burning all day, this would not reduce fatalities. The source of the correlation

3. If the points cluster around either a vertical or a horizontal regression line, the correlation coefficient is also close to zero. For instance, if all the points fell on a horizontal line, this would indicate that whatever the value of one of the variables (say, x), the value of the other (y) would always be the same. In that case, if we were told the (constant) value of y, we could not guess the value of x, which could be anything.

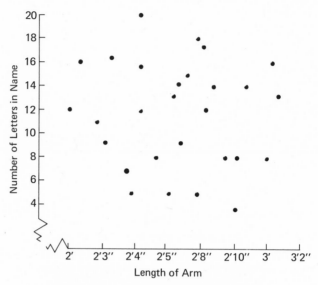

Figure 27 *A hypothetical plot of the lengths of men's full names against the lengths of their arms. Failure of the points to cluster around a regression line indicates that the correlation is near zero.*

is to be found in the fact that, as the weather grows warmer, daylight hours increase *and also* people drive more.

The question of whether a correlation indicates a causal relation can be answered if one of the variables can be manipulated. Thus, failure to reduce fatalities by using more electricity would indicate that no causal relation exists between the use of electricity and fatalities. On the other hand, if a strong drop in the incidence of lung cancer were to follow a sudden removal of cigarettes from the market, this would be evidence of a causal relation between cigarette smoking and lung cancer. Controlled experiments are often designed with the specific aim of establishing or refuting a causal relation initially suggested by a statistical correlation.

Controlled experiment and statistical inference comprise the techniques of induction used in science. As has been shown, these techniques are as far removed from the simple paradigms of induction discussed by Francis Bacon and David Hume as the deductive techniques of mathematics are from the syllogisms of Aristotle.

APPLICATIONS

I. Gather several instances of statistical correlation and present arguments for or against the hypothesis that the correlation represents a direct or indirect causal linkage between events. Examples: change in crime rate vs. change in level of prices; change in automobile fatalities vs. change in admissions to mental hospitals.

II. Some simple psychological experiments can be performed by persons without laboratory experience. Try the following. Make a deck of one hundred cards, some white, some black on one side, all of one color on the other. *N.B.* The "black" cards need not be black. They can be simply marked in some way. Keep the number of black cards (that is, 37, 72, etc.) secret from your subject. Allow him to sample the cards one at a time, always replacing the selected card and shuffling the deck after each sampling. Tell him he can go on choosing as long as he likes. When he stops sampling, ask him to guess the number of black cards in the deck. Make note of how many cards he samples. Make note of the size of the error in his guess. Repeat the experiment with the same subject and with different subjects, using different numbers of black cards in a deck of one hundred. A repetition of an experiment under conditions as similar as possible is called a *replication*. If your patience (and the patience of your subjects) endures, you can get many replications holding a given condition fixed. In one set of replications, you can hold fixed the number of black cards in the deck. Your "variables" will be the size of error in the subject's guess and the number of cards he or she samples. Plot the size of the error against the number of cards sampled. Are the points scattered or do they show a trend? If they do, there is a correlation between the two variables. Is the correlation positive (the larger the number sampled, the larger the error) or negative (the larger the number sampled, the smaller the error)? Now fix the number of cards sampled (require that number to be sampled) and vary the number of black cards in the deck. Plot the size of the error against the number of black cards. Is there a trend? Or, perhaps a trend starts out in one direction, then reverses itself? Do the subjects tend to underestimate or to overestimate the number of black cards? Or does the error tend to be in one direction when there are few black cards and in the other direction when there are many? Answers to these questions will suggest themselves the more clearly the more replications you make.

III. If you think some of the questions have been answered, can you make some inferences about how people make inferences under uncertainty? about how reliable these inferences (yours and theirs) are likely to be? about how much information people think is sufficient to make an inference?

IV. Some people believe in so-called "extrasensory perception," and experiments have been reported in support of this belief. Perform an experiment with a deck of one hundred black and white cards in equal numbers. Shuffle well and invite a friend to guess the cards in succession. If he guesses only by chance, you can expect him to be right about 50 percent of the time. Assuming you do not feel one way or the other about ESP, how many cards will he have to guess for you to admit that there may be something in it? How many if you do *not* believe in ESP? If you believe in ESP, describe an experiment in which specified results would change your mind. Compare your answers with those of others.

1) Assuming again that you are undecided about ESP, how many cards would the subject have to guess if there were only ten cards in the deck, five of which were black?

18/the way of science

Scientific knowledge is said to be reliable and organized. If you understand the full meaning of this description, you understand the way of science.

Many textbooks on various branches of science begin with a description of "scientific method." The scientist in quest of knowledge is pictured first "making observations." Having made several observations and discovered some "regularity" in what he has observed, he may be led to a tentative induction—a hypothesis (cf. Chapter 12). From this hypothesis, stated as a proposition, the scientist deduces other propositions. He then puts the *deduced* propositions to a test by making further observations. If these observations confirm the deduced propositions, the original hypothesis is corroborated, that is, gains credence; if observations fail to confirm the deduced proposition, the original hypothesis is modified or discarded. A new hypothesis is formulated from which appropriate deductions are made and put to a test.

On the whole, this description of "the scientific method" is accurate, but a great deal more must be said if the way of science is to be distinguished from other modes of cognition. Moreover, we must keep in mind that an actual working scientist does much more than follow the successive steps of the "method" in prescribed order. Pursuing science is not a routine.

Before we go deeper into these matters, let us examine a procedure that, though very simple, faithfully reflects the paradigm of scientific cognition as it is conventionally described.

In the World War II novel *Mr. Roberts* by Thomas Heggen, the crew of a navy supply ship continue to wreak vengeance on their despotic captain after Mr. Roberts, the captain's sworn enemy and the crew's champion, leaves the ship. One of Mr. Roberts's last exploits was to throw overboard the captain's potted palm, to the delight of the crew. The captain doggedly replaced the jettisoned plant with *two* potted palms. Another officer, who bravely stepped into Mr. Roberts's role of the avenger, threw the two plants overboard, whereupon the captain promptly replaced them with *four*. Today we call a process of this sort "escalation." The avenger's feat is reported to Mr. Roberts by mail. In his reply, he proposes an experiment with a view of testing a hypothesis. In fact, he offers two hypotheses:

1. The captain is intent on *doubling* the number of potted palms every time the avenger strikes.
2. The captain is intent on *squaring* the number of palms lost.

Mr. Roberts suggests the continuation of the palm-extermination program in the interest of science. If the four palms are replaced by eight, hypothesis 1 will be corroborated; if by sixteen, hypothesis 2.

Unfortunately, by the time Mr. Roberts's letter arrives, he has been killed, and so the novel must be brought to an end, leaving us ignorant of the outcome of the experiment. But we can pursue the investigation hypothetically.

Suppose that, after the disappearance of the four palms, *seven* appeared in their place. In that case, both of Mr. Roberts's hypotheses would have been refuted, and we would have to look for another. The following one easily suggests itself: the captain increases the number of *added* potted palms by one. Thus, after he lost the first, he replaced it and added one more; then there were two. After he lost the two, he replaced them and added *two* more; then there were four. After he lost the four, he replaced them and added *three* more; then there were seven. If the hypothesis is correct, the next number in the sequence should be eleven.

Note that each new hypothesis must account for at least one more observation *not yet made*. In other words, a hypothesis must contain an implicit prediction; and, in addition, the new hypothesis must account for everything that has *already* been observed. Both of Mr.

Roberts's hypotheses satisfy the first criterion, but his second hypothesis does not quite satisfy the second criterion. That hypothesis says that the captain squares the number of palms lost. But when he lost one, he replaced it by two, and two is not the square of one. The squaring started only after the two palms were gone.

The two criteria of a good hypothesis, namely, that it account for everything already observed and that it also lead to a deduced prediction, challenge the scientist's creativity. *The creative act is the recognition of a pattern in what has been observed.* The principle is frequently used in designing intelligence tests. The pupil is presented with a sequence such as 2, 4, 6, 8, . . . or 1, 4, 9, 16, . . . and asked to "predict" the next term of the series. Successful prediction depends on the recognition of a pattern: the even numbers in the first case, the squares of successive integers in the second.

Not many will recognize a pattern in the following sequence: 5, 10, 26, 50, 122, 170, 290, . . . The numbers are obtained by squaring and increasing by one the successive primes (numbers divisible only by themselves): 2, 3, 5, 7, 11, 13, 17. Once the pattern is recognized, the next number can be predicted: 362.

What distinguishes the scientific hypothesis from an ad hoc explanation is its predictive potential. The ad hoc explanation states some principle that accounts for what has already been observed, but it is devoid of predictive power. If new observations fail to fit into the principle, the principle is modified until it accounts for the observations just made, but without suggesting a basis for prediction.

By means of ad hoc explanations, any hypothesis can be made *unfalsifiable.* Hypotheses inherent in magic are typically unfalsifiable. The witch doctor practices his art on the supposition that the performance of a certain ritual will cure a certain disease, unless evil spirits interfere. If recovery occurs, the hypothesis is confirmed. If the patient does not recover, an ad hoc explanation is at hand: evil spirits interfered and rendered the witch doctor's magic ineffective. In order to justify a continued belief in his powers, the witch doctor need not score one hundred percent cures. Nor is it unreasonable to suppose that extraneous intervention renders the cure ineffective. However, if the explanation of failure is to have any "leverage" in the theory, *something* must be indicated about conditions under which failure can be expected. It is not sufficient to infer that these conditions prevailed *just because* a failure occurred.

Superstitions are examples of unfalsifiable hypotheses. A superstition is an assertion in the form "if so, then so." For instance, "If you see a new moon over your left shoulder, you will suffer a mishap." The hypothesis is unfalsifiable because sooner or later all of us suffer mishaps. It would be falsifiable if the time of the expected mishap were approximately specified.

However, even specifying the time of the "then so" may make a hypothesis unfalsifiable. For instance, a Sun Dance may be supposed to make the sun rise. The sun of course rises and the time of sunrise can be specified. In this case the hypothesis is unfalsifiable because "the sun will rise" is a true proposition, a priori. (Recall that any proposition implies a true proposition.) Therefore, "if the Sun Dance is performed, the sun will rise" is a perfectly valid inference. This proposition is worthless as a scientific hypothesis because the a priori probability of the event "The sun will rise" is, for all practical purposes, 1; and, as we have seen, the predictive power of a hypothesis diminishes as the a priori probability of the event predicted becomes larger. When the event predicted is a certainty a priori, the predictive power of the hypothesis vanishes. To test the notion that the Sun Dance "makes the sun rise," we must put the converse on trial: "If the Sun Dance is *not* performed, the sun will *not* rise." Since the a priori probability that the sun will not rise is exceedingly small, a confirmation of the converse hypothesis, even in a single instance, would be an extremely strong corroboration of a causal connection between the ritual and the rising of the sun.

Strong objections may well be raised against this sort of experiment because of the likelihood of disastrous effects should the experiment "succeed." An analogous situation could be observed in connection with the so-called hypothesis of deterrence. It was argued during the early years of the cold war that the threat of retaliation with nuclear weapons deterred the Soviet Union from "taking over Western Europe." The fact that no such attempt was made is still offered by cold warriors as a corroboration of the hypothesis. A much stronger corroboration would be obtained if unilateral atomic disarmament by the United States *did* result in an attack on Western Europe. However, the United States could not be induced to perform this experiment. The disastrous consequences of a positive result could always be counted upon to preclude even the thought of it.

The following story told to me by an anthropologist studying an East African tribe illustrates the proper use of scientific method. He asked the chieftain of the tribe whether his people practiced sex-determination magic. The chieftain replied somewhat as follows:

"No, we don't practice it. Our people don't believe in that magic. But our neighbors to the east do. Personally, I am not sure. You see, my wife gave birth to four daughters, and I became concerned about dying without male issue. So I called in a witch doctor from that tribe. He did his magic, and my wife gave birth to a son. I called him in again the following year, and again my wife gave birth to a son. The next year I didn't call him just to see what would happen. My wife gave birth to a daughter. So I invited him again the following year, and we had a son. After that, my wife died. I have had no more children. So there you are. If you ask me, I think there may be something in this business of sex-determination magic, but I am not sure."

If sex-determination magic works, the chieftain's wife should have had two sons, a daughter, and a son in that order in the four years of the "experiment." The a priori probability of this sequence is 1/16. In most experiments in the behavioral sciences, an a priori probability of 1/20 or less is the conventional criterion for rejecting the null hypothesis (that the events happened by pure chance). Thus the result of the chieftain's experiment did not quite reach the conventional level of significance. His conclusion, however, was a reasonable one.

To repeat, if an observation fails to corroborate the hypothesis, the hypothesis must be discarded or modified. If it is modified, the new hypothesis must account for the observations already made. One way this can always be done is by listing exceptions. However, such modification eventually deprives the hypothesis of its predictive, hence of its explanatory, power.

Before physical science "took off" in the sixteenth century, physical phenomena were explained by philosophers in terms of metaphysically flavored "laws of nature." For example, the action of pumps was explained by the principle "nature abhors vacuum." There was some evidence, aside from the action of pumps, to support this hypothesis. It was known that the space around us is not empty but is filled with air. The presence of air made itself felt through wind (air in motion). Accordingly, the working of pumps was explained by the fact that, when the piston of the pump is displaced, a vacuum (absence of air) is created into which water is impelled to rush because "nature abhors vacuum." All went well until it was noticed that no pump could raise a column of water higher than thirty-two feet.

How could this failure of nature to abhor vacuum be accounted for? An ad hoc explanation always being handy, the "law of nature" could be modified to say that "nature abhors vacuum—except when the vacuum is above a column of water higher than thirty-two feet." Clearly, this sort of modification failed to satisfy even philosophers.

The whole question was then reexamined. Instead of attributing feelings to "nature," the behavior of columns of water was carefully studied. It was found that two connected columns of water could balance each other if they were of the same height, regardless of their cross-sectional areas. This somewhat paradoxical fact could be explained by assuming that in a hydrostatic system in equilibrium the pressure at any given point was equal in all directions and depended only on the height of the liquid above the point. Once this principle was understood, it only remained to include the air as a part of the hydrostatic system: a column of water in a closed pipe emptied of air can be supported by a column of air. But water being heavier than air per unit volume, the column of air supporting a column of water of a given height has to be much higher. In fact, the column of water thirty-two feet high is supported by the column of air stretching all the way to the end of the earth's atmosphere. The entire atmosphere presses on the reservoir from which the water column was raised, and this pressure is just enough to balance the column of water. A higher column cannot be supported because there is no more atmosphere.

To this point the failure of pumps to raise water above thirty-two feet has been explained, but *only* this fact has been explained. There is more to come. A scientific explanation must yield a "dividend." It must explain also other facts that could not be explained before. For example, had we accepted the ad hoc explanation ("nature abhors vacuum but not over thirty-two feet"), we could not explain the fact that only about thirty inches of a column of mercury can be supported in an empty tube. The hydrostatic principle explains this too. Mercury is about thirteen times heavier than water per unit volume. Consequently the column of mercury that can be supported must be about thirteen times shorter than a column of water, and so it is. And there is still more to come. If a column of mercury is supported by atmospheric pressure, it follows that the greater the atmospheric pressure, the higher the column that can be supported. On a high mountain we would expect the atmospheric pressure to be lower than in a valley; therefore we would expect the column of mercury to drop as we ascend the mountain, and so it does. There are more dividends. When the air is humid, the atmospheric pressure drops because water vapor is not as dense as dry air. We would consequently expect the column of mercury (which we can now call a "barometer" = pressure meter) to drop in humid weather and to rise in dry weather. In fact, as the air becomes humid, rain is more likely. If the pressure drops excessively, stormy weather can be expected. Our barometer becomes a rough predictor of weather.

All these dividends are reaped when a philosophical principle ("nature abhors vacuum") is discarded in favor of a careful description of events in terms of firmly established mechanical principles.

Now let us see what happens when firmly established mechanical principles appear to be violated.

We have mentioned the remarkable predictive power of the mathematically formulated law of gravity on the basis of which the motions of heavenly bodies are calculated in advance with clockwork precision. Take the incident of the discovery of a new planet by Sir William Herschel in 1781. A few observations of its position sufficed to calculate its orbit, and once the orbit of a planet is calculated, its future positions for all time to come can be predicted; that is, all future positions can be mathematically deduced from the laws of motion and the law of gravity. As Uranus's path across the sky was observed from year to year (it takes about eighty-four years to go once around the sun), it became apparent that the path deviated to some extent from the predicted one. Could the law of gravity be inexact? If so, how did it account for the motions of all the other heavenly bodies so exactly? If one made corrections in the law to account for the aberrant behavior of Uranus, what would happen to the exact predictions deduced elsewhere from the law? Could one suppose that Uranus obeyed a law different from the one obeyed by other heavenly bodies? To assume this would be to make the type of ad hoc assumption spurned by the scientist.

There was, however, another way out. If there were another planet about which we had not known, then *its* gravitational action on Uranus's perturbations might account for the deviations. If the unknown planet were sufficiently far away beyond the orbit of Uranus, then its gravitational pull on the other known planets might be negligible, and so the corrections in the orbit of Uranus would not affect predicted behavior of the other planets that *did* follow their prescribed paths. This prospect seemed attractive. If the existence of the hitherto unknown planet could be demonstrated, the apparent failure of the exact law of universal gravitation would be turned into a triumph. But where in the vast sky would one start to look for this planet?

The British astronomer John C. Adams (1819–92) and the Frenchman U. Jean Joseph Leverrier (1811–77) worked on the problem independently of each other. They calculated the position, the orbit, and the mass of the unknown planet that would account for the perturbations in the orbit of Uranus. The results were communicated to the Berlin observatory where there was a telescope powerful enough to catch the supposed planet in its visual field. On the basis of this information, the telescope was turned to the direction specified, and the planet was discovered (September 1846). Never did the law of universal gravitation receive such definitive confirmation because the a priori probability of finding a new planet in a specified direction in the sky is practically negligible.

So firmly was confidence established in the universal law of gravitation that, when a tiny irregularity was observed in the behavior of Mercury, it was assumed as a matter of course that some hitherto unknown planet was also responsible for these perturbations. The planet was even named in anticipation of its discovery: Vulcan. Its orbit was supposed to be inside Mercury's, that is, even closer to the sun than the hitherto closest known planet. However, Vulcan was never discovered. Here the classical law of gravitation actually failed and had to be modified. As expected, the modification was exceedingly minute but of epochal importance. It came about through the theory of relativity. The theory of relativity would seem to belong to the realm of physics, but its underpinnings involve semantic analysis and so are directly related to our discussion.

In the sixteenth century, the Polish astronomer Nicolaus Copernicus (1473–1543) advanced the heliocentric theory of the solar system, according to which the planets, including the earth, revolve around the motionless sun. Almost a century later, Galileo, a proponent of the theory, was ordered by the church authorities to renounce it, since it apparently contradicted the Scriptures. As the grip of the church on the intellectual life of Europe relaxed, the heliocentric theory came to be almost universally accepted by astronomers.

So matters stood until more refined astronomical observations revealed that the sun itself was in motion relative to the other "fixed" stars. The word "relative" here is of vital importance, for without further evidence it was impossible to determine the "absolute" motion of the sun; that is to say, an observation might show that the distance between some distant star and the sun was diminishing. But such an observation was equally consistent with the supposition that the sun was standing still and the star was approaching it or with the supposition that the star was standing still and the sun was approaching it or with the supposition that both the sun and the star were moving in any of a number of ways that would account for the diminishing distance between them.

It seemed at the time that the question "What is the *actual* direction and speed of the sun through space?" had a perfectly definite meaning. The Newtonian system of celestial mechanics[1] pictured space as a rigid framework. If one imagined three mutually perpendicular axes in space (the *coordinate axes*), the position and the velocity of every body in the universe with respect to these axes would be defined. Although the point of intersection and the directions of the three axes could be chosen arbitrarily, there was no doubt that the proposition "the axes are at rest in space" was not a matter of conventional agreement but a matter of fact.[2] That being so, then the speed and direction of any body "through space" were also facts to be ascertained. In the 1880s Albert Abraham Michelson and Edward W. Morley undertook to ascertain these facts by an ingenious experiment.

It was known that light consists of electromagnetic waves propagated through the "ether," a substance that was assumed to fill all space, defining, in fact, the "absolute framework" at rest. Michelson and Morley undertook to measure the speed of light in every direction. If the earth is traveling through space in some particular

---

1. A mathematical theory based on Newton's three laws of motion and the law of universal gravitation, according to which the motions of the heavenly bodies can be calculated.

2. Imagine a city with a rectangular grid of streets. A north-south street and an east-west street can be the coordinate axes. These two streets can be chosen arbitrarily, as a matter of convention or agreement. But that the entire grid is "at rest" appears at first to be a matter of fact, not just agreement. Upon some reflection, we will probably admit that the grid is at rest only relative to the earth but not relative to the sun because the earth is itself in motion relative to the sun. Further, to say that the sun itself is "in motion" makes sense only if we specify with relation to what. The Newtonian system assumes that there is a coordinate system that is "absolutely at rest" so that the absolute, or "real", motion of any body can be specified as the motion of that body relative to the assumed absolute grid.

direction, then the speed of light in that direction *relative to the earth* ought to be smaller than in the opposite direction because the earth is moving with the light beam sent in the same direction and opposite the beam of light sent in the opposite direction. (In the same way, two trains moving in the same direction on parallel tracks are moving more slowly with respect to each other than with respect to the tracks, while two trains moving in opposite directions are moving faster with respect to each other.)

There was no question that, if the speed of the earth through space was comparable to its speed around the sun, the instruments used by Michelson and Morley were sufficiently precise to detect the difference in the speed of light. Surprisingly, no such effect was detected. Some explanations of the negative result were offered, but they were of an ad hoc nature. (It was suggested, for example, that all bodies in motion, in particular also the measuring rods, undergo a contraction in the direction of their motion just sufficient to suppress the difference in the speed of light.)

The final resolution of the paradox in light of the special theory of relativity, formulated by Albert Einstein in 1905, is a foremost example of how *semantic* analysis instigated a profound revolution in science.

The revolution was instigated by examining the meanings of the words we use when we speak of motion. When we speak of velocity, we use words like "space interval" and "time interval between two events" without further analyzing the meaning of these expressions. Their "intuitive" meanings have been so firmly embedded in our way of thinking that we feel no need to delve into their origins. For the scientist, however, a *term* has meaning only if it is ultimately related to some specifiable, concrete experience. The meaning of length or distance is derived from measuring operations, the meaning of a time interval from readings of a clock, and so on.

Ordinarily, when we speak of a distance between two accessible points, we can define it in terms of the familiar yardstick operation. When we speak of a time interval at the same place, we can define it as the difference between the readings of the same clock. But what if we have to deal with the distance between the earth and, say, Mars? Or with the time interval between two events, one on earth and one on Mars? Yardstick operations for measuring distance are out of the question; as for the measurement of time intervals, we must depend on readings of *two* clocks, one on the earth and one on Mars—assuming that a human being has been sent there to help with the observations.

To avoid unnecessary complications, let us pretend that the earth and Mars are the only two bodies in the universe. Our problem is to determine the time of occurrence of an event on Mars. Before our confederate departed, we synchronized our watches. Can we assume that his watch shows the same time as ours when he is on Mars? To decide the question, we send a light signal to the man on Mars, which (by prearrangement) is an instruction to him to report the reading on his clock as soon as he receives the signal. Assume first that the distance between us remains constant during this operation. If we sent the signal at 12 o'clock and received the return signal at 12:20, the report stating that the Martian clock read 12:10, we conclude that his clock has remained synchronized with ours, since this conclusion tallies with the assumption that the light took as long to reach him as the return signal to reach us.

Matters would look different if the distance between us and Mars were, let us say, increasing. For, should we receive the return signal at 12.22 and the report is that our signal reached Mars at 12.11, the result can be interpreted in two ways:

1. We are at rest relative to the "ether," and Mars is receding from us; therefore it took longer for our light signal to reach him (eleven minutes instead of ten)—because our light signal was "chasing" Mars. But once the return signal was sent on its way, it took exactly the same time to reach us as it took our signal to reach Mars—because we are at rest. The results tally with the assumption that the Martian watch is synchronized with ours.

2. Mars is at rest, and we are moving through the ether away from Mars. Under this assumption, the return signal should have taken longer to come back to us than it took ours to reach Mars; therefore, we conclude that our man on Mars must have received our signal earlier than 12:11 by our watch. In other words, our watches are *not* synchronized.

We could decide the question of whether the earth or Mars is moving if we could compare the readings of the clocks and so find out whether they are or are not synchronized. But the reading of the clocks requires that signals be sent along with information about when they were sent. This information is reliable only if the clocks are synchronized, and that is what we set out to find out in the first place!

There remains making a direct comparison of the clocks: we could go to Mars, taking our clock with us, and look at both clocks at the same time. But wait. If the clocks are not synchronized, how do we know that it was not the journey to Mars that has unsynchronized them? If so, then *our* journey may have the same effect on *our* clock. The clocks will then be synchronized on Mars, but we still shall have no way of knowing whether they were or were not synchronized when they were apart. We are caught in a vicious cycle.

The cycle is broken when we stop thinking in terms of categories that cannot in principle be linked to concrete experience. If there is no way of determining, say, the "true" time interval between two events, then "time interval" without further specification has no meaning. A time interval has meaning only when it is related to a particular observer and to *his* clock readings. For another observer, the time interval between the same two events may be different. And this difference does not mean that either or both observers are mistaken. It means that the time interval between two events is not an absolutely invariant quantity. It turns out, however, that there *are* absolutely invariant quantities, one of them being the speed of light through "empty space," which is the same for all observers regardless of the way they move with respect to each other.

Taking the constancy of the speed of light as a fundamental assumption (like a postulate), we can deduce many consequences from it. Some of them may seem strange indeed. It turns out, for example, that the length of an object moving with respect to us shrinks in the direction of its motion.[3] This shrinkage is not to be thought of as a mechanical compression of some sort but rather as an inevitable result of performing measuring operations on the moving object. It turns out that clocks on bodies moving with respect to us "run slower," again not in the mechanical sense but in the sense of "their" time actually running slower with respect to "our" time.

The theory of relativity has even stranger consequences. Since space and time turn out to be "intertwined" as it were, other physical quantities also become intertwined, in particular, matter and

---

3. Note that this shrinkage appears now as a *consequence* of the fundamental assumption of the theory of relativity (the constancy of the speed of light with respect to all observers), not as an ad hoc assumption to explain the specific result of an experiment (cf. p. 328).

energy. There is no need at this writing to stress the awesome implications of that discovery which led to the invention of the atomic bomb. It is, however, worthwhile to ponder the productive consequences of subjecting the most firmly established concepts (like the distance between two points or the time interval between two events) to careful *operational* analysis. To illustrate, consider that when we ask ourselves "What do we mean when we say the distance between the earth and Mars, as of this moment, is 112,800,000 miles," we must answer in terms of what we must *do* in order to determine that distance, not by offering synonyms for "distance." This is what scientists mean when they talk about *operational definitions*. Likewise, when we say that an event on Mars happened at the same moment that some other event happened on the earth, we must specify what we mean by "the same moment." And it will not do to specify "the same moment" by reference to the moment recorded on our clock because we must make allowances for the time it takes light to reach us from Mars. If the earth and Mars are in motion with respect to each other, we shall get a different answer depending on whether we take earth or Mars to be the point of reference of motion. Moreover, since this question cannot be decided by any conceivable experiment, it cannot be decided at all. Hence, whether two events far apart occurred simultaneously or not depends on the observer; that is to say, "time interval" is not an absolute but a relative quantity.

The full significance of this revolutionary idea reveals itself in the consequences drawn from it—logical consequences, obtained by mathematical *deduction*. Some are so startling and unexpected that observations corroborating them provide us with an almost compelling proof of the correctness of the theory. (Recall that the corroboration of a scientific hypothesis is the stronger, the less expected are the events predicted by the consequences of the hypothesis.) Following is a list of comparisons between predictions made on the basis of classical (Newtonian) theory of space, time, and motion and those made on the basis of the theory of relativity, now extended to the so-called general theory of relativity that includes the analysis of nonuniform motion and its relation to gravitation.

1. According to Newtonian theory, the mass of a moving body is independent of the velocity of the body.

According to relativity theory, the mass of a moving body increases with its velocity; moreover, *how* the mass increases with velocity is explicitly stated.

Measurements of velocities of very rapidly moving particles—electrons, for example—fully confirm the conclusion of the theory of relativity.

2. According to Newtonian theory, the speed of light should be different with respect to observers moving relative to each other.

According to the theory of relativity, the speed of light should be the same relative to all observers.

Results of the Michelson-Morley experiment corroborated the conclusion of relativity theory and refuted the conclusion of Newtonian theory.

3. According to Newtonian theory, "the flow of time" is independent of locality, in particular, of the strength of the gravitational field in a given locality.

According to the theory of relativity, all "clocks" go slower in strong gravitational fields, not merely in the sense of the movement of their mechanical parts but in the fundamental sense involving "the flow of time." [4]

Oscillations of subatomic particles constitute "atomic clocks." The rate of oscillation is reflected in the spectra of the substances composed of the corresponding atoms. It has been observed that these spectra are shifted toward the red end of the spectrum in the sun's gravitational field. That is to say, "atomic clocks" go slower in the sun's gravitational field. This effect is predicted by the theory of relativity.

4. According to the classical theory of the propagation of electromagnetic waves, light travels in straight lines. According to the theory of relativity, light rays are deflected in the neighborhood of large masses.

The crucial observation was made during the eclipse of the sun in 1919. The prediction of the theory of relativity was fully confirmed. Moreover, the magnitude of the deflection of light beams from distant stars in the neighborhood of the sun was just what it was calculated to be. Being wholly unexpected (never observed before), this result was an especially strong corroboration of the theory of relativity.

5. According to classical theory, the axis of a planet's orbit rotates

4. This result is a consequence of the general theory of relativity, which extends assumptions of the special theory to include motions not in straight lines and with variable velocity.

with respect to the stars. The rate of this rotation (called *precession*) can be calculated. In the case of the planet Mercury, a discrepancy was found between the calculated and the observed rates of precession. The discrepancy was extremely minute, amounting to no more than forty seconds of an arc per century. As already mentioned (cf. p. 326), confidence in the classical theory was so complete that this discrepancy was attributed to the existence of a hitherto unknown planet, which, however, was never found. The theory of relativity led to a deduced correction in the classical theory that almost completely accounted for the discrepancy.

6. According to classical theory, mass and energy are qualitatively different, and a body may possess energy by being in a force field. For example, a weight lifted above the surface of the earth has potential energy. In descending, it can be made to lift another weight. A moving body, such as a bullet, has kinetic energy. When it is stopped in its path, it becomes heated. But according to the classical theory, the mass of a body is not *identical* to a quantity of energy. A conclusion of the theory of relativity essentially identifies mass and energy and supplies a conversion formula which reveals the amount of energy contained in each gram of matter.

The release of atomic energy (essentially a "conversion" of matter into energy) was a dramatic confirmation of the relativity theory.

The triumphs of the theory of relativity represent perhaps the most important example of how a dogged, hard-headed persistence in asking the two fundamental questions of epistemology ("What do we mean?" and "How do we know?") ushered in a scientific revolution.

A scientific revolution occurs when the entire conceptual foundation of a science is changed. Here we have described two such revolutions. The one in mathematics resulted when the fundamental propositions (the postulates) of a mathematical system were no longer held to be "incontrovertible truths" but now were regarded merely as agreements that neither could nor needed to be proved. This change of outlook cut the connections between mathematics and experience but at the same time emancipated mathematics. Freed from the necessity of relating their findings to events in the observable world, mathematicians could construct any mathematical system they liked. Paradoxically, this enlarged the range of experience to which mathematical reasoning could be applied. Contrarily, the second, relativity revolution, strengthened the bond between theory and experience by demanding that every theoretical construct be *eventually* linked to concrete experience, such as a strictly spelled out measurement procedure.

The fusion of the two methods—the completely formal but strictly rigorous method of mathematical deduction and a theory rooted in operationally defined concepts—gave us a science with predictive power that has no equal. Mathematicized physical science is the closest approach to the "certainty" that philosophers have searched for through the ages.

The immense power of a fully mathematicized science derives from the precision of its language. The syntactics of this language is embodied in the completely unambivalent rules of mathematical deduction. Its semantics is embodied in the operational definitions of its terms—definitions that reflect also the restricted pragmatics of the language of science: the symbol user tests propositions by performing exactly specified operations and observations; his "individuality" affects the meaning of propositions only to the extent that his role as observer must be taken into account (cf. p. 329). His internalized concepts, intentions, beliefs, or predilections are excluded.

Because of the dramatic successes of mathematicized physical science (not only in creating modern technology but also in revealing a rational and consistent picture of the material universe), it is often held up as a model for the other sciences that deal with life processes and with human and animal behavior. Whether these sciences can follow the paths blazed by physical science is a subject of intense controversy.

Those who are skeptical about extending the methods of the physical sciences to the biological and the behavioral sciences often advance the following objections.

1. Life processes, especially human behavior, are too complex to be described mathematically.

This argument carries little force. Physical processes also were far too complex to be analyzed and understood until appropriate tools of observation and effective symbolic systems were developed to describe them. There is no reason why these tools of cognition cannot be extended further so as to bring life processes and even behavior within the scope of "hard" analysis.

2. Physical events are governed by mechanical principles, but living beings are governed by goals and purposes; in particular, human

beings are endowed with "free will" and so are not subject to laws of causality on which the consistency of the physical sciences depends.

This argument mimics an orientation in biology known as *vitalism*. The vitalists argued that life processes cannot be fully explained by physical or chemical laws; that living beings develop and behave so as to achieve some *future* state; that the influence "of the future on the present" (teleology) is an inherent feature of biological causality.

In response to this argument, it can be pointed out that goals and purposes were once attributed also to physical events. Recall the principle "nature abhors vacuum" offered as an explanation of why pumps work (cf. pp. 323–24). Evolution itself was once thought to be a goal-directed process, an expression of "strivings" of plants and animals to achieve more perfect adaptation to their environment. Eventually, reasons entirely apart from "goals and purposes" were found to explain both physical events and evolution, which accounted not only for observed events but which also became the foundation for predicting events hitherto unexplained.[5] Moreover, a new technology arose, based on the principles of cybernetics, making it possible to build machines that "simulate" goal-directed, purposeful, and even "intelligent" behavior (cf. p. 266). Someone ignorant of the way these machines are constructed might well conclude that their "behavior" cannot be explained by ordinary cause-effect relations. We may be similarly handicapped with regard to many life processes that have not yet been completely analyzed in the terms of physical events. On the other hand, vast advances have been made in this sort of analysis, and many physiological processes that for ages were explained in terms of the "purposes" they serve are now fully understood in terms of specific causally related physical and chemical reactions. As for the existence of "free will," it is a speculation that cannot be decided by objective evidence and so falls outside the scope of science. Our belief that we have "free will" is an *internal* conviction. Asked to demonstate it, we can only do so by declaring what we intend to do and then doing it. However, it is conceivable that someone who is able to observe the workings of our nervous system

5. According to the theory of natural selection, proposed by Darwin and Wallace, direction in biological evolution is determined by the fact that the better-adapted organisms have more surviving offspring than the less well adapted. The variations in the genetic make-up that result in better or poorer adaptations are governed only by chance.

might predict just what we are about to announce and carry out, and to him it would appear that we had no choice in the matter. Recall Schopenhauer's pessimistic judgment, "Man can do what he will, but he cannot will what he will." Were there a way to put this judgment to a test, we might still be caught in an infinite regress; for, if it turns out that man *can* will what he will, the question then looms whether man can will what he wills to will, etc. The existence of "free will," even if the proposition can be put clearly (which is doubtful), is a question decided by our attitudes, not by ascertaining facts.

3. Applying "scientific method" to the study of human behavior denigrates the dignity of the individual or of the human race.

This argument is also an expression of an attitude rather than a judgment on the application of science to the study of man. Not so long ago the discovery of man's descent from nonhuman ancestors was vociferously rejected on the grounds that it was degrading. This basis of resistance has largely dissipated. Current objections to "meddling" with behavior are aroused more by the fear that science is manipulative—fear reinforced, admittedly, by crass emphasis on "social engineering" as a device for applying scientific knowledge to the management of human affairs. At any rate, the foregoing argument against extending scientific methods of cognition to the study of human affairs opposes certain *uses* of science; it does not refute the possibility of extending it to enlighten human conduct.

A much more serious objection to transferring the methods of the physical sciences to the biological and behavioral sciences stems from entirely different considerations. As noted, the power of the physical sciences resides in their language, which derives its precision from the completely rigorous "grammar" of mathematical deduction. In principle, all propositions of physical science can be reduced to statements about results of measurements. These measurements are made on a comparatively small array of quantities: distances, time intervals, intensities of electric currents, temperatures, and so forth. In other words, *recognition* is no problem in the methodology of the physical sciences: when all observations are reduced to reading instruments, any two or more observers can agree on the result—or the "answer"—of an observation.

Insofar as much biological science *has* been reduced to the analysis of physiochemical processes (as in physiology, biophysics, and biochemistry), the problem of recognition does not arise here either. But a great expanse of biology remains outside the scope of physical measurement. For instance, an organism is recognized as an organism not via measurements but via an intuitive act. Recognition is an all-important aspect of observation in identifying instances of behavior. When we observe that an animal eats, fights, or mates, we can identify these acts because we *recognize* them, not in consequence of measuring them. This is particularly true with regard to human behavior. To identify a human action such as "voting," "quarreling," "taking out insurance," or "protesting" certainly involves recognition. Turning to language behavior, we *recognize* the very wide difference between the meanings of the two utterances

1. We gave him a gun for his money.
2. We gave him a run for his money.

Despite the fact that the physical events (the "measurable" speech sounds) associated with these utterances are nearly identical, we are fully aware of the significant difference in meaning.

The primacy of recognition in the behavioral sciences requires that the observer be *sensitized*. What he is sensitized to, and to what extent, depends on what has become meaningful in his culture and in his personal experience. For this reason, subjective elements can never be completely eliminated from the study of the individual or social behavior of human beings. Those who insist on applying the methods of physical science to the study of human behavior *believe* they have expelled subjectivism from psychology, sociology, and political science. Actually, however, successes scored in these directions (and they have been noteworthy) were achieved by *singling out* for investigation only such events in human affairs as are easily observable and recognizable.

For example, in the early decades of this century, psychologists of the so-called behaviorist persuasion declared that, since only directly observable units of behavior can be talked about in the context of scientific psychology, the task of psychological science is to note how these units are linked to "stimuli" impinging on the behaving organism. In this way the propositions of psychology can be reduced to the propositional "If . . ., then" form, where the "if" refers to a stimulus and the "then" to the observable behavioral response. What goes on between the stimulus and the response—say, the "mental state" of the organism," its "desires" or "aversions," and so on—was declared by the behaviorists to be outside the scope of scientific psychology, being inaccessible to observation.[6]

Similar attitudes turned sociologists away from tackling theoretical problems and toward "demonstrable" tasks of gathering large masses of data, such as public opinion polls, occupational migrations, and so forth. The "objectivity" of such data is indisputable, and the subject matter yields easily to statistical analysis, which became the principal content of "fact-oriented" social science.

The charge of "dehumanization" leveled against the "Higher Statisticians," as C. Wright Mills called them, is related partly to this "reduction of people to statistics," but partly also to the inclination of the quantifiers to accept the conventional conceptualization of current society and of prevailing social values. For example, by analogy to "stable" physical and biological systems, many social scientists conceive of "social equilibrium" in organismic terms, as the ability of the social system to resist or "correct" "deviations" from a "norm." Thus value judgments creep into the social scientists' model of society without their being aware of this departure from "objectivity." Because of the connotations of words like "equilibrium," instances of social tensions and upheavals may appear as pathological manifestations. A theory emerging from the stability concept may then become an implicit defense of the status quo and hence an obstacle to the development of new formulations of social organization and of social values. Scientific revolutions of the sort that spawned the heliocentric theory of the solar system in the sixteenth century and the theory of relativity in the twentieth are thus inhibited. The exactness of the physical sciences virtually ordained that such revolutions eventually had to occur because even minute discrepancies between accepted theories and "real," observed facts could not be tolerated. In contrast, because of the relative inexactness of the social sciences, there are no comparable pressures to force a reconceptualization. In fact, whatever radical reorientations have occurred in the social sciences were instigated by the *value systems* of social philosophers. The social scientist who declares all science to be value-free is not motivated to reexamine the basic assumptions of his science.

6. I am reminded of Kenneth Boulding's jingle, satirizing the behaviorist outlook:
> *That is labeled wisdom which*
> *Describes the scratch but not the itch.*

A case in point is the tacit acceptance by many economists of the gross national product (GNP), especially of its growth, as an index of economic health. Being a "hard quantity," the GNP can serve as a basis of an operational definition of "economic wealth," in the way the IQ ("intelligence quotient") can serve as a basis of an operational definition of "intelligence," and as the size of a nuclear stockpile can serve as an operational definition of "national security," or, for that matter, body weight can be taken as an operational definition of "robustness." In our day, it hardly occurs to anyone to view obesity as a manifestation of robustness, and the significance of the IQ as an index of intelligence is accepted only with considerable reservations. In these instances, we are put on guard against supine acceptance of facile indices as the carriers of equivalent meanings. On the other hand, global concepts like "economic health" and "national security" are not linked to intuitively perceived meanings because these concepts are not crystallized from personal experience. In the interest of mathematizing his science, the economist or political scientist accepts whatever quantitative indices are suggested by conventional wisdom or whatever can be easily explained to the decision makers. In this respect, the economist or the political scientist follows the example of the physicist, whose concepts have long since broken away from personal experience. He often forgets, however, that the abstruse concepts of the physicist, far from being selected for convenience, have emerged from arduous examinations and insights of a unifying theory. In contrast, the only thing that can be said of many numerical indices used in applied social science is that they give the impression of a "scientific approach" and so can be used for rationalizing and "expertizing" decisions.

In short, what the "hard heads" of behavioral science have abstracted from the lessons of physical science is the importance of "objective data," often to the neglect of the crucial role played by unifying theories. While the absence of analogous unifying theories in the behavioral sciences is often lamented, efforts to create them are often dismissed as "speculative." Freud's theory of psychodynamics and Marx's theory of the class struggle as the "prime mover of history" come readily to mind. These formulations, although immensely appealing to their adherents as explanatory frameworks, have little predictive power and so do not qualify as scientific theories in the "hard" sense of the word discussed above. Nevertheless, we need to develop a science of man that can probe beneath the surface of facts that, however readily verifiable, are for the most part disconnected, and whose relevance to a comprehensive theory is difficult to assess. There is no escape from the necessity of exercising imagination, of resorting to analogies and to similar allegedly "unscientific" modes of cognition.

Those who hold up the physical sciences as a model for all science tend to forget that many centuries of speculation, analogizing—even hallucinating, not to mention sterile detours—marked the history of those sciences. Forgotten also is that the mode of cognition that we call science emerged as something altogether opposite to the previously established modes—those of religion, of magic, and of philosophy. Nevertheless some aspects of those earlier modes remain in modern science; for, underlying all quest for scientifically established truth is a *faith* that there is such truth to be found—an element in the philosophy of science analogous to religious experience. And underlying the applications of science to the manipulation of nature is the *will* to adapt the world to man's desires—an element found also in magic. As for philosophy, science has certainly been an outgrowth of it and shares with it the outlook that, in the quest of knowledge, man exercises the noblest aspect of his being.

APPLICATIONS

I. Consider the rain dance ceremony of the Hopi Indians. The Hopi live in a semiarid land which requires rain for the support of life. On regular occasions, the Hopi perform a rain dance which supposedly will induce the "rain god" to let his favors fall on the land. Rain comes seldom. The Hopi must know that the rain dance is usually *not* followed by rain. Why then do they continue to perform the ceremony?

II. We have spoken about "operational definitions" several times in this chapter. In the event that the term is not clear, an operational definition tells you "*what to do* and *what to observe* in order to bring the thing defined or its effects within the range of one's experience."

Give an operational definition of the italicized words in the following sentences. Which are more difficult to define in this way? Can you tell why?

1) I enjoy a meal of *steak tartare.*
2) Erik Erikson warned against the abstract use of the term *aggression.*
3) I prefer to live in a *constitutional democracy.*

4) It is unfortunate that some people must live in countries that have *fascist* regimes.
5) The *radicals* cause all the trouble at the colleges.
6) He received a traffic ticket for driving at excessive *speed*.
7) He was *cultivating* his garden in the morning.
8) He is *cultivating* a taste for spicy foods.
9) Life *processes* are too complex to be described mathematically.
10) The Watergate scandal is an instance of *"white-collar crime."*

III. The symbol user who tests propositions by performing operations must exclude internalized concepts, intentions, beliefs, or predilections. Do you think it is possible for human beings to be "value-free"?

For example, Lawrence Durrell writes in *Spirit of Place*: "Come. Enter into the creative activity in which you do not need your understandings. Do not mistake truth for the possessive process any longer—ratiocination, knowledge. The real desire is *to be possessed*." How would a scientist "test" the possibility that Durrell may have found in the East the greatest, the most significant, the only truth there is?

IV. One way to understand a basic difference between science and other forms of inquiry is to answer these questions:

1) What happened in the past and what happens today when a dogma of the church is challenged? What happens if a dogma seems to be disproven (say, the Creation myth)?
2) What happens when a scientific theory or law is shown to be incompatible with observations (say, the phlogiston theory or Newton's laws of motion applied to high-velocity particles)?
3) What happens when a doctrine of spiritualism, astrology, scientism, cosmic transcendentalism, or palm reading is seriously challenged? Are the challenges welcomed or regarded as potentially constructive?

Can you express in 500 words or less some of the general conclusions you would draw from your examination of these questions?

V. In the year 1610, Galileo discovered Ganymede and three other moons orbiting the planet Jupiter. He maintained that this discovery—four objects revolving regularly around a planet—was a strong argument for the then-controversial Copernican theory which held that the earth and all the planets revolved around the sun. Indirectly this discovery led to his historic troubles with the Roman Catholic Inquisition which maintained that the earth was the center of the universe.

1) Why, when the evidence seems now to be so clear, did the church oppose the Copernican theory? And why did the Inquisition feel that it had to make Galileo recant *in words*? (Reportedly, after he said that the earth did not move around the sun, he muttered under his breath, "*Eppur si muove.*")

2) Does it seem to you that a man of faith is more "loyal" to his faith than a man of science is to his science? As Albert Camus says in *The Myth of Sisyphus*, Galileo was not interested in defending scientific truth against the Inquisition with any degree of intensity.

VI. Here is an analogy to explain "cracking an atom." You believe there is a piano inside a room with lead walls that are three feet thick. You don't know where the piano is, but you would like to hear sound come out of it. You cannot get into the room. Therefore you shoot armor-piercing bullets into the room in the hope that by spraying the room with bullets you will hit the piano wires. When you do, you will produce a sound. Perhaps you have never seen the piano and never will, but you know it is there by the sounds it produces when you hit by chance.

By means of a similar analogy, explain and clarify for an uninitiated reader a sophisticated scientific idea, a technological process, or an electronic device.

VII. If you are interested in magic, then you should read a brilliant and thoughtful book by Keith Thomas called *Religion and the Decline of Magic*, New York: (Charles Scribner's, Sons, 1971). The book deals with the systems of belief that were current in sixteenth- and seventeenth-century England and the survival of these beliefs, especially in astrology, witchcraft, spiritualism, and the occult, into our own times. It is a detailed, scholarly, and detached examination of systems of belief now disdained by most intelligent persons.

1) How do you account for the revival of interest in such matters as astrology, magical healing, divination, prophecy, and clairvoyance?

2) Thomas asks: "If magical acts are ineffective rituals employed as an alternative to sheer helplessness in the face of events, then how are we to classify the status of 'scientific' remedies in which we place faith, but which are subsequently exposed as useless?" After reading this chapter, how would you respond to this question?

/IV
FROM
KNOWLEDGE
TO
RESPONSIBILITY

19/a critical look at language

We said at the outset that man's symbolic language is a mixed blessing. Ever since man became man, symbolic language has been his principal survival mechanism. The *organ* that has enabled man to survive, handicapped as he is physically, is his brain. But this organ functions not as a physical tool, such as fleet legs or sharp teeth, but as a storage center of knowledge. The brain stores knowledge in the form of symbolic language patterns that serve as vehicles for transmitting knowledge from man to man and for accumulating knowledge over generations. Knowledge of how things are, how they were, how they are likely to be, and how they might be is what helps man to survive. On the other hand, "knowledge" stored in words can also be false, even suicidal, and this kind of false knowledge also is transmitted by language from man to man and accumulates from generation to generation. Knowledge that makes possible weapons of mass destruction is one such example. It is not easy to distinguish false knowledge from true knowledge nor knowledge conducive to survival from knowledge conducive to self-destruction. Therein lies the danger to the species and the source of much human misery.

To be "enlightened" is to have developed the capacity for distinguishing truth from falsehood, or delusion. Symbolic language does not confer enlightenment on man, being of itself as frequently the repository and the carrier of delusion as of truth. Enlightenment depends in large measure on one's ability to examine and evaluate what one takes to be knowledge. Fortunately, each of us can acquire this ability by a critical appraisal of language and its roles.

Basically, we use language in two ways: (1) as an instrument of cognition, as when we tell *ourselves* what we experience, when we classify or generalize our experiences, reason about them, draw conclusions, and construct theories on the basis of what we "know" or learn; (2) as an instrument of communication, as when we articulate our experiences *to others*, elicit an account of their experiences, or use our ability to verbalize ideas to influence the behavior of others.

In a way, the cognitive function of language serves to "digest" our experiences; the communicative function of language serves to enlarge our range of experience. Through communication, we can know not only what we ourselves know but also what others know and not only what we ourselves feel but also what others feel. Through both of these functions, language gives us the opportunity to acquire knowledge without direct experience. When we reason, generalize, theorize, we get to know what is, or may be, implied by our experiences. When we communicate, we incorporate the experiences of others and their implications into our store of knowledge.

Like all social animals, humans cooperate. Though they also compete (and so harm one another as well)—whatever other relations develop man-to-man, humans must cooperate to survive because that is the way social animals survive. Without communication, human cooperation would be impossible, and human communication depends above all on symbolic language.

The communicative function of language, however, also has an obverse side. Just as language in its cognitive function can be an instrument of storing false knowledge or knowledge conducive to self-destruction, so language in its communicative function can divide men as well as join them in a cooperative effort. Mankind is divided into language communities. People of one language community rarely understand the speech of other communities. Language, then, more than any other difference, separates friend from stranger. Typically, in tribal cultures, obligations to others, such as taboos against killing and stealing, extend only to members of the same community. Those unable to communicate in the familiar language naturally are excluded "foreigners."

The biblical legend of the Tower of Babel attests to an awareness early in man's history of language as it pertains to cooperation. It tells of a community embarked on a cooperative project. A jealous God, deciding to wreck the plan, confused the people's speech. Unable to communicate, they had to abandon the project.

Languages need not be altogether mutually unintelligible to separate people. Many peoples speaking different dialects of the same language can understand one another, yet they perceive each other as strangers. Usually they come from different localities and so literally are strangers. Another Bible story illustrates this point. Ephraimite infiltrators in the Gileadite army were betrayed by their mispronunciation of the Hebrew word *shibboleth* (they pronounced it *siboleth*).

Nor is geographical distance the only "distance" factor that makes for different language habits. Disparities in wealth, education, and social position also separate people to the extent that they develop widely different dialects. In Bernard Shaw's play *Pygmalion*, a professor of linguistics undertakes to pass a street urchin for a princess by teaching her to speak English as it is spoken by people of the upper class. He succeeds. However, because language habits are deeply imbedded, it takes herculean efforts. Moreover, the girl becomes despondent because, with her newly acquired language habits, she feels she cannot return to her original community and because she expects to be rejected on other grounds by "society" whose "dialect" she has mastered.

There is still another, more subtle way in which language separates people. We believe many things, not because we have tested our beliefs by experience, but because we have been told what to believe. Moreover, many of these beliefs simply *cannot* be tested by experience. Such are many religious beliefs formulated as *creeds*. The child memorizing the catechism learns to *say* "God is a Supreme Being, ubiquitous, omnipotent, and omniscient." These words may or may not evoke mental images in those who speak them, but certainly they do not have denotations in the world experienced in common with all other people. Assertions found in creeds can be neither proved nor disproved; they are simply believed, and frequently belief in what the words say is demonstrated simply by reciting the words.

In the Middle Ages, belief in "the words"—the tenets of faith—was taken very seriously by the learned elite, while to the unlettered believer "knowing the creed" may have meant no more than knowing the words of a few prayers and the answers to questions in the catechism. A branch of learning, called theology, to which scholars devoted many years of study, purported to be an investigation into the nature of God and the meaning of His works. Though the words used in theological discussions had no observable referents, there was no demand to put the assertions of theologians to empirical tests.

Theology flowered in Europe at a time when it occurred to few, if any, learned men to use empirical verification as a test for truth. Some assertions were accepted as true because they stemmed from authority assumed to be unimpeachable (for example, the Holy Script); some were purportedly deduced logically from assertions accepted as true on grounds of "self-evidence"—but the "self-evident" assertions were self-evident only because they were said to be so.

The method of theology, because of its heavy reliance on reasoning that resembles deduction, somewhat resembles the method of mathematics. Recall that mathematical "truths" neither can nor need be put to empirical tests. Unlike mathematicians, however, theologians have traditionally engaged in most bitter controversies. These controversies were no mere academic discussions. Time after time, church authorities proclaimed the assertions of some people to be true and those of others false. If the latter persisted in repeating the proscribed assertions, they were called heretics. Repeatedly, heretics were dealt with harshly—ostracized, imprisoned, burned alive. At times, military campaigns were undertaken against whole populations that became followers of this or that variety of religious belief declared to be "false" by the prevailing "true" believers.

The mischievous divisiveness of language is illustrated in a satirical story, an upside-down version of the Tower of Babel legend. According to this version, each individual had his own private language. Verbal communication was impossible. Nonetheless people got along very well. They became quite adept in using sign language, and since sign language must be confined almost entirely to concrete references (cf. p. 41), the people were not bothered by philosophical, theological, or political controversies. Once someone got the idea of building a tower. Others, seeing him enjoying the work, joined in and the tower grew rapidly.

And the Lord came down to see the city and the tower which the children of men builded. And the Lord was frankly angry. . . . And . . . bethought himself of a way to curb and punish [their] pride. "Go to," he said. "Let us go down, and consolidate their language, that they may understand one another's speech." And it was done. And the whole earth was of one language, and of one speech.[1]

1. Louis B. Salmon, "A Gospel-True Fable," in *Our Language and Our World*, ed. S. I. Hayakawa (New York: Harper and Brothers, 1959), pp. 3–11.

Thereupon the people got into interminable arguments about the purpose of the tower, what to name it, and so on. The arguments grew in intensity and erupted into violence. People split into warring factions and their cooperation ended. God remained unchallenged in his heaven.

All records of human endeavor—historical and legendary— surely make it seem that if the cognitive and the communicative functions of language were better understood, the delusive and disruptive influence of language habits on the human condition could be reduced!

The ancients were concerned with that proposition. Socrates taught his students by asking questions, hoping in this way to get them to arrive at truth by examining their own beliefs, that is, by clarifying in their own minds what they *meant* by "virtue," "duty," and other names of moral qualities. However, since Socrates concerned himself almost entirely with moral questions, the links that he tried to establish were between words and inner experiences, not between words and observable things. He believed that every person could by an honest exercise of reason arrive at "self-evident" truths concerning the meaning of virtue and other qualities.

In the Middle Ages a quasi-critique of language was undertaken by the nominalists, who represented a direction in scholastic philosophy. The nominalists argued that names of classes, such as "man," were no more than names; in other words, that "existence" was to be attributed only to individual men, not to Man writ large. Opposed to this school of thought was another called realism. The realists ascribed "real existence" to so-called universals, such as Man.

One of the most renowned exponents of nominalism was William of Occam (c1349). His motto (*entia non sunt multiplicanda praeter necessitatem*) goes under the name of Occam's Razor and is still often quoted in modern philosophy of science. The principle is an injunction to avoid inventing concepts unless they are necessary; in other words, to use economy of thought. It is also called the principle of parsimony which states that, if two explanations are equally acceptable, the simpler one is to be preferred. Actually the principle warns against freewheeling philosophical speculations in which new concepts are invented promiscuously, giving the impression that something profound is being said while it actually lacks semantic content.

As exemplified by Occam's thought, the thrust of the nominalist idea is toward keeping intact the link between symbols and concrete referents. In the age of scholastic philosophy, this idea appeared in ontological rather than in semantic garb; that is, it was expressed in assertions about what "really exists" rather than in a far-reaching examination of language. Nevertheless the idea carried within it the germ of the philosophy of science, a philosophy of knowledge that holds intact the link between language and experience.

With the advent of the experimental method, science split off from philosophy. In fact early scientific endeavor resembled arts and crafts more than philosophy, if only because the experimental scientist was preoccupied more with things and actions than with abstract ideas. It was not until the nineteenth and twentieth centuries, when first the world of mathematics, then the world of natural science, were shaken by conceptual revolutions, that a philosophy became indispensable for keeping the epistemological foundations of science from crumbling. At that time a critical examination of language as a vehicle of scientific thought began in earnest.

Among the pioneers of the new philosophy was Bertrand Russell in the role of logician. Russell pointed out a fundamental difference between the denotative and the connotative meanings of a word, even where no vagueness of language was apparently involved. Example:

"William IV wanted to know whether Sir Walter Scott was the author of *Waverley*." This is a true proposition in the sense that William IV indeed asked for this information. "The author of *Waverley* was Sir Walter Scott" is also a true proposition.

The last proposition seems to assert that the author of *Waverley* and Sir Walter Scott are the same person. One of the axioms of mathematics states that in any equation one quantity may be substituted for another quantity equal to it. We might think that this principle applies as well in logic, and so we ought to be allowed to substitute "the author of *Waverley*" and "Sir Walter Scott" for each other wherever they occur in propositions. However, when we substitute "Sir Walter Scott" for "the author of *Waverley*" in the proposition about William IV, we get an absurdity or, at any rate, we make William IV look silly. For then the proposition reads: "William IV wanted to know whether Sir Walter Scott was Sir Walter Scott."

This teaser illustrates the trouble that arises when we confuse connotative meaning with denotative meaning. "The author of *Waver-*

ley" is a connotative definition of "Sir Walter Scott." Sir Walter Scott (the person, not the name, hence without quotation marks) is the referent (denotative meaning) of "the author of *Waverley*." The two belong to different logical types and so cannot be substituted for each other in all cases. "The author of *Waverley* was Sir Walter Scott" actually says that the *referents* of (a) "the author of *Waverley*" and of (b) "Sir Walter Scott" are identical. But this does not mean that the phrases in quotation marks may always be substituted for each other. Another example:

Mr. Phi thinks that Budapest is the capital of Rumania. (True: he has simply got Budapest and Bucharest confused.) But Budapest is the capital of Hungary. (True.) Therefore Mr. Phi thinks that the capital of Hungary is the capital of Rumania. (False: he thinks nothing of the sort.)

Other types of paradox pointed out by Russell are so-called antinomies. Example:

It is asserted that in a certain village the single (male) barber shaves every man in the village who does not shave himself, and only those men. Let us assume that men who shave themselves and those who do not comprise all the men in the village; that is to say, very young men who do not yet shave are classified as boys. In that case, the assertion above implies unambiguously that a man either shaves himself or is shaved by the barber. If every proposition is either true or false, then the proposition "The barber shaves himself" must be either true or false. However, if it is true, it contradicts our starting assumption. Because it says that the barber shaves a man who shaves himself. If it is false, it also contradicts the assertion because the barber fails to shave a man who does not shave himself.

Antinomies are not mere curiosities. They strike at the very foundation of traditional two-valued logic, in particular, at one of its fundamental axioms, the law of excluded middle (cf. p. 255).

The prototype of an antinomy is a contradiction inherent in some propositions that refer to themselves. The simplest example is shown in Figure 28.

If the proposition is true, then it is false because that is what it says. If the proposition is false, then there must be true propositions in the box. But there is only one proposition in the box; therefore, it must be true.

Every Proposition
in This Box
Is
False

Figure 28

Russell proposed to solve the problem of antinomies by distinguishing types of propositions. Some propositions assert something about the state of affairs in the world. They belong to one type. There are also propositions that assert something about *propositions*. They belong to another type. On the next level are propositions that refer to propositions about propositions, and so on. A self-consistent logic must distinguish among the types of propositions.

The notation of symbolic logic enables us to keep the distinction in mind. For instance, p may be a proposition about something in the world; $(p \rightarrow q)$ is a proposition about propositions p and q; $[(p \rightarrow q) \rightarrow r]$ is a proposition about the proposition $(p \rightarrow q)$ and the proposition r. Propositions about propositions about propositions occur also in ordinary language, but ordinary language is too clumsy to allow much compounding of this sort in the way we speak and write. For instance, the meaning of "That is obvious" is clear (obvious!). We can go another step and say "That 'that is obvious' is obvious." But if we continue, we soon run out of distinguishing quotation marks. If we omit quotation marks, we get gibberish: "that that that is obvious is obvious is obvious." Nevertheless the sentence ought to make sense. We can unscramble it by circumlocutions like "It is clear to everyone that the proposition 'That is obvious' cannot be denied." Problems of this sort belong as much to semantics as to logic.

Semantics once was concerned primarily with matters that belong to what we now call lexicology, the dictionary makers' field of expertise. A turning point is marked by the remarkable article in the 1911 edition of the *Encyclopedia Britannica* under the entry "Significs" by Lady Viola Welby.

Lady Welby stressed the importance of the pragmatic aspect of language. Her article is essentially a plea for what later came to be called "language hygiene." In her view, the function of language, once adapted to the cognitive and communicative needs of primitive man, has been impaired. She writes:

The very fact that the significating and interpretative function is the actual, though as yet little recognized and quite unstudied condition of mental advance and human achievement, accounts for such a function to be taken for granted and left to take care of itself.[2] This indeed, in pre-civilized ages (since it was then the very condition of safety and practically of survival), it was well able to do. But the innumerable forms of protection, precaution, artificial aid and special facilities which modern civilization implies and provides and to which it is always adding, have entirely and dangerously changed the situation. It has become imperative to realize the fact that through disuse we have partly lost the greatest as well as the most universal of human prerogatives.

And further:

The biological history of Man has been, indeed a long series of transmutations of form to subserve higher functions. In language he has so far failed to accomplish this. There has even in some directions been loss of advantage already gained. While his nature has been plastic and adaptive, language, the most centrally important of his acquirements has remained relatively rigid or, what is just as calamitous, fortuitously elastic.

Lady Welby was concerned with the inadequacy of ordinary speech as a tool for organizing and expressing ideas. This inadequacy

2. Lady Welby exemplifies the "havoc . . . wrought by persistent neglect" by what she calls "logical absurdities which are not only tolerated but taught without correction or warning to children. . . .

"We speak of beginning and ending as complementary, and then of 'both ends' but never of both beginnings. . . . We speak of an eternal sleep when the very raison d'être of sleep is to end in waking—it is not sleep unless it does. . . . Again we use the word 'passion' for the highest activity while we keep 'passive' for its negative."

These examples could be taken as a symptom of linguistic innocence of the author, who apparently assumes that eliminating idiomatic and metaphorical expressions would make everyday language a more effective instrument of survival. It is more likely, however, that Lady Welby warns against letting our language "do our thinking for us," against mistaking the idiosyncrasies of language for reality, against taking metaphorical expressions literally. This warning was expressed more emphatically and more explicitly some twenty years later by Alfred Korzybski (cf. Chapter 21).

inhibits man's intellectual development, which, she assumes, would continue if language had kept pace. Lady Welby does not touch upon the language of science which in its development does reflect just such advance.

In the 1920s the analysis of language was linked to the philosophy of science by a group of scholars that came to be known as the Vienna Circle. One of the foremost exponents of that school, Ludwig Wittgenstein, published a book in 1922 entitled *Tractatus Logico-philosophicus*, now regarded as the fundamental exposition of *logical positivism*, as the views of the Vienna Circle came to be known. The book begins with the sentence "Alles ist wahr, was der Fall ist" (Everything is true which is the case). It ends with the sentence "Worüber man nicht sprechen kann, muss man schweigen" (About that which one cannot talk about, one must remain silent). The first sentence defines truth in terms of what actually occurs *in a particular case* (an echo of the nominalist thesis). Although the body of Wittgenstein's work is essentially a demonstration that all of the traditional problems of philosophy are meaningless, the last sentence is not as paralyzing as it seems if coupled with a more constructive dictum implied: everything that can be said at all can be said clearly.

The logical positivists insisted that the only constructive task of philosophy was the analysis of language, in particular, the language of science. If science is the pursuit of truth, then the language of science ought to be a model of clarity. Also the words used in science ought to be related to what a scientist does in his quest for truth. Since the truth he seeks is truth about "what is the case," as Wittgenstein put it, the scientist must verify truth by observing "cases." He can, of course, make generalizations (induction) and can reason about what he has observed or assumed (deduction), but all of this activity must ultimately be related to finding out what is actually "the case." Therefore the words (terms) used in science must be defined *operationally*, that is, in terms of operations performed by the scientists.

Scientists perform operations of two kinds, observational and logical (or mathematical). Both are involved in operational definitions. As an example, take a term used in physics, say, "power." It is also a term used in ordinary language, and it means a variety of things in a variety of contexts. We speak of the power of an engine, the power of a state, the power of love, the power of conviction, a bureaucrat's power over his subordinates, and so on. In each case we may think we have an intuitive understanding of what the word means. But this intuitive understanding does not meet the scientist's standard of meaningfulness. To use the word in the context of a scientific utterance, one must define it operationally. As the term is used by the physicist, "power" is defined as the rate of doing work. "Work," in turn, is defined in mechanics in terms of force and distance: if a force acting in a given direction is constant during an interval of time, then the amount of work done is the magnitude of the force multiplied by the distance through which it acts. "Force," in turn, is defined as the mass of the body it acts upon multiplied by the acceleration suffered by the body in the direction of the force. Acceleration is the rate of change of velocity; velocity is the rate of change of position in a given direction. Position is defined in terms of distance from a fixed point or coordinate axis. Distance is defined in terms of operations with yardsticks, optical instruments, etc., and time in terms of the reading of a clock. Thus, in the last analysis, "power" is defined in terms of specifiable mathematical and observational operations.

We have already seen in Chapter 18 how the operational definitions of space and time intervals revealed that these terms must be defined relative to a given observer and how this *semantic analysis* led to the formulations of the theory of relativity. Thus, the positive, constructive role of the logical positivist view is readily apparent in the exact sciences. On the other hand, the logical positivist analysis of traditional philosophy was entirely destructive, as can be seen from the following example.

Hans Reichenbach, another exponent of the logical positivist school, begins his book *The Rise of Scientific Philosophy* with a quotation from G. W. F. Hegel (1770–1831).

Reason is substance, as well as infinite power, its own infinite material underlying all the natural and spiritual life; as also the infinite form, that which sets the material in motion. Reason is the substance from which all things derive their being.

Reichenbach comments on this passage as follows:

Many a reader has no patience with linguistic products of this brand. Failing to see any meaning in them, he may feel inclined to throw the book into the fire. In order to progress from this emotional response to logical critique, such a reader is invited to study so-called philosophical language with the attitude of a neutral observer, as the naturalist studies a rare specimen of beetle. Analysis of error begins with analysis of language.

The student of philosophy usually is not irritated by obscure formulations. On the contrary, reading the quoted passage, he would presumably be convinced that it must be his fault if he does not understand it. He therefore would read it again and again and thus would eventually reach a state in which he thinks he has understood it. [Cf. our discussion of "meaningfulness" in Chapter 4.—A. R.] At this point it would appear quite obvious to him that reason consists of an infinite material which underlies all natural and spiritual life and is therefore the substance of all things. He has been so conditioned to this way of talking as to forget all criticisms which a less "educated" man would make.

Now consider a scientist trained to use his words in such a way that every sentence has a meaning. His statements are so phrased that he is always able to prove their truth. He does not mind if long chains of thought are involved in the proof: he is not afraid of abstract reasoning. But he demands that somehow the abstract thought be connected with what his eyes see and his ears hear and the fingers feel. What would such a man say if he read the quoted passage?

The words "material" and "substance" are no strangers to him. He has applied them in his description of many an experiment: he has learned to measure the weight and the solidity of a material or a substance. He knows that a material may consist of several substances, each of which may look very different from the material. So these words do not offer any difficulty in themselves.

But what kind of material is that which underlies life? One would like to assume that it is the substance of which our bodies are made. How then can it be identical with reason? Reason is an abstract capacity of human beings, manifesting itself in their behavior, or to be modest, in parts of their behavior. Does the philosopher quoted wish to say that our bodies are made of an abstract capacity of themselves?

Even a philosopher cannot mean such an absurdity. What then does he mean? Presumably he means to say that all happenings in the universe are so arranged that they serve a reasonable purpose. That is a questionable assumption, but at least a comprehensible one. Yet if it is all the philosopher wants to say, why must he say it in a cryptic way?

That is the question I wish to answer before I can say what philosophy is and what it should be.[3]

3. Hans Reichenbach, *The Rise of Scientific Philosophy* (Berkeley: University of California Press, 1951), pp. 3–4.

When scientific standards of meaning are applied to most of the verbal output of traditional philosophy, very little of it remains that can lay claim to "meaning," and therefore the scientific criteria of truth cannot even be applied; for in order to ascertain the truth of an utterance, we must first know what it means. Whether philosophy can lay claim to some other kind of truth is a question that logical positivists cannot answer because they recognize no other than scientific truth. At any rate, the strongest impact of the semantic analysis undertaken by the logical positivists has been on science. For example, from the time when the Vienna Circle flourished, many psychologists and sociologists started to apply scientific standards of meaning and of truth in their disciplines and to look askance at theories that failed to satisfy these criteria.

Especially relevant to the theme of this book is the manifestation of these ideas in a popular movement aimed at promoting a sort of "language hygiene." The movement is centered mostly in the United States and derives much of its inspiration from a philosophy of language called *general semantics*. We shall be concerned with general semantics in Chapters 21 and 22. First we shall examine the ideas of an early American exponent of language hygiene.

APPLICATION

In *Extraterritorial*, George Steiner suggests that the certainties of language have become a privilege of the past and that the Tower of Babel is once again an appropriate metaphor: "Increasingly every act of communication between human beings takes on the shape of an act of translation." According to Steiner, the crisis in language began between 1900 and 1925 in Central Europe. In Vienna, Ludwig Wittgenstein tried to prove that philosophy was "speech therapy." In Prague, Franz Kafka made art out of what Steiner calls "the resistance of language to truth." In different ways, Steiner suggests, both men were signaling a loss of faith—the sudden awareness of a credibility gap between meanings and the words used to express them.

1) What other events in Europe in the twenties could be used as evidence to support Steiner's thesis?
2) What signs are there, both in public and in private life, that such a credibility gap still exists?

20/an early american semanticist

Alexander Bryan Johnson was born in England in 1786 and settled in Utica, New York, in 1801. His major work, *The Philosophy of Human Knowledge or A Treatise on Language*, appeared in 1828. An expanded edition entitled *A Treatise on Language or The Relation which Words Bear to Things* was published in 1836. It was followed by *The Meaning of Words Analyzed into Words and Unverbal Things* (1854).

Johnson's views on language bear such a striking resemblance to those of Alfred Korzybski (1879–1950) that one wonders whether they served as a point of departure for the latter's *Science and Sanity* published in 1933. This is not likely because Johnson's work remained obscure until it was rediscovered by David Rynin of the University of California, Berkeley, and republished in 1947.

It is interesting to note that major figures in the development of a critical philosophy of language in the United States were "amateurs," that is, people outside of professional philosophy. Alfred Korzybski was an engineer; Benjamin Lee Whorf (cf. pp. 208–9) was an employee of an insurance company; Alexander Bryan Johnson was a business man and banker. *A Treatise on Language* was based on lectures delivered by Johnson not at a university but at a place called the Lyceum, which later became the YMCA in Utica, New York. Another book of Johnson's, *Morality and Manners*, was based on lectures delivered at the YMCA. Incidentally, his first book (published in 1813) was entitled *An Inquiry into the Nature of Value and Capital, and into the Operation of Government Loans, Banking Institutions and Private Credit with an Appendix Containing an Inquiry into the Causes which Regulate the Rate of Interest and the Price of Stocks.*

I believe that the interest in language philosophy on the part of "nonprofessional philosophers" (especially in the United States) reflects an impatience with the methods of traditional philosophical inquiry. The traditional philosopher weaves theories from threads of speculation spun in his own mind. The ideas expounded in such theories, like all ideas, must have originated in some experiences of the philosophers, but words have a way of acquiring a life of their own, unrelated to nonverbal experience. In the mind of the philosopher, words combine and recombine on the strength of their metaphorical connotations. Since the philosophical method of inquiry does not impose an obligation to keep intact the links that connect assertions to experiences, the philosopher is easily led to assertions that cannot even in principle be related to any observable events. Americans, with their strongly developed sense of practicality, are especially prone to view philosophical speculations with mistrust. The layman may simply dismiss them as irrelevant to his interests and pursuits. The thinker with a pragmatic bent, however, will not leave it at that. He is distressed by what appears to him as nonsense masquerading as wisdom. Frequently he is motivated to "debunk" abstruse philosophy. One is tempted to say that this pragmatic attitude, so congenial to Americans, is actually antiphilosophical. It turned out, however, that this attitude itself crystallized into a well-formulated philosophy (pragmatism) of which William James and John Dewey became leading exponents.[1] Alexander Bryan Johnson's critical examination of language anticipated pragmatism.

The content of *A Treatise on Language* has been summarized by Johnson himself in a number of assertions interspersed with paragraphs that elaborate, explain, or illustrate the assertions. The very

1. William James (1842–1910) and John Dewey (1859–1952) are perhaps the most important figures in American philosophy since Emerson. Both made notable contributions to psychology. James, psychologist and philosopher, was the foremost leader in pragmatic philosophy, foreshadowed by Charles S. Peirce. For the clearest exposition of American pragmatism, see James's *Pragmatism: A New Name for Old Ways of Thinking* (1907) and *Essays in Radical Empiricism* (1912, posthumous), both published by Longmans, Green and Company, New York.

Dewey, like James, was a psychologist and philosopher, and while also labeled a pragmatist, he preferred to call his outlook *instrumentalism*. He championed scientific investigation as a model of inquiry and based his educational philosophy (for which he is most noted) on its spirit. The ideas of "progressive education" with their emphasis on process and growth have been largely inspired by Dewey.

first assertion states the main thesis of Johnson's philosophy of language: "To understand the relation which words bear to created existences, we must contemplate creation apart from words." [2]

By "created existences," Johnson means reality. In order to understand the relation between language and reality, says Johnson, we must contemplate reality *directly*, not through language.

What, then, is "reality"? Johnson tells us in the next assertion: "The external creations may be divided into sights, sounds, tastes, feels, and smells." [3]

In other words, reality is what is accessible to our senses. Names of objects—for example, "lemon"—are associations of four of the five sensations. Next, "We must discriminate between the extent and variety of creation and the paucity of language." [4]

In other words, the name of an object cannot incorporate all of the properties of the "real" object. Every lemon is different from every other lemon, but the name "lemon" stands for any lemon and fails to distinguish individual differences. Later, "Words are confounded with things." [5]

"We must subordinate language to what we discover in nature." [6]

Here in a nutshell is what Korzybski a century later was to call the extensional orientation: the recognition that (1) the word is not the thing; (2) the word cannot describe the thing in all its intricate detail; (3) we ought to evaluate language by how well it describes reality, not impute to reality what language tells us about it.

Next Johnson warns against imputing to reality what we deduce from language. "We seek in nature for a unit which exists in language only." [7]

Here again is the nominalist thesis (cf. p. 349): Men exist: Every man is different from every other man. But all men have some characteristics in common. These happen to be important to us, so we *abstract* the characteristics and give the abstraction a name—man. The error of the realists (as the nominalists saw it) was to assume

2. Alexander Bryan Johnson, *A Treatise on Language*, ed. David Rynin (Berkeley and Los Angeles: University of California Press, 1947), p. 47.
3. Ibid.
4. Ibid., p. 49.
5. Ibid., p. 53.
6. Ibid., p. 56.
7. Ibid., p. 73.

tacitly that, because we have the word "man" in our language, something called "man" must exist as a unit in nature.

One example cited by Johnson to illustrate this point is especially interesting:

Medical science is probably embarrassed by our imputing to diseases and their incidents, the oneness which pertains to their names only.
The medical question of contagion [Johnson goes on] is embarrassed by not discriminating the oneness of language from the plurality of nature. The contagiousness of cholera generally is less a unit than the contagiousness of a single case. Even the contagiousness of a single case, during its whole continuance, is less a unit than its contagiousness on any given moment:—hence to investigate the contagiousness of cholera and to proceed by supposing that the contagiousness possesses the oneness which the word contagion imports, is like seeking for magnetism as a unit among the numerous magnetic phenomena. It is seeking in nature for a unit that exists in language only.

"But cholera itself is not a unit. Whether medical science suffers not by the implied oneness of each disease merits the consideration of physicians. Many medical theories seem to owe their origin to this errour [sic]. But not only is cholera in general not a unit, the particular cholera of Thomas is not a unit. It consists of many feels, sights, and other phenomena. I admit the propriety of combining them under one name; but if we would escape delusion, we must construe their oneness by nature, and not by the oneness of their name.[8]

As it turned out, "cholera" is *more* of a unit than many other so-called diseases common in Johnson's time ("fever," "ague," "catarrh," etc.). Before the advent of microbiology and biochemistry, diseases were classified by associations of symptoms; consequently, the often very different etiology of different diseases went unnoticed. With the discovery of pathogenic microorganisms, diseases came to be classified in accordance with specific pathogenic organisms associated with them. Thus "cholera" remained as a name of the disease. While its *etymology* ("cholera" is derived from *cholerikos*, meaning heat, hence fever) may mislead by suggesting a kinship with typhus and meningitis (also characterized by high fever), the *etiology* of cholera is specific and constant. There is no cholera without the *vibrio*

8. Ibid., pp. 75–76.

cholerae, an identifiable organism. True, every bacillus *vibrio cholerae* is in some way different from every other *vibrio cholerae*, yet a considerable degree of "oneness" can be ascribed to the bacillus, at least a larger degree than to the symptoms that are manifested in individual cases or to the general event called "contagion." Had Johnson chosen another example, say, "the ague," he would have a much stronger case in warning against attributing "oneness" to nature on the basis of how we happen to classify things and events.

Vestiges of primitive nomenclature have persisted in medicine and in psychiatry to our day. It is now known that "cancer" is a name given to many diseases, some of which are probably quite unrelated to each other from the point of view of etiology. Schizophrenia is still a catchall name for possibly several diseases with different etiologies but with similar symptoms. However, demonstrated etiology of a disease does provide a better base for ascribing an entity to the disease than the name originally given to an "association of sensations," that is, roughly perceived symptoms which are themselves names of impressions. A case in point is "magnetism," another example used by Johnson. There *is* something in nature to which the name magnetism applies. That something is not an object; it is a principle. Based on that principle, many different events can be shown to be related in a very real way, not only because they have been given the same name.

Nevertheless the original injunction, "To understand the relation which words bear to created existences, we must contemplate creation apart from words," must be taken seriously. We can evaluate critically the degree of correspondence between our accustomed language and reality (the relation which words bear to things) only by constantly checking the oneness of names against what we actually find in nature. Korzybski formulated this principle more sharply by emphasizing the correspondence (or the lack of it) between the *structure* of a language and that of reality. As we shall see in the next chapters, examination of structural correspondence involves considerably more than awareness of sensations.

The injunction against seeking a "unit" in nature suggested by a word warns against *reification* of abstractions. The first words we learn are mostly names of objects. The expectation of finding an object behind a word is a carry-over of infantile semantics. Thus, writes Johnson, "The word gravity names many interesting and important phenomena; but if, in addition to these, we look for gravity itself we act as ignorantly as the child at the opera who, after listening with impatience to the musick [sic], singing, and dancing, said 'I am tired of these; I want the opera.'" [9]

Linguistic innocence (cf. Chapter 2) is not confined to childhood. Early conceptions of disease as a thing that entered a body (especially believed of mental disease) led to corresponding therapeutic practices. A person gone mad was supposed to be possessed by a demon. It was easy to imagine the demon residing in the person. The disease was attacked by "exorcising" the demon, that is, by ritual designed to make the demon leave the person's body. The difference between life and death was often attributed (and still is in popular conception) to the presence or absence of a "soul" in the body of a person: when the person dies, the "soul" leaves the body. The idea leads naturally to speculations about the subsequent whereabouts or fate of the "soul."

Reification suggests questions like "Where does the flame go when we blow out the candle?" or "Where does the hole go when we eat a doughnut?"

The second question may appear silly even to a child, yet it is no less and no more justified than the question about the flame or about the soul. All such questions are suggested by a tacit assumption that whatever is named is a thing. Ordinary things do not just vanish. When they are not in sight, they must be somewhere else. It is therefore legitimate to ask where they are.

Besides suggesting reification (looking for a "thing" that the word is thought to name), words also erase the differences between the individual members of a class.

We should not confound the verbal identity with the realities of nature.[10]

Johnson recognizes that verbal identities are inevitable:

I complain not of language for its implied identities. We can construct a language on no other principle. A whale and an anchovy present sufficient similarities to render the word fish [sic!] appropriate to both: still we need not confound the verbal identity with the realities of nature. In

9. Ibid., pp. 77–78.
10. Ibid., p. 81.

nature, the identity is just as we discover it to be. It must not be measured by names, but ascertained by observation. We reverse this rule: we interpret the natural identity by the verbal.[11]

By ascribing primacy to observation rather than to concepts, Johnson stands in diametric opposition to the idealist philosophy of Plato. Recall that for Plato "reality" consisted of idealized conceptions reflected in language. Somewhere (perhaps in the mind of God) there exists, Plato supposed, a perfect Man, a perfect Tree, perhaps even a perfect Hammer or a perfect Language. Actual men, trees, hammers, and languages appeared to Plato as imperfect copies of those Ideals. Differences between men, trees, and so on, were due to accidental deviations from idealized models. True knowledge, therefore, was to be sought in the contemplation of these Ideals and of their properties, revealed to men by the exercise of pure reason.

Johnson, on the contrary, takes the material world to be the real world. We may form a concept of Man, of Tree, and so on, but these concepts are derivatives of our experience. We abstract properties of objects we perceive and give these abstracted properties a name. The name "identifies" members of the class to which the name refers. The differences between distinct members of a class are not "errors," as Plato supposed; they are the facts of existence. Reality *is* diverse. Our language turns diversity into unity, but this unity is of our own making. Says Johnson:

The diversity which we discover among natural objects, etc., that possess the same name, should teach us to correct the identity implied by their name; but we employ the verbal identity to excite wonder at the natural diversity.[12]

The identification of language with reality may lead to a failure of language as a means of communication:

Two men who assent to the same general proposition may possess very diverse meanings.[13]

Johnson illustrates this point by a situation where both he and the reader "agree" that "George is good." However, Johnson may have

11. Ibid.
12. Ibid., p. 82.
13. Ibid., p. 91.

in mind qualities of George, unknown to the reader, which Johnson regards as good but which the reader would have judged to be bad, and vice versa.

The opposite situation is also frequently observed. In the simplest case, two men may disagree as to whether a house is on the right or the left side of the street merely because one means that it is on the right side if one faces north, while the other means that it is on the left side when one faces south. Having omitted the orientation, each man has made an unwarranted generalization. In the same way, in Johnson's example, the men who judge George's character have made an unwarranted generalization. Instead of referring to specific traits or acts which led them to their judgments, they attached a general label to George. They thought they agreed because they applied the same label. They did not know that the ranges of denotation of the label did not coincide. The two men who argued about the location of the house attached an incomplete label to its position. "Right" and "left" do not specify direction unless the direction in which one faces is also specified.

Again, quoting Johnson:

No general proposition is significant of more than certain particulars.
A father once said 'My son, in water exists a principle which is destructive of life, and in brandy a principle preservative of life.' The father meant that immersion in water would produce death, and that a small quantity of brandy was occasionally salutary. The proposition was correct while confined to the particulars to which the father alluded; but the son, supposing its application universal, refrained from the use of water, and substituted brandy. We all err in a similar manner, though not always in a like degree, when we consider any proposition significant of more than certain particulars; and if those who promulge [sic] general propositions, will not announce the particulars to which they refer, we have still every thing to learn.[14]

Knowledge, according to Johnson, comes to us only through our senses:

Our sense alone can answer questions. Words can only refer us to what our senses reveal.[15]

14. Ibid., p. 131.
15. Ibid., p. 244.

In this view, any discrepancy between what language asserts and what the senses reveal must be resolved in favor of the evidence of the senses. Not only can verbal assertions be false; they can also be meaningless if they do not refer to something that the senses can reveal. However,

We are vigilant in detecting verbal contradictions, but we never detect the sensible contradictions which exist in affirming the presence of sensible existences, where none are discoverable by the senses.[16]

Philosophers, in Johnson's view, are especially prone to take seriously assertions that are only consequences of verbal deductions. Johnson's view is representative of what we shall call extreme positivism, an orientation that has been especially influential in the United States in both professional and popular philosophy. It underlies what has come to be known as general semantics, although, as we shall see, Alfred Korzybski, the founder (or, some would say, the guru) of general semantics did not explicitly expound the extreme positivist veiw. In later chapters we shall examine the shortcomings of extreme positivism in its philosophical and social context.

APPLICATIONS

I. Having reached this point in the text, you should be developing the ability to read more critically, more thoughtfully, and with greater understanding of the author's intentions. Of course, such an assumption should not be automatic. If you wish to check your own interpretative processes at this stage of your reading, decide whether the following statements *agree with*, *disagree with*, or *bear no relation to* what has been said in this chapter. Find the place in the chapter that corroborates your response. If you seem to have made an error, try to determine whether a) you made an unjustified inference, b) you missed a connotative meaning, or c) the author's exposition lacked sufficient clarity.

1) Alfred Korzybski's *Science and Sanity* was influenced by the work of Alexander Johnson.
2) As philosophical method of inquiry is defined in this chapter, existentialism would not be regarded as a philosophy.

16. Ibid., p. 99.

3) Most people think that the philosophical method of inquiry does not impose an obligation to keep intact the links that connect assertions to experiences.

4) The pragmatic attitude of Americans toward philosophy is actually antiphilosophical.

5) Reality for Johnson was the experience created by words.

6) At its heart, the Johnson position is antinominalist.

7) Man may be succeeded by a race of giant rats if he does not correct the errors of language.

8) In all likelihood, cholera is a concept invented by physicians who indulged in overabstracting—at least, according to Johnson.

9) A Greek physician is likely to have a better understanding of what cholera means because the word comes from the Greek word *cholerikos* meaning "heat."

10) Schizophrenia is a catchall name for several diseases with similar symptoms but different etiologies.

11) People should try to understand what magnetism is because, according to Johnson, it exists as a principle in nature and relates different events.

12) *Reification* is risky because it means regarding an abstraction as a real thing.

13) Fortunately, most linguistic innocence is confined to childhood.

14) Johnson admired the philosophy of Aristotle and sought to develop a system within that framework.

15) The author agrees with Johnson's assertion that knowledge comes to us only through our senses.

II. Which of the following statements are examples of *reification* and which are not? Briefly defend your answer, using an *operational procedure* whenever possible.

1) How many angels (an angel being incorporeal) can dance on the head of a pin?

2) Where do flies go in the winter?

3) Where does the darkness go?

4) When the epidemic subsided, where did the cholera go?

5) Why does virtue so often go unrewarded?

6) Why does God allow things like cancer and infant death to happen to his children?

7) Where did that supernova go?

8) Is life worth living?

9) Is Liffey worth leaving? (James Joyce).

10) Society is hypocritical.

11) Drugs can be valuable because they are mind-expanding.

12) He wrote a dissertation on "The Unicorn in Medieval Life."

13) Proof that the modern age is more liberal is that we no longer burn witches.

14) The trouble with middle-class whites is that they have no "soul."

15) Why can't you see ghosts during the day?

21/korzybski's general semantics, or the non-aristotelian system

Language, said Korzybski, is a map of reality. The metaphor is a good one. An ordinary map purports to mark the positions of points of interest in a territory. These points are fixed in spatial relations to each other. The map is a good one if the spatial relations between the points marked on it reflect accurately the spatial relations between the locations they represent. Thus a map of the United States should show Chicago between New York and San Francisco. If it shows San Francisco between New York and Chicago, it is a bad map, and we shall be misled if we try to travel by it. In short, the structure of the map should correspond to the structure of the territory it represents.

The three postulates of Korzybski's "non-Aristotelian system" can be stated as assertions about the "map." These are:

1. The map is not the territory.
2. The map is not all of the territory.
3. The map is self-reflexive.[1]

"The map is not the territory" is a paraphrase of A. B. Johnson's "The word is not the thing"—the latter phrase being one of Korzybski's also. What the dictum is getting at is this: the word "chair" has five letters. The object CHAIR is not composed of letters. You can sit on the nonverbal chair. You cannot sit on the word "chair."

1. The reader wishing to acquaint himself with a précis of Korzybski's ideas will find it in "A Non-Aristotelian System and Its Necessity for Rigor in Mathematical Physics," a paper he presented to the American Mathematical Society on December 28, 1931, and included as Supplement III in the second edition of *Science and Sanity*.

"The map is not all of the territory" paraphrases Johnson's "We must discriminate between the extent and variety of creation and the paucity of language." Indeed, no map can represent all of the territory, if only because the map is so much smaller than the territory. My house cannot be represented on a map of Canada which shows the whole of my town only as a tiny circle. Korzybski would challenge his students to describe some object "completely." Needless to say, no matter how minutely they described it, he could always point to features they had left out. If they said the apple he held up for inspection was "red," he would call their attention to streaks of green or to a black spot; if they included these, he would challenge them to specify exactly the shape of the green streaks or the position of the spot, to describe the inside of the apple, and so on. The demonstration proved conclusively that when we name objects or even describe them minutely we *must* leave out some things. Similarly a map omits things, not only because of the limitations of its scale but also because different maps serve different purposes.

Consider that I want to invite to dinner a colleague who is about to visit Toronto. In my letter I enclose a crude "map"—a piece of paper with some lines on it and two crosses. One of the crosses represents the hotel where he will stop; the other, my house. I assume that he will recognize that the lines stand for streets and the words near them are names of streets. I expect that he will take the piece of paper with him as he leaves his hotel, check its words against the words written on signposts placed on Toronto street corners, and so follow the way to my house. If he finds my house without getting lost, the map has fulfilled its purpose. But the same map is worthless to a real estate agent who is interested in boundaries between properties in Toronto; it is worthless also to the surveyor who wants to know the elevations of sites. Every map is designed to fit a specific purpose. No map can represent all of the territory. Nor should it attempt to represent more than what is required for its purpose since the irrelevant markings will only distract our attention and make our task (learning the relations that interest us) more difficult.

By the assertion "the map is self-reflexive" Korzybski meant that, if a map were located on the territory it represented and if it contained enough detail, it would have to include a representation of itself. If it did, think of the difficulties that would arise. For example, consider packages such as most of us have seen (of cereal, soap powder—or the familiar "Pet Milk" can) on which the package itself is pictured. To be accurate, the smaller picture of the package must show a still smaller picture-of-the-picture, and on and on. (Perhaps, as children, we wondered where all this must end! It may have been our first encounter with infinity.)

The principle of self-reflexiveness is clearly related to self-referring propositions discussed on page 351 where it was shown that, upon analysis, some of these propositions turned out to be neither true nor false, a result incompatible with Aristotle's postulates.

Korzybski maintained that self-reflexiveness is inherent in all language. Therefore, to use language at all, we must do one of two things: either abandon the principle of noncontradiction or abandon the principle of the excluded middle. Korzybski was not a logician and did not have a clear idea about these alternatives. He was satisfied that in stating the three "map" principles he had laid the foundation of a "non-Aristotelian" system. However, for our part, if logic is to continue to serve as a tool of deduction and if its foundation is to be self-consistent, we must make a decision—which of the two Aristotelian postulates to drop.

Actually there is little choice. If the Aristotelian system of logic turned out to be inadequate because in it an analysis of some propositions leads to contradictions, then we should not *allow* contradictions in order to save the system. It is because we want to avoid contradiction that we started looking for ways to modify the system.

Dropping the principle of the excluded middle is the more promising because in doing so the principle of noncontradiction remains in force: a proposition cannot be *both* true and false. By dropping the principle of the excluded middle, we simply admit that a proposition may be *neither* true nor false. We shall call such propositions *undecidable*. As it later turned out, the admission of undecidable propositions is indispensable in mathematical logic.

A system of logic which does not accommodate the principle of the excluded middle can be legitimately called a "non-Aristotelian" logic, by analogy with "non-Euclidean" geometry and "non-Newtonian" physics. Non-Euclidean geometry was discussed in Chapter 16 and non-Newtonian physics (based on the theory of relativity) in Chapter 18. In each case, the prefix "non" refers to replacing a postulate of the "classical" (Euclidean, Newtonian) system by another: in non-Euclidean geometry, Euclid's fifth postulate is replaced by another; in non-Newtonian physics, the equations governing the transformation of coordinates of a moving body with respect to a coordinate system which is itself in motion were replaced by other equations (these equations being essentially postulates).

Similarly a non-Aristotelian logic is one in which the principle of the excluded middle is replaced by another. There are several such logics, including a three-valued logic in which a proposition has one of three truth values instead of one of two (true or false), and we have seen that probability theory (cf. Chapter 15) can be viewed as an infinite-valued logic. In calling his system non-Aristotelian, Korzybski stressed the analogy with non-Euclidean geometries and non-Newtonian physics.

If this were the sense in which Korzybski's system is non-Aristotelian—that it admits undecidable propositions and so points to many-valued logics—his contribution would be nil because multivalued logics had already been constructed.[2] Also, the theory of probability had been systematically developed since the seventeenth century,[3] and its equivalence to an extension of two-valued logic was already apparent in the nineteenth century.

It is on quite different grounds that Korzybski bases his claim to having constructed a non-Aristotelian system. He has repeatedly emphasized that general semantics is not to be viewed as a system of logic, nor even as a philosophy, but as an empirical science.

Now, an empirical science, unlike a system of logic and unlike many systems of philosophy, deals with observations and experiments. As far as is known, Korzybski performed no experiments, but he did observe people's behavior. His claim to having laid the foundations of a new empirical science then must be evaluated on the basis of the generalizations that he made from his observations.

Korzybski maintained that people behave as if they confounded their linguistic maps with the territory of reality, or words with things—an observation made by Alexander Bryan Johnson more than one hundred years before Korzybski wrote his major book, *Science and Sanity* (1933). Many other thinkers have made the same observation. Korzybski, however, put special emphasis on what he

2. In fact, Korzybski acknowledges an intellectual debt to a compatriot, Jan Lukasiewicz, whose paper on three-valued logic appeared in 1921. In English, see, for example, A. N. Prior, "Three-Valued Logic and Future Contingents," *Philosophical Quarterly* 3 (1953).
3. See Note 10, Chapter 15.

thought was the root of identifying the structure of reality with the structure of language. He believed it to be the result of "internalizing" Aristotelian logic.

Of course, few people have formally studied Aristotelian logic. Korzybski pointed out, however, that this logic is reflected in the peculiar structure of Indo-European languages and so became incorporated into the language habits, therefore into the thought habits, of the people who spoke these languages. The structure of propositions that Korzybski considered to be the foundation of Indo-European languages is the subject and predicate connected by the copula "is"—the structure of all propositions that enter the syllogism: "All A are B," "Some X are Y," "No M is N," and so forth.

Now, the word "is" ["are"] has several meanings. When I say "A bachelor is an unmarried man," I use "is" in the sense of establishing an identicalness. In this sense, the word "bachelor" may be substituted for "an unmarried man" in a chain of reasoning. Aristotle's principle of identity allows this, once we agree that the range of denotation of two words is the same: A is A.

In another sense, "is" denotes class inclusion. When I say "A Frenchman is a European," I do not mean to identify Frenchmen with all Europeans. The class of Europeans is larger than the class of Frenchmen, and "Frenchman" cannot be substituted for "Europeans" in every case. For example, from the truth of the proposition "All Frenchmen speak French," I cannot deduce "All Europeans speak French." Clearly in this case the meaning of "is" is quite different from that of identifying the referents of two words.

Another meaning of "is" appears when I say "The rose is red." Here I am describing a property of the rose, certainly not identifying the flower with the color. If we twist language, we can interpret "The rose is red" as a proposition denoting class inclusion, namely, "The rose belongs to the class of red objects." Such interpretations, however, are artificial. It is more convenient to allow another meaning to "is"—that of connecting an object with one of its attributes.

Still another meaning of "is" manifests itself in the act of naming. When I say (pointing to a rose) "This is a rose," I am naming what I am pointing to. This statement can also be interpreted as class inclusion: "This object belongs to the class of roses." There may be a logical equivalence between the two statements, but the intended meanings are different. When I classify a flower as a rose, I assume that the hearer already has a conception of a class of flowers called roses. When I name the flower, I may be assuming that the hearer does not know the English word with which to refer to it.

Korzybski thought that the subject-predicate structure of sentences in Indo-European languages predisposed people to "understand" the copula "is" primarily as the "is" of identity, neglecting the other meanings. Here it is important to grasp that Korzybski meant by "understanding" not the ability to explain something in words, but a process inside the skin of an individual, which Korzybski described in terms of neural events. He called the process a *semantic reaction* and related it to the conditioning processes discovered by the great Russian physiologist Ivan Pavlov.

Specifically, Pavlov discovered the so-called *conditioned response.* Pavlov's work is now a rubric of "scientific psychology," the method that aims to explain behavior by systematic experiments and theories deduced from their results. Pavlov's work provides a solid link between physiology and psychology; that is, makes it possible to relate some aspects of behavior of organisms possessing complex nervous systems to events in the nervous system—neural events.

Pavlov's experiments are now "classical." They are described in most textbooks of psychology and in many popular writings on behavior. They will be briefly reviewed here for the sake of continuity.

When a dog eats, the flow of saliva from his salivary glands increases. Saliva serves to facilitate the preliminary digestion of food. Even before the food is in the dog's mouth, copious saliva begins to flow, stimulated by the smell of food. (This also happens to people, whence the expression that something "makes our mouth water.") This process is the result of what physiologists call a *reflex.* A reflex is a nervous impulse that is started by some external stimulus, then passes along an *afferent* nerve fiber from the periphery toward a central location, where it jumps across a *synapse* (a connection between nerve fibers), and next proceeds along an *efferent* nerve fiber to a muscle or gland which is thereby activated.

To demonstrate, when your finger touches something hot, you jerk it away. The action is *not* the result of a deduction. You do not reason: "This object is hot; therefore if I keep in contact with it, it will hurt me; therefore I must pull my hand away." The action is independent of your volition. The stimulus from the hot object passes along an afferent nerve through your finger and arm to your spinal cord, where there is a junction with a nerve fiber leading to the muscles, which are thereby made to contract and so pull your hand away. In fact, the hand is pulled away before you feel the heat because there are no sensory centers in the spinal cord. *Other* impulses are sent along the cord to the sensory center in your brain, and you feel the heat when the center is activated. That is why you will usually have the sensation of heat after you have already jerked your hand away.

The survival value of this arrangement is obvious. It enables you to protect your body against injury without taking the time to reason things out or even to recognize the source of the danger.

An automatic response of this sort is called an *unconditioned response*. It is built into the nervous system. All animals with nervous systems have such built-in responses. By and large, they are arrangements that enable the animal to avoid dangers automatically and to approach sources of food or mates. The salivation of the dog in the presence of food is an unconditioned response that prepares the dog for eating.

In Pavlov's conditioning experiments, another stimulus is presented to the dog a short time before the food is presented. This other stimulus may be the sound of a bell or of a buzzer. Ordinarily the sound does not elicit salivation. However, after, say, a buzzer has been followed by food a number of times, the dog begins to salivate at the sound of the buzzer before the food is presented. And even if the buzzer is not followed by food, the dog nevertheless continues to salivate at the sound of the buzzer. This salivation is called a *conditioned* response. In a way, we can say that the buzzer has come to "mean" food to the dog; he reacts to the buzzer as if it were food.

It is possible further to condition a stimulus to another stimulus that has been previously linked to a conditioned response. For instance, after the dog has "learned" to salivate at the sound of a buzzer, he can be conditioned to salivate when a light is turned on *without* the use of food. The light is turned on, followed by the buzzer to which the dog has been conditioned to salivate. Eventually the dog will salivate when the light is turned on. It can then be said that for the dog the light has come to "mean" the buzzer, and he reacts to the light as if it were the buzzer.

Conditioned responses have been demonstrated in human beings. In fact, habit formation may well depend on a complex of conditioned responses. In learning a muscular skill, such as typing or playing the piano, we learn to make conditioned responses. If we type to dictation, we learn to respond with certain coordinated finger movements to the sounds of words. If we play from sheet music, we acquire conditioned responses to the musical symbols. In learning any skill, a teacher can explain to us only to a certain extent what we are supposed to do; the bulk of the skill is acquired by processes in our nervous system of which we are unaware. It is supposed that these processes effect changes, largely in the synapses, in ways that channel the nervous impulses along the proper paths.

The discovery of conditioning has provided psychologists with a method for systematically investigating "learning." Pavlov's method was enlarged to encompass so-called *instrumental conditioning* and *operant conditioning*.

In instrumental conditioning, the subject (usually an animal) is presented with stimuli to which it is to learn to respond "properly." For example, a rat is confined in a cage with two doors, one marked with a circle, the other with a square. Some stimulus is given, say, an electric shock, to elicit an attempt to escape. The door with the square is locked, but the door with the circle opens when the rat pushes against it. Eventually the rat will learn to go directly to the door with the circle. The positions of the doors are frequently reversed to make sure that the rat has learned the "meaning" of the symbols (circle = escape; square = no escape) rather than merely the position of the escape door.

In operant conditioning, the animal learns by trial and error, as it were, without having a clear-cut choice of alternatives. For example, a rat may be put in a cage with a bar which, upon being pressed, causes a food pellet to drop into the cage. In exploring the cage (as rats are wont to do), he may accidentally press the bar and so get the "reward." Eventually he will "learn" that he can get food by pressing the bar. The rat can also be taught that bar pressing will get him food only if a light goes on. He can even be taught that food will come only if he waits a specified time after the light goes on before pressing the bar and so on.

Experiments in conditioning suggest many interesting questions about the learning process in animals, and they also answer some of them. Psychologists study the relations between the rate at which a conditioned response is acquired in reinforcement conditioning and the magnitude or the scheduling of the rewards and punishments used; the degree to which learned tasks are retained under various conditions; the way a conditioned response can be transferred from one stimulus to another; and so forth.

Those professionals wanting psychology to be divested of "mentalistic" concepts (that is, concepts that could not be easily operationalized or linked to observable events) looked upon the theory of conditioning as the solid base on which to build a science of behavior. Foremost among them was the American psychologist B. F. Skinner. Skinner's book *Verbal Behavior* is an attempt to explain language behavior in terms of operant conditioning.[4] Up to a point, the theory seems plausible. Before an infant learns to speak, he babbles. This is the trial-and-error phase. Occasionally the infant makes a noise that sounds like a word or part of a word. The attention and approval of parents, siblings, and others serve as the infant's reward (reinforcement). Eventually the child acquires words as conditioned responses to objects and events. He learns to verbalize his wants, somewhat in the way the rat learns to press a bar to get food. The complex acts of speech appear in Skinner's scheme as results of chains of operant conditioning.

Korzybski in his theory of language behavior also took the conditioning process as a point of departure. However, he insisted that this way of acquiring language habits leads to "false-to-fact semantic reactions." When a word becomes a conditioned response to the thing it represents, it is *identified* with the thing. Thereupon we react to the thing by evoking its name and react to the *name* as if it were the thing.

For example, persons allergic to roses have been known to sneeze in the presence of *artificial* roses. Allergy is a physiological response elicited by chemical reactions of body tissues to substances ingested, inhaled, or coming in contact with the skin. Obviously paper roses do not contain substances responsible for allergy to real roses, so how can the reaction be explained? Korzybski would explain it as follows. The sight of an artificial rose elicits the conditioned verbal response "rose." The word need not be spoken. It is enough to think it, since the thought, like the spoken word, is associated with certain neural activity. This is a semantic reaction. Next, the body reacts to the

4. See Notes 5 and 6, Chapter 4.

word "rose" as it would to a real rose. This, too, is a semantic reaction. Hypnosis provides ample evidence that physiological reactions can be elicited by words alone, to the extent even of making burns appear on the surface of the skin of a hypnotized subject by the mere suggestion that he has touched a hot object. Faith healing and hexing work on the same principle.

Unlike most language philosophers, Korzybski puts the human nervous system at the center of attention. Recall the reference triangle of Ogden and Richards (cf. p. 154) where meaning is defined not as a direct relation between the word and its referent but as a relation mediated by the language user, represented by the apex of the triangle. In language philosophy, this apex plays the part of a "black box." [5] Korzybski theorized about the events in that black box, that is, about actual physicochemical events associated with the creation and perception of meaning. He thought that he could infer the nature of these events by observing language behavior. In particular, he thought he could construct a theory of sanity on the basis of these inferred events.

Sanity, in Korzybski's theory, is defined as a close correspondence between the structure of reality and the structure of language (whether in thought or in speech) used to represent and to interpret reality. Since there are degrees of correspondence, there are degrees of sanity. At one extreme, the closest approach to sanity is reflected in the language of the exact sciences. At the other extreme is "insanity," reflected in the semantic reactions of the mentally ill. In between is "*un*sanity," reflected in ordinary, uncritically accepted, everyday language.

As cited at the beginning of this chapter, Korzybski stressed the influence of the subject-predicate structure of Indo-European languages, in particular its pernicious effects of internalizing the "is" of identity. When we say "This is a rose," Korzybski argued, we are reinforcing a conditioned response to the word "rose" as if it were the object rose. We identify "this" with "rose." Actually "this" (pointing) refers to a nonverbal thing, something neither identical

---

5. Consider an automation of the sort described on pages 264–65. It receives "inputs" and responds with "outputs." An output may depend not only on the input just presented but also on the internal state of the automaton, which may depend on previous inputs and outputs. We may set for ourselves the task of *inferring* the internal structure of the automaton, inaccessible to direct inspection, by studying the dependence of outputs upon inputs (including previous ones). This sort of automaton is called a "black box."

with a word nor describable by any combination of words. In naming "this," we deprive ourselves of awareness of its sensory, nonverbal reality. The first step toward sanity, then, according to Korzybski, is to acquire a habit of *delaying* the semantic reaction. Look at a rose, he said, and refrain from naming it. Take it in as a complex of sense impressions. The same goes for any other situation. We must learn, Korzybski insisted, to experience and observe without naming, classifying, or categorizing. In so doing, we *internalize* the realization that every rose is different from every other rose, that $rose_1$ is not identical with $rose_2$, and also that $rose_1$ is not identical with *itself*, for it is continually changing. The changes are not apparent to us, but we have evidence provided by scientific findings that they go on all the time. The fragrance of the rose attests to the fact that substances from it are constantly diffusing through the air. Chemical changes are continually taking place in the substances of which the "nonverbal" rose is composed. Further, the appearance of the rose as a solid object is only an abstraction created by our senses that cannot penetrate the detailed structure of the rose. On another level of observation, a rose is not a solid object at all. Matter consists of minute particles (molecules, atoms, electrons, etc.) in constant motion. If our vision were sufficiently acute, a rose would appear to us more like a swarm of flies than a solid object. Indeed, on the so-called subatomic level of reality, there are no such things as "objects," much less are there permanently existing objects: there are only "events"—happenings without permanence. Our senses organize our impressions so as to present to us a world of objects in the way that similarly the limitations of our vision make a whirling fan appear as a solid disc (a favorite demonstration of Korzybski's). Our language fixates our belief in the reality of permanent objects.

It is in this sense that Korzybski's denial of the principle of identity must be understood—not as a denial of a logical principle but as a warning against projecting that principle upon reality. The principle of identity says "A is A." Identifying the word with its referent, we tend to understand this to mean "A rose is a rose," that is, that a rose is identical with itself.[6] But it is not.

Are the discrepancies important that occur between the identities

6. Gertrude Stein went further. In "A rose is a rose is a rose," she identifies the "identity" ("A rose is a rose") with a rose. Korzybski would call it compounding false-to-fact identification, but, of course, logical or empirical standards of validity ought not be applied to the language of poetry.

established in language and the nonidentities found in nature? In some contexts they are. When we categorize human beings or situations, we impair our awareness of individual human beings and of specific situations. The assertion "A Jew is a Jew" is structurally similar to "A rose is a rose" and to "A is A." In certain social contexts, however, such an assertion reinforces ethnic or religious prejudices. The slogan "Once an Englishman, always an Englishman" was used to justify the conscription of American seamen into British service during the Napoleonic wars. The practice was said to have been a contributing factor to the War of 1812. Categorization also encourages us to perceive individuals as members of classes rather than as themselves.

Established categorizations, moreover, reinforced by word labels, obscure the fact that categorizing may be done in many ways that distort perceptions. Inevitably we internalize just those categorizations that are imposed on us by the language habits of our speech community; other categorizations then seem bizarre to us. For example, in the United States, persons are usually categorized as "Negroes" if they have discernible traces of African ancestry, and as "whites" if they have none (aside from Orientals and Indians). This categorization is no more "logical" than one that would label as "whites" all persons that had discernible traces of European descent and as "Negroes" all those that had none. According to this categorization, most people now labeled Negroes would be labeled "whites" because a majority of them have discernible traces of European ancestry. In Czarist Russia, people were categorized as Jews only if they professed Judaism. If they submitted to a ceremony (baptism) in which they declared acceptance of the Greek Orthodox faith, they were no longer Jews in the eyes of the law and so acquired civil rights denied to professed Jews. In Nazi Germany, on the other hand, a Jew was defined as a person who had at least one Jewish grandparent, and there was nothing he could do to change his label.

The principle of noncontradiction and the principle of the excluded middle, when projected on reality, induce what Korzybski called the *two-valued orientation*. The logical principles as such assert no more than that a proposition must be either true or false but not both. But internalized as a language habit, the principles of noncontradiction and of the excluded middle induce a division of properties and situations into mutually exclusive opposite categories. The principle of the excluded middle does not say that a thing is black if it is not white. It says only that a thing is either white or not-white. But the word "not" tends to induce the notion of "opposite." Most people will readily admit that if something is not white, it need not be black. Still many behave as if whatever is not good were bad, as if whoever is not a friend were an enemy ("Who is not with us is against us"), as if "success" or "failure" were the only outcomes of an enterprise, as if the alternative to freedom were slavery, the alternative to victory, defeat, and so on. The either-or habit of thought pervades theology, philosophy, and politics. On Judgment Day, mortals will be categorized, we are told, as *either* the Saved *or* the Damned and will proceed respectively *either* to Heaven *or* to Hell. Descartes (1596–1650) was a foremost exponent of *dualism*, where human existence is pictured as two separate entities composed of a Body and a Mind—a conception still dominant in popular philosophy. American foreign policy after World War II has been depicted by its proponents in either-or terms, as a defense of the Free World Against Communism. In the Soviet Union, where politics is rationalized in terms of a philosophy, the either-or style of polemics is especially pervasive. Soviet political doctrine is declared by its proponents to be derived from Karl Marx's theory of the class struggle.[7]

Associated with this polarized struggle is a cleavage of philosophy into two irreconcilable (either-or) camps—*materialism*, the philosophy of progress, and *idealism*, the philosophy of reaction. (These labels are not to be confused with their popular meaning related to attitudes toward material and spiritual values.) Materialism is a world view that declares matter to be "primary" reality, and ideas, consciousness, and so on, to be derived from properties of matter. Idealism is said to hold ideas, mind, and so forth, as "primary reality," agencies that shape the material world.

Relevant to our discussion is not the alleged philosophical issue between materialism and idealism but rather the compulsive either-or orientation in Soviet philosophy. The orientation stems from Lenin's polemical style. Lenin, in turn, got it from Engels.

7. The class struggle, according to Marx, has been the principal driving force of social evolution, hence of history. Ever since the division of labor led to the stratification of human societies into classes, there have been struggles between the exploiters and exploited; plebeians against patricians, feudal lords against serfs, the nobility against the bourgeoisie, the bourgeoisie (capitalists) against the proletariat (industrial workers). Each struggle culminated in a social revolution, as a result of which a new class became dominant, organized the social order in accordance with its class interests, and developed its particular mode of exploitation.

Materialism [wrote Lenin] regards nature as primary and spirit as secondary. Idealism holds the contrary view. The fundamental difference between the two great camps, into which the philosophies of the various schools of idealism and materialism are divided, Engels regards as the cornerstone of philosophy, accusing those who give another interpretation to idealism and materialism, of "confusion." [8]

and later:

Fully in the spirit of Marx and in close collaboration with him, Engels in all his philosophical works briefly and clearly contrasts in *all* questions, without taking seriously . . . the innumerable endeavors to "transcend" the "one-sidedness" of materialism and idealism, or proclaiming a *new* tendency whatever "positivism," "realism" or other professional charlatanism might have been current. The struggle . . . was led by Engels *wholly* under the slogan of consistent pursuit of materialism . . . either a materialism consistent to the end, or the falsehood and confusion of idealism—that is the alternative. . . . Only people whose minds have been corrupted by reactionary official philosophers can fail to notice it.[9]

Throughout the half century of Soviet history, this theme has pervaded all philosophical discussion in the Soviet Union.[10]

Scientific concepts, filtered through popularizations, also tend to polarize. For many years arguments raged over whether certain abilities and predispositions were inherited or acquired, whether the "causes of war" are political or economic, whether mental illnesses are due to "organic" or to "functional" disorders, and so forth.

---

8. V. I. Lenin, *Materialism and Empiriocriticism* (New York: International Publishers, 1947), p. 74.
9. Ibid., p. 292.
10. In the Stalinist era, "philosophical vigilance" marked also the science policy of the Soviet Union. Periodical purges were conducted in research centers and educational institutions to eliminate sources of heretical views. Once the label of "idealism" or of some other onerous "ism" (usually traced to "idealism," the Original Sin of philosophy) was attached to a professor or an investigator, he was a marked man, and so were his close associates and students, unless they denounced their colleague or teacher with equal vehemence. The idealism heresy was found in linguistics, in statistics, in biology, and in psychology. These purges all but crippled many sectors of Soviet science and scholarship. Following Stalin's death, the craze subsided; many scientists were "rehabilitated" (some posthumously); and many centers, institutes, and university departments were reconstructed. However, the dogma of the life-and-death struggles between two irreconcilable camps of philosophy was at this writing still not renounced. The roots of the two-valued orientation, once embedded, penetrate deeply into the human psyche.

A discrimination between two conditions, situations, causes, or the like is called *dichotomy*. It is the simplest possible discrimination. Actions, commitments, decisions require a choice. The choice between only two alternatives is the simplest. Dichotomies made in language simplify our choices. Perhaps succumbing to the two-valued orientation reflects a "short circuit" in our nervous system when we are troubled by uncertainty.

A third source of delusion, according to Korzybski, is reflected in the tacit assumption that the structure of language corresponds faithfully to the structure of the world. We may avoid the identification of "rose" and "red" suggested by the assertion "The rose is red," yet we may tacitly assume that the red rose is a combination of "roseness" and "redness."

In the Middle Ages, alchemists worked on the assumption (stemming from Aristotle's philosophy) that substances are composed of an "essential" substance common to all of them *and* specific properties superimposed on that essential substance. Thus lead was supposed to be the essential substance *plus* "grayness," "dullness," "heaviness," "poor malleability," and so on. Gold was the essential substance plus "yellowness," "luster," "good malleability," and so forth. Alchemists, supported by greedy princes, sought to transform base metals, like lead or tin, into gold. They thought they could do this by replacing the properties of lead with those of gold in the "essential substance."

Belief in werewolves was a natural consequence of similar notions. Some persons were supposed to be able to take the shape of an animal, as if, in replacing one's shape, one was composed of "himself" and some shape he assumed.

The simplistic view of the world as an array of things, properties, actions, etc., in various combinations, Korzybski called *elementalism* —the error of separating in language what is not separated in nature. Heredity and environment are separate words. But heredity cannot manifest itself except in environment, and the environment molds an organism only within certain limits set by heredity. A seed will not grow without nutrients, and no environment will make an oak tree grow out of a tomato seed, nor mold a chicken embryo into a crocodile. Economics and politics are separate words. But all economic events take place in some political system, and no political system exists without an economy. There is no husband without a wife, no wife without a husband. The structure of reality consists of *relations* rather than of things or categories. It is this structure that is obscured by language in which names of things, properties, categories, and so on, play a predominant role.

Korzybski cites the theory of relativity as a dramatic break with a particularly stubborn elementalistic conception. Recall from Chapter 18 that in Newtonian physics, space and time are entirely separate, independent categories, while relativistic physics deals with *space-time*, a four-dimensional continuum in which spatial and temporal elements are inseparable. The emergence of "hybrid sciences" attests to the increasing recognition that the division of knowledge into separate compartments does not reflect the structure of the world which science purports to study. There is no sharp dividing line between physics and chemistry. Physical chemistry, a fusion of both the older disciplines, studies the physical aspect of chemical events. We now have geophysics, astrophysics, and biophysics. Organic chemistry, biochemistry, and physiology have been linked by common methods and concepts. A better understanding of how nervous systems work is revealing the emptiness of the body-mind dichotomy. The world does not fit into the pigeonholes prepared for it by our language.

In summary, Korzybski pointed out three cognitive errors induced by language habits: the false-to-fact identification, the two-valued orientation, and elementalism. Collectively these errors, he said, reflect an "Aristotelian" orientation. General semantics was offered as a discipline designed to correct the errors of the Aristotelian orientation and was called by Korzybski a non-Aristotelian system. He called it also an extensional, nonelementalistic, and infinite-valued orientation.

Korzybski sought to explain cognitive errors by the fact that we do not make full use of the uniquely human properties of our nervous systems. Instead, he said, we "copy animals." Animals, not having a symbolic language, react to stimuli as to signals, not symbols. Thus a dog, trained to make "proper" responses to verbal commands and so appearing to "understand" speech, is actually reacting with conditioned responses. The sounds of the words are simply channeled into the learned responses to commands. Our reactions to words as if they were things are basically of the same sort, in Korzybski's estimation. He even went so far as to specify the neural paths leading to the responses. He pictured the path going through the thalamus, a region of the midbrain, thought to be a mediator of rapid emotional responses.

An awareness of the world as a *symbol* rather than a signal involves, Korzybski thought, a longer path through the cortex of the brain, the seat of specifically human intellectual activity. In this way the passage of the neural impulse through the thalamus was pictured by Korzybski as a short-circuited path.[11]

Much of Korzybski's *Science and Sanity* is devoted to what he presented as a method of training the human nervous system to respond appropriately to language and to the world. The aim of the training is to impart awareness of *levels of abstraction*. Knowledge of the world comes to us through our senses. However, our senses give us only partial information about physical reality. What we perceive as an object is "in reality" a tremendously complex array of events impossible to describe or even to perceive in its completeness. But our nervous system so organizes our sensory impressions that we perceive an object as "something." This perceived object is the first level of abstraction. The name of the object is another (higher) level of abstraction.[12] Names of classes of objects, properties defining classes, generalizations, theories, and so forth, are on successively higher levels of abstraction. According to Korzybski, the "natural" order of abstraction is from the lower levels to the higher ones. He repeats Alexander Bryan Johnson's dictum on judging an assertion of language by comparing it with sensory impressions rather than projecting upon nature the relations established verbally. However, Korzybski does not take the position of extreme positivism, as does Johnson. Korzybski has a much better understanding of what constitutes scientific knowledge, especially the role of the hypothetico-deductive method (cf. Chapter 16), and particularly of mathematics.

Korzybski recognized mathematics as a language of relations rather than of things-plus-properties; hence, he believed that the cognitive power of mature sciences derives from the structure of their (mathematicized) language and from the recognition that a scientific theory is a map to be constantly checked against the territory of concrete

11. Cf. Korzybski, *Science and Sanity*, 2d ed., p. 193.
12. For some reason Korzybski put great stress on illustrating this idea by referring to a wooden gadget that he called "the structural differential." The "nonverbal" level was represented in this object by a parabolic segment (symbolizing infinite extent), the first level of abstracton by a disk, successive levels by rectangles. All of these wooden blocks were perforated. Bits of string connected holes from one level to another, some being left dangling. I have always remained in the dark about the point of this demonstration (cf. Korzybski, *Science and Sanity*, 2d ed., Chapter 25).

experience by comparing the predictions of the theory with observations. Indeed, the paradigm of an assertion in the language of, say, mathematical physics, is not "A is B." It is a set of relations expressed in the symbolism of mathematics. For example, the formula

$$F = \frac{m\,v^2}{R}$$

states that the centripetal force (F), acting on a body moving in a circle, equals the mass of the body (m) multiplied by the square of its velocity (v^2) divided by the radius of the circle (R). This assertion includes an infinite number of predictions, for example:

If the force is doubled while the mass and the velocity remain constant, the radius of the circle along which the body is moving will be reduced by one half.

If the velocity is tripled while the mass and the radius remain the same, the force will be increased nine times.

If the radius is quadrupled while the force and the mass remain the same, the velocity will be doubled.

And so on.

Note that the formula says nothing about "cause and effect," whether, for example, the force "causes" the body to move in a circle or whether the circular motion is the "cause" of the force. The formula says only how force, mass, and the elements of the circular motion (velocity and radius) are *related*. In *manipulating* portions of the world, we may find it useful to speak of causes and effects. Suppose, for instance, the body is an airplane in a circling pattern over an airport. The centripetal force is the force of the surrounding air on the control surfaces of the plane. The pilot can increase this force by changing the angle of the bank. At the same time he can keep the velocity constant. The mass of the plane, of course, also remains constant. As soon as the force on the control surfaces increases—no sooner, *but also no later*—the radius of the circle described by the plane will decrease. Here, since it is "we" (that is, the pilot) who initiate the change, the change in force appears to us the "cause" and the change in radius the "effect." We may even think that the change in force comes first and the change in radius follows. This, however, is not the case; the two changes occur simultaneously. There is nothing "in nature" that distinguishes one of these changes as the cause and the other as the effect.

The pilot can also change the mass of the plane, say, by jettisoning a load. If the velocity and the centripetal force are kept constant, the radius of the circular path will increase. In this case, we might think of the change in mass as the "cause," but it appears so to us only because the pilot has initiated this change.

If the body is a ball on a string that we twirl around our finger, we can change the radius by pulling the string in or out. In this case the change of radius will appear to us as the "cause" and the resulting change in velocity or force (depending on which is kept constant) will appear as the "effect." In reality, "cause" and "effect" are not separable. Mathematical language brings this interrelatedness to our attention and helps us to avoid the error of elementalism—projecting on nature the "cause-effect" relations that we abstract from crude experience and verbal descriptions of it.

Can ordinary language acquire some of the structural features of the language of the exact sciences? Should we communicate in mathematical formulas rather than in English or Hindi or Swahili? Certainly a program of language reform of this sort would be as quixotic as those described by Swift (cf. p. 41). Korzybski did not, of course, recommend discarding "vernacular" language in favor of strict scientific terminology. As a matter of fact, contrary to a rather widespread misunderstanding, Korzybski did not recommend any sort of language reform. He recommended rather an awareness of abstraction levels that are far from clear in ordinary language. To see what this means, let us return to the formula on page 386.

The left side of the equation stands for force. Force is defined in physics as mass times acceleration. In cgs. units, this is symbolized as

$$\frac{(\text{grams}) \ (\text{centimeters})}{(\text{seconds})^2}.$$

Now look at the right side of the equation $F = \dfrac{m \, v^2}{R}$. The expression denotes grams (mass) times velocity squared, that is (centimeters)^2, divided by (seconds)^2, the whole divided by distance (centimeters). The result of these symbolic operations is precisely the expression shown above.

If the units of the two sides of the equation were not the same, the physicist would know that the formula could not be right. In other words, the *grammar* of mathematical physics has a built-in checking procedure which forewarns the theoretician against "confusing levels of abstraction," as Korzybski would say. Ordinary language has no such built-in safeguards. Recall the extended ranges of denotation that words acquire through their *metaphorical* meanings. We say, "The boy is nibbling an apple." Our politicians say, "The Communists are nibbling at the edges of the Free World."

Clearly, the levels of abstraction of the two meanings of "nibbling" are widely disparate. But there is no way of discovering this disparity through analysis of the language itself (as there is by way of analyzing the expressions of exact science). We can discover this disparity only by constantly checking the meanings of words against the experiences, if any, to which they are supposed to refer.

Next, compare the meanings of the repeated words in the following pairs of sentences.

1a. John hates Peter.	**1b.** John hates hatred.
2a. We should tolerate dissent.	**2b.** We should tolerate intolerance.
3a. I am afraid of tarantulas.	**3b.** I am afraid that when confronted with a tarantula, I shall be afraid.
4a. I am telling a falsehood.	**4b.** I was telling a falsehood.

Let us examine 4a and 4b first. Assertion 4a is our old acquaintance, the self-referring proposition. We have seen (cf. p. 41) that neither the truth nor the falsehood of some such assertions can be established without inducing contradictions. On the other hand, assertion 4b refers not to itself but to another assertion made previously. Hence 4b can very well be true, or it could be false, depending on whether a previous assertion made by the speaker was false or true. Here the different levels of abstraction of the phrase "telling a falsehood" are apparent, since 4b is *explicitly* an assertion about an assertion. In 4a, on the other hand, the levels are mixed. This assertion is only implicitly an assertion about an assertion (namely about itself). It constitutes an antinomy.

Difference of levels of assertions is easily discerned in a purely logical context, but not always in a psychological context. Fear of tarantulas and fear of fear are two quite different kinds of fear. One can take specific precautions against being bitten by a tarantula. Precautions against the *feeling* of fear are not nearly so clearly indicated. In fact, precautions of this sort are likely to aggravate the condition.

This is well known to speech therapists. Stutterers who become self-conscious about their stuttering often undergo severe psychological strains trying to avoid stuttering. The more they try, the worse their speech defect becomes.

Next, "tolerance of intolerance" means something quite different from tolerance of dissent. A society may well enforce a tolerance of dissent by invoking sanctions against intolerance of dissent. "Tolerance of intolerance," on the other hand, involves an ambiguity. Is a society which tolerates intolerance tolerant or intolerant?

Finally, hatred$_2$ of hatred$_1$ is something quite different from hatred$_1$ of Peter. It may *become* hatred$_1$ of Peter who exhibits hatred. If so, he who hates Peter because he hates Peter's hatred is confusing levels of abstraction. Korzybski's third postulate, "The map is self-reflexive," points out the danger.

Korzybski insisted that general semantics is an empirical science, concerned not with logic but with semantic reactions, the functioning of the human nervous system. Since Korzybski did not support his conclusions with the sort of evidence demanded in the empirical sciences (like results of controlled experiments), the claim can be questioned. General semantics, as conceived by Korzybski, would be more accurately described as a therapeutic technique, especially in view of the way Korzybski related semantic reactions with degrees of sanity and "unsanity." Korzybski sought to impart to his students the extensional orientation, a constant awareness of abstraction levels and of the discrepancies between the structure of ordinary language and the structure of reality. To achieve this end, he recommended the use of so-called extensional devices.

When we say "dog," Korzybski taught, we should mentally affix indexes on the word: dog$_1$, dog$_2$, and so on, in order to maintain an awareness that "dog" is an abstraction and that the *extensional* meaning of the word refers to individual, distinct dogs. Failure to sustain this awareness is what induces prejudice against bus drivers (or stockbrokers or red-headed people) after an unfortunate encounter with bus driver$_1$ (or stockbroker$_1$ or red-headed person$_1$).

Further, dog$_{1(Monday)}$ is not the same dog as dog$_{1(Sunday)}$. Failure to realize that dogs (and persons and governments of countries) undergo constant change may induce rigid attitudes toward a particular dog (or person or government of a country) and so make us unreceptive to possibly quite different circumstances involving the same dog (or person or country) at another time. In fact, dog$_1$ is itself an abstraction of the nonverbal reality ("process" dog) which our senses organize into the impression of the "entity" dog$_1$.

When we speak of abstractions not easily related to concrete experiences, we should mentally put the words that designate them in quotation marks, that is, "virtue," "love," "hatred," "duty," "democracy," and so forth.

When, to explain our meaning, we resort to definitions, we should try to *descend* rather than *ascend* the ladder of abstractions. For example, from "dog" we come down the ladder when we think of a collie, further down when we think of Fido; we go up the ladder when we think of "animal," still higher when we think of "living thing." Extensional definitions, according to Korzybski, are to be preferred to intensional ones. Thus, in explaining what we mean by "love," we should mention situations that exemplify it rather than try to define "love" in terms of even higher order abstractions, such as "an attitude composed of ardent affection, empathetic understanding, . . . " and so on. When we try to explain what we mean by "democracy," we should mention examples of actual cultures or societies that we would designate as democratic, or, if such do not exist, we should at least spell out more or less concretely the specific political and social arrangements that in our opinion constitute democracy. Formal textbook definitions such as "Democracy is a form of government in which the people rule" are no more informative than the word "democracy" itself because "people" and "rule" in these contexts are as high on the abstraction level as "democracy." The idea of explicating meaning is to bring the word defined closer to the hearer's experience. Generally this is accomplished by relating the word to words on lower levels of abstraction.[13]

In using extensional definitions, we should mentally fix "etc." to our descriptions in order to reinforce the awareness that no description can exhaust *completely* the characteristics of the referent.

To counteract elementalism, we should mentally connect words by hyphens. The physicist still speaks of space *and* time. In situations where Newtonian physics is an adequate map, this dichotomy is harmless. It is nevertheless "false-to-fact." Space-time is a more accurate designation of the framework in which physical events occur.

13. The *Peanuts* comic book, *Happiness Is a Warm Puppy*, is an exercise in extensional definitions.

The foremost military thinker of the nineteenth century, Karl von Clausewitz, wrote that the military and the political goals of a modern state are inseparable. The social and ethical implications of this doctrine may have been disastrous, but at the time Clausewitz wrote, the definition of war as "the continuation of policy by other means" was an accurate one. In some circles this conception has persisted to our day, so that it makes sense to speak of diplo-military strategies that guide the foreign policies of major powers.

Finally, Korzybski never tired of repeating his warning against the dangers lurking in the promiscuous use of the "is of identity," which, as already explained, was in his estimation the root of all errors resulting from our failure to use symbolic language as it ought to be used—as a means of survival and an instrument of the time-binding process.

The effectiveness of general semantics as a psychotherapeutic technique is as difficult to evaluate as the effectiveness of any other psychotherapeutic technique. Aside from recognizing some clear cases of mental illness, people studying mental health are still very much in the dark concerning criteria by means of which the effectiveness of therapy can be evaluated. It has been said that general semantics therapy can possibly be of value at most in the treatment of neuroses, as distinct from psychoses. However, criteria of neuroses are vague and depend strongly on the subjective feelings of the patient. Moreover, "neurotics" who seek help are not a representative sample of "neurotics" (the quotes are to remind us of the vagueness of this category); they are a self-selected sample, and so are the ones most likely to cooperate in an attempt to restore them to a more comfortable state of mind. Frequently, the neurotic feels better after following any course of therapy that seems promising to him. Feeling better, he may also function better in relation to his work and to other people. Because of the strong subjective component of therapy of this sort, it is next to impossible to compare the effectiveness of different therapies. Some people are helped (or think they are helped or say they are helped) by psychoanalysis, some by group therapy, some by religion, some by ministrations of outright cranks and charlatans, some by general semantics. To the extent that they function better, not only in their own estimation but also in the estimation of others, any "method" that achieves this effect has therapeutic value. However, there is no justification on that account for attributing therapeutic value to the *method*. The improvement, if any, is to be attributed to a reorganization of evaluations or of behavior patterns by the patient who believes in the method. From the practical viewpoint of helping people by alleviating their misery, it makes little difference to what the success of the therapy it attributed. However, interpreting the "success" of the method as a corroboration of the underlying "theory" not only fails to help but actually hinders the improvement of our understanding of how our nervous systems work, of why we behave as we do, and of the difficulties we face in coming to terms with reality.

The scientific attitude that holds the truth of an assertion to be contained in the verifiable predictions implied by it can be easily perverted into the attitude of vulgar pragmatism: truth is "what works." A case in point is "dianetics," a variant of quack psychotherapy that swept the United States in the early 1950s. The founder of this cult, one L. Ron Hubbard, earlier known as a science fiction writer, succeeded in building a vast "psychotherapy" business by exploiting the belief in "science." The "theory" expounded in his best seller *Dianetics* is a mélange of pseudoscientific mumbo jumbo, references to "experiments" in nonexistent laboratories, formulas that are immediately recognized as utterly meaningless by anyone with a minimal literacy in mathematics, and glowing accounts of miracles achieved by a quick, easy, do-it-yourself, foolproof method of "clearing engrams"—those snags that clutter up the brain and prevent it from functioning like a "perfect computer."

What was remarkable about the dianetics affair was not the gullibility of a large sector of the public (this is commonplace) but the number of highly educated persons who sprang to the defense of Hubbard's "method" on the grounds that "it worked." The fact that water dowsing and rainmaking dances also "work," without in the least deserving serious consideration as rational procedures, somehow makes no difference to people with a will to believe.

And so the therapeutic value of general semantics must for the time being remain a matter of conjecture. Whatever else it is, it provides no justification for Korzybski's conjecture about the workings of the human nervous system, particularly on the physiological level. Korzybski, a voracious reader, was impressed by the rapid advances stimulated in psychology by Pavlov's discovery of the conditioned response and in histology by developments in colloid chemistry. He must have been particularly impressed by the latter because he made almost compulsively repeated allusions to "events on the colloidal level," referring presumably to changes in the structure of nerve cells associated with the acquisition of proper or improper semantic reactions. Just what these changes are and how they are associated with semantic reactions are not indicated in any of Korzybski's writings. Allusions of this sort are evidence of "scientism"—the use of technical terms to create an impression of a scientific formulation of a theory. In view of Korzybski's fundamental thesis, his misuse of scientific terminology is ironic, and many scholars and scientists were quick to dismiss Korzybski as a dilettante, at times a crank. This impression was reinforced by Korzybski himself. On occasions he lectured to scientists in the manner of a patronizing schoolmaster on subjects to which they had devoted many years of hard, careful work and of which he had only a smattering of knowledge.

On the whole, the impact of Korzybski's ideas on the scientific community was weak or negative. However, the seeds of his thought did fall on fertile soil, particularly in the United States, and they sprouted. We shall examine the resulting growth in the next chapter.

APPLICATIONS

I. You may think that only the naïve still attribute magical power to words. But stop for a moment to consider these questions:

1) Does "word magic" operate in the "rhetoric of politics"? For example, what explanation is there for the force of such expressions as "Power to the people" or "America—love it or leave it"?
2) Are people propelled into buying things by an almost mysterious "power of the phrase"? What kind of advertising "magic" do you recall that has been effective? Is Madison Avenue's "magic" black magic or white magic?
3) Does poetry have magical dimensions in its use of language?
4) Look up the original meaning of the word "glamour" in the dictionary. Are you surprised? Is it still true that people who have the power to move others through words recall the ancient wizard who "made things happen" with his occult incantations?
5) What is the best defense against the ministrations of someone who wants to persuade you to buy something, do something, say something, and so on, that you did not think of yourself?

6) Write a 500-word paper on "The Science of Word Magic." If you can, choose an area or a subject in which there is a specific "word magic" (i.e., military communiques, psychology, sociology).

II. The poet tries to make his reader feel the presence or be in the presence of the thing he describes. In other words, if you actually hear the beat of the waves on the shore, Homer has succeeded; or if you see the hare limping through the snow, Keats has succeeded—or so we say. Is this a form of "false-to-fact" conditioning? How does poetry differ from publicity? Recall that Plato would bar poets from the ideal Republic because their powers are persuasive and irrational—that is, they tell lies. Would you agree with Plato?

III.   Is it always unwise to react to the word as though it were the thing? For example, is it generally a good idea to leave a theater when someone shouts "Fire!"?

IV.   Read Robert Lindner's "The Jet-Propelled Couch" in *The Fifty-Minute Hour*. Does Lindner's experience with the physicist bear out Korzybski's theory of sanity? Note that the definition puts emphasis on the correspondence of *structures*.

V.   What determines how we set up our categories (that is, personally and collectively)? Why is a person who is half-black more likely to be regarded as half-black than half-white?

Sometimes an act of categorizing is also the act of euphemizing. For instance, during the student unrest at the City College of New York, students "liberated" the cafeteria by taking food without paying for it. This act could also be categorized by other people as "stealing." How it is categorized may determine how we feel about it. Can you cite similar examples from your own experience?

VI.   S. I. Hayakawa told a *Time* reporter (May 28, 1973, p. 55), "To some of you, I am a racist pig. To others, I am the savior of the university." How would you classify him? A research paper might help you to answer the question.

22/semantics for everyman

The principal impact of Korzybski's general semantics has been on education. The curricula of many high schools and colleges include courses in general semantics. Another entry was via adult education programs, such as informal evening classes offered by many educational institutions and "seminars" organized by various groups associated with the "general semantics movement." Korzybski himself, from the last years of the 1930s to his death in 1950, was involved principally in teaching at the Institute of General Semantics founded by him and supported by interested people (established first in Chicago, later at Lakeville, Connecticut). Students came to the Institute to take "seminars," that is, to listen to several hours of lectures by Korzybski and to participate in "workshops" conducted by his assistants.

Korzybski taught students rather than a "subject." In fact, the principles of general semantics, or, so to speak, the foundations of the "non-Aristotelian system," like those of Christianity, could be stated in a few sentences. Unlike a science that has an elaborate theoretical superstructure on its postulational base, general semantics had no such superstructure, unless one counts as a theoretical contribution Korzybski's conjectures about neural events "on the colloidal level" associated with so-called "semantic reactions." In short, general semantics, as presented by Korzybski, was anything but an organized body of knowledge that could be taught systematically along a logical line of developing ideas, as one would teach mathematics or physics or genetics or, for that matter, a foreign language. "Knowledge" of general semantics, as Korzybski himself insisted, is not of the sort that one demonstrates by answering examination questions or by performing a well-designed experiment or by building a bridge or by translating a book. According to Korzybski and his assistants at the Institute of General Semantics, general semantics had to be "internalized" rather than understood "intellectually"—on the verbal level, that is. In this respect, general semantics resembled Zen Buddhism rather than, say, symbolic logic or mathematical physics, in spite of the fact that Korzybski paid glowing homage to the language of the exact sciences as the prototype of a language of sanity.

Understandably, the number of people who came into direct contact with Korzybski during the twelve years of his leadership at the Institute was rather limited. Some of these people, however, turned out to be most effective and enthusiastic teachers. They became the "apostles" of general semantics, and through them it received rather wide attention, especially in the United States. Indeed, widespread popular interest in *semantics* is largely the result of the work of the popularizers of Korzybski's ideas.

The first widely read book on "semantics" (as the outlook recommended by A. B. Johnson and Korzybski came to be known) was *The Tyranny of Words* by Stuart Chase, published in 1938 by Harcourt, Brace and Company. Three years later, the same house published S. I. Hayakawa's *Language in Action*, which enjoyed an even greater success. It was mainly through these two books that "semantics" became a household and newspaper word in the United States.

The 1930s saw the rise of militant totalitarianism. Mussolini, the dictator of Italy, set out to restore the Roman Empire by conquering Ethiopia. This sortie was soon dwarfed by Hitler, who, having convinced the Germans that they were a master race destined to rule the world, took Austria and announced a blueprint for conquest that included all of Eastern Europe and European Russia. A civil war was raging in Spain, where an insurgent general, Franco, equipped by Hitler and Mussolini, was destroying the republic established after the collapse of monarchy. Japan was carving out an empire in East Asia, turning Manchuria into a puppet state and invading China proper.

The forces that instigated these waves of violent aggression were doubtless complex, but one feature was strikingly in evidence—the adroit use of language by the totalitarian leaders. Hitler and Mussolini revived the art of oratorical exhortation. In hours-long harangues, punctuated by war whoops from their audiences, they whipped their listeners into a frenzy. The people were told that they were the noblest, the bravest, and the most civilized men that ever walked the earth and that cunning and cowardly enemies had robbed them of their greatness. The dictators shouted that greatness could be restored only by force of arms; that, in war, victory goes to the bold, the ruthless, and the disciplined; that these manly virtues were subverted by spineless pacificism and decadent democracy. Hitler was especially explicit on this point. He told the Germans that the debilitating viruses of pacifism and democracy were deliberately injected into the German people by their enemies, the Jews, a corrupt and evil race, who also sapped the vitality of the German "race" by miscegenation. Hitler called upon the German people to eliminate the parasitic Jew in their midst and to prepare for deeds of glory. Germans, he said, need living space; they should secure it by the sword; the rich soil of the East was theirs for the taking; the subhuman Slavs were to be either exterminated or reduced to serfs working for the German masters. Above all, the humiliation imposed on Germany by the Treaty of Versailles was to be wiped out. The Nazis declared that the German armies had never been defeated in World War I, rather Germany had been stabbed in the back by Jews and traitors, and now the day of vengeance was approaching.

In the United States, the general public was becoming slowly aware of what was happening in Germany and in other totalitarian states and of the dangers portended by those events to the rest of the world. The United States was beset by its own severe problems. The debilitating economic depression that followed the stock market crash of 1929 dragged on. Rising unemployment depressed the buying power of wage earners. Mounting inventories led to shutdowns and curtailment of production and so to even greater unemployment. Franklin D. Roosevelt's "New Deal" administration attempted to break the vicious cycle by introducing a measure of control into the economic life of the nation. Some social legislation was enacted, providing for unemployment insurance and old-age pensions. Federal funds were assigned to public works projects. Laws were passed to protect workers seeking to organize labor unions from intimidation by employers. These measures, although largely supported by the bulk of the population, particularly by labor, met with considerable resistance, especially in business circles. Government interference in business was declared to be a gross violation of the free-enterprise principles on which the American republic was founded. The source of American greatness, it was argued, derived from "rugged individualism," the virtue of the pioneer who eschewed anything that made him dependent on others, particularly on outside authority. Government regulation of business, argued the opponents of New Deal policies, was undermining the self-reliance of Americans and sapping the nation's strength.

There is a certain similarity between the way Hitler diagnosed Germany's plight and the way conservatives in the United States characterized America's difficulties. Both laid great stress on subversion of national virtues by alien ideas. Hitler pointed to un-German "democracy"; the champions of free enterprise pointed to un-American "socialism," with which they identified the New Deal policies. Of course, the images of "national virtue" invoked were quite different. The ideal German in the Nazi conception was the embodiment of a "national will," emanating from the *Führer*. The individual was a link in a rigid chain of command, expected to render instantaneous and unquestioning obedience to his immediate superior and to exact the same obedience from his subordinates. The prototype of the nation in the Nazi conception was an army. The ideal American, on the other hand, was, in the conservative conception, a man who played the game to win. Certain rules of the game were recognized as necessary, most significantly the rules that guaranteed private property against seizure by force or government decree. Within these rules, however, the player (a person or a firm) was entitled to pursue "success." In this view, the prototype of a democracy was a society that offered everyone an equal opportunity to compete.

Despite his apparent violation of traditional American values by the various measures undertaken to regulate the economy, Roosevelt enjoyed wide popular support, primarily from people hard hit by the Depression. He consolidated this support by frequent nation-wide radio talks (the "fireside chats") in which he explained and justified his policies in simple, straightforward language. Although not an orator in the traditional sense, Roosevelt was an exceptionally effective speaker. He was the first President to utilize the radio on a large scale, a practice which gave him the opportunity to test the persuasive power of the spoken word addressed simultaneously to tens of millions. The tremendous potentiality of instantaneous mass communication was quickly recognized by all who, for one reason or another, wanted direct access to a large public: advertisers, preachers, politicians, and demagogues. Access to the airwaves offered a means of manipulating attitudes and behavior far more effectively than through the press because of the more direct emotional impact of the spoken word.

These developments turned the attention of thoughtful people to the vital role of language in large-scale human affairs, particularly to the possibility of inducing highly predictable and exploitable patterns of behavior in large masses of people. The dictators showed that supposedly rational and well-informed people could be driven to mass insanity, that they could be made to believe anything by an adroit use of slogans that somehow activated deep-seated hatreds, fears, and desires.

In the United States, dogged resistance to what seemed reasonable and practical measures undertaken to relieve human misery appeared to be based on rigid beliefs in the inviolability of certain verbally reiterated principles that upon careful examination bore little relation to any concrete experience. Korzybski's insistence on the close correspondence between language habits and a position on the sanity spectrum came exactly at a time when these ideas could elicit wide interest and acceptance.

Stuart Chase was a prominent figure in the New Deal Administration. *The Tyranny of Words*, written in simple, straightforward language, was conceived as "antipropaganda." It offered the "intelligent reader" a means of orientating himself in the blizzard of words descending on him, a barrage calculated to get him to do what someone else wanted him to do: to buy this or that product, to vote for this or that candidate, to give his loyalty to this or that cause, to get him to want, to fear, or to hate.

Communication that aims to change an orientation or an attitude must locate a sympathetic response in the listener or reader. To be accepted, even to be attended to, the communication must meet some felt need of the audience. In the 1930s, there was a widespread need to resist the barrage of propaganda. The flowering of demagogy stimulated a search for defenses against it, a search for means to escape from the tyranny of words.

Chase's book struck an immediately responsive chord in the American public because it attacked the authority of abstractions. It was a debunking job in a long-established American tradition: it challenged clichés, dogmas, and slogans, not by arguing that they were false, but by insisting that they were meaningless. It ridiculed the "ghostly concepts" of the contemporary economic scene with its "parade of demons": money, property, profit, production, decentralization, public ownership—all words around which politicians rallied their cohorts. The book applied the acid test of "concrete reference" to all these words, and all were found wanting. The demolition job proved to be delightfully easy. "Show me!" Chase says in effect. He refuses to accept any definition unless it relates to things or events directly perceived by the senses. He writes, for example:

Consider the term "inflation." When the verbal fire got too warm, the Washington administration in self-defense adopted the word "reflation." I have yet to find any general agreement upon what "inflation," let alone "reflation" means. A man has just written a book about seven kinds of inflation. Definitions are sometimes attempted, but references are hard to come by. Does one mean credit, currency, stock-market or land-value inflation? Some of my friends go about shaking their heads, observing that inflation is already here. Others say it is inevitably coming. Others that it may come. Others that it will not come at all. Still others hold that a headlong "deflation" is just around the corner. Think of it calmly; thousands of so-called intelligent people arguing for millions of hours, filling acres of newspaper columns, and heaven knows how many magazine and book pages, with reflections on a term that no single one of them understands.[1]

The law fares no better:

Semantically considered, "the law" is a parade of abstractions, normally without referents. As in the case of classical economic theory, it can be used and is used to make citizens more uncomfortable than they need be. Legal machinery for settling disputes and enacting statutes, on the other hand, is vitally necessary in civilized communities. Those judges, juries, arbitrators, who make the decisions are human beings, limited by their own experience, by the Thingumbobs they have met and the "principles" they have digested. If they are very old and full of principles derived from an earlier cultural era, the decisions they hand down may be

1. Stuart Chase, *The Tyranny of Words* (New York: Harcourt, Brace, 1938), p. 291.

inapplicable to the current situation, and sometimes really disastrous. Certain authorities believe that the decision of Mr. Justice Taney in the Dred Scott case was a major reason for the Civil War. Many decisions of the Supreme Court in the past two generations have checked and bedeviled the doing of things which ultimately had to be done. The income-tax law, the minimum wage law, were thrown out because judges personally did not like these ideas, but responsibility was shifted to the due-process clause of the Constitution. Later it was found that the process was not violated, and both pieces of legislation were admitted. By concentrating on the sublimities of due process, we lose sight of the judges. I suggest that we keep looking steadily at the man on the bench, a metaphorical pop bottle in either hand. If he is unable to surmount his stock of 1880 Thingumbobs, we had best begin looking about for an arbitrator who can do so.[2]

Mathematics does not escape:

Certain Greek philosophers took this useful tool and made a dull fetish out of it. They lifted it from the market place and put it in the cloister. They believed bedrock had been reached when they had isolated a point, a line, an angle—something changeless, timeless, eternal. From these absolutes, truth could be reared by reason. The intellectuals of Athens and Alexandria rarely examined the sort of things about which these words can be intelligently used. They dealt with pure theory, not with a living world. In Euclid the analysis of flatness reached its climax, so perfect and often so unreal that it has been a major educational subject ever since. No wonder so many schoolboys are bored by geometry. . . .[3]

As remarked earlier, the enormous popular success of *The Tyranny of Words* indicates that it met a deeply felt need in many people: for a point of anchorage in resisting propaganda, for a way to escape the sense of helplessness when confronted with symbol manipulators. In the United States, however, resentment against the tyranny of words has been traditionally coupled with a deep-seated anti-intellectualism; practical men of action tend to reject speculation, "theory," abstract thought, and involved reasoning.

Inspired, like *The Tyranny of Words*, by Korzybski's ideas, S. I. Hayakawa's *Language in Action* was also conceived as "antipropa-

2. Ibid., p. 326.
3. Ibid., p. 144.

ganda" rooted in pragmatism. But it is considerably more. Hayakawa does not confine his analysis of language to the debunking of "abstractions," as does Chase. *Language in Action* is a primer on the *use* of language as well as a defense against it, and has in consequence become a vastly popular textbook of English.

Hayakawa teaches English as a tool to be used rather than as a system of rules to be learned. He agrees with Korzybski that language is man's principal instrument of survival, and adds that language performs this function by enabling men to cooperate, to make use of each other's nervous systems, as it were.

When someone shouts at you, "Look out!" and you jump in time to avoid being hit by an automobile, you owe your escape from injury to the fundamental cooperative act by which most of the higher animals survive, namely by communication by means of noises. You did not see the car coming: nevertheless, someone did, and he made certain *noises to communicate* his alarm to you.[4]

Hayakawa goes on to examine the ways in which this "instrument of survival" performs its function. Unlike *The Tyranny of Words*, *Language in Action* is not just an angry tirade against "abstractions." For Hayakawa, all aspects of language have their uses. The value of his book as a textbook of English lies in the diversity of its explorations and in the way the content of a school subject ("English") is always linked to situations familiar and, presumably, important to the students.

To establish these links, Hayakawa went beyond the traditional subject matter of English courses, such as grammar, syntax, rhetoric, and so on. If language is to be shown in action, matters discussed in psychology, sociology, and anthropology must be touched upon. Example:

The white Southerner's apparently illogical attitude toward Negroes can . . . be accounted for on symbolic grounds. People from outside the South often find it difficult to understand how many white Southerners accept close physical contact with Negro servants and yet become extremely upset at the idea of sitting beside Negroes in restaurants or buses.

4. This and the following quotations are from a later expanded edition. S. I. Hayakawa, *Language in Thought and Action*, 2d ed. (London: George Allen and Unwin, Ltd.) p. 10.

The attitude of the Southerner rests on the fact that the ministrations of a Negro servant—even personal care, such as nursing—have the symbolic implication of social inequality; while admission of Negroes to buses, restaurants, and nonsegregated schools has the symbolic implication of social equality.[5]

By repeatedly pointing out the role of symbols in human affairs, Hayakawa calls attention to something that young people may have known for a long time without realizing that they have known it. Frequently this "revelation" is the first step toward arousing a lively interest in a subject.

In the traditional approach to "composition," distinctions are made among "exposition," "argument," "narrative," and so on. Hayakawa brings this analysis down to the level of the utterance and bases it on semantic instead of formal criteria. A sentence may be a report, an inference, or a judgment. A report refers the utterance to events that have been actually observed. An inference refers it to something that has been inferred by the speaker but can in principle be checked by observations. Judgments are assertions of value; they tell only of the speaker's (or writer's) attitudes and opinions: in general, they express his feelings. In order to distinguish among the three kinds of utterances, one must ask what procedures, if any, can be undertaken to verify what is being said. If events or their immediate consequences actually mentioned in the utterance are directly observable (by the eyes or an extension of the senses), we are dealing with a report. If events are involved which are not observed by the speaker or are altogether unobservable, we are dealing with an inference. If the only relevant evidence is that which relates to the speaker's attitudes, we are dealing with a judgment.

Thus "She goes to church only in order to show off her clothes" is an inference with overtones of judgment. "And the days of Adam after he had begotten Seth were eight hundred years" is a report. (*N.B.* A report need not be true.) "Cary Grant has lots of personality" is a judgment, since the utterance says almost nothing except that the speaker is impressed by Cary Grant.

Of special significance are *slanted* reports, where the events related are observable but selected with a view of inducing a certain attitude. Example:

5. Ibid., p. 26.

Commuter—one who spends his life
In riding to and from his wife;
A man who shaves and takes a train
And then rides back to shave again.

Hayakawa is a firm believer in learning by doing, and he is able to add zest to the traditionally tedious assignments in "English Composition." After warning of the dangers of making or accepting unwarranted inferences, he invites his students to try their hand at them. Sample exercise:

"Harry Thompson visited Russia in 1958." "Rex Davis is a millionaire." "Betty Armstrong does not believe in God." "Dr. Baxter is in disagreement with the policies of the American Medical Association." Accepting these statements as true, write several hundred words of unfounded inferences, and inferences upon inferences about these people. Of course, you don't know who they are, but don't let that stop you. Just go ahead and make inferences.

English can be fun.[6]

Hayakawa not only emphasizes the importance of distinguishing between levels of abstraction, but he also applies the idea to writing effectively. A common failure of inexperienced or dull writers is that they stay on the same level of specificity or generality (the same level of abstraction). A child's first composition is often an inventory: "We went on a picnic. There were many good things to eat. Harry and I played catch. It started to rain." And so on.

And here is an example of a man who stays on the same level of vague generality.

PRESIDENT EISENHOWER: Let me tell you this: we are concerned about it. I mean we want to see it just as strong as you want to see it. I'd like to point out that supporting this kind of thing is the necessity for broadening our contact in the world. . . . I believe we've got to have better exchange of ideas, of the products and conclusions of scientific people; we have got to have more in books; but above all the people.[7]

6. Ibid., p. 53.
7. From a television discussion, "Issues Confronting the West," 1 September 1959.

Effective communication depends on using different levels of abstraction appropriately: general statements are indispensable to drive a point home and to organize ideas; getting down to cases is indispensable for indicating the range of denotation of an assertion, for supporting arguments, for specifying the evidence from which inferences have been made.

In teaching the "extensional orientation" in the context of the language arts, Hayakawa discloses the source of the persuasive power of great literature. Poetry induces feelings by evoking specific, vivid images. Effective characterization in fiction derives not from the author's commenting on the personal qualities of the characters but by his having them say and do things from which their springs of motivation become apparent to the reader. In drama, for example, the author does not even have the opportunity to comment on what is going on. The message must emerge entirely from the behavior of the characters involved in the action. Thus, an extensional orientation, an ear for spoken language, a sympathetic perceptiveness of a large variety of modes of feeling and thinking, each is indispensable for communicating through literature—and equally indispensable to the appreciation of literature.

Language hygiene is for Hayakawa not simply a mistrust of abstractions but an awareness of abstraction levels and, above all, the use of appropriate language for appropriate purposes on appropriate occasions. Thus, he is able to give a vivid description of the language of science, of artistic expression, of social cohesion, and of social control. His orientation is pragmatic, like that of Chase, but also functional. Implicit in his outlook is a view, shared by many sociologists and anthropologists, that most, if not all social institutions have some positive value. The view is characteristic of a school of thought called functionalism.

Instead of teaching what is "proper" and "improper" English, Hayakawa points out differences of connotation inherent in saying the same thing in different words. Example: "I have the honor to inform Your Excellency. . . ."; "This is to advise you. . . ."; "I should like to tell you, sir. . ."; "I am telling you, Mister. . . ."; "Cheez, boss, git a load of dis. . . ." [8]

8. Ibid., pp. 85–86.

Other comparative examples:

Finest quality filet mignon.	—First-class piece of dead cow.
Cubs trounce Giants 5–3.	—Score: Clubs 5, Giants 3.
Urban Redevelopment Bill steamrollered through Senate.	—Senate passes Urban Redevelopment Bill over strong opposition.
She has her husband under her thumb.	—She takes a deep interest in her husband's affairs.
The governor appeared to be gravely concerned and said that a statement should be issued in a few days after careful examination of the facts.	—The governor was on the spot.[9]

These are, of course, further adaptations of the principle exemplified in Bertrand Russell's game (cf. p. 129). In the broadened context, semantic analysis of alternative expressions leads to an appreciation of social situations and social attitudes as determinants of verbal expression.

In this way the entire range of usage from scientific exposition to advertising copy, from poetry to merchandise catalogues, comes under the scrutiny of semantic analysis. The study of the native tongue comes alive and engages the student by constantly inviting him to find connections between symbols and experiences.

Language in Action carries a social message, as every book on language rooted in experience must. Substantially, the message is: societies function by virtue of the cooperation among their members. Breakdowns of communication or of cooperation are instances of social pathology. Positive social and political action consists of improving communication and of enlarging the areas of cooperative endeavor within a society. Language hygiene is a most important precondition of effective communication, hence of cooperation, hence of proper functioning of society.

Hygienic language habits are not inculcated by a list of do's and don'ts, but by imparting an understanding of how language functions. Above all, it is necessary to encourage an extensional orientation in people, as Korzybski kept insisting. The job of the language teacher, therefore, is to induce awareness of the experiences that underlie

9. Ibid.

language and to further habits of comparing verbal maps with non-verbal territories.

If I have stated Hayakawa's position fairly, you may find it difficult to disagree with its basic tenets. Nevertheless, I intend to challenge the fundamental assumption of pragmatism which Hayakawa espouses so eloquently. These assumptions and their consequences will be examined in the next chapter.

In 1943, Hayakawa founded a magazine, *ETC.: A Review of General Semantics*. ("Etc.," recall, is one of the "extensional devices" recommended by Korzybski to remind us that language cannot exhaustively describe any situation.) The first issue of *ETC.* reprinted a poem by e. e. cummings in which a soldier recalls his sweetheart's corporeal charms:

> *... meanwhile my*
>
> *self etcetera lay quietly*
> *in the deep mud et*
>
> *cetera*
> *(dreaming,*
> *et*
> *   cetera, of*
> *Your smile*
> *eyes knees and of your Etcetera)* [10]

The magazine became the organ of the International Society for General Semantics, or "the semantics movement" as it is sometimes called. The membership includes people who are interested in language for many different reasons: teachers impressed with the importance of language analysis in pedagogy; professional and business men concerned with problems of communication; people active in community organizations, and so on. The society has also attracted those who look to language awareness as a means of coming to grips with their personal problems and as a way of achieving mental health. The proselytizing efforts of these people, typically accompanied by promiscuous use of Korzybskian terminology, have created the impression that the "semantics movement" is a cult. In view of the life styles

---

10. e. e. cummings, "Etcetera," from *Collected Poems of e. e. cummings*, in *ETC.: A Review of General Semantics* 1 (1 August 1943): 24.

and activities of some "Korzybski-ites," the impression may be justified. Nevertheless, the salutary effects of the "movement" should not
be discounted. It brought to millions an awareness of the crucial role
of language habits in personal and social relations.

Other writers influenced by Korzybski include Wendell Johnson
(1906–65), Irving J. Lee (1909–55), and J. Samuel Bois (1892–).
Wendell Johnson was a clinical psychologist and speech therapist. In
his book *People in Quandaries* (1946), he offered a perceptive analysis of symbolic factors in the etiology of neuroses. A stutterer himself who learned to control the affliction, he also undertook an
analysis of stuttering in the light of Korzybski's principle of self-
reflexiveness. Irving J. Lee was a teacher of speech. His book *Language Habits in Human Affairs* stresses the sources of communication
failure. *How to Talk with People* (note *with*, not *to*) is a primer on
communication as a process of personal interaction. Bois's book
Explorations of Awareness brings the principles of general semantics
to bear on problems of human relations in management and organization.

In short, Korzybski's disciples must be credited with bringing
language philosophy out of its shell and to the people. This was not
always done well, and sometimes it encouraged serious misconceptions; but such are inevitable by-products of the democratization of
knowledge.

APPLICATIONS

I. Do you agree with the view of the "functionalists" who maintain
that most, if not all, social institutions are of some positive value? What
"positive value" would you attribute to the following social institutions?

1) slavery
2) the caste system
3) war
4) dating
5) voting
6) prostitution
7) the Mafia
8) the electoral college

II. The increased awareness of language habits in personal and social relations probably gave rise to such organizations as Esalen and such activities as "group sensitivity training." Can "awareness of awareness" sometimes be overzealous? Comment on the following story that appeared in the *Los Angeles Times* of 3 September 1971:

Washington—Senate investigators are checking complaints from government employees that they are being pressured into joining race relations group encounters that border on invasion of privacy. One woman identified as Alice D. walked out on one session because she said "it got down to sex life and just downright uncalled-for vulgar language."

Her boss in an Agricultural Department agency insisted that the meetings were an earnest attempt "to carry out President Nixon's directives to end racial discrimination in government."

An editorial in the *Los Angeles Times* of 7 September 1971 called "Official Dabbling with Minds" comments: "Secretary Richardson says attendance, once compulsory, is now voluntary. Voluntary or not, officially sponsored group encounters should stop." What is your view of officially sponsored programs that deal with race questions?

23/a critical look
at pragmatism

In Part III we described the three-pronged tool of science: induction, deduction, and observation. Observation establishes what is seen to be the case. Induction suggests that there are regularities in nature. Deduction binds the generalizations into theories, which observation puts to a further test. In the pursuit of scientific truth, the three "arms" must be coordinated. None is sufficient alone. However, it took a long time to integrate observation, induction, and deduction into a single method.

Prescientific man certainly made observations and tacit, hence uncritical, generalizations. Systematic deduction was first used by the Greeks, and, as we have seen, some Greek philosophers were so impressed by the power of deductive reasoning that they held it to be the sole source of true knowledge. It has remained the sole source of mathematical knowledge, but the Greek philosophers did not confine deductive reasoning to mathematics. Recall how Plato believed he had discovered the nature of the Deity by pure deduction (cf. pp. 260–61).

The philosophical tradition established by Plato persisted through the Middle Ages and beyond. The Dutch-Jewish philosopher Spinoza (1632–77) attempted to construct a system of ethics by pure deduction, analogous to Euclid's geometry. Hegel's insistence that reason was the "substance" underlying all existence was in accord with the same tradition.

Emphasis on reasoning, especially deductive reasoning, as a way of getting at truth, has been called *rationalism*. Opposed to this conception of truth was *empiricism*, the notion that observation and induction were the only productive methods of discovering truth. Empiricists conceived of truth as that which is actually the case and which is accessible to the senses. In later philosophy of science, empiricism appears as *positivism*, still emphasizing the primacy of sense data as the source of knowledge but admitting deduction as an auxiliary method. *Logical positivism* (cf. p. 354) was another outgrowth of empiricism, coupled with a critical analysis of the language of science. (Later, logical positivists called themselves logical empiricists.)

The history of the philosophy of knowledge, like many other historical processes, developed in a seesaw fashion. Empiricist attitudes emerged as a reaction to rationalism carried too far, and rationalist attitudes were stimulated by the necessity to "make sense" of accumulated masses of facts.

Galileo, contrary to many popular accounts, was more a rationalist than an empiricist. Had he been an empiricist, he might have believed with Aristotle that heavier bodies fall faster than lighter ones, for that is what observation tells us. To be sure, Galileo performed experiments with heavy falling bodies (cannonballs) and showed that *their* rate of fall was independent of weight. But it is important to note that he chose *this* evidence for his theory rather than the evidence of falling leaves or raindrops. He chose cannonballs because their manner of falling (or rolling down inclined planes) could be fitted into a relatively simple mathematical, hence rational, theory (cf. p. 295), whereas the manner of falling of light bodies, complicated by air resistance, could not. Had Galileo been a pure empiricist like, say, Francis Bacon or Alexander Bryan Johnson, he would never have formulated his law of falling bodies and would not have started mathematical physics on its way. Rather, he would have accepted the infinite diversity of nature as evidenced by the senses unencumbered by verbal reasoning. In fact, if "scientists" had remained either pure empiricists or pure rationalists, there would be no science.

By and large, empirical philosophy is concomitant with an orientation toward action; rationalist philosophy reflects a predisposition to contemplation. I believe it is not an accident that the home of the empirical direction in both science and philosophy was England, and of the rationalist outlook, Germany.

American pragmatism, developed as a system of philosophy by

William James and John Dewey,[1] is an outgrowth of the empirical
tradition, nurtured in a social climate that placed a high premium on
practical activity. Spiked with Korzybski's critique of language and
linked to the concerns of the 1930s, this philosophy became a sort of
populist positivism, an expression of down-to-earth practicality rebelling against "effete" speculations of traditional philosophy, at times
against "theory" of all kinds. Thomas Edison remarked on one occasion that, in selecting the trainees for his laboratories, he favored
a young man who could give an immediate accurate answer to "What
is the speed of sound?" over one who was facile with mathematics.
In what follows, I shall mean by "pragmatism" this populist version
of empiricism. Its motto is "Truth is that which works," somewhat a
vulgarization of the positivist definition of truth as that which leads
to a realized prediction.

In the context of semantics, the pragmatic attitude manifests itself
in a demand for "immediate cash payment" in every intellectual
transaction. A word is dismissed as meaningless as soon as a difficulty
arises in relating it to a concrete referent. A theory is dismissed as
"non-sense" if it cannot immediately predict concrete observable
events. If applied seriously to an economy, this attitude would do
away with all credit. "Symbolic payments," such as promissory notes,
would be unacceptable unless they were backed by existing assets;
even money would not be acceptable as payment unless it could be
demonstrated to represent immediately available goods and services.
Strictly speaking, such an economy would be reduced to a barter
system.

Let us now examine in greater detail the manifestations of pragmatism in American language philosophy, beginning with the interpretation of mathematics.

For A. B. Johnson (Chapter 20), mathematics was an intellectual
tool for discovering empirically verifiable quantitative relations, and
no more. Here is the way he addresses himself to the celebrated
Achilles paradox proposed by the Greek philosopher Zeno (c490–
c430 B.C.).

Zeno says, suppose Achilles, a champion runner, is matched in a
foot race with the tortoise, a notoriously slow runner. Since the tortoise clearly deserves a handicap, he gets a mile head start. In order to
overtake the tortoise, Achilles must pass this mile. By the time he has

1. See Note 1, Chapter 20.

passed it, the tortoise, who runs with one-tenth the speed of Achilles, is one-tenth of a mile ahead. If the tortoise is to be overtaken, this tenth of a mile must be passed. But by the time Achilles has passed this distance, the tortoise is still one-*hundredth* of a mile ahead. By the time Achilles has passed this distance, the tortoise is .001 miles ahead. By the time this distance is passed, the tortoise is .0001 miles ahead. And so on. No matter how many times Achilles traverses the distance that had separated him from the tortoise, the tortoise is still ahead—granted, by a very short distance, but still ahead—for the distance separating the two can never be reduced to zero. The logical conclusion is that Achilles, for all his running prowess, can never pass the tortoise. Paradox.

Johnson's reply:

Though the proposition is palpably preposterous, the defect of its reasoning has never been explained; nor is it explicable on any other principle, than that its words become insignificant the moment they are used where nothing sensible is discoverable: for instance, "while Achilles passes over the hundredth part of a mile, the tortoise moves on the ten thousandth part of a mile." [In Johnson's version, Achilles runs 100 times faster than the tortoise, which makes no difference.] The ten thousandth part of a mile is between six and seven inches. It names a sight and a feel; hence the tortoise is not yet overtaken:—but the proposition proceeds,—"whilst Achilles passes over this ten thousandth part of a mile, the tortoise moves on the millionth part of a mile." The millionth part of a mile leaves them asunder about the fifteenth part of an inch, which names a sight and a feel; hence the tortoise is not yet overtaken. But the next step is a quibble. It affirms, that whilst Achilles passes over this millionth part of a mile, the tortoise moves on the hundredth millionth part of a mile. This is a name without any corresponding existence in nature, hence the sophistry is a quibble. The last step is absurd, not from any defect of logick [sic], but because the words are become divested of signification.

The new *Edinburgh Encyclopedia* says, "it would not be easy to solve this quibble were we to measure motion by space merely, without taking in the idea of time. This explication is only the substitution of a new quibble. The tortoise will not be overtaken so long as it is a minute the start of Achilles" [sic] but when the time which separates them is the hundred millionth part of a minute, the words will have no archetype among sensible phenomena, and will be divested of signification.[2]

2. Alexander Bryan Johnson, *A Treatise on Language*, ed. David Rynin (Berkeley and Los Angeles: University of California Press, 1947), pp. 100–1.

In short, Johnson *dismisses* the paradox instead of solving it. He thinks he has "solved" it by pointing out that names which do not refer to "sights" or "feels" are "divested of signification." Hence Zeno's argument is empty; it is not about anything to be found in reality.

Curiously, Johnson fails to mention that the microscope extends to an enormous extent the range of things we can see. Supposedly, he would not consider this objection as in any way an invalidation of his argument; he would probably point out that no microscope has infinite resolving power. The real crux of Johnson's argument is the denial of the "reality" of the mathematical continuum. To say that space is infinitely divisible is, according to Johnson, to talk nonsense because our senses cannot be infinitely refined. Arguments of this sort amount to divesting mathematics of all its cognitive power. Stuart Chase "solves" Zeno's paradox in another way. He writes:

Dealing in words alone, the logic is unimpeachable. Let it whirl around your cortex from reference to symbol and the chances are that you will be unable to discover anything wrong with it. You may settle yourself in an armchair and think until kingdom come, or until you go mad, and you cannot get around it. But the moment you begin to look for referents, to perform an operation, to place an actual turtle there, and a young athlete there, and start them off, the mental blockage dissolves. When I hear a problem of this nature, my impulse is to reach for a pencil and paper, and undoubtedly you share this impulse. It is a sign of semantic progress. The ancients had no scribbling paper and no adequate symbols for attacking such problems. They knew of course that Achilles could lick the tar out of the tortoise, but how were they to prove it? Let us translate the problem into simple algebra. Let r be the rate of the tortoise. Then Achilles's rate will be 10r. Let x be the time in seconds taken by the tortoise before they meet. We know that the distance traveled by the tortoise equals the distance traveled by Achilles. The distance a body travels is its rate of travel multiplied by the time traveled. Using this formula:

$$\text{Tortoise's distance} = rx$$
$$\text{Achilles's distance} = 10r\,(x - 100)$$
$$\text{or } rx = 10rx - 1000r$$
$$\text{or } 9x = 1000$$

Therefore $x = 111.11$ seconds. They will meet 111.11 seconds after the tortoise starts, or, 111.11 yards down the course. [In Chase's version, the tortoise gets 100 yards head start.] [3]

Chase, like Johnson, dismisses the paradox. He does not raise the metaphysical question of whether space is infinitely divisible, nor does he raise the question of whether the name of a distance that cannot be perceived by "sight or feel" has any meaning. He first resorts to horse sense: anyone knows that Achilles can "lick the tar out of the tortoise." Then for proof he proposes to put this knowledge to a test. Let them race and see what happens. Still he does not let it go at that; he tries to explain why the Greeks got into the difficulty: they did not know algebra. So he reaches for pencil and paper and sets up a problem in algebraic notation. Quite different from setting up the race, this is an attempt to check the result by mathematical reasoning.

It is the mathematical reasoning that constitutes the "semantic advance" over the purely logical reasoning of the Greeks. Algebra gives the answer dictated by common sense, and Chase is satisfied. However, in his "proof" he resorted to a device inadmissible in mathematical logic: he assumed what he set out to prove, namely, that Achilles and the tortoise *will* meet. "We know," he writes, "that the distance traveled by the tortoise [when they meet] equals the distance traveled by Achilles." The words in brackets are inserted to call attention to the *tacit* assumption made by Chase, that Achilles will overtake the tortoise. *Given* this assumption, we can readily calculate the time of the meeting or the distance traveled. But that was not the problem posed by Zeno. The problem was to prove that Achilles *will* overtake the tortoise, as, of course, we know he will in spite of the fact that a "logical" argument makes it seem impossible.[4]

---

3. Stuart Chase, *The Tyranny of Words* (New York: Harcourt, Brace, 1938), p. 152–54.

4. The demand that a solution be shown to exist before it is offered as a solution of a problem is not a quibble To illustrate, suppose a body is revolving clockwise in a circular path with constant speed. Let the center of the circle be at the intersection of two mutually perpendicular coordinate axes (cf. Note 2, Chapter 18). Call x the horizontal distance of the body from the vertical axis (positive to the right, negative to the left) and y the vertical distance from the horizontal axis (positive up, negative down). Then the equations of motion of the body are:

$$\frac{dx}{dt} = a\,y \quad \text{(the horizontal component of velocity is proportional to the vertical distance)}$$

$$\frac{dy}{dt} = -a\,x \quad \text{(the vertical component of velocity is proportional to the negative of the horizontal distance)}$$

Although lack of an adequate mathematical symbolism was indeed what prevented the Greeks from seeing through Zeno's paradox, the symbolism of algebra would not have been sufficient. More is involved in the semantic analysis of the paradox than either finding concrete referents of words or translating the problem into algebra.

The paradox hinges on the meaning of "never" in the assertion "Achilles will never overtake the tortoise." Clearly there is no concreate referent of "never." If "never" means anything at all, it means "not after any span of time however long." Thus we cannot demonstrate by any experiment that an event will "never" occur, for, no matter how much time has elapsed without the event occurring, we cannot logically infer that it will not occur at some time in the future. The concept "never" rests on the concept of "infinite" time, which Johnson would have dismissed as meaningless because no one can live forever. However, the concept of infinity is indispensable in modern mathematics. To repeat, the concepts of mathematics neither can nor need be related to any actual experience; they are tools of reasoning, and the power of mathematical reasoning has been amply demonstrated. And so the problem is to demonstrate *logically* that the assertion "Achilles will never overtake the tortoise" is false, something we already know empirically or, at any rate, on common sense grounds.

Zeno's argument rests on a tacit assumption which we will now make explicit. To do this, we will consider the time intervals between the moments when Achilles passes the points occupied by the tortoise —the mile, the tenth of a mile, and so on. In shifting the attention to the time intervals, the *Edinburgh Encyclopedia* was on the right

---

Here a is the constant of proportionality (cf. p. 295).

Consider the question "Is the body ever at rest?" If it *is* at rest, both components of its velocity must be zero. So, following Stuart Chase's method, we set dx/dt and dy/dt equal to zero and solve the following equations for x and y:

$$a\ x = 0$$
$$a\ y = 0$$

Ignoring the trivial result when $a = 0$ (meaning that the body is *always* at rest), we divide the left sides of the last two equations by a and get $x = 0$, $y = 0$. We interpret the result as saying that the body is at rest when it is at the intersection of the coordinate axes, that is, at the center of the circle. But a body moving around a circle is never at the center. The formal solution of the problem is *vacuous*: it points to an event that does not occur. Actually the solution says "If the body is at rest, it must be at the center." Similarly, Chase's solution of Zeno's paradox says only "If Achilles passes the tortoise, he must pass it 111.11 yards down the track." But his "solution" does not prove that Achilles actually passes the tortoise.

track. The tacit assumption made by Zeno was that the number of these time intervals being infinite, they add up to an infinite span of time, and hence that Achilles will not overtake the tortoise in any finite span of time. Taking as a unit the time required for Achilles to pass the first interval, this infinite sum can be written as

$$1 + 1/10 + 1/100 + 1/000 + \ldots$$

and so on ad infinitum. It is shown in modern mathematics that this "infinite series," as it is called, approaches a *limit*. This limit is 10/9. That is to say, no matter how many terms of the series are added, the sum will always remain smaller than 10/9 but will approach nearer to 10/9 than to any smaller number we specify. Translated into the relation between the positions of the runners, this means that at any time before 10/9 units following the start of the race, Achilles will be behind the tortoise, but at any time after 10/9 units he will be ahead. In other words, Achilles will pass the tortoise 10/9 units of time after the start of the race. This is the same result Chase obtained by elementary algebra, but to obtain it we have made no a priori assumption that the two will meet (as Chase did). We *proved* that they will meet by showing that the total time used by Achilles in passing an *infinite* number of space intervals was finite, not infinite. Nor have we appealed to the evidence of the senses, which is irrelevant in a mathematical proof. The power of mathematical reasoning resides precisely in its independence from observation. This is what makes mathematical reasoning exact. This is the core of truth in Plato's conviction that only pure reasoning can reveal truth. Plato's error was in dismissing empirical truth and its consequences. Those who take the extreme positivist position make the opposite error: they dismiss truths arrived at by pure reasoning if these truths cannot be translated into direct observation or experience. In doing so, they misunderstand the source from which scientific reasoning derives its immense power.

Here is another instructive example from Johnson's *A Treatise on Language*:

In the Polynesian Researches, published lately in London, the author, in speaking of some islands in the Pacifick [sic] ocean says "The tide is here very singular. If influenced at all by the moon, it is in a very small degree only. The height to which the water rises, varies but a few inches during the whole year. Whatever be the age or situation of the moon, the water is lowest at six in the morning, and the same hour in the evening, and highest at noon and at midnight." The writer seems embarrassed by the usual confusion of words with sensible realities. He evidently is seeking in nature for "the influence of the moon," instead of seeking in nature for the sensible meaning of those words. To me, nothing is less surprising than the fact to which he refers, because I know that the sensible signification of those words is nothing but numerous and various sensible incidents which we discover in different seas. If the seas to which the writer alludes exhibit nothing that can yield those words a sensible signification, I shall not deem the circumstance a wonder of nature, but an instance of inapplicability in an ingenious verbal contrivance of man.[5]

That is positivism in its most extreme form. Facts as revealed by the senses are truth; if the facts do not fit a theory, so much the worse for the theory. On these grounds, the failure of Uranus to move as prescribed by the theory of gravitation would be taken as an indication that the theory is "mere words." The behavior of Uranus would in no way surprise Johnson because he would never inquire as to why Uranus behaves as it does. It behaves as it does; that is the truth. Had the astronomers of the nineteenth century taken this stand, Neptune might never have been discovered. Had the physicists simply accepted the negative results of the Michelson-Morley experiment, there would have been no theory of relativity. Had the mathematicians dismissed the concept of incommensurables on the grounds that it corresponds to nothing that can be "seen" or "felt," mathematics would have been confined to land measurement and bookkeeping.

We find illuminating examples of pragmatism in Stuart Chase's treatment of abstractions in the language of economics and politics; for instance, in his critique of Marx's theory of value. Marx defined the "value" (more properly, the exchange value, as distinguished from use value) of a commodity in terms of the amount of labor time absorbed in making it. Clearly the definition is not operational because it does not indicate whose labor is to be taken into account, and the productivity of labor varies from worker to worker. Marx overcame this variance by introducing the notion of an "average" which he designated socially necessary labor time. Chase attempts to demolish this concept as meaningless, and so it is from the operational point of view, since

5. Johnson, *A Treatise on Language*, p. 176.

procedures for calculating the "socially necessary labor time" of any given article are nowhere indicated.

Nevertheless it is evident that commodities do get bought and sold, hence, in effect, exchanged in certain proportions. These proportions are certainly of central interest in economics. If economics is to be a science, something more ought to be said about these proportions than that they-are-what-they-are. In fact, other assertions in so-called classical economics do say more. The "law of supply and demand," for example, asserts that if the supply of commodity A increases, more of this commodity will be exchanged for a unit of some fixed commodity B; if the demand for commodity A increases, less will be given in exchange for B. Although this "law" can be easily refuted by citing frequent exceptions and violations, nevertheless it provides some anchorage for developing a science of economics. Possibly, when other conditions are taken into account, more accurate statements can be made about the proportions in which commodities are exchanged under given conditions.

Marx's theory of value should be understood in this spirit. Marx sought some common denominator of commodities enabling him to make general statements about how commodities are exchanged in the market. He thought he had found it in the "average" amount of labor time that went into the commodity. The usefulness of this concept depends in no way on our ability to measure it directly, any more than the usefulness of the concept "intensity of electric current" depends on our ability to measure electric current directly. We do not in fact measure electric current directly; to do so would require counting the number of electrons that pass a given point in a unit time, which is impossible. Instead we measure the intensity of an electric current indirectly, by noting, for example, the angle of deviation of a magnetic needle. The connection between the deviation and the intensity of the electric current is established by a *theory*, only few of whose assertions are verifiable by direct observations.

The extreme positivist does not appreciate this facet of theory construction. He demands immediate redemption of concepts in terms of direct observations. Here is how Chase understands the theory of value:

Most books on economic theory revolve around value. If the task of the student of semantics is to find the referent, the task of the economist has been to find the value. He has not found it yet, and I am afraid he never will. For "value," apart from a price or a sum of money, is a meaningless absolute. No operation can be performed to establish it. There is no magnitude of value apart from money. The measurable value is what B will actually give for A's old fishing rod, not A's claim that he would not take $500 for it.[6]

This way of looking at value is analogous to declaring that there is no such thing as "mass" apart from the reading we get when we put a body on a scale, for this reading is the only thing we observe. True, the weighing operation may be part of the operational definition of mass, but it is not the whole definition. If we weigh an object on a spring scale, we shall find that it registers a larger weight in Alaska than at the equator, a smaller weight on the top of a mountain than in the adjoining valley. Different scales will give different readings. Moreover, if we weigh the object on a beam scale, we shall find that it then will weigh the same everywhere. A. B. Johnson would declare that all these facts merely indicate the diversity of nature and that we err when we try to impose a "one-ness on nature by means of verbal labels." Stuart Chase would declare that the different results are the only things we could make meaningful statements about, that "mass" is simply an empty word that might as well be "blab."

For the physicist, however, the concept of "mass" is indispensable. He knows very well that the weighing operation does not determine the mass directly, perhaps that the exact mass of an object cannot be determined at all. But, without the concept, there would be no science of physics, only a catalogue of disconnected observations. Having a theory which relates the hypothetical mass of an object to its weight measured under different circumstances, the physicist can actually explain the variations in weight as the object is moved from a high latitude to a low one or from a high altitude to a low one. He also knows why these variations are observed when the object is weighed on a spring scale but not when it is weighed on a beam scale. For him, the results of all these experiments are not simply a "pile of facts." They make sense in their *totality*. They fit into a theory.

Again the positivist attitude toward law characteristically avoids going beyond brute facts. The dictum of Oliver Wendell Holmes, Jr., expresses it: "The prophesies of what the courts will do in fact, and

6. Chase, *The Tyranny of Words*, p. 290

nothing more pretentious are what I mean by law." If law is nothing but the totality of judges' decisions, there is no point in considering the economic, cultural, historical, or psychological roots of different legal systems, and varying philosophies of law then become idle speculations. From such a conclusion, it is only a step to believing that a jurist's task is simply to know the precedents, or the attorney's, to be able to predict the foibles of this or that judge.

A similar attitude in an even more extreme form is found in some conceptions of international law. International law, it is declared, is nothing more than established patterns of behavior of states toward each other. To paraphrase Holmes's definition, "The prophecies of what the *litigants* will do, and nothing more pretentious are what is meant by international law." The definition certainly brings the law down to cases in the literal sense. The trouble is that such a definition chokes off any ideas of supranational law based on principles other than the relative power of the litigants, just as Holmes's conception dismisses in advance any question that one might raise regarding the relation between law and justice. Justice eludes an operational definition.

Consider another pragmatic exercise on "meaning." To demonstrate the meaninglessness of the word "fascism," Stuart Chase collected almost one hundred reactions from chance acquaintances and friends during 1937, asking them what came into their minds when they heard the word. The answers were inconsistent, as one would expect; typically:

Schoolteacher: A dictator suppressing all opposition.
Author: One-party government. "Outs" unrepresented.
Governess: Obtaining one's desires by sacrifice of human lives.
College student: Hitler and Mussolini.
United States Senator: Deception, duplicity, and professing to do what one is not doing.
Schoolboy: War. Concentration camps. Bad treatment of workers. Something that's got to be licked.
Lawyer: A coercive capitalistic state.
Housewife: Same thing as communism.
Italian hairdresser: A bunch, all together.
Housewife: A large Florida rattlesnake in summer.[7]

7. Ibid., pp. 189–90.

Chase goes on to conjecture (correctly, in my opinion) that "democracy," "communism," and so on, would have evoked a similar diversity of replies. One could add that *any* word would have done the same, an effect well-known to psychologists who conduct experiments on associations evoked by words (cf. p. 155). If the variety of associations which a sample of people gave to the word "fascism" is offered as evidence that the word is devoid of meaning, then practically any word can be shown to be devoid of meaning.

In summary, the pragmatist answers the two fundamental questions of semantics as follows. To the question "What has meaning?" his answer is "That which has an observable referent." To the question "What is true?" his answer is "That which works." The latter answer bespeaks the pragmatist's primary orientation toward action. He would probably agree with the definition of a rational man as the "problem-solving animal." According to the pragmatist's conception, a rational man faced with a difficulty should pose the question "What is the problem?" Then, to formulate the problem, the rational man should take stock of the existing state of affairs and specify a desired state of affairs. Next, he should seek ways and means of reaching the desired state, starting with the existing state.

Two tacit assumptions are involved in this formulation of "the problem." (1) What is wanted is known. (2) It is possible to get from "here" to "there" by available means. There are, of course, situations where both assumptions are justified. In building a bridge, what is wanted is clearly a bridge. When the decision to build a bridge is made, materials and labor are usually available or can be made available. "Know-how" relevant to building bridges is also at hand. It remains to put the know-how to work. The pragmatist is most comfortable in situations of this sort, for this is where his attitude is most easily vindicated. Consequently, posing problems solvable by applications of technological know-how has become for the pragmatist the paradigm of rational action.

Our own age has brought "social problems" to the forefront of attention. The pragmatist sees them as extensions of technological problems. A thoughtful person (there are thoughtful persons among the pragmatists) cannot remain unaware of the fact that social problems differ from technological ones in that "what is desired" in the social sphere is never as clear as a goal posed by a technological problem. Faced with this disjunction, the pragmatist tends to stress the purely instrumental nature of science.

In his book *Can Science Save Us?* (1947), George A. Lundberg argued that science can never tell us what goals we should strive for; it can only tell us how we can reach specified goals, including the costs and consequences of alternative ways of reaching them; that choice of goals is not a matter that can be decided by scientific investigation because the results of such investigations must always be put in terms of "If so . . ., then so" propositions, and propositions such as "X is good" or "Y is bad" are outside the language of science.

In light of what was said in Part III about the semantics of science, we cannot disagree with Lundberg's argument. Let us, however, look at its consequences. If science is powerless to prescribe goals, how are goals to be chosen? Lundberg's answer, that the choice of goals is a political act, is granted. But political systems vary. In an autocracy, goals are chosen by the autocrat; in a plutocracy, by a ruling elite. Most Americans are convinced that they live in a democracy, where goals are chosen by "the people." Applying the pragmatist's standards of analysis, we cannot be satisfied with verbal descriptions of the political processes (as found in constitutions and civics textbooks). We must trace the actual decision-making processes as they occur, specifying who makes what decisions under what circumstances, as well as possible discrepancies between stated and implemented goals.

Pragmatists often recommend "social engineering" as a method of social problem-solving. Yet, remarkably enough, they seldom pursue inquiries as to which problems are actually posed for solution, by whom, and with what aim in mind. They are more often content to assume that in a democracy "national goals" reflect the interests of the people.

Though one cannot demand expertise from someone who does not claim it, one can question whether the pragmatically oriented social engineers are as willing to serve goals chosen by an autocrat, or by a power elite unresponsive to the needs of the people, as to serve the goals chosen "by the people." Some would say yes, pointing out that the choice of goals is not their "department." Others might say no, adding, however, that favoring democratically chosen goals is only a matter of personal preference, not of a reasoned conclusion. Still others might suggest that a preference for democracy *can* be justified on pragmatic grounds if it can be shown that democratically chosen goals are more likely to satisfy human needs than goals dictated by interests of special groups. However, shifting the goals to another level (say, "human needs") does not eliminate the distinction between ethical choice and scientific truth.

In short, the separation of science and values is inherent in the *instrumental view* of science, which, in turn, is a consequence of the pragmatic outlook. Nevertheless some pragmatists shy away from this consequence. S. I. Hayakawa, for instance, who defends the pragmatic outlook throughout his writings and relates it to language awareness, starts with an ethical postulate, namely, that cooperation is preferable to conflict. He believes that the language of science is common to all scientists regardless of nationality, cultural background, and even political conviction, and that therefore the very commitment to science as a way of life implies the acceptance of certain values, such as a preference for truth, defined as a correspondence between language and experience, rather than the acceptance of dogma and authority, and so on. This commitment, in turn, encourages and is nurtured by cooperative attitudes. This is a view that Werner Heisenberg, a Nobel Prize winner in physics, asserted repeatedly after the holocaust of World War II.

I myself once subscribed to this view. In a book written in 1950 (*Science and the Goals of Man*), I argued that science is not just a product of a particular culture and so of a certain special system of values (the Western), but rather a supracultural phenomenon. Since science can *examine* and compare cultures and value systems, it can lead to insights transcending the parochial culture-bound value systems of the presently existing cultures.

Today I would say that whether science can create a new supraculture, one in which what is good and what is true are more closely related, depends in large measure on what the practitioners of science do. The fact of the matter is that a large majority of practicing scientists, to the extent that their research is put to practical use, serve not humanity but special interests—national, military, or corporate. Scientific knowledge so applied serves to promote the interests of power-wielding groups, largely to enhance or to consolidate their power vis-à-vis other similar groups, which is the antithesis of cooperation. Research of demonstrable value to humanity (for example, medical research) is more than offset by increased efficiency of death technology. Research that makes possible a more "efficient" exploitation of resources hastens the depletion of the resources and contributes to pollution of the environment and to further concentration of power.

Why should there be such wide discrepancy between the supposed humanitarian functions of science and the exploitative uses to which it is put? This question leads to even deeper inquiries about the nature of modern societies, especially about the actual (rather than constitutionally defined) distribution of power in human societies. It would be well if questions of this sort could be put in a form amenable to scientific investigation. The trouble is that standard "scientific method" is applicable only when a definite *conceptualization* has crystallized. New conceptualizations are results of strenuous intellectual effort of the sort not usually congenial to the pragmatist's way of thinking. The pragmatist presses for getting on with solving problems, as they appear, within the customary frameworks of thought.

An old ideology (framework of thought) can be displaced only by a new ideology, and an ideology is indispensable to any system of organized knowledge, scientific or otherwise. However, "ideology" is a bad word in the lexicon of the pragmatist, who is inclined to celebrate his emancipation from ideology. In this respect he repeats the error of the "pure" empiricist who says "Never mind theories; give me facts!"—forgetting that the hardest "fact" cannot even be stated without tacit theoretical assumptions.

The pragmatist believes himself to be free of ideology because he usually is imbued with the current one. He may be convinced, for example, that the political system of the United States has outgrown the "ideological stage" (by which he means explicit formulation of political creeds or social philosophies) and has entered the mature "problem-solving stage." Accordingly he often dismisses ideologically couched political arguments, regarding them as instances of demagogy or dogmatism standing in the way of practical problem-solving.

Hayakawa and Goldfield, commenting on the 1966 riots in Watts (a slum district in Los Angeles), wrote:

Power in America is always limited and shared power, exerted by alliances and coalitions of political parties, business groups, churches, unions, minority blocs, and the like. New Left leaders adroitly escape power (and therefore responsibility) by refusing to enter into alliances or coalitions, which they term "making deals" and "selling out." Standing on their ideological purity, they prefer blazing rhetoric of moral denunciation to the give-and-take and the hemming-and-hawing of practical negotiation—for jobs, for better schools, for housing, for political support.

From the New Left, therefore, Negroes can expect nothing: not money, nor power, nor jobs, nor better schools, nor housing, nor political leverage.

The only hope for minorities, including the Negroes of Watts, lies in the broad center of both major parties—in those whose minds are neither in an imaginary past or a visionary future, but in the realities of the present —in those who in the pragmatic, commonsense tradition of American life, will continue to hammer out the agreements and accommodations that we all must make to live together in peace and progress.[8]

One difficulty with the problem-solving ("common sense" . . . "hammer out") approach to social evils is that, even if a solution of a problem is available, there may be no one who can make use of it. Return to the example of building a bridge: an engineer solves mechanical problems; his solutions are incorporated into a blueprint, and the bridge is built according to the directions specified in it. Or when a drug is discovered to be effective against some disease, pharmaceutical houses prepare it and physicians prescribe it. In other words, when it comes to technological (including medical) problems, institutions already exist empowered to put new knowledge to work. Moreover, there are institutions ready to *test* the dependability of proposed solutions. For instance, before the efficacy of a drug becomes apparent, it must be tried. Procedures exist for trial administration, and hospital staffs are authorized to carry out these procedures, even though they involve some risk to patients.

Oppositely, there are few if any institutions empowered to "try out" proposed solutions of large-scale social problems. War is one example of such a "problem" which confronts all humanity. Many well-meaning people agree that it would be a good thing if social scientists would make progress toward a "solution" that eliminated the threat of war. By analogy with medical problems, knowledge of conditions that make war more likely or less likely should bring us closer to the solution, just as knowledge of etiology of diseases brings us closer to means of inhibiting them.

Suppose, for the sake of argument, social scientists do come up with

8. S. I. Hayakawa and Barry A. Goldfield, "Reflections on a Visit to Watts," *ETC.: A Review of General Semantics* 23, no. 3 (1966): 305.

a finding that universal disarmament and certain limitations on the sovereignty of nation states are vital steps toward the abolition of war. Who could take these steps? It might be argued that the efficacy of disarmament has not been proven. Then how can it be proven if it is not tried? It might be argued further especially by the major powers asked to disarm, that the risks involved in trying such a step would be too great. But how can these risks be weighed against the risks involved in the present state of affairs?

From the point of view of applying "science" to human affairs, there can be no argument against viewing social evils as "problems." However, if we pursue the analysis far enough, we see that a paramount problem is precisely the absence of institutions for applying whatever knowledge is gained in a scientific investigation of large-scale human behavior. Worse, there are institutions that actually *prevent* putting into a new perspective certain problems that are unsolvable within the conventional framework of political thinking. Take, for instance, military establishments. With their tremendous political influence in countries like the United States and, possibly, the Soviet Union, their very existence helps to perpetuate ways of thinking that preclude the emergence of fresh outlooks and creative solutions to the urgent problem of burgeoning war-making institutions.

Ways of thinking being ideologies, ideologies do indeed often stand in the way of making the problem-solving approach productive. In declaring pragmatic politics to be "nonideological," the pragmatists typically fail to come to grips with some of the most urgent problems of our age.

Despite the shortcomings of the pragmatic outlook, it is well to keep in mind its positive contributions. For one thing, the extensional orientation urged by Korzybski and his followers, the general semanticists, is a powerful antidote to dogmatism. It is always salutary to shut out verbal cerebration (categorizing, generalizing, inferring) in order to reestablish contact with the world amenable to the senses. In proper proportion, the empirical attitude is indispensable in science. It also makes for mature journalism, represented, for example, by the superb straight reporting practiced by *The New Yorker*, which leaves evaluation to the reader. There is a great deal to be said for problem-solving in the social sphere, unencumbered by ideological commitments, where the goals to be attained clearly reflect *the needs of the people to be affected by the solutions*. Carried to extremes, however, the extensional orientation shuts out the creative role of symbolic language, as in Swift's caricature of the "extensional" philosophers of Lagado (cf. p. 41).

This brings us back to the limitations of the pragmatic approach. For example: the strict denotative meaning of "a dollar" is a paper bill. The most accurate description of a dollar bill, as S. I. Hayakawa himself once pointed out, will reveal nothing about the economic system in which dollars are the common denominator of exchange. Nor will Stuart Chase's "operational definition" of market value of commodities, identified with price, reveal much about the workings of a market economy. The extensional denotation of "disease" is the symptoms of Mr. Chi, who is suffering from it, and the limitations of medicine confined to the treatment of symptoms are well-known. The denotative meaning of "social unrest" is specific riots, protests, and so forth. These can be put down in the name of "law and order," which itself can be extensionally defined as the absence of riots or of demonstrations without permission of the authorities. But this sort of "treatment" may be directly analogous to the treatment of symptoms in medicine.

The extensional denotation of "social evils" is bad housing, bad schools, inadequate or unavailable medical care, abusive police power, and so on. Though social evils are difficult to eliminate, it is not so much because we do not know what to do about them. We already know how to build good houses, how to prevent and cure diseases, but the difficulty lies in the absence of institutions empowered to take appropriate action. To say "If we had such and such institutions, such and such social evils could be eliminated" may be an indisputable proposition, but it does not help to solve the problems. Nor does it help to argue that, if enough people wanted the problems solved, they would initiate appropriate political pressures to create the necessary institutions. Wanting does not necessarily imply acting. Acting requires mobilization of attention and energy, but attention and energy in sufficient force are impossible to mobilize as long as people direct them elsewhere.

Although physical science provides means of solving a great many problems, it took centuries to develop the *concepts* of physical science, and many of these centuries were spent in breaking away from an obsolete ideology that inhibited the empirical approach to natural science.

To recapitulate, the very "reasonableness" of the pragmatic attitude sometimes blinds us to its very serious limitations. Perhaps the greatest handicap of the pragmatic outlook is its antihistorical bias, its resistance to investigating origins and to looking through the time perspective. It was Henry Ford, an eminently practical and immensely successful man, who said "History is bunk." Couched in more sophisticated language, this attitude is echoed in Hayakawa's and Goldfield's disdain for the "imaginary past" and the "visionary future." Yet, in order to solve social problems, we must understand the obstacles in the way of solutions—obstacles which are deeply embedded in the history of societies and their institutions. People cannot dispense with images of the future, no matter how "visionary," if they are to gain any leverage in political action. An image of visionary future is another name for hope, and hope is indispensable to action.

APPLICATIONS

I. You have read the phrase "tacit assumption" in this chapter. If you would like to explore the meaning of this phrase further, read *The Tacit Dimension* by Michael Polanyi, a distinguished scientist-philosopher. Polanyi uncovers the mechanism of an essential process of thinking that he calls "tacit knowing," offering as a paradigm the recognition of moods on a human face. Tacit knowing guides the scientist to problems that promise new discoveries. He finds that hunches and intuitions are essential to all creative thought and to science in particular. From your own reading about science, can you give instances of "tacit knowing" on the part of men who made important scientific discoveries? ("The scientist's surmises or hunches are the spurs and pointers of his search.") Can you recall instances of "tacit knowing" from your own experience?

II. In September of 1971, speaking before the Western Hemisphere Nutrition Congress, Dr. Norman Borlaugh, winner of the 1970 Nobel Peace Prize, said the failure of scientists to communicate their knowledge has contributed to human misery in the form of poor diet, hunger, and a cynicism regarding environmental protection which could set food production back to a primitive level. He said that scientists have failed to lead the way to proper application of resources and have taken either a standoffish attitude about conveying their information to the public or have neglected to get their message across to political leaders.

1) What advice do you think a trained semanticist might give these scientists if he agreed with Dr. Borlaugh?
2) What advice would you give the trained semanticist?

III. If the very existence of the military helps to perpetuate ways of thinking that preclude the emergence of fresh outlooks on war-making institutions, perhaps *your* very existence (and mine) helps to perpetuate the existence of a powerful military establishment. Before you scoff, respond "yes" or "no" to the following statements:

1) If South Vietnam and Thailand are permitted to move out of the Western sphere of influence, all of Asia will turn Communist.
2) If the People's Republic of China is seated in the U.N., we will have to increase our military vigilance in the Western Pacific.
3) The withdrawal of American troops from Europe would both irritate our allies and invite invasion from the Soviets.
4) It is necessary for the federal government to spend more money on military matters than on education because in the end there can be no education unless a country is free and strong.
5) A year or two of military service for young people provides good discipline and useful training in a vocation.
6) The military establishment provides thousands of jobs for civilians; to dismantle it rapidly would disrupt the economy.
7) Power resides in the barrel of a gun—even a semanticist should know that. And guns cost money.
8) History proves that countries which have given up strong military establishments have perished in one way or another.
9) War is too important not to leave to the generals.
10) It is almost always the ones who pay the least in taxes who complain the most about military expenditures.

24/toward
responsible use
of language

Consider the following four samples of language.

1.

"There are many details which must be considered before even a crude expression for control of mRNA synthesis by metabolite can be obtained. These include the kinetics of the reaction between DNA templates and activated nucleotides on the one hand and repressors on the other, and the relationship of the repressing complex to the metabolite concentration. It also requires certain assumptions about the 'storage capacity' of the metabolic pool. When the pool size is very small, one would expect very little or no metabolite to 'spill out' of the pool and repress the activity of the genetic locus. But when the pool is large, then a considerable fraction of the metabolite would be expected to serve a repressive function." [1]

2.

"Let us assume again that we have an adequate definition for the concept of confirming case. Then it may happen that the evidence e available to X does not quite suffice to make the individual b a confirming case. For example, let h be the law '(x) (Mx $\supset$ M'X)' ('all

1. Brian C. Goodwin, "A Statistical Mechanics of Temporal Organization in Cells," in *Toward a Theoretical Biology*, ed. C. H. Waddington, I.U.B.S. Symposium, vol. 2, "Sketches" (Chicago: Aldine Publishing Company, 1969), p. 145.

swans are white'), and let *e* contain 'Mb. (M'b ∨ Pb)' ('b is a swan and is either white or small') and nothing else about *b*. Here, X does not know whether the swan *b* is white or not but, still, the information that *b* is either white or small is more than nothing. Should it not count for something in weighing the evidence for the law *h*? But how much?" [2]

3.

"The essential of man as religious is that he is aware of his finite limits. He who recognizes a limit is already in reflection beyond it, and this sense of the beyond, of the infinite, is the source of religion. The finite implies the infinite, the relative the absolute. Thus we experience degrees of good, as the moral argument for the existence of God asserts, and from this we argue to the 'existence' of the infinitely good, to the *ens perfectissimum* implied in it. But this is not a purely empirical argument, for if the sense for the perfect—and 'the lust for the perfect' which goes with it—were not a part of our experience we could never argue to it. Man's sense of imperfection is, as Emerson says, that 'fine innuendo by means of which he makes his immortal claim.' Without the 'sense' for the quality of perfection, the sense of imperfection would have no meaning. This is the essence for all true religious realism." [3]

4.

"Atomic energy (nuclear energy, NR) represents cosmic energy which is freed from matter through disintegration of the atom, which is the constituent of the universe in terms of classical and quantum physics. It is energy *after matter*. OR energy, on the other hand, represents cosmic energy before matter, i.e., energy, which has *not* been caught in or has been transformed into solid matter. It is universally present, penetrating everything, surrounds, as the so-called OR energy envelope, our planet and most likely all other heavenly bodies (sun's

2. Rudolph Carnap, *Logical Foundations of Probability* (Chicago: University of Chicago Press, 1950), p. 229.
3. Wilbur Marshall Urban, *Language and Reality* (London: George Allen and Unwin, Ltd.; New York: Macmillan, 1939, 1951), ch. XII, p. 690.

corona, Saturn's ring, etc.). Cosmic OR energy, moving freely within the living organism, is called bio-energy or organismic OR energy." [4]

For most readers, at least three of these four passages will not be immediately comprehensible. At any rate, each requires some effort to be understood. If the reader considers such effort sufficiently worthwhile, he may seek the help of someone who is familiar with the meanings of the words used in these passages and with the way these meanings combine into the meanings of the total utterances.

For example, to gain an understanding of the first passage, the reader can enlist the assistance of a biologist with competence in physiological genetics. If both the informant and the reader have sufficient time (possibly several years) and sufficient patience (for intense instruction and study), the meaning of the passage will become quite clear to the reader. That is to say, he will know what words like "mRNA synthesis" and "genetic locus" stand for, and also (important to note) how the meanings emerging from their combinations inform us about certain aspects of the vastly complex process we call life. The information contained in the passage is far removed from our everyday experiences. It is, as a matter of fact, "information of the second order," so to speak—information about what information we must have (or what sort of assumptions we must make) in order to infer a very small portion of what goes on in a living cell. The passage is written in the language of science, which, we have seen, is so constructed that connections (no matter how tortuous and complex) between symbols and referents *in the outside world* are kept intact. In principle, any normally intelligent person can learn to perceive these connections, for they lead ultimately to experiences or observations of external events that all human beings have in common. Such is the language of science.

To understand the second passage, the reader should enlist the assistance of a logician. Here, too, with sufficient effort, the reader can fathom completely and without ambiguity the exact meaning of what is being said. The meanings in this passage relate not to the external world but to the world of thought; moreover, not to just any sort of thought but to rigorous thought—thought that follows perfectly clear

4. Wilhelm Reich, "Basic Premises of the Oranur Project," *Orgone Energy Bulletin* 3, no. 41 (October 1951): 270.

rules such as those that govern a game of chess, checkers, or tick-tack-toe. In fact, the author of this passage is discussing matters closely related to those discussed in Chapter 15 of this book, as the reader may have surmised by the glimpse of everyday language provided by the proposition "all swans are white." In this passage, as in the first, the language is *disciplined*. It operates under constraints imposed on it by the rules of deductive and inductive reasoning. *Anyone* can learn these rules and, having learned them, can decide whether a sample of discourse of this sort makes or fails to make sense and whether, if it makes sense, it leads to valid conclusions. Such is the language of logic.

The meanings of the third passage, like those of the second, relate to the world of thought, but not of thought that adheres to well-defined rules. The author says that the concept of the finite generates its complement—that of the infinite; that the awareness of imperfections is coupled with "the lust for the perfect." Many of us will agree that *some* sort of truth is being asserted here. In Chapter 15, I described Plato's philosophy as one dominated by the concept of the ideal, and I am convinced that Plato did not merely invent that concept but, rather, that his philosophy was simply a clear formulation of an idea conceived by many people of his day. Thus the passage cited seems to me to assert something about the way some people think about "the meaning of existence" and matters of that sort. I would be hard put, however, to explain the passage to someone unless he were *already attuned* to the ideas expressed in it. That is, I could not begin with the simplest concrete experiences (as I would in explaining a scientific theory, no matter how abstruse), nor with the simplest forms of reasoning (as I would in explaining a system of logic, no matter how complex). There is, therefore, no guarantee *in principle* that I could make *any* reasonably intelligent person, however willing to make the effort, fathom the meaning of religious feeling, any more than I could make *anyone* appreciate the beauty of a Beethoven symphony: some people, "normal" in all other respects, are tone-deaf. Such is the language of inner experience.

The fourth passage was written by a once-outstanding psychiatrist, who possibly became psychotic. At any rate, on close examination, the passage shows every indication of pathological thought, as do the examples of schizophrenic writing discussed in Chapter 9. Observe, however, how difficult it is for an uninitiated reader to distinguish the quality of that passage from the quality of the first, a genuine example of scientific discourse. This last passage, written by the apparent psychotic, *mimics* the language of science. The words in it are words used in physics: "energy," "disintegration of atoms," "quantum physics," "matter," "living organism." Neologisms like "bio-energy" appear to be "defined" after the manner of newly introduced terms in a scientific paper. Yet, put together, these words mean precisely nothing.

This last passage differs in one important respect from our samples of schizophrenic writing. The latter give themselves away by their bizarre syntax, by bursting through the frames of sentence structure. In contrast, there is nothing wrong with the syntax of the pseudoscientific passage: the sentences in it are all properly constructed. They just do not make *semantic* sense. As assertions, they refer to nothing in the external world, nor to any thought process that adheres to any discernible logical rules. They do not even invoke any recognizable images in the mind of a nondeluded reader, as does "Jabberwocky" or the third passage or even, to some extent, the passage from Hegel ridiculed by Reichenbach (cf. pp. 355–56).

How are we to account for verbal behavior exemplified by the fourth passage? One answer has already been suggested: it may be that the utterance makes private sense to the author—that it represents some sort of images in his mind alone. His being apparently unaware of the fact that the utterances are meaningless to others is part of the syndrome of a mental illness. The other possibility is that the author is deliberately engaging in an act of deception. "Scientific-sounding" language lends an aura of authority to what is being said. People, by and large, accept the authority of science, even though not many understand the nature of the evidence or of the arguments that support scientific findings. Those with medical or mental health problems, strongly motivated to believe that they can be helped, and for that reason hoping that an imminent "scientific discovery" will alleviate their suffering, are especially vulnerable to exploitation by charlatans.

The "journal" from which the pseudoscientific mumbo-jumbo passage was quoted is an authentic-looking imitation of a scientific publication. It has the typical format; it bristles with graphs, charts, and tables of figures, purporting to be recorded data. It exhibits photographs of impressive-looking "apparatus." The lay reader is not in a position to distinguish this counterfeit article from genuine ones because the latter are no more comprehensible to him than the former.

It is not certain whether Dr. Wilhelm Reich, the publisher of the

Orgone Energy Bulletin, himself suffered from delusions or perpetrated delusions on others or both. A significant and alarming fact is that for several years Dr. Reich headed a large "therapeutic" establishment to which people came in search of help. They paid money to sit in wooden boxes, supposedly absorbing "orgone energy" and being charged with its miraculous powers. That is to say, if Dr. Reich's intention was to induce delusions in his patients in order to milk them, he succeeded. If he was himself deluded (which, in light of the circumstances of Dr. Reich's career, seems more likely), then delusions appear to be strongly contagious.

That delusions are inherent in the human condition is a truism, and it is not our purpose to belabor it. The point to be made is that, when we give some thought to the matter, we realize how difficult it is to define and to identify delusions and to make general statements about what should be done about them, if anything.

On the level of the individual, delusions are sometimes symptomatic of clearly recognizable mental illness. At least some mental illnesses, such as hallucinations, are *defined* in terms of symptoms of delusion. If I see a crocodile in my bedroom that no one else sees, it is agreed that I am suffering from hallucinations and need help. Here the distinction between delusion and normal perception is clear because we *define* "objective reality" in terms of agreement among reports of independent sensory impressions of several individuals.

However, we must use different criteria if we are to decide whether *beliefs* held by entire populations or by large majorities or, for that matter, by minorities, are or are not delusions. Beliefs are not simply consequences of direct perceptions. Applying the test of immediate sensory perception to beliefs will not distinguish a scientist's belief in atoms from Dr. Reich's patients' belief in "orgones." The scientific definition of reality, in contrast to the common-sense definition of the "real world perceived by the senses," is an intricate one. The acceptance or rejection of that definition *itself* depends on deeply seated metaphysical assumptions about the "ultimate" nature of reality. These cannot usually be affected by "rational arguments" because rational arguments can be built only on a common base of fundamental assumptions.

Now, beliefs are propagated by language. The point of departure in this book was the view that language is the survival mechanism characteristic of the human species: language mediates our acquisition of knowledge about the world we live in and is the vehicle by which knowledge is communicated, not only among contemporaries but across generations. It was pointed out that, because of the way language functions, false knowledge can be internalized as readily as true knowledge. In Part III, however, we developed the idea that criteria for distinguishing truth from falsehood do exist and can be discovered by a certain method of analysis. This method—the scientific mode of reasoning and cognition—appears valid, provided we embrace the conception of truth inherent in *that* mode of reasoning and cognition. Therefore the "appeal to reason" based on a *tacit* acceptance of the scientific mode of thought is, in the last analysis, an attempt to reinforce certain perceptions if they already exist or to change certain perceptions if they are at variance with those inherent in the scientific outlook. The appeal is an attempt to persuade by affecting the perceptions of the target.

In Chapter 11 we distinguished between the informative and the persuasive functions of language and also between exploitative and nonexploitative aspects of persuasion. We mentioned instances of clearly exploitative persuasion of the sort that manipulates the perceptions of the targets in order to make them serve the interests of the persuader. In Chapter 22 we traced the beginnings of the general semantics movement in the United States to a defensive reaction against manipulation of populations by demagogues. We saw how this movement was stimulated by Korzybski's identification of science (the scientific mode of thought) with sanity. We saw also how simple-minded conceptions of the relation between language and reality introduced new sources of delusion—first, a belief that an immediate connection between words and concretely perceived referents is the only guarantee of meaningfulness; second, a naïve faith in the universal applicability of the technological mode of "solving problems."

The errors of vulgarization can be easily dispensed with. The scientific mode of cognition is not coextensive with either the debunking of "abstractions," as Stuart Chase pictured it, nor with translating the difficulties and dilemmas of the human condition into analogues of technological problems, as the pragmatists insist. In fact, the entire outlook called "the scientific method" (even when it is described with full competence) must be reexamined before it can be recommended as a way to make the human survival mechanism work.

The strongest argument in favor of the scientific outlook as a basis of a sane and humane society is that it disavows exploitative persuasion. Scientifically established truth does not depend on the interests or appetites of individuals or groups. For this reason, the scientific mode of thought, although it is disciplined and must operate under constraints of that discipline, provides a greater measure of autonomy even in its persuasive role than do other modes. The scientific outlook, however, is limited by language that serves only the cognitive and the informative functions. It cannot serve the persuasive function except in the context of accepting true propositions or rejecting false ones which may be insufficient for inducing urgently needed action. The language of science cannot at all serve the *expressive* function of communication (such as is served by poetry, the language of religious experience, etc.), although Edna St. Vincent Millay said that only Euclid had looked on beauty bare.

It has been suggested that if language is to function properly, its different roles should be strictly separated. Where it is important to know and to disseminate "objective truth," the cognitive and the informative uses of language should be subjected to the strict syntactic and semantic discipline of scientific discourse. The expressive and the persuasive uses of language should be clearly identified as such. Moreover, when conflicts arise among individuals or groups, large or small, as many as possible of the underlying issues should be translated into propositions verifiable by the scientific mode of cognition. In this way the scientific outlook, it is argued, can serve in a conflict-resolving, integrative role, in addition to its role of enhancing the survival potential of the human race. This is essentially the language hygiene program implicit in the ideas of the general semanticists and other "scientific humanists." It amounts to a *particular* definition of responsibility in the use of language, both on the part of the speaker and on the part of the hearer.

To be "responsible" (in the ethical sense of the word) means to be aware of the probable consequences of one's actions and to be guided by a concordance between these consequences and certain values. For instance, a "responsible" driver obeys traffic rules because he is aware that violation of the rules increases the probability of an accident and because he respects the generally accepted value of protecting people against being killed or maimed.

Responsibility in the use of language, as the general semanticists have understood it, relates to two sets of values: those of reality testing and those of cooperation. Sanity involves, among other things, a concordance between perceptions and beliefs on the one hand and "reality" on the other. Therefore reality testing is a symptom of sanity. A viable society depends on cooperation among its members. Since the scientific outlook is certainly conducive to reality testing, it is related to sanity. It is said to be also related to the cooperative attitude because science is a cooperative enterprise; and so, on these grounds, the scientific outlook is considered to be conducive to preserving a viable society. Since both sanity and a viable society represent commonly accepted values, a plausible case appears to have been made for the scientific outlook as a contribution to the responsible use of language.

Nevertheless, this view of language hygiene is vulnerable to criticism. We have already seen that the "reality testing" attitude can be easily perverted into one that summarily dismisses any attempt to transcend the level of immediate sensory experience. Stuart Chase, at least at the time when he was writing *The Tyranny of Words*, would not have bothered trying to fathom the meaning of *any* of the four passages cited in the beginning of this chapter. He would have dismissed all four as gibberish. To be sure, we need not hold the proponents of the scientific outlook responsible for the excesses of vulgar pragmatism. However, even if the scientific outlook is properly understood as the epistemology of science rather than as a crude "show me" attitude, still the range of experience to which "reality testing" can be applied with confidence is limited to what is investigated by contemporary science. It would be inaccurate to insist that this range is thereby restricted to the areas illuminated by the natural sciences. Nevertheless, the illumination grows dimmer the more we penetrate into areas involving human behavior, the human psyche, and the factors that determine the nature of human society. This is not to argue that those areas are closed to scientific investigation but only to acknowledge that formidable obstacles impede the extension of scientific methods to those areas.

The obstacles are of two sorts. First, there is the enormous disparity in the amount of public support given to the natural as compared to the "human" sciences. The reason for this disparity is that investments in natural science research, unlike investments in the social sciences or the humanities, give relatively quick and recognizable returns. Moreover, the "utility" of the knowledge derived from the natural sciences can be rationalized in terms of the dominant values of the dominant classes in the dominant societies: understanding nature confers power over the environment (recall Francis Bacon's dictum "Knowledge is power"). Ever since the Renaissance, pursuit of power has replaced the thousand-year preoccupation with "salvation" as the foremost perceived goal of Western civilization. The needs of military technology defined the leading edge of scientific research. The needs of industrial technology followed closely behind. The flowering of the biological sciences, spurred by the needs of the healing arts, came much later, not until the second half of the nineteenth century. Note how this sequence followed the transformation of Western society. The end of the Middle Ages saw the rise of absolute monarchies. The prime concern of absolute monarchs was the extension of power by war. In the eighteenth century, a new source of power appeared— industry and trade. Attention was turned then to sciences with applications in industrial technology, mechanics, thermodynamics, chemistry. Only with the spread of democratic ideas did the rapid advance begin in the sciences most relevant to medicine. Scientific medicine can confer its benefits on the people directly (provided its services are available), not as a by-product of a select group's appetite for power. Nevertheless, whether the natural sciences served the needs of naked power of military establishments or the needs of covert power (of industrial entrepreneurs) or the needs of the people through easing toil and prolonging life, they nevertheless served a common purpose— mastery over nature. Once man's attention was turned to this end, the natural sciences embarked on their phenomenally successful progress. Success insures support. Support generates further successes. In the present cultural climate, sciences dealing with man and his works, directed toward ends other than mastery over something external, simply cannot compete with the prestige of the natural sciences. Comparative lack of support impedes progress. The lack of dramatic successes of an obvious utilitarian nature inhibits support.

The second obstacle to including a science of man as an equal partner in the scientific enterprise was touched upon at the end of Chapter 18. A science of man requires the infusion of a new cognitive orientation into the method of science, in quite the same way that the development of the natural sciences required a new orientation. The new orientation that provided the stimulus to the natural sciences in the sixteenth century emphasized the empirical component of knowledge (careful observation, induction, controlled experiment) and an initial *de*-emphasis of the hitherto paramount search for purpose in the natural scheme of things. The scientists learned to hold the question "why?" in abeyance until the "how" of events was thoroughly understood. Later the "why" question was put again, but now not in the context of cosmic or divine purpose but in the context of verifiable relations among events. Moreover, scientists learned to manipulate the material world they were studying. They became craftsmen as well as thinkers. Without the infusion of these new approaches into the process of acquiring knowledge, superimposed on the approach already developed (deduction), natural science would not have flourished.

It seems reasonable to suppose that new additions to the scientific method of cognition are required if the method is to be successfully extended to include the study of man and his works. Following the old formula of the "scientific method" as it developed in the natural sciences will not do. This does not mean, of course, that the time-honored method will be abandoned, any more than deduction was abandoned when quantitative observation and the controlled experiment were added to the scientist's tool kit. On the contrary, deduction, combined with the experimental method, was incorporated into the enormously powerful mathematical method. So if, spurred by the need for a science of man, new modes of cognition appear on the scene, the old method will still continue to function. Hypotheses will still be formulated and put to the test of observation or experiment. Mathematics will certainly continue to serve deductive techniques. But the *generation* of hypotheses will have to depend not simply on observation of regularly occurring events (the traditional source of hypotheses in the natural sciences) *but rather on insights acquired by the exercise of the imagination, in the course of social action, and through commitment to values.* Reasons for this were suggested in Chapter 18. First, the social sciences depend far more than the natural sciences on *acts of recognition,* hence, on the development of certain sensitivities in the social scientist. Second, the self-predictive assumption, unimportant in the natural sciences, plays a crucial role in human affairs.

If these conjectures are justified, the limitations of traditional scientific humanism and its program of language hygiene are clear. Scientific knowledge and commitment to values, which had to be separated at the dawn of the scientific era, can no longer remain separated if the method of science is to be fruitfully extended to the study of man. The implication for language hygiene is that responsibility in the use of language is no longer discharged by simply separating statements of fact from assertions of values (as in the established principle of responsible journalism) or reports of direct observations from theoretical inference (as in traditional scientific discourse). The point is that, in the "human" sciences, the *selection of facts* to be ascertained is already a reflection of values, and reports of these facts may profoundly influence the subsequent course of events. Moreover, there are hardly any theories pertaining to man and his behavior that are established nearly as firmly as the theories of natural science. Consequently, in the construction of a science of man, theories must still be continually reformulated. The way such theories are formulated, even more than the way events are selected for study, may influence profoundly the course of human history. Therefore the formulation of theories related to human affairs involves a responsibility ordinarily not assumed by the scientist. My reservation about "extending the scientific method," as it has been traditionally understood, to a science of man revolves around this point.

The positivist attitude in the social sciences, which purports to start investigations by describing "societies as they are," is actually a disavowal of this responsibility because it does not take into account that *any* description of what purports to be "social reality" contributes to a *conception* of social reality, and thereby influences its nature.

A case in point is the "realist" position in theories of international relations. In the realists' view, the "actors" in the international arena are sovereign states. Sovereignty means absence of responsibility to any supranational authority, such as the United Nations. The goals governing the behavior of nation states appear to be those of preserving and, if possible, extending their power vis-à-vis other states. This conception of the "international system" may well be historically accurate. It may explain a great deal about how nation states relate to each other. It accounts for the existence and the burgeoning growth of military machines, exhibits the "causes" of many wars, and so on. In short, the realist conception of international relations provides a framework for explaining the observed conduct of foreign policies of states. However, it does more than that. As we have seen, a scientific theory not only explains what has already been observed but also predicts what will occur under given conditions. Indeed, the "realist" theory of international relations does generate predictions. It is maintained, for example, that the probability of war increases when the "balance of power" in the international system is disturbed. Here we seem to have a useful finding: if wars are to be avoided (as practically everyone in our day professes to believe), the "balance of power" in the international system should be preserved. Today, two superstates, the United States and the Soviet Union, possess between them the bulk of total "power" (as the realists understand the term). Consequently it appears as though the preservation of a "balance of power" between the Big Two is a way of "insuring peace," at least of preventing the holocaust that a war between them would entail.

However, it turns out that, when the "balance of power" appears to be disturbed, the only measures undertaken for restoring it are those that aim to increase the war potential of the party that feels itself to be behind, never those that decrease the war potential of the party that feels itself to be ahead. Each side, of course, wants the *other's* war potential to be reduced. But since the states are sovereign, there is no authority to force such reductions, and the identification of "national security" with military prowess makes it virtually impossible for the decision makers of either state to effect such reductions voluntarily. The result is the disastrously costly and utterly senseless nuclear arms race that has dominated our age.

Note that neither errors of reasoning nor a pathological misperception of "reality" nor a lack of commitment to "problem-solving" drove the United States and the Soviet Union into this impasse. The "realist" conception of international relations is a defensible one. The best brains of both countries are mobilized to work on very real problems generated by the "balance of power" theory. In working on these problems, they apply the latest scientific knowledge and most sophisticated techniques. Still the result is a nightmare.

Consider the following passage.

Almost certainly the primary purpose of the side that strikes first would be to destroy the military power of the other. Our strategic force is the target of highest priority at the outset of such a war. How much of the aggressor's force would be available for use against our cities would depend on the ability of our strategic force to "soak up" his attack. We plan on having a well-protected force and such a force, by definition, is able to withstand the entire weight of the enemy assault and survive. The aggressor might save little for use against cities. Might not both sides have an incentive to avoid cities? The aggressor might attempt to minimize the defender's civil damage in order to hold his cities as hostage and to force a quick end to the war. How about the side that strikes second? Suppose its cities are not attacked initially? If it carries out a policy of only city attack with its surviving forces, it may be condemning its own cities to destruction. Moreover, it is feasible to avoid most cities. Clean weapons can be used instead of dirty ones, airbursts against soft targets rather than ground bursts, relatively small-yield weapons rather than very large. If the surviving force were a minimum-deterrence force designed to be just large enough to assure unacceptable civil damage to the enemy, how credible would its deterrent strength look in this situation? If the war were to begin in a favorable way for the defender, if it managed to have a large part of its force available, a policy of hitting only civil targets would give up the prospect of a favorable military outcome. And the prospect of civil damage is not the only deterrent. The aggressor is not as likely to start a war if it appears he stands a good chance of losing it—as well as receiving some civil damage.[5]

Unlike the pseudoscientific excerpt cited at the beginning of this chapter, this passage is not an example of psychotic discourse. It makes semantic sense. The words have identifiable referents. Assertions are supported by sound reasoning. The writer poses problems to which solutions can perhaps be found. In short, the passage is written in the mode of scientific discourse. Only when the meaning of the passage is seen in another perspective does the character of its insanity become apparent. It is not the insanity of a clinically mentally ill individual, but rather the insanity of an entire conception, one which equates "security" with its opposite, the maintenance of terror. (Recall the slogan in Orwell's *1984:* "War is Peace.") To be sure, if one accepts the basic position of the "realists," the "security" of each side seems to depend on maintaining the terror. But certainly the security of *both* sides is not assured by the mutual threat of annihilation. Here is the hangup. The language in which the idea of "national security" is couched does not permit the user to adopt the perspective from which both sides are seen as a single "actor." From *this* perspective, "the actor" certainly appears insane because the uses to which he puts "his" knowledge, the formidable technical and scientific problem that "he"

5. Henry S. Rowen, "The Future of General War," in *American National Security: A Reader in Theory and Policy,* eds. M. Berkowitz and P. G. Bock (New York: Free Press, 1965), p. 71.

solves, lead him closer to self-destruction instead of away from it. Given that practically everyone prefers self-preservation to self-destruction, those who promote, develop, elaborate, and rationalize the concepts that make the insane acts of the two superstates appear "rational" are subverting language and, with it, man's mechanism of survival. They are, in fact, contributing to "semantic pollution"—the poisoning of the ocean of words in which we must continue to live and from which we derive the nourishment for our ideas.

Cleaning up the semantic environment involves more than clarifying meanings of words and bringing the structure of language into closer correspondence with "reality." No one is aware of the entire reality, only of certain portions or aspects of it. What aspect of "reality" will command our attention is influenced, but not determined, by the purely cognitive and informative functions of language. Since their beginnings, human societies have been held together primarily by the *expressive* functions of language, manifested in poetry, myth, and religion. Susanne Langer writes:

Ritual "expresses feelings" in the logical rather than the physiological sense. It may have what Aristotle called "cathartic" value, but that is not its characteristic; it is primarily an *articulation* of feelings. The ultimate product of such articulation is not a simple emotion, but a complex, permanent *attitude*. This attitude, which is the worshipers' response to the insight given by the sacred symbols, is an emotional pattern, which governs all individual lives. It cannot be recognized through any clearer medium than that of formalized gesture; yet in this cryptic form it *is* recognized, and yields a strong sense of tribal or congregational unity, of rightness and security. A rite regularly performed is the constant reiteration of sentiments toward "first and last things"; it is not a free expression of emotions, but a disciplined rehearsal of "right attitudes." [Italics in the original.][6]

The key phrase in the passage is "first and last things." "Right attitudes" in this context means not only proper behavior but also fixing attention on what is important—on the aspect of reality that dominates the culture. Primitive man knew little about the structure of physical reality. Accordingly, he manufactured his own "reality,"

6. Susanne K. Langer, *Philosophy in a New Key* (New York and Harmondsworth, Middlesex: Penguin Books, 1948), p. 124.

embodied in myth and religion. These inventions did not give him much control over nature, but *sharing* the images kept the tribe together and promoted survival through cooperation. Shared meanings are the mortar of group cohesion.

Science drove myth out of our conception of the physical world. This does not mean, of course, that myth has disappeared in "civilized" societies: it still performs the function of fixing the attention upon what is perceived to be important. Our rituals (inaugurations, weddings, graduations, elections) are its manifestations. The crisis of our time is no different from similar crises of other ages. The myths are being challenged. Attention is being directed to aspects of reality neglected heretofore in our "traditional" culture with its preoccupation with personal "success," unlimited growth of production and consumption, and security through military power. The neglected aspect of reality is the common fate of the human race, now threatened from one direction by a spasm of self-destruction, from the other by the prospect of plundered and poisoned environment. To shift attention to this aspect of reality, new symbols are needed. It is not enough to invent them; they must be grafted onto our consciousness, and the grafts must "take" so as to displace the old symbols and shibboleths. This is a painful process, for men tend to cling desperately to the symbols by which they have lived.

We value security. We have traditionally thought of personal security in terms of money in the bank, insurance policies, and steady jobs; of national security, in terms of preparedness to go to war. In this way, we have circumscribed the meaning of security, identifying it with "my security" or "our security," assuming tacitly that security means protection against external threats. Once we become aware of the actual state of the world, this concept of security reveals itself as inadequate. No one is secure unless everyone is secure. But the myth that depicts security as a shield against an external danger dies hard. We have dispensed with walled cities, but we are still dominated by fortress mentality.

We value cooperation. We have traditionally thought of cooperation as teamwork. Members of a business firm, of a political party, and of a football squad cooperate. It turns out that cooperation in all these instances is directed toward effective competition. In war, the more perfect is the cooperation within each of the opposing military establishments, the more destruction each can wreak on the other.

Hence, more "cooperation" in this case means more violence, the opposite of cooperation. But the beatific connotations of "cooperation" persist.

S. I. Hayakawa writes: *"It will be the basic assumption in this book that widespread intraspecific cooperation . . . is the fundamental mechanism of human survival"* (his italics).[7] If, as often appears, cooperation within a group is strengthened to the extent that the group must compete or struggle against other groups, how is "widespread intraspecific cooperation" to be achieved? Perhaps it can be enhanced by de-emphasizing conflicts between groups. But does this not mean that other motivations for cooperation, besides the perception of a common rival or enemy, must be suggested to human beings? If so, how can this be done? One can imagine that conflicting parties can resolve their conflict and start cooperating if both see that they can gain thereby. But what if the gain is to one side only? Should a man being executed cooperate with the executioner? a slave, with his master? an insurgent people, with an oppressive government? Is collaborating with a foreign army of occupation "cooperation"? Apparently, how one understands "cooperation" depends on what myths one has internalized. Some myths are functional, some are vestigial and dysfunctional. But all myths die hard.

We value education. We have traditionally thought of education as preparation for productive participation in the life of one's society. The life of a society flows in channels defined by a social order. The purpose of education, therefore, has been traditionally that of preserving the existing social order. The young are trained for jobs and professions, and they are "socialized"; that is, their attention is turned to the "first and last things," toward an aspect of reality that a culture has singled out as *the* reality. What happens, or should happen, to education when current conceptions of reality are challenged? As this is written (July 1970), the question is an ominous one.

We value law and order. We have traditionally thought of law and order as a guarantee of personal security from wanton violence and as a safeguard of accustomed channels of social life. When a social order is challenged by a large segment of the population, law and order may become an instrument for suppressing the challenge instead of meeting it. Those committed to the established order see the

7. S. I. Hayakawa, *Language in Thought and Action*, 2d ed. (London: George Allen and Unwin, Ltd.), p. 18.

forces of suppression as protection; those who have rejected the established values see the forces of law and order as oppression. Society is rent asunder. We read of the upheavals of the past and in retrospect see many of them as harbingers of social rebirth and of progress. To contemporaries, however, especially to those who do not see the deep underlying causes of the upheavals and do not share the despair of the alienated, impending social revolutions appear as unbearable threats to be removed at any cost, even at the cost of jettisoning the values that law and order was supposed to save. Consequently the social orders change anyway, whether revolutions are successful or suppressed. Myths, however, die hard. They outlive the functions they had served. When myths do not even correspond to *perceived* reality, the stability of the society that clings to them becomes precarious.

Security, education, cooperation, law, and hundreds of other words of that sort are symbols that at one time or another have united portions of humanity into societies. In human societies, symbols serve the same purpose that biologically programmed signals serve in animal societies. However, as was pointed out in Chapter 1, there is a vast difference between the way signals and symbols perform their functions. Signals, by which social animals communicate, are firmly built-in. Changes in the nature of the signals or in their effects on behavior occur very slowly, only as a consequence of the animals' evolutionary adaptation. As long as their way of life remains adapted to their environment, the "social order" of social animals undergoes no changes. Oppositely symbols that unite human beings into societies are not built-in. They are learned and they are fluid. That is, the coupling between them and the behavior they elicit remains loose, varies among individuals, groups, and generations. Most important, man can become aware of the role symbols play in his life and can manipulate and change them, thereby altering the quality of his life and affecting the quality of life of generations to come.

Men who attempt to reorganize our perceptions by introducing new symbols and by making them meaningful are called prophets or visionaries or revolutionaries, or gods. Their responsibility is the most awesome of all, since it is impossible to predict what sort of existence is in store for people who adopt the new symbols by which to live. This is why the responsible use of language concerns not only the producers but also the receivers of symbols, the reader as well as the writer, the listener as well as the speaker, the governed as well as the rulers. Socrates' famous remark "Life without investigation is not worth living" applies to nothing more directly than to our critical awareness of our unique gift—symbolic language.

APPLICATIONS

I. Is it possible for an entire culture or society to be delusional? Is there such a thing as a "mass neurosis"? Consider the following instances and decide to what degree if any faulty communications systems or deliberately distorted communications systems are involved:

1) Carlos Castanada in *The Teachings of Don Juan* apprenticed himself to a shaman who allegedly preserved the wisdom of certain Amerindian tribes that used to enter into mystical communication with the universe through the use of mescal, the jimson weed, and other hallucinogens. Would you regard an individual belonging to this tribe as "mentally ill"? Would you regard the entire tribe as "delusional" with respect to reality?

2) Under the dictatorship of Hitler, the German people appeared to believe during the 1930s and 1940s that through the force of arms and their superiority as "Aryans" they could create a new millennium for the world. Would you regard this as an instance of "mass madness"?

3) The Madison Avenue advertising firms help to persuade millions of young people that smoking is a happy pastime. It is done by unscrupulous but skillful use of language. Are there parallels between the German propaganda machine under Hitler and the functioning of Madison Avenue advertising experts?

4) Read *The Penal Colony* by Franz Kafka. Write a short paper about it relating the theme to this application.

5) Read *The Politics of Experience* by R. D. Laing and similarly write a short paper relating it to this application.

II. The "expression theory" of art was given currency by Ernst Cassirer and Susanne Langer. The most recent advocate of this position, Richard Wollheim, holds that a work of art is not a symptom of emotion or even emotion recollected in tranquillity (Wordsworth), but a *symbol* of that emotion. The work of art is a "presentational" symbol in contrast to the "discursive" symbolism that associates St. Mark with a lion. The "presentational" symbol "presents," just as a Mercator map *exhibits* the true compass directions among all of its points, although it only *refers* to (by a complicated system of mathematical translation) their relative distances. What a work of art exhibits or expresses, according to this notion, is not feeling as such but the forms of feeling—both dynamic forms (tension and release) and static forms. Works of art are therefore the cognitive instruments through which we learn the *structure* of the life of feeling, something general rather than particular. The *content* of the particular emotional states of others and even ourselves (as distinct from the artist's), we must infer from the symptomatic ways in which they are evinced or betrayed, not expressed.

What are some of the difficulties of this theory? Does it seem to apply more to one art than to others?

III.   Jean Piaget has written an intellectual autobiography called *Insights and Illusions of Philosophy* (New York: World, 1971) in which he explores "the boundary that separates verification from speculation" in the areas of science and philosophy. The famous Swiss psychologist does not question the value of philosophy—"man lives, takes sides, believes in a multiplicity of values, orders them hierarchically and thus gives meaning to his existence by decisions that constantly go beyond the limits of his actual knowledge"—but he does maintain that we often confuse "wisdom," a set of beliefs, with "knowledge," or verifiable perceptions.

Return to Application I. Castanada calls the teachings of his master Don Juan a "lost wisdom." If a culture or a society bases its behavior on a wisdom that ignores the knowledge of a more "advanced" or more powerful society, is there any justification for describing that culture as "delusional" or "mad"? Read Ruth Benedict's *Patterns of Culture* and decide how you feel about the Dobuans, who achieve status in direct proportion to their ability to steal successfully.

IV.   "How is 'widespread intraspecific cooperation' to be achieved?" remains the question to be answered if civilization as we know it is to survive beyond the century of atomic weaponry.

1) It has been argued by "social engineers" that war is an institution like slavery or the caste system, and just as those two institutions were modified or gradually eliminated when they were regarded as incompatible with humane goals, so can war be abolished and the institutions of "intraspecific cooperation" substituted for it. This argument has merits, but can you recognize what may be its essential weakness?

2) Dr. Kenneth Clark, president of the American Psychological Association for 1971–72, proposed a cure for international aggression: the world's leaders should be required to take "psychotechnical medication" —pills or other treatments to curb their aggressive behavior and induce them to govern more humanely. Such a pharmacological fix, Clark

argued, "would provide the masses with the security that their leaders would not or could not sacrifice them on the altars of the leaders' personal ego pathos."

3) Writers such as Aldous Huxley and Agatha Christie have treated this idea as more or less prophetic fiction, and it is an extension of B. F. Skinner's argument that man must be controlled to survive, even if it requires tampering with the mind of man. What do you think of this possibility? What are the arguments in favor of it? The arguments against it?

V.   The theme of Eugene O'Neill's *The Iceman Cometh* is that men need their illusions in order to live. Are myths like illusions (first decide what you mean by "myth")? Do we need myths in order to live? What risk is there in continuing to believe in myths that may not correspond to *perceived* reality?

VI.   Following times of crisis, the hunger for belief and personal salvation becomes palpable. This appetite appears to be strong today in America. People are turning to mysticism and meditation; the mantic arts flourish again, communes are growing, numbers of young people are turning to Jesus as their personal savior, others to the religions and disciplines of the East: Aikido, Yoga, Zen, Hasidism, and I Ching.

1) Can there be any useful dialogues between people who are turning in this direction and those who accept the scientific definition of truth? Are there any necessary contradictions between the two positions?

2) Write a short dialogue between an advocate of the new popular religions and a semanticist.

index